2009
EDITION

McGraw-Hill's

GRE

Graduate Record Examination General Test

Steven W. Dulan
and the Faculty of Advantage Education

New York | Chicago | San Francisco | Lisbon | London
Madrid | Mexico City | Milan | New Delhi | San Juan | Seoul
Singapore | Sydney | Toronto

Copyright © 2009 by The McGraw-Hill Companies, Inc. All rights reserved. Printed in the United States of America. Except as permitted under the United States Copyright Act of 1976, no part of this publication may be reproduced or distributed in any form or by any means, or stored in a database or retrieval system, without the prior written permission of the publisher.

1 2 3 4 5 6 7 8 9 0   QPD/QPD   0 1 4 3 2 1 0 9 8

Book alone:
ISBN 978-0-07-160305-8
MHID 0-07-160305-0

Book/CD set:
ISBN: P/N 978-0-07-160308-9 of set
        978-0-07-160307-2

ISBN: P/N 0-07-160308-5 of set
        0-07-160307-7

Printed and bound by Quebecor/Dubuque

McGraw-Hill books are available at special quantity discounts to use as premiums and sales promotions, or for use in corporate training programs. For more information, please write to the Director of Special Sales, McGraw-Hill Professional, Two Penn Plaza, New York, NY 10121-2298. Or contact your local bookstore.

GRE® is a registered trademark of Educational Testing Service (ETS), which was not involved in the production of, and does not endorse, this product.

Product or brand names used in this book may be trade names or trademarks. Where we believe that there may be proprietary claims to such trade names or trademarks, the name has been used with an initial capital or it has been capitalized in the style used by the name claimant. Regardless of the capitalization used, all such names have been used in an editorial manner without any intent to convey endorsement of or other affiliation with the name claimant. Neither the author nor the publisher intends to express any judgment as to the validity or legal status of any such proprietary claims.

Library of Congress Cataloging-in-Publication Data

Dulan, Steven W.
    McGraw-Hill's GRE with CD-ROM : Graduate Record Examination general test / Steven W. Dulan.
    -- 2009 ed.
        p.   cm.
    Includes bibliographical references and index.
    ISBN-13: 978-0-07-160305-8
    ISBN-10: 0-07-160305-0
    ISBN-13: 978-0-07-160307-2 (Book-CD set)
    ISBN-10: 0-07-160307-7 (Book-CD set)
    1. Graduate Record Examination—Study guides. I. Title.
    LB2367.4.D854 2009
    378.1'662--dc22
                                                                                2008018680

Contents at a Glance

Contents

Part I: Introduction to the GRE General Test

Part II: Preparing for the GRE General Test

Part III: Content Area Review

Part IV: Practicing for the GRE General Test

Appendixes

How to Use This Book

This book includes general information about the GRE General Test and chapters with specific information on each of the test sections, as well as additional simulated practice tests. In an ideal situation, you will be reading this book at least three to four weeks before you take the actual GRE General Test. In our experience, the students who see the largest increases in their scores are those who put in consistent effort over several weeks. Try to keep your frustration to a minimum if you are struggling. In addition, try to keep from becoming overconfident when everything is going your way. The GRE Training Schedule shown on the next page will help you to manage your time effectively and stay focused during your preparation.

> **GRE Tip**
>
> If you have already registered for a specific test date but do not feel that you are ready for the test, it might be better to reschedule your GRE. There may be additional fees, but you will have a more positive testing experience and achieve your maximum score if you are sufficiently prepared.

How to Use the Practice Tests

The practice tests found in this book are reasonably accurate simulations written by GRE experts. They contain basically the same mix of question types as a real GRE. If you work through all the material provided, you can rest assured that there won't be any surprises on test day.

The biggest difference between the practice tests in this book and your real GRE is the fact that these are not computer adaptive tests (see Chapter 1 for more information on the CAT format). You should use these practice tests to become familiar with the different question types and reveal any gaps in your knowledge. Generally, students tend to score a little better on each successive practice test.

Keep in mind that GRE test results are sensitive to individual conditions such as fatigue and stress. Therefore, the time of day that you take your practice tests, your environment, and other things that might be going on in your life can have an impact on your scores. Don't get worried if you see some score fluctuation because of a bad day or because the practice tests indicate weaknesses in your knowledge or skills. Simply use this information to help you improve. Plan to do some practicing with POWERPREP®, the free software from the authors of the GRE that is made available at www.gre.org, to get a good feel for how the questions will be presented on test day.

GRE TRAINING SCHEDULE

At least 4 weeks before your GRE

Take the Diagnostic Test (Chapter 4) under realistic conditions. Time yourself strictly. Take the test in a place that approximates actual test conditions. Evaluate your results and pinpoint your areas of strength and weakness. Read Chapters 1 and 2 (and Chapter 3 if you are an international student). Download the POWERPREP® software if you haven't done so already. Register for your GRE test following the procedures set out at www.gre.org. Purchase a Mozart CD if you don't already have one.

The first 3 to 4 weeks of training

Don't worry about timing. Work through the first two simulated GRE tests (Chapters 12 and 13) at your leisure. Think about how the questions and passages are put together and read Chapters 5–11 so that you can start to acquire good testing skills and fill any holes in your knowledge base. Listen to your Mozart CD while you are reading and reviewing material, but not while you're testing.

2 weeks before your GRE

Take your first "dress rehearsal" test—we recommend Practice Test 1 from POWERPREP®. Use the results to fine-tune the last part of your training. Work through at least one more simulated test in the book, untimed, making sure that you understand the questions and explanations. If you haven't yet received confirmation of your test date, follow up with GRE and make sure that your registration was processed properly.

1 week before your GRE

Take your second "dress rehearsal" test (POWERPREP® Practice Test 2). If it doesn't go well, don't get too worried. Try to determine what went wrong and review the relevant portions of this book. If it does go well, don't rest on your laurels. There is still time to consolidate your gains and continue to improve. Review all relevant portions of this book. Start planning a fun event for after your GRE test! (Remember that there is a pretty good chance you will want a nap after your GRE.)

2 to 3 days before your GRE

Make a practice run to the testing center. Figure out what you are going to wear on test day. Gather your materials together (Test Center Admissions information, ID, and so on). Review the results of the tests you've taken, and work through any remaining test material. Confirm your plans for fun after the test!

The day before your GRE

Do little or no practice or studying. Get some physical activity so that you are better able to sleep, and because the endorphins that you release in your brain will help with stress management. Rest and relaxation are the order of the day. Make sure that your transportation issues and wake up plan are taken care of.

Test Day!

Get up early. Eat breakfast. Read something to get you "warmed up." Tear out the "Top Strategies" section of this book to bring to the Testing Center. Listen to your Mozart CD. Be on time. Follow all Testing Center protocol. Avoid contact with any fellow test-takers who are "stress monsters." Don't forget to breathe deeply and evenly, and don't tire yourself out with needless physical exertion like tensing up your muscles while taking your GRE. When the test is finished, relax and try not to think about it until you get your score report. Good Luck!

In addition, there are times when you will want to work through some material without a time limit. Refer to the Training Schedule for more information regarding when you should switch the focus of your training from studying knowledge to practicing skills and when to make the shift to working on your timing.

There is an explanation for each of the practice questions in this book. You will probably not need to read all of them. Sometimes, you can tell right away why you got a particular question wrong. We have seen countless students smack themselves on the forehead and say "Stupid mistake!" We refer to these errors as "concentration errors." Everyone makes them from time to time, and you should not worry when they occur. There is a good chance that your focus will be a little better on the real test as long as you train yourself properly with the aid of this book. You should distinguish between concentration errors and any understanding issues or holes in your knowledge base. If you have the time, it is worth reading the explanations for any of the questions that were at all challenging for you. Sometimes, students get questions correct but for the wrong reason, or because they guessed correctly. While you are practicing, you should mark any questions that you want to revisit and be sure to read the explanations for those questions.

Take the GRE Diagnostic Test (Chapter 4) after reading this section. It will help you to pinpoint areas of strength and weakness in your knowledge base and your skill set. Take it under realistic conditions. The best setting would be a library where there are other people around and they are being relatively quiet, just like at a testing center. Time yourself strictly on this first test. You need to have an accurate picture of what your performance would be like if test day were today. After you have scored it, you should review the parts of the chapters that cover any content areas that you need to review.

A Note on Scoring the Practice Tests

The tests in this book are simulations created by experts to replicate the question types, difficulty level, and content areas that you will find on your real GRE. The Scoring Guidelines provided for each test are guides to computing approximate scores. Each Scoring Guidelines has formulae for you to work out an approximate scaled score for each section. Each computation includes a "correction factor," which is an average correction derived from analysis of recent GRE tests. The correction factor is most valid for students whose scores are in the middle 50 percent of all scores; it starts to lose a bit of its effectiveness at the top and bottom of the scoring scale.

Actual GRE tests are scored from tables that are unique to each test. The actual scaled scores depend on several factors, which include: the number of students who take the test, the difficulty level of the items (questions and answer choices), and the performance of all of the students who take the test. We include a more detailed discussion of scoring the Computer Adaptive Tests (CAT) in Chapter 1. Do not get too hung up on your practice test scores; the idea is to learn something from each practice experience and to get used to the "look and feel" of the GRE.

What's Next?

Part I includes detailed descriptions of the GRE format, question types, and registration and scoring processes. We recommend that you visit www.gre.org to check for any updates prior to taking your GRE.

PART I

Introduction to the GRE General Test

1

Overview of the GRE

- Learn how the GRE is structured.
- Find out what kinds of questions are on the test.
- Study examples of each question type.
- Learn about the computer adaptive test format.

The Graduate Record Examinations (GRE) General Test is required by most institutions and programs granting Master or Doctorate degrees, although it is not required by all programs. Not surprisingly, the most competitive programs generally have higher score requirements. Some programs also require Subject Tests, which are beyond the scope of this volume. You should speak to the admissions department at the school to which you are applying to confirm whether you will need to take one or more of the subject tests. For more information on the GRE Subject Tests, visit www.gre.org.

The GRE does not measure your knowledge of business procedures or law, or any specific content area. In addition, it does not measure your value as a person, nor does it predict your success in life. However, the GRE does a fairly good job of predicting how hard you will have to work to understand the material in your chosen program. If you prepare for this test seriously now, you'll sharpen your comprehension, math, and reasoning skills, and be able to focus on the relevant information in your course work much more easily once you start graduate school.

GRE Format

The GRE General Test is a computer-based test that includes four scored sections: Analytical Writing Assessment Issue Task, Analytical Writing Assessment Argument Task, Quantitative, and Verbal. Your test will also include an experimental section, called the "pretest" section, which is mixed in with the other sections of the test and appears as either a Verbal or a Quantitative section. There might also be a "research" section, which will always be the final section presented if you have one included in your test. The answers on the pretest and research sections will not count toward your GRE score. The questions are meant to help the test writers at Educational Testing Service (ETS) refine their methods and try out new material that may be included in future GRE tests. The pretest is not identified and will seem like just another test section as you work through it. The research section, if you have one on your test, will be identified as such.

You are allowed up to 3 hours to complete the GRE. If you have a research section, you are given additional time. The test always begins with the two Analytical Writing Assessment (AWA) tasks: the Issue task and the Argument task. In the Issue task, you get to choose one of two topics on which to write. In the Argument task, you do not get a choice; there is only one argument presented and you must respond to it. For both tasks, you will write your response using the word processor that is built into the GRE software. Chapter 7 of this book discusses the AWA in detail, while Chapters 8 and 9 cover the Quantitative and Verbal sections, respectively.

The basic time breakdown is shown in the following chart. (Note that all sections after the AWA can appear in any order on your actual test, except for the research section, which will come last.)

GRE Test Format

Section	Number of Questions	Time Limit
Analytical Writing	Issue task Argument task	45 minutes 30 minutes
Verbal	30	30 minutes
Quantitative (math)	28	45 minutes
Pretest (experimental Verbal or Quantitative)	Varies; you will be told the number when you begin	Varies; you will be told the time limit when you begin
Research (your GRE might not include this section)	Varies	Varies

Your GRE may contain questions that are the same or similar to released GRE questions that appear on the POWERPREP® software or in official GRE publications, such as *Practicing to Take the General Test,* 10th edition (ETS, 2002). Be very careful when responding to these questions because they might be slightly different from the questions that you remember. There might be different facts in the stimuli and there might be different answer choices.

GRE Question Types

In order to simplify the sometimes complicated information on the GRE, you must first understand what you're looking at. The following section provides a simple overview of the kinds of GRE questions that you will encounter.

Analytical Writing

The Analytical Writing Assessment consists of an Issue Task and an Argument Task. You are expected to write essays that address each task. Here is a typical example of what you might see:

Issue Task

Present your viewpoint on one of the claims made below. Use relevant reasons and examples to support your point of view.

Topic 1

> "Leaders should focus more on the needs of the majority than on the needs of the minority."

Topic 2

> "The study of mathematics has value only to the extent that it is relevant in our daily lives."

Argument Task

Critique the reasoning used in the argument below.

> The following appeared as part of an article in a health and fitness magazine: "Several volunteers participated in a study of consumer responses to the new Exer-Core exercise machine. Every day for a month, they worked out on the machine for 30 minutes in addition to maintaining their normal fitness regime. At the end of that month, most of the volunteers reported a significant improvement in both their stamina and muscle condition. Therefore, it appears that the Exer-Core exercise machine is truly effective in improving a person's overall general health and fitness."

Strategies to help you write high-scoring essays are included in Chapter 7, "GRE Analytical Writing Assessment."

Verbal

The verbal sections of the GRE General Test include Antonym, Analogy, Sentence Completion, Reading Comprehension, and Text Completion questions. The questions do not appear in any predetermined order, nor is there any set number of each question type on any given GRE General Test. You should take as many practice tests as you can in order to become familiar with the format of the GRE verbal section.

Strategies specific to each of the question types outlined below can be found in Chapter 9, "GRE Verbal."

Antonym

Select the word or phrase that best expresses a meaning opposite to the word in capital letters.

CREDULOUS:

(A) skeptical

(B) naive

(C) spontaneous

(D) sensitive

(E) discrete

Analogy

Select the set of words that represents a relationship similar to the relationship between the words in capital letters.

APPRENTICE : PLUMBER ::

(A) player : coach

(B) child : parent

(C) student : teacher

(D) author : publisher

(E) intern : doctor

Sentence Completion

Select the word or set of words that, when inserted in the blank(s), best fits the context of the sentence.

Because of his --------, Brian's guests felt very welcome and comfortable staying at his house for the weekend.

(A) animosity

(B) hospitality

(C) determination

(D) wittiness

(E) severity

Reading Comprehension

Read the passage and choose the best answer for each question.

Scientists know very little about the eating habits of our ancestors who
Line lived over two and a half million years ago. To solve this problem, scientists have
started examining chimpanzees' hunting behavior and diet to find clues about our
own prehistoric past. It is not difficult to determine why studying chimpanzees
(5) might be beneficial. Modern humans and chimpanzees are actually very closely
related. Experts believe that chimpanzees share about 98.5 percent of our DNA
sequence. If this is true, humans are more closely related to chimpanzees than
they are to any other animal species.

The main purpose of the passage is to

(A) explore biological and physiological similarities between humans and chimpanzees

(B) examine the hunting behavior and diet of chimpanzees and compare it to human activity

(C) discuss the health benefits of eating and hunting meat while simultaneously predicting the effect of this behavior on chimpanzee offspring

(D) bring attention to the pioneering research of Dr. Jane Goodall in Tanzania

(E) educate the public on the impact that tool use had on early human societies

Text Completion

Choose one entry for each blank from the corresponding column of choices. Fill in the blanks in the way that best completes the sentence.

Experts believe that humans have 10 trillion cells in their bodies, which (i) _____ any number of essential genetic elements; scientists often marvel at what incredible (ii) _____ would ensue should the cells become jumbled or misunderstand their purpose.

Blank (i)	Blank (ii)
govern	order
organize	method
dislocate	chaos

Quantitative

The quantitative sections on the GRE General Test include Discrete Problem Solving (multiple-choice), Numeric Entry, and Quantitative Comparison (multiple-choice) questions. The questions do not appear in any predetermined order, nor is there any set number of each question type on any given GRE General Test. You should take as many practice tests as you can in order to become familiar with the format of the GRE quantitative section.

Strategies specific to each of the question types outlined below can be found in Chapter 8, "GRE Quantitative."

Discrete Problem Solving

Select the best answer.

When jogging, a certain person takes 24 complete steps in 10 seconds. At this rate, approximately how many complete steps does the person take in 144 seconds?

(A) 34

(B) 104

(C) 154

(D) 240

(E) 346

Numeric Entry

Enter your answer in the box provided.

Solve the equation for x: $2(x - 3) + 9 = 4x - 7$

$x =$ ☐

Quantitative Comparison

Compare the quantities in Column A and Column B and select:

A if Quantity A is greater;

B if Quantity B is greater;

C if the two quantities are equal;

D if the relationship cannot be determined from the information given.

<u>Column A</u>	<u>Column B</u>
$-(3)^4$	$(-3)^4$

NOTE

Some Quantitative Comparison questions provide additional information centered between the columns. This information will help you to compare the two quantities. Refer to Chapter 8, "GRE Quantitative," for more details.

More on the Computer Adaptive Test (CAT)

The GRE is a Computer Adaptive Test, which means that the level of difficulty of the questions will adapt according to your skill level. Questions appear on your computer screen one at a time. You must answer and confirm each question before you can move forward to the next question. Once you have answered a question, you cannot change your answer. Within each set of multiple-choice questions, the computer software selects your test items depending on your response to the previous question. The first question is always a medium-difficulty question. If you answer it correctly, your next question will be more difficult and worth more points. If you answer the first question incorrectly, your next question will be less difficult and worth fewer points, which means that your GRE score is arrived at through a complex formula that includes the number of questions that you answer correctly and the difficulty level of each question. This process allows for an accurate assessment of your individual ability level in a given subject area. There are some experimental questions that appear randomly in each set that do not count toward your score. You will not be able to tell which ones they are, so you must do your best on all questions as you work through your exam.

GRE Tip

The GRE is offered as a paper-based test in certain areas of the world where computer testing is not available. International test-takers can find more information in Chapter 3.

Only minimal computer skills are required to take the GRE. We suggest that you familiarize yourself with the computer adaptive system by downloading the free POWERPREP® software available at www.gre.org. Review the tutorials and testing tools prior to test day so that you know how the process works.

Because you cannot go back to review or change your confirmed answers, it is important that you prepare sufficiently and be able to proceed through the test with confidence. The chapters in Part II, "Preparing for the GRE General Test," give you the strategies that you need to successfully tackle the questions on your GRE, and the simulated tests contained in Part IV, "Practicing for the GRE General Test," provide you with material on which to practice and hone your test-taking skills. It is imperative that you do enough practice to develop the proper pace to complete the GRE, as there are penalties for not completing the test.

What's Next?

Chapter 2, "Taking the GRE," includes information on how to register for the GRE, what to expect at the testing center, and how the GRE is scored. We also provide a review of the policies governing test-takers with disabilities. Chapter 3 includes more information for international test-takers.

2

Taking the GRE

CHAPTER GOALS

- Get information about registering for the GRE.
- Find out what rules you must follow at the testing center.
- Learn how each part of the test is scored.

As mentioned in Chapter 1, the GRE General Test is designed to help graduate school admissions departments assess applicants. GRE scores are used to augment undergraduate records and transcripts and to provide a standard of measure for comparing all applicants.

The first step in taking the GRE is to register for an appropriate test date and location. If you are an international student, please read Chapter 3.

Registering for the GRE General Test

You can register for the GRE on the Internet, by telephone, or by U.S. mail. You will schedule your GRE test on a first-come, first-served basis at a testing location near you. The test is offered throughout the year at many locations around the United States. The GRE is also given in many countries worldwide. The full list of locations, and other registration details, can be found online at www.ets.org.

You can register via telephone by calling 1-800-GRE-CALL (1-800-473-2255). Registrations sent by mail can take up to four weeks to process. You must send the appropriate forms, either those printed directly from the GRE website or those found in the GRE Bulletin. The latter is available at many college counseling offices, as well as online. After you register, you will receive both detailed information about your testing center and free test prep materials, including the POWERPREP® software mentioned previously.

As of the printing of this book, you can take one GRE per calendar month. In addition, you can take a maximum of five GRE tests within any 12-month period. When you send your GRE scores to graduate schools, they see all scores from all

GRE tests that you have taken within the past five years. You cannot choose to reveal scores only from a certain test date. How schools treat multiple-test scores varies. Some use only your most recent score, while others average the scores of each of your tests. Contact the admissions department of the programs to which you are applying for more information.

Taking the GRE General Test

One of the reasons the GRE is a useful tool for admissions departments is that it is a standardized test administered in the same way to all test-takers. In order to maintain this level of standardization, administration of the GRE is governed by some very specific rules, including, but not limited to, the following:

- You must have acceptable and valid ID; if you do not, you will not be admitted into the test center.
- You must use exactly the name that appears on your primary ID to register for the GRE and gain admittance to the test center.
- You must adhere to test center personnel requirements; failure to do so could result in expulsion from the test center.
- You cannot bring personal items such as cell phones, pagers, cameras, calculators, and the like.
- You must sign the confidentiality statement at the test center.

NOTE

The rules governing the Computer Adaptive Test (CAT) are different from those governing the paper-and-pencil test. Visit www.ets.org for more information on the test administration process.

Scoring the GRE General Test

The process for scoring the CAT version of the GRE is similar to the process for scoring the traditional paper-based GRE: The number of questions answered correctly is adjusted according to the difficulty level of the questions on each particular test. However, with adaptive testing, the scoring process incorporates the statistical properties of the questions, the test-taker's performance on the questions, and the number of questions that are answered. Depending on how you progress through the exam, you might be presented with fewer questions than another test-taker might be presented with. In addition, the same number of correct answers on different tests might not yield the same reported score.

On the CAT, wrong answers do not decrease your score directly, but they do lead to subsequent questions that are worth fewer points. Always make the best selection for each of the questions you are presented with; use the strategies presented later in this book to help you select the correct answer and avoid random guessing.

Scoring the General Test Analytical Writing Section

Each essay receives a score from two highly trained readers using a 6-point holistic scale. This means that the readers are trained to assign a score based on the overall quality of an essay in response to a specific task. If the two scores differ by more than one point on the scale, a third reader steps in to resolve the discrepancy. In this case, the first two scores are dropped and the score given by the third reader is used. Otherwise, the scores from the two readers are averaged so that a single score from 0 to 6 (in half-point increments) is reported. If no essay response is given, a No Score (NS) is reported for this section. If an essay response is provided for one of the two writing tasks, the task for which no response is written receives a score of zero. Scoring guidelines are provided in Chapter 7, "GRE Analytical Writing Assessment." Your actual essays will also be reviewed by the Essay-Similarity-Detection software at Educational Testing Service (ETS) to ensure that your work is original.

Scoring the General Test Verbal and Quantitative Sections

These scores will depend on your specific performance on the questions given as well as the number of questions answered in the allotted time. The Verbal and Quantitative scores are reported on a 200–800 score scale, in 10-point increments. Each section receives a separate score. If you answer no questions at all in either section, a No Score (NS) is reported.

A Note on Scoring the Practice Exams in this Book

Because actual GRE tests are scored using scales that are unique to each test form, this book only includes a guideline for interpreting scores on the simulated practice tests. After you work through this book, you should take additional practice exams with the official POWERPREP® software. It contains the same scoring "engine" as the real GRE exam and can give you a very good idea of how you should expect to do on test day. At this stage, and throughout most of your practice, you should not worry excessively about your test scores; your goal should be to learn something from every practice experience and to become familiar with the format and types of questions on the GRE.

What Your Scores Mean to Schools

You can select up to four institutions to receive your score report. Generally, score reports will be sent to you and the institutions selected 10 to 15 days after you complete the test. Most graduate programs elect to use GRE scores as an admissions tool because GRE scores are a reliable measure of an individual's capacity to perform at the graduate level, and because GRE scores provide a consistent means by which to evaluate applicants. Admissions professionals also take into account an applicant's grade point average, personal interviews, and letters of recommendation. However, because each of these methods of evaluation is variable and subjective, admissions departments need a standardized tool to provide a more objective measure of academic success.

Test-Takers with Disabilities

ETS provides additional information for test-takers with disabilities that includes guidelines for documenting disabilities, suggestions for test-takers, and the necessary forms required to obtain special accommodations. For test-takers with documented disabilities, these accommodations might include the following:

- Additional or extended testing time and breaks
- Allowance of medical devices in the testing center and special computer equipment
- A reader, a sign language interpreter, and recording devices

Accommodation requests must be made in advance and by following the guidelines set forth in *The 2007–2008 Bulletin Supplement for Test Takers with Disabilities,* available as a download on www.ets.org. Documentation review could take several weeks, so be sure to submit all of the required forms and information at least two months prior to your desired test date.

What's Next?

The Diagnostic Test in Chapter 4 should be your next step. It will help you to focus on areas of strength and weakness in your knowledge base and skill set. After you've assessed your current readiness for the GRE, focus on the remaining chapters in this book to maximize your GRE score. If you are an international test-taker, read Chapter 3.

3

Information for International Test-Takers

Each year, more and more international students take the GRE General Test. This chapter provides information for those students who might be taking the test outside their country of citizenship. We suggest that you visit www.gre.org for further details and updates.

The General Test is currently offered as a computer-based test in the United States, Canada, and many other countries. The test is offered in a paper-based format in areas of the world where computer-based testing is not available. In addition, China offers split-test administration, in which the Analytical Writing section is given on the computer and the Verbal and Quantitative sections are paper-based. Test-Takers in China are required to take both versions in the same testing year, completing the Analytical Writing section first.

Educational Testing Service (ETS) is very careful to make sure that the GRE is not biased against international test-takers. The test-makers pretest all questions by including them in experimental test sections (which are not scored) given to both U.S. and international test-takers. If statistics prove that any of the new questions put the international test-takers at a disadvantage, those items never appear on the test. Still, international test-takers face certain challenges.

The Language Barrier

The biggest and most obvious difficulty for international test-takers is the language barrier. Many people residing outside of the United States who sign up to take the GRE are non-native English speakers. The entire test, including instructions and questions, is in English. If you are testing outside your country of citizenship, be aware that other factors exist that might affect your testing experience and your score. For example, if you are testing in the United States or Canada and your native language is not English, you might be required to take the Test of English as a Foreign Language (TOEFL) before being allowed to take the GRE. Admissions committees use your TOEFL score to judge your language skills and make sure you will be able to succeed in classes that are taught in English. In fact, more than 6,000 institutions and agencies in 110 countries rely on TOEFL scores. Contact the admissions department of the graduate program to which you are applying for details on particular requirements.

The Registration Process

Register early to get your preferred test date and to receive your test preparation material in time to prepare for the test. Remember that testing appointments are scheduled on a first-come, first-served basis.

There are four ways you can register for the computer-based General Test: on the Internet, by phone, by fax, and by mail. Major credit cards are accepted to pay for registration.

- To register via the Internet, visit www.gre.org.

- To register by phone, call your local test center directly, or call the Prometric® Candidate Services Call Center Monday through Friday, 8 a.m.–8 p.m., Eastern Time (New York), (excluding holidays), at 1-443-751-4820 or 1-800-GRE-CALL (1-800-473-2255). You will receive a confirmation number, reporting time, and test center address when you call.

- To register by fax, you must download and complete the International Test Scheduling form, then fax it to the appropriate Regional Registration Center (RRC). The form must be received at least seven days before your first-choice test date. A confirmation number, reporting time, and the test center address will be faxed or mailed to you. If you provide an e-mail address, you may receive a confirmation by e-mail.The list of RRCs is updated frequently, so be sure to visit www.gre.org for the most current information.

- To register by mail, download and complete the Authorization Voucher Request Form, and mail the appropriate payment and voucher request form to the address printed on the voucher. Allow up to four weeks for processing and mail delivery. When you receive your voucher, call to schedule an appointment; be sure to make your appointment prior to the expiration date on the voucher.

Standby testing is available at permanent test centers on a first-come, first-served, space available basis in the United States, American Samoa, Guam, U.S. Virgin Islands, Puerto Rico, and Canada only.

If you must cancel or reschedule a testing appointment, contact the appropriate registration center no later than 10 full days before your appointment (not including the day of your test or the day of your request). Keep in mind that you cannot reschedule between sites served by different Regional Registration Centers.

> **NOTE**
>
> You can register for the paper-based General Test either online or by mail. Use a credit card, a money order, or a certified check when registering by mail. Download and complete the registration form and mail the completed form with payment to the address printed on the form. ETS must receive your registration form by the registration deadline, which can be found on www.gre.org. Allow at least four weeks for processing.

We suggest that international students register for the GRE well in advance. This is especially good advice if you plan to take the test outside the United States. First, it may take you some time to decide where exactly you will take the test. Also, the application process in general will take longer for you because of the necessary paperwork.

The Day of the Test

If you are testing outside your country of origin, then you must present your signed passport as your primary identification document. If you do not, ETS may automatically cancel your test scores. In addition, if your passport is not written using English language letters, you must also present another form of identification that includes a recent, recognizable photo and is written in English.

If you are taking the test within a European Union country, you may use your valid national European identity card. Your card must be signed.

Be sure to follow all testing center instructions and procedures set by the testing center. Some of these procedures have been outlined in Chapter 2, "Taking the GRE."

The Student Visa

Another thing that sets international applicants apart from domestic students is their need for a visa to live in the United States. Once you have been accepted to your graduate program and have chosen an institution to attend, the process of obtaining a student visa must begin.

Getting a student visa to study in the United States is not as hard as getting an H1-B visa to work in the country after graduation. Experts, including the U.S. government, suggest that students begin the student visa process as soon as possible. Besides needing the time to complete the requisite forms, you will also need to schedule an appointment for the required embassy consular interview, and the waiting times for this vary and can be lengthy.

Visa Requirements

During the student visa process, you are expected to prove that you have adequate financing to study in the United States, ties to your home country, and a likelihood that you will return home after finishing your studies. In addition, you will have to participate in an ink-free, digital fingerprint scan and provide a passport valid for travel to the United States that has a validity date at least six months beyond your intended period of stay.

The school will provide you with an I-20 form to complete. Your school will use this to register you with the Student and Exchange Visitor Information System (SEVIS), an Internet-based system that maintains accurate and current information on nonimmigrant students and exchange visitors and their families. If you have a spouse and/or children who will be joining you, then you must register them with SEVIS as well. You'll also need to submit a completed and signed nonimmigrant visa application with forms DS-156 and DS-158. A 2 x 2 inch photo that meets certain requirements, which you can find at the U.S. Department of State site, www.travel.state.gov, is necessary as well.

Transcripts, diplomas from previous institutions, scores from standardized tests such as the GRE and TOEFL, and proof you can afford the school fees (income tax records, original bank books and statements, and so on) are things you should have on hand when applying for your visa. If you have dependents, you will also need documents that prove your relationship to your spouse and children, such as a marriage license and birth certificates.

What's Next?

The GRE Diagnostic Test in Chapter 4 should be your next step. It will help you to focus on areas of strength and weakness in your knowledge base and skill set. After you've assessed your current readiness for the GRE, focus on the remaining chapters in the book to help you to maximize your GRE score.

PART II

Preparing for the GRE General Test

4

GRE Diagnostic Test

This diagnostic test can assist you in evaluating your current readiness for the Graduate Record Examination (GRE). Sample questions representing each section of the GRE are included to help you pinpoint areas of strength and weakness in your knowledge base and your skill set. Don't worry if you are unable to answer many or most of the questions at this point. The rest of the book contains information and resources to help you to maximize your GRE score.

We suggest that you make this diagnostic test as much like the real test as possible. Find a quiet location, free from distractions, and make sure that you have pencils and a timepiece.

The simulated GRE in this chapter consists of 4 sections for a total of 58 multiple-choice questions and 2 essay tasks. Please allow approximately 2 hours and 30 minutes to complete the following test. The test sections should be completed in the time indicated at the beginning of each of the sections and in the order in which they appear on this test. There are several types of questions within each section. Make sure that you read and understand all directions before you begin. To achieve the best results, time yourself strictly on each section. You should answer each question before you move on to the next question to make this simulated test as much like the actual Computer Adaptive Test as possible. Remember to circle your answers on the practice test so that you can compare your answers to the correct answers listed on the Answer Key on page 48. Carefully review the explanations, paying close attention to the questions you missed. Reviewing explanations for questions you answered correctly is helpful because it reinforces "GRE thinking."

Remember, your score on the actual GRE will depend on many factors, including your level of preparedness and your fatigue level on test day.

As you work through this and the other simulated tests in the book, you should be aware that they are not actual tests. They are reasonably accurate simulations written by GRE experts. They contain basically the same mix of question types as a real GRE. If you work through all of the material provided, you can rest assured that there won't be any surprises on test day.

The biggest difference between these tests and the real GRE is the fact that these are paper tests and you will take the GRE using a computer. We've tried to mimic the computer test as much as possible, but you should definitely plan to do some practicing with POWERPREP®, the free software available at www.gre.org from the authors of the GRE. For more information regarding the differences between the simulated test in this book and your actual GRE, please refer to Chapter 1, "Overview of the GRE," and Chapter 2, "Taking the GRE."

The Diagnostic Test begins on the next page.

SECTION 1—ISSUE TASK

45 Minutes

1 Question

You will have 45 minutes to select one topic from the two options presented, organize your thoughts, and compose a response that represents your point of view on the topic that you choose. Do not respond to any topic other than the one you select; a response to any other topic will receive a score of 0.

You will be given a choice between two general issues on a broad range of topics. You will be required to discuss your perspective on one of the issues, using examples and reasons drawn from your own experiences and observations.

Use scratch paper to organize your response before you begin writing. Write your response on the pages provided.

Present your viewpoint on *one* of the following claims. Use relevant reasons and examples to support your point of view.

Topic 1

> "All college students should be required to take math courses, even if the students have no interest in math."

Topic 2

> "The government should provide funding for school music programs so that music can flourish and be available to all members of the community."

Math is the fundmental for everything in our everyday basies. Thus I agree with the view that all college student should take Math course even if they are not intrested in Math, because meath is not only the fundmental to all subjects, it is also a very useful and basic tool that one will need in everyday life.

Math is very where. No matter which subject or math the student studies in college, math is there. From art, to chemistry, from science to social study math is hidden in every little corner of each subject. Many of the non-science student think that they do not need math, and some choose those non-science majors because they went to avoid taking math classes. However, what they do not realise is that no matter what they study, it will involve meath here and there. In art, one need to study the proportion of between different objects and compose them in a way that is please to the eyes. Thus, learning porportion is very important. Also, when one is learning how to draw a human face or body, he/she will know that human body features are very proportional, the artist need to do a very close calculation when drawing the the features, otherwise it will be unrealistic. For social science students, they need to know the population, and the make up of a society learn how to

thus, calculation of land, man power, and resources
are very important in term of their study. Every
subject is inter change and connected in different fields
when we start study deeper and deeper in our field,
and math is the basic of the basics, thus
the college students need to study at least one or two
math course in there college life.

Not only math is inbedded in every subject in different
studies and fields. It is a very important part of
our life. After graduation, and started working, 'I'
realized that basic math skills are very important
in ones life. After graduation, I started to earn money
on my own, and I need to file tax, do basic
budgeting and manage my bank account by myself.
without basic math skills, it would be very hard
to manage and learn to do those chores. Also
at work, no matter what position and field the
student is in, there is always some thing related
to math. From closing cash drawer for the cashier
to budgeting company's expenses, to submitt
your own expenses to the company for compensition
Very thing we do requires math.

There fore, it is very important for college
students to have math skills before they graduated
from college, because it will prepare them for their
future life and career.

SECTION 2—ARGUMENT TASK

30 Minutes

1 Question

You will have 30 minutes to organize your thoughts and compose a response that critiques the given argument. Do not respond to any topic other than the one given; a response to any other topic will receive a score of 0.

You are not being asked to discuss your point of view on the statement. You should identify and analyze the central elements of the argument, the underlying assumptions that are being made, and any supporting information that is given. Your critique can also discuss other information that would strengthen or weaken the argument or make it more logical.

Use scratch paper to organize your response before you begin writing. Write your response on the pages provided.

Critique the reasoning used in the following argument.

"When Marion Park first opened, it was the largest, most popular park in town. While it is still the largest park, it is no longer as popular as it once was. Recently collected statistics reveal the park's drop in popularity: On average, only 45 cars per day enter the park. Conversely, tiny Midtown Park in the center of downtown is visited by more than 125 people on a typical weekday. One obvious difference is that Midtown Park, unlike Marion Park, can utilize parking spaces along Main Street and along various side streets. Therefore, if Marion Park is to regain its popularity, then the town council will obviously need to approve funding for additional parking."

Martion Park's popularity dropped due to limited parking spaces for the vistors.

Comparing to the Midtown Park, Martion Park is not as convienent to park. Thus, resulting the potential vistors switched to Midtown Park instead of the Martion Park.

SECTION 3—VERBAL

30 Minutes

30 Questions

This section consists of five different types of questions: Sentence Completion, Analogies, Antonyms, Reading Comprehension, and Text Completion with Two or Three Blanks (this is a new question type; you will typically see only one of these questions on your GRE). To answer the questions, select the best answer from the answer choices given. Circle the letter or word(s) of your choice.

<u>Directions</u> for Sentence Completion Questions: The following sentences each contain one or two blanks, indicating that something has been left out of the sentence. Each answer choice contains one word or a set of words. Select the word or set of words that, when inserted in the blank(s), best fits the context of the sentence.

Example: Because of his --------, Brian's guests felt very welcome and comfortable staying at his house for the weekend.

(A) animosity

(B) hospitality

(C) determination

(D) wittiness

(E) severity

<u>Directions</u> for Analogies Questions: The following questions contain a set of related words in capital letters and five answer choices. Each answer choice also contains a set of words. Select the set of words that represents a relationship similar to the original set of words.

Example: APPRENTICE : PLUMBER ::

(A) player : coach

(B) child : parent

(C) student : teacher

(D) author : publisher

(E) intern : doctor

Directions for Antonyms Questions: The following questions contain a word in capital letters and five answer choices. Each answer choice contains a word or phrase. Select the word or phrase that best expresses a meaning opposite to the word in capital letters.

Example: CREDULOUS:

(A) skeptical

(B) naive   C

(C) spontaneous

(D) sensitive

(E) discrete

Directions for Text Completion with Two or Three Blanks Questions: These questions consist of a short passage with two or three numbered blanks, indicating that something has been left out of the text. Select the word or set of words that, when inserted in the blanks, best completes the text.

Example: Experts believe that humans have ten trillion cells in their bodies that (i) _____ any number of essential genetic elements; scientists often marvel at what incredible (ii) _____ would ensue should the cells become jumbled or misunderstand their purpose.

Blank (i)	Blank (ii)
govern	order
organize	method
dislocate	chaos

Directions for Reading Comprehension Questions: The passages in this section are followed by several questions. The questions correspond to information that is stated or implied in the passage. Read the passage and choose the best answer for each question.

Answer the questions in the order presented.

The Verbal section questions begin on the next page.

1. CULPABLE : GUILTY ::

    (A) marginal : necessary

    (B) sociable : ambivalent

    (C) venerable : esteemed

    C

    (D) factual : suspect

    (E) reasonable : superlative

2. PILGRIMAGE : ZEALOT ::

    (A) chef : recipe

    (B) journey : path

    (C) sleet : hail

    (D) genesis : citizen

    (E) expedition : pioneer

3. As we traveled to college for the first time, the family car was -------- with books, clothing, appliances, and other necessities.

    (A) keen

    (B) indigent

    (C) barren

     E

    (D) pallid

    (E) laden

4. The -------- of sediment in the river caused concern among environmentalists and industrialists alike; the water levels in the river were being reduced almost daily.

    (A) accretion

    P

    (B) disposal

    (C) catalyst

    (D) alienation

    (E) ethnology

5. UTILITARIAN : QUIXOTIC ::

    (A) disconcerting : unsettling

    (B) ephemeral : fleeting

    (C) malevolent : kind

    (D) loquacious : talkative

    (E) obdurate : stubborn

6. ABATE:

    (A) abdicate

    (B) augment

    (C) annihilate

    (D) lessen

    (E) contradict

7. Body language involves a combination of multiple facial (i) _____ and various physical positions to convey its unique (ii) _____ message.

Blank (i)	Blank (ii)
terminology	oral
expressions	strident
appearance	nonverbal

8. FIRE : WOOD ::

    (A) motor : boat

    (B) sunlight : forest

    (C) oil : water

    (D) gears : bicycle

    (E) automobile : gasoline

9. PLACATE:

   (A) to pacify

   (B) to infuriate

B (C) to percolate

   (D) to promulgate

   (E) to manipulate

10. SKEPTICISM:

   (A) intricacy

   (B) qualmishness

C (C) credulity

   (D) disbelief

   (E) narcissism

11. WARY:

   (A) waning

   (B) vigilant

E (C) arbitrary

   (D) cautious

   (E) foolhardy

12. ABROGATE:

   (A) to institute

   (B) to annul

A (C) to abate

   (D) to abuse

   (E) to bargain for

13. OBLIQUE : INDIRECT ::

   (A) par : standard

   (B) inherent : direct

A (C) resonant : equitable

   (D) justified : logical

   (E) circular : animated

14. Although the scientist's recommendations may have been --------, the students had trouble following his -------- presentation and were, therefore, against his proposal.

    (A) plausible . . organized

    (B) absurd . . intricate

    (C) realistic . . convoluted

    (D) judicious . . dynamic

    (E) ubiquitous . . empirical

15. ASSIMILATE:

    (A) to ascertain

    (B) to befuddle

    (C) to suffocate

    (D) to dissipate

    (E) to incorporate into

16. Running a marathon is an -------- task, taking months of both physical and mental preparation and training before actually running a grueling 26.2 miles.

    (A) arduous

    (B) ambiguous

    (C) involuntary

    (D) eloquent

    (E) overt

Questions 17 and 18 are based on the following passage.

Line

(5)

(10)

　　When I was preparing for my two-week vacation in southern Africa, I realized that the continent would be like nothing I had ever seen. I wanted to explore the urban streets as well as the savannah; it's always been my goal to have experiences on vacation that most other tourists fail to find. When my plans were finalized, I left for Africa. The cultural differences were stunning, and made for plenty of laughter and confusion, but always ended up bringing smiles to our faces. What's funny now, though, more than ever, is how ridiculous I must have seemed to the people of one village when I played with their dog. Apparently, the role of dogs in America is nothing like it is in the third world.

　　When I walk the streets of my hometown now, I often find myself staring at all of the dogs and dog owners on the sidewalk. The way I see it, the American dog lives for the thrill: a hug, a scratch behind the ears, a new chew toy, another

chance to fight against the leash it knows is only six feet long. Dog owners love to believe their animal is smart, while people who've never owned a dog tend to
(15)   believe the opposite. With a little training, the dogs don't bark, bite, or use the sofa as a toilet, but they do provide years of unconditional affection and loyalty, plus the occasional lame-brained escapade at which human onlookers can laugh.

I am convinced African dogs could clobber their American counterparts. The relationship between a typical African and his dog is one of tangible mutualism.
(20)   I say tangible because the African sees himself as the dominant creature not to be bothered by the dog, but nevertheless responsible for providing for it. Hence, no attempts at behavioral training are ever made on African dogs. Instead, the African seizes power with a chunk of scrap meat and a bowl of water. The dog soon learns to quit yapping and biting at the hand that feeds him. Never does
(25)   the African speak to the animal. I'm not even sure such dogs get names. Their behavior becomes interestingly balanced, however, much to the surprise of the compassionate American dog lover.

17. The author of the passage is primarily concerned with presenting

   (A) a description of cultural differences

   (B) an overview of animal behavior

   (C) a history of international tourism

   (D) evidence to refute a global theory

   (E) an account of animal cruelty

18. According to information provided by the passage, which of the following traits would the author most likely ascribe to African dog owners?

   (A) Affectionate

   (B) Abusive

   (C) Pragmatic

   (D) Deceitful

   (E) Antagonistic

19. MUFFLED : NOISE ::

   (A) heightened : awareness

   (B) pervasive : tone

   (C) condensed : version

   (D) subdued : emotion

   (E) increased : capacity

20. When practicing with a bow and arrow, it is necessary to be aware of both the -------- and the -------- of one's arrows if one wishes to hit the target.

    (A) rigor . . tenacity

    (B) direction . . imminence

    (C) breadth . . cessation

    (D) divergence . . expulsion

    (E) velocity . . trajectory

Questions 21−24 are based on the following passage.

Over the years there have been countless fans of the classic Hanna-Barbera cartoon character Yogi Bear. The cartoon series enjoyed by young and old alike revolved mostly around the misadventures of this loveable bear and his sidekick Boo-Boo as they attempted to snag "pic-a-nic" baskets in the made-up land of Jellystone Park. It's not often that people think about where the ideas for these cartoon characters came from, which brings up an interesting point: Do bears actually search for food left in picnic baskets and unattended campsites? Anyone who has watched an episode of the classic cartoon can see that the bears' behavior goes far beyond the limits of what is natural. The thing that must be explored, then, is which of those humorous antics were imagined by the writers at Hanna-Barbera, and which were actually based on a bear's normal behaviors.

Remarkably enough, bears have been known to seek out food from some unlikely sources, including picnic baskets, to supplement their usual diet of berries, insects, and fish. Bears work throughout the summer and fall to build up fat stores to have energy enough to last them through their winter hibernations. Related to this is their need to replenish their depleted reserves when they wake up in the spring. Food is generally scarce in the early spring and consequently the bears will gladly indulge in any foods that are high in proteins or fats. This is the main reason for any incidents involving bears after they enter campsites in search of food.

Although this behavior may seem strange, it is merely the result of nature equipping the bears with a variety of traits that allow them to remain well fed in increasingly human-populated habitats. Specifically, the American black bear, *Ursus americanus*, has color vision, which most other animals lack. Black bears have been observed by scientists using this unique enhancement to distinguish between varying food items at close range. On top of this, bears have an acute sense of smell and can use their especially sensitive lips to locate food. These sensory talents contribute to the bears' remarkably high intelligence and curiosity, giving them the ability to open closed containers if they believe food is inside. Their exploratory and navigational skills are also worthy of note—most bears will maintain vast territories to be sure they can obtain food from a varity of sources. Bears may even vary their sleep cycles in areas where there is a large degree of human activity, either feasting on road-side garbage during the day or scouring campsites for leftovers at night.

21. The primary purpose of the passage is to

    (A) offer a comparison between television programming and real-world events

    (B) describe the conditions under which a bear will enter human habitats

    (C) explain the different means by which bears secure nutritious food

    (D) discuss new evidence concerning the difficulty of controlling bears

    (E) resolve a controversy surrounding the foraging behavior of bears

22. The author mentions all of the following as potential food sources for bears EXCEPT:

    (A) berries

    (B) general stores

    (C) insects

    (D) fish

    (E) picnic baskets

23. It can be inferred from the passage that which of the following is true of bears?

    (A) They are particularly resourceful.

    (B) They must enter human habitats in order to survive.

    (C) They cannot tolerate human food.

    (D) They eat voraciously throughout the winter.

    (E) They have only one method of obtaining food.

24. The author includes a discussion of the American black bear, *Ursus americanus*, most likely in order to

    (A) provide additional support for the unique feeding habits of bears

    (B) discount the theory regarding a bear's ability to remain well fed

    (C) evaluate the dispute between advocates of differing theories regarding bear behavior

    (D) challenge recent research on the way in which bears secure food

    (E) suggest further investigation of human interaction with bears

Questions 25 and 26 are based on the following passage.

Line

(5)

(10)

(15)

(20)

Sending a robot into space to gather information is certainly a viable option, but should be regarded only as that—an option. Even the most technologically advanced robots cannot and should not replace manned missions to outer space.

Certainly it is cheaper and less dangerous to launch a computer probe that can gather reams of data, but often the information obtained by a machine serves only to produce more questions than it answers. Therefore, the space program should allow manned missions to follow up on those initial information-gathering robotic ventures.

While manned missions are more costly than are unmanned missions, they are also more successful. Robots and astronauts use much of the same equipment in space, but a human is much more capable of calibrating those instruments correctly and placing them in appropriate and useful positions. A computer is often neither as sensitive nor as accurate as a human in managing the same terrain or environmental circumstances. Robots are also not as equipped as humans to solve problems as they arise, and robots often collect data that is not helpful or even desired. A human, on the other hand, can make instant decisions about what to explore further and what to ignore.

While technological advances have allowed us to make incredible strides in space exploration, they still cannot match the power of the human brain. This "supercomputer" is necessary in order to maintain a space program that can truly advance to the next level.

25. The passage supplies information to answer which of the following questions?

(A) What is the cost of launching a computer probe into space?

(B) What type of information can safely be ignored when exploring outer space?

(C) How much information can a computer probe gather in outer space?

(D) What is the next level in space exploration?

(E) Are unmanned space missions more economical than manned space missions?

26. According to the passage, all of the following are advantages of humans over robots EXCEPT:

(A) humans can more accurately manage the data collected

(B) humans can apply critical thinking skills to new situations

(C) humans can typically stay in outer space for longer periods of time

(D) humans are more sensitive to environmental changes

(E) humans are better at preparing instrumentation for use in space

27. The problem with activists is that far too often they merely -------- the protection of various ecosystems, instead of taking a lead role in their --------.

    (A) circumvent . . stability

    (B) abridge . . solution

    (C) diversify . . precedent

    (D) advocate . . management

    (E) abhor . . demise

28. BRAZEN:

    (A) insolent

    (B) prudent

    (C) uncouth

    (D) undaunted

    (E) materialistic

29. ENIGMATIC:

    (A) abstruse

    (B) puzzling

    (C) enlightening

    (D) disconcerting

    (E) worrisome

30. FORAGE : HUNGRY ::

    (A) pillage : content

    (B) steal : incarcerated

    (C) celebrate : dejected

    (D) leap : caustic

    (E) sleep : exhausted

END OF SECTION 3

SECTION 4—QUANTITATIVE

30 Minutes

28 Questions

This section includes three types of questions: Quantitative Comparison, Problem Solving, and Numeric Entry. (Your actual GRE will likely have only one Numeric Entry question, because it is a new question type.) For each question, circle the letter of your choice or write your answer as instructed.

General Information:

Numbers: All of the numbers used in this section are real numbers.

Figures: Assume that the position of all points, angles, etc., are in the order shown and the measures of angles are positive.

Straight lines can be assumed to be straight.

All figures lie in a plane unless otherwise stated.

The figures given for each question provide information to solve the problem. The figures are not drawn to scale unless otherwise stated. To solve the problems, use your knowledge of mathematics; do not estimate lengths and sizes of the figures to answer questions.

Directions for Quantitative Comparison Questions: Some of the following questions give you two quantities, one in Column A and one in Column B. Compare the two quantities and choose one of the following answer choices:

A if the quantity in Column A is greater;

B if the quantity in Column B is greater;

C if the two quantities are equal;

D if you cannot determine the relationship based on the given information

Do not mark answer choice E, as there are only four choices from which to choose.

Note: Information and/or figures pertaining to one or both of the quantities may appear above the two columns. Any information that appears in both columns has the same meaning in Column A and in Column B.

Example: <u>Column A</u>   <u>Column B</u>

$-(3)^4$ $(-3)^4$

<u>Directions</u> for Problem Solving Questions: Select the best answer for these multiple-choice questions.

Example: If $y = 5x$ and $z = 3y$, then in terms of x, $x + y + z =$

(A) 21x

$z = 15x$

$x + 5x + 15x = 21x$

(B) 16x

(C) 15x

(D) 9x

(E) 8x

<u>Directions</u> for Numeric Entry Questions: Enter your answer in the box below the question.

Example: Solve the equation for x: $2(x - 3) + 9 = 4x - 7$

$x =$

Answer the questions in the order presented.

The Quantitative Section questions begin on the next page.

	Column A	**Column B**
1.	40,000	$(201.70)^2$

$(200)^2$
40000

2.	15 percent of 90	90 percent of 15

$$9x - 2y = 16$$
$$3x + 7y = 82$$

3.	$x + y$	10

$$x = 4$$

4.	$3x^4$	750

5. $(22 - 20 - 18 - 16) - (20 - 18 - 16 - 14) =$

(A) -100

(B) -4

(C) 4

(D) 8

(E) 36

6. If $5x - 6 = 14$, then $8x =$

(A) $\frac{8}{5}$

(B) 4

(C) $\frac{64}{5}$

(D) 20

(E) 32

Column A   **Column B**

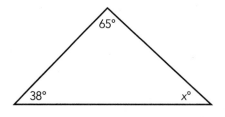

7.	x	87°

8.	The average (arithmetic mean) of 16, 23, and 52	The average (arithmetic mean) of 15, 24, and 51

9.	The number of hours in a week	The number of months in 14 years

10. Of the following, which is closest to $\sqrt[4]{80}$?

    (A) 5

    (B) 4

    (C) 3

    (D) 2

    (E) 1

Column A	**Column B**
11. 8.7(3.5)	8(3.5) + 0.7(3.5)

12. Solve the equation for x: $2(x - 3) + 9 = 4x - 7$

$$x = \boxed{2}$$

Column A	**Column B**
x is an integer greater than 2.	
13. 3^{2x-3}	3^{x}

Refer to the following graphs for Questions 14–18.

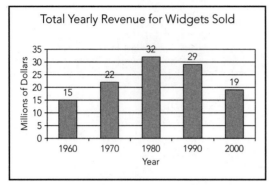

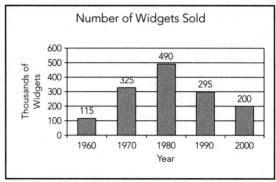

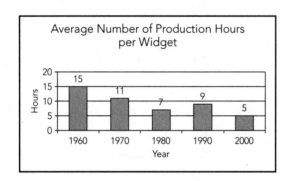

14. In 1990, the total revenue for widgets sold was about how many times as great as the number of widgets sold?

    (A) 3

    (B) 10

    (C) 65

    (D) 98

    (E) 120

15. In 1970, if the cost to produce one widget was $0.07, what would have been the total cost to produce the number of widgets sold during that year?

    (A) $1,540

    (B) $14,000

    (C) $20,650

    (D) $22,750

    (E) $34,300

16. The percent decrease in average number of production hours per widget from 1990 to 2000 was approximately

    (A) 44%

    (B) 36%

    (C) 34%

    (D) 32%

    (E) 27%

17. In how many of the years shown was the number of widgets sold at least three times the number of widgets sold in 1960?

    (A) Four

    (B) Three

    (C) Two

    (D) One

    (E) None

18. Which of the following statements can be inferred from the data?

    I. The greatest increase in total yearly revenue over any 10-year period shown was $7 million.

    II. In each of the 10-year periods shown in which total yearly revenue increased, the average number of production hours per widget decreased.

    III. From 1980 to 1990, fewer widgets were sold because each widget took longer to produce.

    (A) I only

    (B) II only

    (C) III only

    (D) I and III

    (E) II and III

	Column A	Column B
19.	The cost of p apples at a cost of $r + 7$ cents each	The cost of 7 peaches at a cost of $(p + r)$ cents each

A rectangular box is 5 feet wide and 6 feet high
and has a volume of 120 cubic feet.

20.	4 feet	The length of the box

21. Which of the following is equivalent to the inequality $3x - 6 > 6x + 9$?

    (A) $x > -5$

    (B) $x < -5$

    (C) $x > -2$

    (D) $x < 3$

    (E) $x > 3$

22. If Tom traveled 45 miles in 12 hours and Jim traveled four times as far in one-third the time, what was Jim's average speed, in miles per hour?

    (A) 5

    (B) 15

    (C) 30

    (D) 45

    (E) 90

Column A	**Column B**
In the rectangular coordinate plane, points A, B, and C have coordinates (8, 9), (5, 9), and (5, 6), respectively.	

23. AB AC

The height of right circular cylinder K is 3 times the radius of its base.

24.   The height of K The area of the base of K

25. On the following line AD, if $AC = 15$ and $BD = 35$, and CD is three times AB, what is the value of BC?

    (A) 5

    (B) 10

    (C) 15

    (D) 25

    (E) It cannot be determined from the information given.

26. For senior class pictures, a photographer charges x dollars to make a negative, $\frac{7x}{10}$ dollars for each of the first 20 prints, and $\frac{x}{10}$ dollars for each print in excess of 20 prints. If \$80 is the total charge to make a negative and 30 prints, what is the value of x?

(A) 3

(B) 4

(C) 5

(D) 6

(E) 7

C

27. Which of the following is equal to $\frac{1}{4}$ of 0.1 percent?

(A) 0.000025

(B) 0.00025

(C) 0.0025

(D) 0.025

(E) 0.25

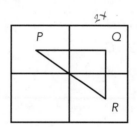

28. In the preceding figure, each of the four squares has sides of length $2x$. If triangle PQR is formed by joining the centers of three of the squares, what is the perimeter of triangle PQR in terms of x?

(A) $4x\sqrt{2}$

(B) $2x\sqrt{2}$

(C) $4x + \sqrt{2}$

(D) $4x + 2x\sqrt{2}$

(E) $4 + 2x\sqrt{2}$

END OF SECTION 4

GRE Diagnostic Test Answer Key

Section 3

1. C
2. E
3. E
4. A
5. C
6. B
7. expressions; nonverbal
8. E
9. B
10. C
11. E
12. A
13. A
14. C
15. D
16. A
17. A
18. C
19. D
20. E
21. B
22. B
23. A
24. A
25. E
26. C
27. D
28. B
29. C
30. E

Section 4

1. B
2. C
3. A
4. A
5. B
6. E
7. B
8. A
9. C
10. C
11. C
12. 5
13. D
14. D
15. D
16. A
17. D
18. B
19. D
20. C
21. B
22. D
23. B
24. D
25. A
26. C
27. B
28. D

Scoring Guidelines

To calculate your approximate Scaled Score, count the number of questions that you answered correctly on the Verbal and Quantitative sections. This is your Raw Score, which can then be converted to a Scaled Score for each section using the table below. Remember that this is just an *approximation* of what you might expect to score on the GRE if you took the test today!

SCORE CONVERSION TABLE FOR GRE GENERAL TEST

Raw Score	Scaled Score	
	Verbal	Quantitative
30	800	
29	780	
28	750	800
27	730	780
26	710	750
25	690	720
24	660	700
23	640	680
22	620	650
21	600	630
20	580	610
19	570	600
18	550	590
17	520	570
16	490	540
15	470	500
14	450	480
13	440	460
12	400	430
11	380	400
10	360	390

Continued on Next Page

9	320	370
8	240	320
7	200	290
6	200	240
5	200	200
4	200	200
0–3	200	200

NOTE: Your actual scaled GRE score may vary by as much as 60 points.

GRE Diagnostic Test Answers and Explanations

Sections 1 and 2—Analytical Writing

Because grading the essay is subjective, we've chosen not to include any "graded" essays here. Your best bet is to have someone you trust, such as your personal tutor, read your essays and give you an honest critique. Make the grading criteria mentioned in Chapter 7, "GRE Analytical Writing Assessment," available to whomever grades your essays. If you plan on grading your own essays, review the grading criteria and be as honest as possible regarding the structure, development, organization, technique, and appropriateness of your writing. Focus on your weak areas and continue to practice in order to improve your writing skills.

Section 3—Verbal

1. **The best answer is C.** *Culpable* means "guilty," so the best answer will include two words that are synonyms. *Venerable* means "esteemed," so this word pair has the same relationship as do the words in the question stem. None of the other word pairs are synonyms.

2. **The best answer is E.** A *zealot* is generally someone who is committed to a certain cause, and a *pilgrimage* is a long journey or search of some significance. A general sentence that can be used to describe the analogy is: "A -------- is likely to embark upon a --------." The word pair that best fits the sentence is *pioneer* and *expedition*; a *pioneer* embarks upon an *expedition* in search of land, adventure, and often, a new beginning.

3. **The best answer is E.** The word *laden* means "weighed down with a heavy load," which best fits the description in this sentence of the family car. The other words do not fit the context of the sentence.

4. **The best answer is A.** *Accretion* means "the gradual buildup" of something, and is often used in reference to geologic phenomena. If water levels were being reduced because of the buildup of sediment, then both environmentalists and industrialists might have cause for concern. The other words do not fit the context of the sentence.

5. **The best answer is C.** *Utilitarian* is an adjective that is used to describe something that is "useful" and "practical." Conversely, the adjective *quixotic* means "idealistic" or "impractical." A general sentence that can be used to describe the analogy is: "Something that is appropriately described as ------- cannot be --------." To answer this question, determine

which of the answer choices contains two words that are antonyms. Something that is *malevolent* would never be described as *kind* because the two words are opposite in meaning; therefore, answer choice C is correct. The other word pairs are synonyms.

6. **The best answer is B.** *Abate* means to "diminish or reduce," and *augment* means to "add to or increase." The word *abdicate*, while it sounds similar to *abate*, means "to give up power or rights," which is not an antonym of *abate*. Both *annihilate* and *lessen* have meanings similar to *abate*. *Contradict* means to "deny."

7. **The answers are: *expressions*; *nonverbal*.** In the first blank, think what word would fit best with "multiple facial." *Terminology* does not make sense, and *appearance* does not mesh with *multiple*. In the second blank, *strident* and *oral* do not work because body language is not audible.

8. **The best answer is E.** A *fire* consumes *wood* as fuel. The word pair with the same relationship is *automobile* and *gasoline*. The other answer choices contain word pairs that are related, but not in the same ways as *fire* and *wood*. Although a *boat* is powered by a *motor*, the *boat* does not consume the *motor*. In addition, the words in this answer choice are in the wrong order.

9. **The best answer is B.** *Placate* means to "pacify," which is the opposite of *infuriate*, which means to "anger." Answer choice A is a synonym of *placate*. The other answer choices do not have meanings that are opposite to that of *placate*.

10. **The best answer is C.** The word *skepticism* indicates an inclination to be "doubtful or questioning," whereas the word *credulity* indicates an inclination to be "easily deceived." These words are most opposite in meaning. Answer choice D is a synonym of *skepticism*. The other answer choices do not have meanings that are opposite to that of *skepticism*.

11. **The best answer is E.** The word *wary* means "cautious of danger," whereas *foolhardy* means "reckless." *Waning* sounds like *wary*, but it means "decreasing in size." *Vigilant* means "alert to danger," which is a synonym of *wary*. Likewise, *cautious* is a synonym of *wary*. *Arbitrary* means "unregulated or unreasonable" and is not an antonym of *wary*.

12. **The best answer is A.** *Abrogate* means to "repeal," usually by an act of authority. To *institute* means to "establish," often by an act of authority. These words are most opposite in meaning. The other answer choices do not have meanings that are opposite to that of *abrogate*.

13. **The best answer is A.** *Oblique* means "indirectly aimed or expressed," so the words in the question stem are synonyms. *Par* means "an accepted standard," so the words in answer choice A are also synonyms. None of the other answer choices contain word pairs that are synonymous.

14. **The best answer is C.** The word *although* suggests a conflict between the words that best fit in the blanks. Because the students were against the scientist's proposal, it makes sense that the word in the second blank would have a somewhat negative connotation. Answer choice C best fits the context of the sentence; even though the students thought the recommendations were realistic, the presentation was so hard to follow that the students did not support the scientist's proposal. None of the other answer choices fit the context of the sentence.

15. **The best answer is D.** To *assimilate* is to "incorporate or absorb," whereas *dissipate* means to "drive away or disperse." None of the other answer choices have meanings that are opposite to that of *assimilate*.

16. **The best answer is A.** The context of the sentence indicates that running a marathon is quite challenging and takes a lot of preparation. *Arduous* means "difficult or demanding great effort," which best fits the context of the sentence.

17. **The best answer is A.** The main focus of the passage is on the differences between American dogs and dog owners, and African dogs and dog owners. According to the passage, the author thought that the cultural differences between him and the African people "were stunning," and then he goes on to describe one particular difference. This best supports answer choice A. The other answer choices are either too broad, or do not effectively describe the main point of the passage.

18. **The best answer is C.** The author states, "The relationship between a typical African and his dog is one of tangible mutualism. I say tangible because the African sees himself as the dominant creature not to be bothered by the dog, but nevertheless responsible for providing for it." There is nothing in the passage to suggest that African dog owners are either affectionate or abusive to their animals; rather, African dog owners are quite pragmatic, or practical, in their approach to interacting with their dogs. Likewise, the passage does not indicate that African dog owners are deceitful or antagonistic.

19. **The best answer is D.** The word *muffled* means "repressed or quieted." Likewise, *subdued* means "quieted or brought under control." A *noise* can be *muffled* in the same way that an *emotion* can be *subdued*. None of the other answer choices have the same relationship as that of the words in the question stem.

20. **The best answer is E.** If you were shooting a bow and arrow, it makes sense that you would want to be aware of things such as direction, speed, and so on. Only answer choices B and E contain words that are appropriate for the first blank. *Imminence*, which means "the likelihood of something happening," does not make sense in the second blank, whereas *trajectory*, which refers to "the path of a projectile," does.

21. **The best answer is B.** The passage focuses primarily on describing some unusual eating habits of bears, including seeking food from campsites. According to the passage, "Food is generally scarce in the early spring and consequently the bears will gladly indulge in any foods that are high in proteins or fats. This is the main reason for any incidents involving bears after they enter campsites in search of food." This best supports answer choice B. The other answer choices are either too broad, or do not effectively describe the main point of the passage.

22. **The best answer is B.** The passage states that ". . . bears have been known to seek out food from some unlikely sources, including picnic baskets, to supplement their usual diet of berries, insects, and fish." The passage mentions that bears need to build up their "fat stores," but the passage does not mention "general stores" as a food source for bears.

23. **The best answer is A.** According to the passage, bears often engage in seemingly unbearlike behavior when it comes to securing food: entering campsites and searching through picnic baskets. This suggests that bears are particularly resourceful when it comes to making sure that they have enough to eat. The other answer choices are not supported by the passage.

24. **The best answer is A.** The passage points out a unique characteristic of the American black bear: It has color vision, and can, as a result, easily "distinguish between varying food items at close range." This detail was most likely provided to offer additional support for the unique feeding habits of bears. The other answer choices are not supported by the passage.

25. **The best answer is E.** The passage states that "Certainly it is cheaper and less dangerous to launch a computer probe . . . ," which answers the question posed in answer choice E. There is not enough information in the passage to answer any of the other questions.

26. **The best answer is C.** There is nothing in the passage to suggest that humans can stay in outer space for longer periods of time than can robots. All of the other answer choices are mentioned specifically in the passage as advantages that humans have over robots.

27. **The best answer is D.** The context of the sentence indicates that activists should be taking a lead role in something that has to do with the protection of ecosystems. *Advocate* means "to speak out in favor of," and it makes sense that there might be a problem if activists simply speak out in favor of protecting ecosystems, and don't actually do anything to help manage the ecosystems. The other answer choices do not fit the context of the sentence.

28. **The best answer is B.** *Brazen* means "shameless or unrestrained," whereas *prudent* means "wise and practical." Both *insolent* and *uncouth* have meanings similar to that of *brazen*. The other answer choices do not include words that have meanings opposite to that of *brazen*.

29. **The best answer is C.** *Enigmatic* refers to something that is "ambiguous," which is the opposite of *enlightening*. Both *abstruse* and *puzzling* are synonyms of *enigmatic*. The other answer choices do not include words that have meanings opposite to that of *enigmatic*.

30. **The best answer is E.** The word *forage* refers to "the act of searching for food." Therefore, one *forages* when one is *hungry*. A general sentence that can be used to describe the analogy is: "Individuals -------- when they are --------." The words that have the same relationship and can be inserted into the sentence are *sleep* and *exhausted*.

Section 4—Quantitative

1. **The correct answer is B.** The quantity in Column A, 40,000, is equal to $(200)^2$, which is less than $(201.7)^2$. Therefore, the quantity in Column B is greater than the quantity in Column A.

2. **The correct answer is C.** In order to calculate 15 percent of 90, multiply 90 by 0.15, the decimal equivalent of 15 percent. Likewise, to calculate 90 percent of 15, multiply 15 by 0.90, the decimal equivalent of 90 percent:

    $$(0.15)(90) = 13.5$$
    $$(0.90)(15) = 13.5$$

    The quantities are equal.

3. **The correct answer is A.** To answer this question, first multiply the bottom equation by -3 to get $-9x - 21y = -246$. Now you can add the two equations in the system together and eliminate one of the variables, as follows:

    $$
    \begin{aligned}
    (9x - 2y &= 16) \\
    + (-9x - 21y &= -246) \\
    \hline
    -23y &= -230 \\
    y &= 10
    \end{aligned}
    $$

Substitute 10 for y in the first equation and solve for x:

$$9x - 2(10) = 16$$
$$9x - 20 = 16$$
$$9x = 36$$
$$x = 4$$

Column A, $(x + y)$, is equivalent to $4 + 10$, or 14, and Column B = 10; therefore, the quantity in Column A is greater than the quantity in Column B.

4. **The correct answer is A.** When $x = 4$, Column A is equivalent to $3(4)^4$, or $3(256)$; Column B = 750, which is equivalent to $3(250)$. Therefore, the quantity in Column A is greater than the quantity in Column B.

5. **The correct answer is B.** To solve this problem, perform the operations within the parentheses first:

$$(22 - 20 - 18 - 16) = -32$$

and

$$(20 - 18 - 16 - 14) = -28$$

Now, subtract the second value from the first:

$$-32 - (-28) =$$
$$-32 + 28 = -4$$

6. **The correct answer is E.** To solve this problem, first solve for x, as follows:

$$5x - 6 = 14$$
$$5x = 20$$
$$x = 4$$

Now substitute 4 for x: $8x = 8(4) = 32$.

7. **The correct answer is B.** To answer this question correctly you must remember that the sum of the interior angles of a triangle is 180°. Therefore, $x = 180 - 65 - 38$, or 77. Therefore, the quantity in Column B (87) is greater than the quantity in Column A (77).

8. **The correct answer is A.** The sum of the values in Column A (91) is greater than the sum of the values in Column B (90), so the average of Column A is greater than the average of Column B.

9. **The correct answer is C.** To answer this question, simply calculate the number of hours in a week (24×7, or 168) and the number of months in 14 years (12×14, or 168). The quantities are equal.

10. **The correct answer is C.** To easily solve this problem, recognize that $\sqrt[4]{81}$ (the fourth root of 81) is equivalent to 3, because $3^4 = 81$. Therefore, of the choices given, 3 is closest to $\sqrt[4]{80}$. You could have eliminated answer choice E, because 1 raised to any power will always be 1.

11. **The correct answer is C.** To solve this problem, factor 3.5 out of Column B to get $3.5(8 + 0.7)$, which is equivalent to $3.5(8.7)$. This is the same value as that in Column A; the quantities are equal.

12. **The correct answer is 5.** To solve this problem, isolate x on the left side of the equation by performing the necessary calculations:

$$2(x - 3) + 9 = 4x - 7$$

First, distribute the 2:

$$2x - 6 + 9 = 4x - 7$$

Next, perform the addition on the left side:

$$2x + 3 = 4x - 7$$

Now, subtract 3 from both sides:

$$2x = 4x - 10$$

Next, subtract $4x$ from each side:

$$-2x = -10$$

Finally, divide both sides by -2:

$$x = 5$$

13. **The correct answer is D.** Because you do not know the value of x, you cannot determine a relationship between the two columns. For example, when $x = 3$, the quantities are equal. However, when x is an integer greater than 3, the quantity in Column B is greater.

14. **The correct answer is D.** According to the graphs, in 1990 total revenue was $29 million and the number of widgets sold was 295,000. Because 295,000 is slightly less than 10 percent of 29,000,000, the total revenue must have been just under 100 times greater than the number of widgets sold.

15. **The correct answer is D.** According to the graphs, in 1970, 325,000 widgets were sold; at $0.07 per widget, the total cost would have been 325,000($0.07), or $22,750.

16. **The correct answer is A.** According to the graphs, from 1990 to 2000, the average number of production hours per widget decreased from 9 to 5. To calculate the percent decrease, divide the starting value (9) by the difference between the starting value and ending value (9 − 5):

$$\frac{4}{9} = 0.44, \text{ which is equivalent to } 44\%$$

17. **The correct answer is D.** The first step in solving this problem is to calculate three times the number of widgets sold in 1960. According to the graphs, the number of widgets sold in 1960 was 115,000; 115,000(3) = 345,000. The only year in which more than 345,000 widgets sold was 1980 (490,000 widgets sold).

18. **The correct answer is B.** According to the graphs, the greatest increase in total yearly revenue over any 10-year period shown was $10 million—from 1970 to 1980. Therefore, Roman numeral I is not true, and you can eliminate answer choices A and D, which include Roman numeral I. According to the graphs, from 1960 to 1970 and from 1970 to 1980, total yearly revenue increased while average production hours per widget decreased; therefore, Roman numeral II is true. Eliminate answer choice C because it does not include Roman numeral II. According to the graphs, from 1980 to 1990, the number of widgets sold decreased while the average number of production hours per widget increased; you might be tempted to infer that the reduced number of widgets sold was due to the increased production time, but there could have been other factors that you are not aware of; therefore, you cannot safely accept Roman numeral III as true. Eliminate answer choice E.

19. **The correct answer is D.** The values of p and r are not given, so you cannot determine the relationship between Column A and Column B.

20. **The correct answer is C.** To solve this problem remember that the volume is calculated by multiplying the length by the width by the height ($l \times w \times h$). Set up an equation to find the length of the box:

$$l \times 5 \times 6 = 120$$
$$l \times 30 = 120$$
$$l = 4$$

The quantities are equal.

21. **The correct answer is B.** To quickly solve this problem, recall the perfect squares that are closest to $\sqrt{42}$:

$$\sqrt{36} = 6$$
$$\sqrt{49} = 7$$

Because the question asks for the largest integer *less* than $\sqrt{42}$, the correct answer must be 6.

22. **The correct answer is D.** You are given that Tom traveled 45 miles in 12 hours and that Jim traveled four times as far in one-third the time. That means that Jim traveled 45×4, or 180 miles in $12 \times \left(\frac{1}{3}\right)$, or 4 hours. Therefore, Jim traveled $\frac{180}{4}$, or 45 miles per hour.

23. **The correct answer is B.** To solve this problem, plot the points in the coordinate plane, as shown below:

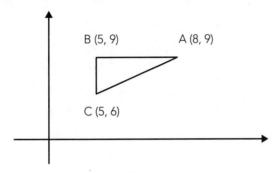

    AC is the hypotenuse of the right triangle that you just created, and AB is a side; the hypotenuse is always longer than either of the sides, so the quantity in Column B (AC) is greater than the quantity in Column A (AB).

24. **The correct answer is D.** To solve this problem, set the radius equal to x; therefore, the height is $3x$. The base of a circular cylinder is a circle, and the formula for the area of a circle is πr^2. Therefore, the area (Column B) is πx^2, which will be greater than $3x$ (Column A) when $x > \frac{3}{\pi}$. Conversely, if $x = \frac{3}{\pi}$, then the height would equal the area. Because you don't know what x is, you cannot determine a relationship between the quantities.

25. **The correct answer is A.** To solve this problem, break down the lengths of each of the segments, as follows:

    You are given that CD is three times AB, which means that $CD = 3AB$.
    You are also given that $AC = 15$, which means that $BC = 15 - AB$.
    Since $BD = 35$, then BC also equals $35 - CD$.
    Substitute $3AB$ for CD to get $BC = 35 - 3AB$.

Now, set the two values for BC equal to one another and solve for AB, as follows:

$$15 - AB = 35 - 3AB$$
$$2AB = 20$$
$$AB = 10$$

Finally, because $AB = 10$ and $AC = 15$, BC must equal $AC - AB$, or $15 - 10$, which is 5.

26. **The correct answer is C.** You are given that the cost of the negative is x dollars and that the cost of the first 20 prints is $\frac{7x}{10}$ dollars per print. You are also given that any number of prints over 20 is $\frac{x}{10}$ dollars per print. The question stem indicates that $80 is the total charge to make a negative and 30 prints. You know that the first 20 prints will cost $\frac{7x}{10}$ dollars per print and the remaining 10 prints will cost $\frac{x}{10}$ dollars per print. Set up and equation and solve for x, as follows:

$$x + 20\left(\frac{7x}{10}\right) + 10\left(\frac{x}{10}\right) = 80$$
$$x + \left(\frac{140x}{10}\right) + \left(\frac{10x}{10}\right) = 80$$
$$x + 14x + x = 80$$
$$16x = 80$$
$$x = 5$$

27. **The correct answer is B.** To solve this problem, remember that $\frac{1}{4}$ is equivalent to 0.25, and that 0.1 percent is equivalent to $0.001 \left(\frac{0.1}{100}\right)$. Therefore, $\frac{1}{4}$, or 0.25 of $0.001 = 0.00025$; do not get confused and simply find $\frac{1}{4}$ of 0.1, (0.025) because the question asks for $\frac{1}{4}$ of 0.1 percent.

28. **The correct answer is D.** You are given that the length of each side of the square is $2x$. Because triangle PQR is formed by joining the centers of the squares, the length of sides PQ and QR is also $2x$. To find the length of PR, use the Pythagorean theorem, which states that $a^2 + b^2 = c^2$, where c is the hypotenuse (PR):

$$(2x)^2 + (2x)^2 = (PR)^2$$
$$4x^2 + 4x^2 = (PR)^2$$
$$8x^2 = (PR)^2$$
$$2x\sqrt{2} = PR$$

The perimeter is equal to the distance around the triangle, so add the lengths of the sides:

$$2x + 2x + 2x\sqrt{2} = 4x + 2x\sqrt{2}.$$

5

GRE General Testing Strategies

CHAPTER GOALS

- Understand the importance of developing test-taking skills.
- Discover specific test-taking strategies that can help you raise your score.
- Find out how to eliminate stress and build confidence.
- Learn how to deal with the computerized testing format.
- Get last-minute tips for test day.

Now that you've assessed your strengths and weaknesses, it's time to take a look at some general test-taking strategies that should help you approach the GRE with confidence. This chapter discusses the importance of acquiring the skills necessary to maximize your GRE score. At the end of the chapter you'll find some tips on how to handle stress before, during, and after the GRE.

Later chapters in this book present strategies and techniques specific to each of the GRE sections.

Knowledge, Skills, and Abilities (KSA)

Cognitive psychologists, those who study learning and thinking, use the letters KSA to refer to the basic components of human performance in all human activities, from academics to athletics, from playing music to playing games. The letters stand for *Knowledge, Skills, and Abilities.* As mentioned previously, the GRE measures a specific set of skills. Many thousands of students have successfully raised their GRE scores by acquiring the requisite skills through study and practice.

GRE Tip
The GRE measures both knowledge and skills. Study to acquire knowledge, but practice to acquire skills.

The human brain stores and retrieves factual knowledge a little differently from the way it acquires and executes skills. You learn factual information by studying, and you acquire skills through practice. There is some overlap between these actions; you will learn while you practice, and vice versa. In fact, research shows that repetition is important for both information storage and skills acquisition.

Repetition is also necessary to improve skills: Knowing *about* a skill, or understanding how the skill should be executed, is not the same as actually *having* that skill and being able to execute it. For instance, you might be told *about* a skill such as driving a car with a manual transmission, playing the piano, or typing on a computer keyboard. You might have a great teacher, have wonderful learning tools, and pay attention very carefully. You might *understand* everything perfectly. But, the first few times that you actually attempt the skill, you will probably make some mistakes. In fact, you will probably experience some frustration because of the gap between your understanding of the skill and your actual ability to perform the skill. Perfecting skills takes practice. When skills are repeated so many times that they can't be further improved, psychologists use the term *perfectly internalized skills,* which means that the skills are executed automatically, without any conscious thought. You need repetition to create the pathways in your brain that control your skills. Therefore, you shouldn't be satisfied with simply reading this book and then saying to yourself, "I get it." You will not reach your full GRE scoring potential unless you put in sufficient time practicing as well as understanding and learning.

We hope that you will internalize the skills that you need for top performance on the GRE so that you don't have to spend time and energy figuring out what to do during the introduction to the exam. We hope that you will be well into each section while some of your less-prepared classmates are still reading the directions and trying to figure out exactly what they are supposed to be doing. With sufficient practice you will develop your test-taking skills, and, specifically, good GRE-taking skills. While you practice, you should distinguish between practice that is meant to serve as a learning experience and practice that is meant to be a realistic simulation of what will happen on your actual GRE.

NOTE

During practice meant for learning, it is acceptable to "cheat." You should feel free to disregard the time limits to think about how the questions are put together; you can stop to look at the explanations in the back of the book. It is even acceptable to talk to others about what you are learning during your "learning practice."

Be sure to do some simulated testing practice, in which you time yourself carefully and try to control as many variables in your environment as possible. Research shows that you will have an easier time executing your skills and remembering information when the environment in which you are testing is similar to the environment in which you studied and practiced.

You must be realistic about how you spend your time and energy during the preparation process. The psychological term cognitive endurance refers to your ability to perform difficult mental tasks over an extended period of time. Just as with your physical endurance, you can build up your cognitive endurance through training. As you prepare yourself for the GRE, you should start with shorter practice sessions and work up to the point at which you can easily work for 45 minutes without noticeable fatigue. That is the longest period of time you will have to work on test day without a break. Remember to select an answer for each question before you move on to the next question, even if you have to guess. The section "Guess Wisely," later in this chapter, covers guessing in greater detail.

Now, let's explore the skills and strategies important to ensuring your success on the GRE.

> **GRE Tip**
>
> You should not attempt any timed practice tests when you are mentally or physically exhausted. This will add unwanted tension to an already stressful situation.

Focus on the Easy Stuff

You will have to get familiar with the format of each section of the GRE so that you can recognize passages and questions that are likely to give you trouble. Remember that you must select and confirm an answer before you are allowed to move on to the next question, so it is in your best interest to spend less time on the questions that you will probably answer incorrectly, and simply make an educated guess. Focus on the questions that you're sure you can answer correctly in order to maximize your GRE score. The only way to become competent in this strategy is to practice using both the tests in this book and the tests contained in the POWERPREP® software available from Educational Testing Service (ETS) (www.gre.org).

The writers of the GRE know that they are dealing with a group of test-takers who probably share certain characteristics. For example, they know that you probably have evidence that you are intelligent, or you would have self-selected out of the process by now. You probably also have evidence that you are tenacious, perhaps even stubborn. There will be some time-consuming questions in each section that are meant to lure you into wasting time that would be better spent answering some more reasonable questions.

Stay "On Point"

It is important to note that many incorrect GRE answers are incorrect because they are irrelevant. This applies to all the different question types in all the various sections. If you get very good at spotting answer choices that are outside the scope of a reading passage, for example, you'll go a

> **GRE Tip**
>
> A good way to check relevance is to ask yourself, "So what?" when evaluating the answer choices.

long way toward improving your score. This can be more difficult than it sounds because some of the irrelevant choices will use terms, numbers, and ideas from the question or passage.

When your training is finished, you will be able to do this type of analysis on most of the questions and answer choices that you encounter on your GRE. You will be able to quickly and efficiently eliminate all of the answer choices that are irrelevant, or not "on point." This strategy will also help you to write better essays. Many students lose points either by introducing irrelevant information into their essays, or by going "off topic."

Simplify

The GRE contains relatively straightforward, simple ideas that sometimes appear difficult because of a complex sentence structure and an elevated vocabulary level. The best way to simplify the language that you encounter on the GRE is to paraphrase as you go. We suggest to our GRE tutoring students to think first of explaining the gist of what they are reading to an intelligent tenth grade student. After some time spent practicing, the simplification process becomes second nature and can be done quite quickly.

Guess Wisely

Because you must select and confirm an answer before you move on to the next question, it is imperative to learn how to make an educated guess. If you do not know how to solve a math problem, for example, you might still be able to eliminate at least one answer choice that is clearly incorrect; draw pictures and apply logic to assist you during this process. After you have eliminated the answer choices that you know cannot be correct, select the best answer from those choices that remain.

There are specific suggestions in each chapter regarding the process of elimination and how to identify the question types on which you should probably guess and move on. As you practice, you'll also develop likes and dislikes, meaning that you will recognize certain question types that will always be tough for you. By test day you will have done enough timed practice tests that you will also develop a "feel" for how long you should be spending on each question. Be flexible. If a question is of a type that you can usually answer easily, do not spend more time on it than you should.

You also need to find out whether you are an answer-changer or not; if you change an answer, are you more likely to change it to the correct answer, or from the correct answer? You can only learn this about yourself by taking practice exams and paying attention to your tendencies.

GRE Tip

Because of the computer adaptive nature of the GRE, it is important that you eliminate as many incorrect answer choices as possible before you guess and move on.

Manage Stress

In graduate school, stress arises from sources such as family expectations, fear of failure, heavy workload, competition, and difficult subjects. The GRE is designed to create similar stresses. The psychometricians (specialized psychologists who study the measurement of the mind) who contribute to the design of standardized tests use artificial stressors to test how you will respond to the stress of graduate school. In other words, they are actually trying to create a certain level of stress in you.

The main stressor is the time limit. The time limits are set on the GRE so that many students cannot finish all of the questions in the time allowed. Use the specific strategies mentioned in Chapters 6 through 8 to help you select as many correct answers as possible in the time allowed.

Another stressor is the element of surprise that is present for most test-takers. If you practice enough, there should be no surprises on test day. For example, test takers who have not practiced sufficiently are more likely to encounter a question that is unlike any that they saw during their limited practice. A well-prepared test-taker, however, will know what to expect.

> **GRE Tip**
>
> Once you get a handle on the various question types, do most of your practice under timed conditions so that you learn how to pace yourself.

Relax to Succeed

Probably the worst thing that a test-taker can do is to panic. Research shows that there are very predictable results when a person panics. When you panic, you can usually identify a specific set of easily recognizable symptoms, including sweating, shortness of breath, muscle tension, increased pulse rate, tunnel vision, nausea, lightheadedness, and, in rare cases, even loss of consciousness. These symptoms are the result of chemical changes in the brain brought on by some stimulus. The stimulus does not have to be external. Therefore, we can panic ourselves just by thinking about certain things.

The stress chemical in your body called *epinephrine,* more commonly known as *adrenalin,* brings on these symptoms. Adrenalin changes the priorities in your brain activity. It moves blood and electrical energy away from some parts of the brain and over to others. Specifically, it increases brain activity in the areas that control your body and decreases blood flow to the parts of your brain that are involved in complex thinking. Therefore, panic makes a person stronger and faster—and also less able to perform the type of thinking that is important on a GRE exam. It is not a bad thing to have a small amount of adrenalin in your bloodstream brought about by a healthy amount of excitement about your exam. However, you should take steps to avoid panic before or during your GRE.

You can control your adrenalin levels by minimizing the unknown factors in the testing process. The biggest stress-inducing questions are as follows:

- *"What do the GRE writers expect?"*
- *"Am I ready?"*
- *"How will I do on test day?"*

If you spend your time and energy studying and practicing under realistic conditions before test day, then you will have a much better chance of controlling your adrenalin levels and handling the exam with no panic.

The goals of your preparation should be to learn about the test, acquire the skills that are being measured by the test, and learn about yourself and how you respond to the different parts of the test. You should also consider which question types you will answer with certainty on test day and which ones you will give an educated guess. You need to be familiar with the material that is tested on each section of your exam. As you work through this book, make an assessment of the best use of your time and energy. Concentrate on the areas that will give you the highest score in the amount of time that you have until you take the GRE. This will give you a feeling of confidence on test day even when you are facing very challenging questions.

GRE Tip

Preparation goals:

1. Learn about the test
2. Learn about yourself
3. Approach the test with confidence

Specific Relaxation Techniques

The following sections present various ways to help you be as relaxed and confident as possible on test day.

Be Prepared

The more prepared you feel, the less likely it is that you'll be stressed on test day. Study and practice consistently between now and your test day. Be organized. Have your supplies and lucky testing clothes ready in advance. Make a practice trip to the test center before your test day.

Know Yourself

Get to know your strengths and weaknesses on the GRE and the things that help you to relax. Some test-takers feel that being slightly anxious helps them to focus. Others folks do best when they are so relaxed that they are almost asleep. You will learn about yourself through practice.

Rest

The better rested you are, the better things seem. As you become fatigued, you are more likely to look on the dark side of things and worry more, which hurts your test scores. Our favorite Shakespeare quote refers to ". . . sleep that knits up the raveled sleeve of care."

In addition, consider doing something "mindless" the night before your GRE. You should be well prepared by then, so take the night off!

Eat Right

Sugar is bad for stress and brain function in general. Consuming refined sugar creates biological stress that has an impact on your brain chemistry. Keep sugar consumption to a minimum for several days before your test. If you are actually addicted to caffeine, then by all means consume your normal amount. Don't forget to eat regularly while you're preparing for the GRE. It's not a good idea to skip meals simply because you are experiencing some additional stress. It is also important to eat something before you take the GRE. An empty stomach might be distracting and uncomfortable on test day. Consider bringing a high-protein snack to eat during your break.

Breathe

If you feel yourself tensing up, slow down and take deeper breaths. This will relax you and get more oxygen to your brain so that you can think more clearly.

Take Mental Breaks

You cannot stay sharply focused on your GRE for the whole time in the testing center. You will certainly have distracting thoughts or times when you just can't process all the information. When this happens, close your eyes, clear your mind, and then start back on your test. This process should take only a minute or so. You could pray, meditate, or just visualize a place or person that helps you relax. Try thinking of something fun that you have planned to do after your GRE.

Have a Plan of Attack

Know how you are going to work through each part of the exam. There is no time to create a plan of attack on test day. Practice enough that you internalize the skills you need to do your best on each section, and you won't have to stop to think about what to do next.

Be Aware of Time

You should time yourself on test day. You should time yourself on some of your practice exams. We suggest that you use an analog (dial face) watch. You can turn the hands on your watch back from noon to allow enough time for the section that you are working on. Remember, all that matters during the test is your test. All of life's other issues will have to be dealt with after your test is finished. You might find this attitude easier to attain if you lose track of what time it is in the "outside world."

Listen to Music

Some types of music increase measured brain stress and interfere with clear thinking. Specifically, some rock, hip-hop, and dance rhythms, while great for certain occasions, can have detrimental effects on certain types of brain waves that have been measured in labs. Other music seems to help to organize brain waves and create a relaxed state that is conducive to learning and skills acquisition.

Some CAT Strategies

While all of the previously mentioned strategies will help on both the paper and computer adaptive tests, following are some specific guidelines for approaching the CAT with confidence:

- Take the POWERPREP® practice tests. This software includes tutorials that teach you how to use the computer features available to you on test day.

- Practice typing your Analytical Writing Assessment responses. Your goal on test day is to type a complete essay in the time allowed, so practice to improve your typing speed and accuracy.

- You must answer each Verbal and Quantitative question before you can move on to the next one. Budget enough time for each question and work actively through the test material.

- Try to complete the entire test, even if you are running out of time. Most test takers get higher scores if they finish the test—learn to pace yourself so that you have time to consider each question and can avoid making random guesses.

Refer to Chapter 1, "Overview of the GRE," for more information on the CAT (Computer Adaptive Test).

What to Expect on Test Day

If you work through the material in this book and do some additional practice on released GRE exams, then you should be more than adequately prepared for the GRE. Use the following tips to help the entire testing process go smoothly.

Take a Dry Run

Make sure that you know how long it will take to get to the testing center, where you will park, alternative routes, and so on. If you are testing in a place that is new to you, try to get into the building between now and test day so that you can absorb the sounds and smells, find out where the bathrooms and snack machines are, and so on.

Wake Up Early

You will have to be at the testing center by a specified time. Set two alarms if you have to so that you're not late. Leave yourself plenty of time to get fully awake and alert before you have to run out the door. If you have a family member who wants to feel like part of the process, you might want to have him or her act as your wake-up call. If you arrive at the testing center late, you might not be admitted.

Dress for Success

Wear loose, comfortable clothes in layers so that you can adjust to the temperature. Remember your watch. There might not be a clock in your testing room.

Fuel Up

Eat something without too much sugar in it on the morning of your test. Get your normal dose of caffeine, if any. (Test day is not the time to "try coffee" for the first time!)

Bring Supplies

Bring your ID and your admission ticket. If you need them, bring your glasses or contact lenses. You won't be able to eat or drink while the GRE is in progress, but you can bring a snack for the break time.

> **GRE Tip**
> You are not allowed to use a calculator when you take the GRE, so be sure to practice without one!

Warm Up Your Brain

Read a newspaper or something similar, or review some practice material so that the GRE isn't the first thing you read on test day.

Plan a Mini-Vacation

Most students find it easier to concentrate on their exam preparation and on their GRE if they have a plan for some fun right after the test. Plan something that you can look forward to as a reward for all the hard work and energy that you're putting into preparing for and taking the GRE.

What's Next?

Chapter 6 of this book includes an introduction to logic, which will be useful on almost all of the sections of the GRE General Test. Chapters 7 through 9 focus on the specific sections of the GRE, while Chapters 10 and 11 provide an in-depth review of both the quantitative and verbal content that is tested on the exam. Read these chapters carefully, note the particular strategies and techniques, and answer the practice questions included at the end of each chapter. The full-length Practice Tests (Chapters 12 through 14) can be found in Part IV of this book. Plan to take a full-length test approximately one week prior to the actual GRE. Read the explanations for the questions that you missed, and review Chapters 5 through 11 as necessary.

Remember, practice as much as you can under realistic testing conditions to maximize your GRE score.

6

Introduction to GRE Logic

CHAPTER GOALS

- Learn the structure of a logical argument.
- Understand the logic of conditional statements.
- Learn to recognize different kinds of logical fallacies.

A basic understanding of Informal Logic is important for GRE success because the GRE is, primarily, a test of your critical thinking skills. This chapter contains information that applies directly to the Analytical Writing Assessment (especially the Analysis of an Argument task), Reading Comprehension, and Analogy question types on the GRE. It applies indirectly to the Quantitative (both Problem Solving and Quantitative Comparison) and even Antonym question types.

Furthermore, because logic is the foundation of research and analysis in every field, the topics covered in this chapter will certainly be useful during graduate school and for the rest of your professional career.

Before we begin, let's talk briefly about logic and the question types to which it has a less obvious connection. As will be made clear in later chapters, even question types such as Quantitative and Antonym questions that seem most grounded in specific content have a logic component. With antonyms, of course a strong vocabulary is necessary. But it is not all that's needed (this distinction will be explained in detail later in this chapter). If the makers of the GRE had simply wished to test your vocabulary, a synonyms section would have sufficed. Finding an antonym not only forces you to take an extra step, it also requires an understanding of the relationship between the question prompt and the answer choices. Note that Analogy questions simply take this process to the next degree.

Similarly, Quantitative Comparison questions are not asking for an absolute answer, but rather a relative one: Which quantity is greater? Analyzing that relativity requires logic. If you are ever in doubt about the correct answer choice, know that the credited answer is always grounded in logic.

Now let's begin our discussion of Informal Logic.

Arguments

Logic is often defined as "the science of argument." In this context, an argument does not refer to a verbal skirmish, nor does it usually involve shouting. An argument is an orderly process of supporting a *conclusion* with *evidence*. The conclusion is the main point of the argument and the evidence is the information that supports it. An evidentiary statement is also called a *premise*. Breaking an argument down into these component parts is called *analysis*. The Reading Comprehension passages will all contain logical (sound) arguments. The Analysis of an Argument prompts will all contain logical flaws. By understanding how a logical argument is constructed, you can more easily navigate a Reading passage and more thoroughly criticize an Argument prompt.

Some of the words that commonly signal *evidence* are

- Since
- Because
- For
- As
- Due to
- In that

Some of the words that commonly signal *conclusion* are

- Therefore
- Hence
- Thus
- So
- Accordingly
- Consequently
- Ergo

The basic form of an argument is illustrated by the following time-honored example:

Socrates is a man.

Men are mortal.

Therefore, Socrates is mortal.

The first two statements are pieces of evidence; the last statement is the conclusion that follows naturally from them.

Context

The function that a statement serves within an argument is entirely dependent upon *context*. In other words, a mere raw assertion is neither evidence nor conclusion until it is placed in a context of surrounding statements.

Consider the following statement:

Steve wears glasses.

Is this statement evidence or conclusion? The truth is that it is neither evidence nor conclusion without context.

Consider the following two arguments, each of which includes the previous statement:

1. **Steve wears glasses.**

   People who wear glasses are smart.

   Therefore, Steve is smart.

2. **Steve is nearsighted.**

   Nearsighted people wear glasses.

   Therefore, Steve wears glasses.

Both arguments contain the original statement. However, in Argument 1 the statement is evidence. In Argument 2, it is the conclusion.

Chain of Reasoning

Sometimes arguments are linked together in chains, as shown in the following example that combines the two previous arguments:

Steve is nearsighted.

Nearsighted people wear glasses.

Therefore, Steve wears glasses

People who wear glasses are smart.

Therefore, Steve is smart.

In this example, the first conclusion drawn becomes what is known as a *subsidiary conclusion*. The subsidiary conclusion is then used as a piece of evidence to support another conclusion. The last conclusion in such a chain is sometimes referred to as the *ultimate conclusion*.

Sometimes competing evidence can also lead to a conclusion (e.g., "Steve likes to wear disguises. Glasses are effective disguises. Therefore, Steve wears glasses."). When this competing evidence is ignored or omitted by the writer, it's called an *alternative explanation*. Finding *alternative explanations* is useful in evaluating the Analytical Writing Argument task and answering the Reading Comprehension Assumption, Strengthen, and Weaken questions.

Assumptions

GRE Tip

Practice spotting assumptions in arguments that you encounter in daily life. This habit will help you to score higher on the GRE.

Many Reading Comprehension questions directly test your ability to recognize assumptions—they're a common question type. Assumptions also provide many of the flaws in the Argument writing prompts. Sometimes, one or more pieces of evidence are left unstated. Such unstated evidence is called an *assumption*; assumptions are also known as *suppressed premises*.

If you leave out the second piece of evidence in the sample argument, as shown next, you'll have an illustration of an argument that makes an essential assumption:

Socrates is a man.

Therefore, Socrates is mortal.

The only statement that would provide the necessary link between the stated evidence and the stated conclusion is "Men are mortal."

You need a bridge between the unlike terms in the two statements. "Socrates" is a term in both the single stated premise and the conclusion of the argument. The two other terms are "man" and "mortal." This recognition leads you to infer that the missing premise is "Man is mortal."

This is a process that is often performed intuitively. Recognizing key assumptions is very important for several exam question types; as mentioned previously, Reading Comprehension questions will ask about assumptions directly. The GRE also assumes that you will recognize them in the Argument essay prompt. After all, often the easiest way to attack an argument is to attack its assumptions. Finally, when writing your own Issues essay, be aware of your assumptions—not every reader will agree with you.

Validity, Truth, and Soundness

Validity refers to the strength of the structure of an argument, whereas *truth* refers to the factual verifiability of the evidence and the conclusion. An argument that is both valid and true is said to be *sound*.

Here is an example of an argument that is valid but *not* true:

All dogs can fly.

Ralph is a dog.

Therefore, Ralph can fly.

The argument is valid because *if* the evidence is true, *then* the conclusion follows logically. However, the evidence is clearly not true, and therefore, the conclusion is not true. Giving an example of a dog that cannot fly would disprove the argument and show that it is not sound. This is known as a *counterexample*. A counterexample is an example, real or hypothetical, that disproves evidence used in an argument.

Here is an example of an argument that is *not* valid but has a conclusion that is verifiably true:

Bluebirds are blue.

Some things that are blue can fly.

Therefore, bluebirds can fly.

Although it is true that bluebirds can fly, the argument is not valid because the evidence does not fully support the conclusion.

Conditionals

Statements in the form of **"if X, then Y"** are known as *conditionals*; if X occurs, then Y is certain to occur. In other words, X *implies* Y. In fact, another name for a conditional statement is an *implication*. This category, along with negation, is most useful for the Analytical Writing tasks. It will help you to understand exactly what can and cannot be understood from a sound argument.

> **NOTE**
>
> The "if" clause is known as the *antecedent*; the "then" clause is known as the *consequent*.

Consider the following example:

If it rains, then the flowers will grow.

"If it rains . . ." is the antecedent, and ". . . then the flowers will grow" is the consequent.

The sentence means that if the rain comes, then the flowers will certainly grow. Let's accept this as true.

However, if the flowers grow, you cannot be sure that the rain fell. For example, it could be that they were watered by hand.

So, "if the flowers are growing, then it has rained" does not necessarily follow from the previous statement. In fact, this is known as a *fallacy*. (Note that fallacy has the same root as the word *false*.) The fallacy of simply reversing a conditional statement is known as *affirming the consequent*.

In addition, you cannot simply negate the components of the statement by saying, "If it doesn't rain, the flowers will not grow." This is known as the fallacy of *denying the antecedent*.

> **NOTE**
>
> If you reverse the position of the terms and negate both terms, you arrive at a statement that always has exactly the same truth value as the original statement, as shown here:
>
> **If the flowers did not grow, then it did not rain.**
>
> This must be true because the original statement tells you that if it had rained, then the flowers would certainly have grown. This is known as the *contrapositive*.

There are two varieties of conditional statements, *sufficient conditions* and *necessary conditions*. They both include the concept of "If" and "Then," but they can create confusion.

Sufficiency

Consider the following statement:

If my car has gas in it, then it will run.

This is known as a *sufficient condition* because having gasoline in the car is sufficient to guarantee that it will run. The statement implies that there are no other problems with the car and you can rest assured that, as long as there is gas in the tank, this car will run.

The contrapositive of this implication would be: "If the car is not running, then it has no gas."

Necessity

Consider the following statement:

Only if my car has gas in it, will it run.

This is a *necessary condition* because the gas is necessary for the car to run but not sufficient to guarantee that it will certainly run. In other words, the car in this statement might not have an engine in it, and the statement would still be true.

The contrapositive of this statement would be: "If the car has no gas, then it will not run."

Negation

As you can see from the discussion of the previous contrapositive, it is important to be able to negate statements properly. If you negate clumsily, then your logic will fail.

> **NOTE**
>
> Understanding proper negation is important for several reasons, one of which involves a useful technique for Reading Comprehension Assumption and Strengthen questions, which will be discussed later.

For example, try to negate the following statement:

All clocks are round.

You might be tempted to say:

No clocks are round.

But, this is clearly an incorrect statement. In fact, it is just as incorrect as the original statement.

However, suppose you say:

At least one clock is not round.

You have negated the original statement safely and correctly. In other words, you have negated a categorical statement with a single counterexample. Categorical statements are phrased absolutely using words like *all*, *none*, *always*, *every*, and so on. You have probably heard the phrase "Never say 'never'!" This is sound advice because categorical statements are inherently unreliable.

You might find yourself in a position where you must negate a statement such as the following:

Some birds can fly.

In this case, simply use a categorical statement:

No birds can fly.

Because the original statement is *not* categorical, you can use a categorical statement to negate it.

Fallacies

A *fallacy* is a statement or argument that is not logically sound. In other words, it lacks validity. Notice that fallacy looks and sounds a lot like the word *false*. This is not a coincidence. Both words derive from the Latin word *fallere*, which means "to deceive."

The GRE Reading Comprehension section includes EXCEPT questions, in which the fallacy will be the *correct* answer (see Chapter 9). Fallacies are also important in the Analytical Writing Assessment discussed in Chapter 7. Avoid fallacies in your Analysis of an Issue and exploit them in your Analysis of an Argument!

The sections that follow outline several fallacies that appear often on the GRE, either as examples of flawed arguments, or as incorrect answer choices.

- Slippery Slope
- Percent versus Number
- Sampling Error
- Correlation versus Causation
- Equivocation
- *Ad hominem* Arguments
- Appeal to Authority
- Appeal to Majority: The Quantity/Quality Fallacy
- Circular Argument
- Begging the Question
- *Reductio ad Absurdum*

Slippery Slope

Slippery slope arguments are often referred to as "domino arguments," and are more properly called *causal slippery slope arguments*.

Consider the following example:

If you eat one hot, fresh, glazed donut, then you will eat another one, and soon it will become a habit. Eventually, you will eat so many that you will gain a large amount of weight and suffer from the health problems that result from being significantly overweight. These problems include diabetes. So, if you eat that one hot, fresh, glazed donut, you will suffer from diabetes in the future.

The reason that the conclusion does not necessarily follow from the evidence presented is that the evidence is made up of suppositions about the future. Although the suppositions are possible and plausible, they are not certain to occur. The mistake in this kind of argument is that the author is focusing on one possible set of outcomes and stacking them on top of one another to form what looks like an argument but really isn't.

This is not to say that all suppositions about the future are meaningless. If one has accurate data regarding the probability of certain outcomes, one can often make more informed decisions about a given course of action available now, in the present. However, the slippery slope argument is based on pure conjecture and not solid probability.

Percent versus Number

Often, the success of an argument is based on the distinction between percentage and raw number. Consider this example:

> **The gross revenue of Company X increased by more than $1 million when comparing last year to the year before. The gross revenue of Company Y increased by over $10 million during the same period. Clearly Company Y experienced a larger percentage of increase in gross revenue than Company X did.**

The reason that you cannot be convinced by this argument is that there is some very important information missing. You do not know the overall amount of gross revenue for either Company X or Company Y. Therefore, you cannot accept the conclusion that one or the other had a larger percentage of increase in gross revenue.

> **NOTE**
>
> Percent versus Number and Sampling Error fallacies have appeared in Quantitative Comparison questions. Be aware of them when you have to determine which given value is actually larger.

Sampling Error

Here is another fallacy that might trick you into a mistake on the Quantitative Comparison questions. Remember that for any statistical conclusion to be valid, it must be drawn from a proper random sample. Consider the following example:

> **All of the instructors at the community college wear glasses. I know that this is true because I have taken three auto repair classes at the community college and all of my instructors wore glasses.**

The reason that you should not be convinced by this argument is that all of the classes had something in common. They were not a random sample of classes.

They were all auto repair classes. In fact, you can easily suppose that the glasses that were worn by the instructors were safety glasses.

You might also question the sample size. Perhaps three instructors, even if they were randomly chosen, would not be considered a large enough group to fully represent the entire faculty of the community college.

Sampling error results from either an insufficient sample size or a nonrepresentative, or *skewed*, sample.

Correlation versus Causation

Correlation is finding two things that occur together, either simultaneously or consecutively. It is a mistake to conclude that one thing caused the other based only on the correlation. For example:

1. **It rained yesterday and today I have a cold. The rain must have caused my cold.**

2. **As the popularity of cell phones has increased, the prevalence of cheating on college campuses has increased. Cell phone availability must contribute to cheating by college students.**

3. **An Olympic gold medalist eats this brand of breakfast cereal. Therefore, if I eat the same brand of breakfast cereal, I, too, can become an Olympic champion.**

The reason these arguments are not convincing is that, in each case, something else could have caused the result.

In Example 1, the rain happened before the cold but that doesn't mean that it caused the cold. The cold might have some other cause entirely.

In Example 2, two phenomena are seen to be increasing together. There are four possibilities: (a) Cell phones cause cheating; (b) cheating increases cell phone use; (c) some third factor is causing both cell phone use to increase and cheating to increase; or (d) there is no connection at all and the observed correlation is simply a coincidence.

In Example 3, it should be clear that there are many other factors involved in Olympic success than the choice of a certain breakfast cereal. Even if the cereal does contribute in some measure to the athlete's success, it cannot be safely concluded that eating the cereal is a sufficient condition to guarantee any other individual the same kind of success.

Equivocation

Sometimes the author of an argument gets very tricky and uses the fact that words often have more than one meaning. Consider the following:

Hollywood gossip reporting is legitimate news reporting. It is well established that the press has a right to act in the public interest. Everyone would agree that all reporting that is in the public interest is legitimate. The public is obviously interested in gossip reporting based on the large audience that such reporting garners. Since the public is interested in gossip, such reporting is clearly in the public interest and therefore legitimate.

The reason that you should not be persuaded by this argument is that it takes advantage of the flexibility of the English language and uses more than one meaning for the word *interest*. On one hand, when discussing "the public interest" in the first and second sentences, the meaning is closer to "in the best interest of the public" or "to provide a valuable service to the public." In the next two sentences, "interested" means merely "to pay attention to," or "to desire to observe." These two definitions are not interchangeable. As a result, the "argument" about Hollywood gossip is not sound because the same word is used to represent two different meanings. Therefore, the conclusion does not follow from the evidence presented.

Ad Hominem Arguments

The Latin term *ad hominem* means "against the person," and refers to arguments that are directed against the person who is making a given argument rather than against the validity or truth of the argument. Consider the following:

We should not accept Milton's conclusions regarding the soundness of our investment decisions since he is an adult who spends his off time playing video games and lives in his mother's basement.

The reason this argument is not convincing is that it does not actually give you any reason to doubt Milton's conclusions other than some facts about Milton himself. The author of this argument is asking you to follow along on some rather large assumptions about adults who live in their mothers' basements and play video games as a hobby. You are supposed to conclude that there is no way that such a person could be correct about investment decisions. In other words, this is nothing more than an attack on Milton himself with no real logic or argumentation. If you listen closely to many political advertisements and debates, you will easily find many *ad hominem* arguments.

Appeal to Authority

Some purported arguments simply rely on the reputation of some third party rather than any convincing evidence. Consider the following examples:

1. **My conclusions about foreign policy must be correct since they are in accord with the pronouncements of Winston Churchill.**

2. **Pacifism must be the correct course of action since Albert Einstein supported it.**

3. **Dr. Ligenfelder says that houses built of discarded tires are the best way to save energy so you cannot disagree with me when I say the same thing.**

All three examples have a reference to some person who is an authority of some kind as their only evidence to support their argument. As with some other fallacies, you will often find appeal to authority included in popular advertising.

There is no real logic or argumentation. You are expected simply to accept the conclusions offered because someone who is famous, or has some kind of expertise, has reached the same conclusions.

In some cases, such as Example 2, the expert is speaking out on a topic that is not within his area of expertise. In Example 3, you don't even know what Dr. Ligenfelder's area of expertise is; you are expected to agree simply because the person making the assertion is called "Doctor."

Appeal to Majority: The Quantity/Quality Fallacy

Sometimes a position is supported only by the number of people who hold it. Consider the following:

1. **Can 4 million voters be wrong?**

2. **The new game show is the most popular one on television; therefore, it must be the best thing on TV.**

Of course, the implied conclusion in Example 1 is "No. They cannot be wrong." The problem is that, as you are aware, it is possible for any number of individuals to be wrong. So, there is no real evidence offered to provide support for the implied assertion that this particular group of 4 million voters is correct.

In Example 2, you are expected to accept the fact that more people watch this game show than any other game show as evidence of its quality. (Example 2 also asks you to assume that even if it is the best game show, it is therefore ". . . the best thing on TV." This is another fairly sizable assumption that is probably not warranted.)

Circular Argument

A circular argument is characterized by the conclusion appearing as a premise. Consider the following example:

> **All newspaper reporters are biased. Only biased individuals would go into journalism so that they could influence the public's thinking on issues. Such a person tries to influence the public's thinking to create changes in our culture. Therefore, all newspaper reporters are biased.**

This is a glaring example of a fairly common fallacy. This argument assumes the truth of its own conclusion and provides no support for the contention that newspaper reporters are biased.

Begging the Question

The fallacy of begging the question is characterized by an "if, then" implication with a clearly false consequent. Consider the following example:

> **If this isn't the best pizza in the world, then pigs can fly. We all know that pigs can't fly, so clearly this is the best pizza in the world.**

The author of this argument makes it seem that he is simply applying the contrapositive to an implication. However, the original implication contains a statement, "then pigs can fly," that is patently ridiculous, thereby ensuring that the conclusion "this is the best pizza in the world" appears to be inescapably true, even though no real evidence has been offered.

Reductio ad Absurdum

The Latin term *reductio ad absurdum* means "to reduce to the absurd." It is used to convince the listener that an argument seems ridiculous by pointing out the similarities between the original argument and an absurd argument. Consider the following:

> *Mother:* **This copper bracelet must prevent arthritis since I have been wearing it for years and I do not have arthritis.**
>
> *Son:* **That is just like arguing that the brown roof on your house repels meteorites since you have not had any meteorite strikes since installing it.**

The son in this case is using the technique of making an absurd argument using the same structure as his mother's argument, in order to show her that her argument must also be absurd. This technique is sometimes effective to illustrate the flaws in a given argument. However, its value is dependent on the subject matter content chosen for the counterexample and a structure that is perfectly parallel to the original argument. For this reason, it is included in this list of common fallacies.

What's Next?

As we mentioned at the beginning of this chapter, an understanding of logic is essential to success on several of the sections tested on the GRE. Some questions might ask you to analyze an argument, or ask you to identify assumptions or conclusions, while other questions will simply be easier for you to manage if your logic skills are sharp.

Refer to this chapter as necessary while working through the rest of this book. You might want to hang on to it as reference source long after you have taken the GRE.

7

GRE Analytical Writing Assessment

The Analytical Writing Assessment section of the GRE is purely a skills test. This means that you are not tested on any knowledge whatsoever. Instead, you are given an opportunity to demonstrate your ability to reason clearly and write coherently and concisely.

There are two separate tasks within this section:

- "Present Your Perspective on an Issue" (which we'll call the Issue Task)

- "Analysis of an Argument" (which we'll call the Argument Task)

You are allowed 45 minutes for the Issue Task, and 30 minutes for the Argument Task, including reading and prewriting. Note that, despite the time difference, the essays are generally weighted equally by department admissions boards.

Breaking Down the Analytical Writing Assessment

No specialized knowledge is required to complete either writing exercise. You are not tested on what you might know about a particular subject. Instead, you are given the opportunity to demonstrate your ability to reason clearly and write coherently and concisely. Graduate schools are looking for logical reasoning, clarity, organization, writing mechanics, and proper usage of the language.

In addition, how *well* you write is much more important than how *much* you write. The GRE software provides more "space" than you will ever be able to use. You should write enough to clearly support your position or analyze the given argument within the allotted time.

It's very important to note that the Argument Task has a very different purpose than the Issue Task; you're not being asked to write the same type of essay twice. If, after practicing, you still have trouble separating the two in your mind, consider how they might be used in graduate school. The Issue Task is similar to the writing you have done and will continue to do in greater depth: to propose a thesis and defend it. The Argument Task, however, reflects the processes used during research. As an undergraduate, you have probably had most of your academic resources vetted by your professors. As you will discover in graduate school, if you haven't already, not everything published is solid scholarship. Some theses are simply false. Others are justifiable, but are poorly defended by their authors. You will have to be able to evaluate published work and identify any logical flaws, if only to avoid introducing the same mistakes into your own papers. The Argument Task measures your readiness to perform this important part of academic research.

We'll discuss how to approach each task later in the chapter.

Scoring the Analytical Writing Sections

Each essay is scored on a scale of 0 to 6 by two readers. The readers might be college faculty members (often graduate students serving as teaching assistants) or a computer program referred to as an "automated engine." Therefore, your initial scoring might be done by two well-trained human beings, or by one such human and a computer. All readers, human or not, use the same *rubric*, or scoring guide. The process contains several safeguards to ensure fairness. For instance, the essays are randomly assigned to the readers, who have no way of learning the identity of the writer. Also, two readers grade each essay. If the two scores given to a single essay differ by more than one point, a third, senior, reader (always a human being) is called in to resolve the conflict.

Essays are scored *holistically*, which means that a reader simply assigns a single number grade to the essay without assigning any specific point value to the various factors considered in scoring. Although many factors can enter into the reader's decision, the most important factors are clear structure (logic) and analytical writing (also logic).

What the GRE Readers Are Looking For

Logical structure is far more important than mechanics such as spelling and grammar. However, you shouldn't take any chances with mechanics. If you aren't absolutely certain how to use a semicolon properly, don't use one. If you are unsure of the meaning of a word, do not use it. Instead, think of a simpler term with the same meaning and use it instead.

Here is a description of how the essays are scored at each level on both tasks. Essays that receive the following scores exhibit one or more of the characteristics listed:

Score of 0: Response does not address the assigned task, is in a foreign language, is indecipherable, or contains no text (not attempted).

Score of 1: *Fundamentally deficient.* The essay is extremely confusing or mostly irrelevant. There is little or no development of ideas. Contains severe and pervasive errors. Does not present a logical analysis of the argument.

Score of 2: *Seriously weak.* Contains frequent problems in sentence structure or use of language. Errors obscure meaning. The essay lacks analysis or development of ideas.

Score of 3: *Shows some competence.* Contains some analysis and development of ideas. The essay has limited organization with flawed control or numerous sentence structure or language errors. It is vague and lacks clarity.

Score of 4: *Competent.* Main ideas are supported with relevant evidence and examples. The essay shows adequate organization and is reasonably clear. The argument is identified and important features are analyzed. There is adequate control of sentences and language, but the essay might include some errors that reduce overall clarity.

Score of 5: *Generally thoughtful analysis of complex ideas.* Sound reasoning and well-chosen examples support conclusions. The essay is well organized and focused, and includes sentences of varying length and complexity. Any errors are minor and do not affect the meaning of the essay.

Score of 6: Insightful, in-depth analysis of complex ideas. Compelling logic and very persuasive examples. Essay is well organized and focused and displays skill in structuring sentences; vocabulary is precise and relevant. If there are any errors, they do not affect the logic or meaning of the essay.

Writing Techniques

Following are the steps you should take when writing your essays. To write the best essay that you can in the time allotted, these steps should be performed one at a time.

Carefully read the prompt. It's OK to read the prompt more than once to be certain that you understand what you are reading. You must know what the task is before you begin. Rushing through this step can cost valuable points and make some of your hard work worthless.

Plan your essay. Your essay should start out with a clear statement of your position on the issue or a clear evaluation of the strength of the argument. The outline that you create does not have to include complete sentences. It does have to include the ideas that you will put into your final draft. You need to be sure that you have a clear picture of where you are going and how you will get there before you start to write on the answer document. Finally, don't underestimate the effect of stress on memory. You may think the order of your essay is obvious, but it's easy to forget even brilliant insights once you begin the actual writing.

Type your essay out in the space provided. Remember that graduate school admissions professionals will only look at what you've typed on the computer screen. Be sure to save time to review your work in order to make necessary corrections or improvements.

Writing Strategies

As noted earlier in this book, humans acquire skills through practice. Because the Analytical Writing Assessment is a test of your writing skills, you should practice writing under test-like conditions. The best way to make sure that you are on track is to have someone with writing experience, someone you trust (such as your personal tutor), give you specific feedback on your practice essays. It is important to have someone else read and critique your essays because writers tend to develop blind spots when it comes to areas that need improvement in their own essays. It is always a good idea to get a fresh set of eyes to review your work. It will not take long for an experienced reader to give feedback that can be immensely valuable.

If you will be critiquing your own essays, put them away for a week or so after you write them and then take them out for another spin. You might find errors and lapses in logic that were not evident to you as you were writing. Be aware that this process will significantly increase the amount of time required for your overall preparation, so be sure to plan accordingly.

Consider the following strategies to help you write an effective essay.

Clearly State Your Position

GRE Tip
Make sure that you understand the issue or argument that is presented before you begin writing. Remember that responses that are off the topic are not acceptable.

Your essay should start out with a clear statement of your position on the issue. There should be no doubt in the reader's mind about which side you are on from the beginning of your essay. For the Argument Task, clearly identify important flaws in the prompt argument. Use the scratch paper with which you are provided to outline the structure of your essay. This is not the time for multitasking; do not simply read the prompt and then try to write your essay from the beginning to the end. It is very difficult to simultaneously create the logical structure of your essay, anticipate counterarguments, attempt to correctly apply the rules of grammar, punctuation, and spelling, and identify appropriate examples to plug into your essay structure.

Too often, GRE test-takers make broad, general statements in their essays without giving any specific support. Make sure that you provide clear, simple examples of the general statements that you make, and that your evaluations are logical and well supported. In your response to the Argument Task, be sure to include a cause and effect relationship between *your* evidence and *your* conclusion.

Present Your Ideas Logically

As we mentioned, many factors can enter into the reader's scoring decision, but the most important factors are critical thinking (logic) and analytical writing (also, logic). Remember that logic is far more important than mechanics such as spelling and grammar. Be sure to prewrite before you begin to type your essay. This strategy acquaints you with the stimulus and suggests patterns for presenting your thoughts. Carefully consider the prompt and make sure you understand it. Decide which course of action you will support, and jot down your ideas on the topic: this might simply be a list of ideas, reasons, and examples that you will use to explain and support your decision. Think of how best to organize the ideas in your essay. You can refer back to these notes as you type the essay into the space provided by the GRE software.

Review and Correct Your Essay

When you start to write your essay, remember that those who read it will consider it a first draft. Your essay will not be perfect; however, it should be an example of the best writing you can produce under the time constraints and testing conditions. Be sure to take a few minutes before the end of the time period to read over your essay, correcting any mistakes in grammar, usage, punctuation, and spelling.

The practice tests included later in this book contain additional essay prompts. Use these as well as the prompts in the GRE topic pool, which can be found in the

GRE Official Guide or at www.gre.org, to write several practice essays between now and test day. The following section also provides some sample prompts you can use to start practicing and honing your writing skills.

Issue Task

The Issue Task allows you to choose one of two given issues, and then write a short essay supporting your position on that issue. Although you cannot be certain what the issue choices will be in advance, some examples of issue prompts are provided later in this chapter so that you can get an idea of the type of issue that is likely to appear. The topics presented are usually of general public interest. You are expected to think clearly and critically about the topic and create a thoughtful, well-reasoned essay supporting your position. There is never a "correct" answer. Your task is simply to write a good essay from whatever perspective you choose.

The Time Limit

The 45-minute time limit starts running from the moment that the issues are revealed to you on the computer screen. Use the scratch paper you are given to make a few notes about the positives and negatives of various sides to the issue and to outline your response before you begin to type.

The Issues

The issues are carefully chosen so that they aren't biased toward any one college major or profession. However, luck is a bit of a factor on this section of the GRE. If you happen to be presented with an issue that you know something about, you will probably feel more comfortable writing about it. But, be careful to respond to the issue presented. Don't answer a question that wasn't asked just because you happen to know something about the subject matter. Finally, don't assume your reader is an expert in the subject; if you use specialized examples, always explain their significance.

Your Response

There are many possible responses to any Issue prompt. You might agree or disagree in part, or in whole. You might attack the underlying assumptions in the statement that is given. You might decide to discuss the fact that the statement you are writing about has only limited applicability in certain situations. Whatever your decision, tell your reader the position you have taken. This will be your thesis statement. Everything in your essay should work to support your thesis. You should certainly use at least one example to support your position. You may choose to use more than one example, which is fine as long as the examples you select are relevant and you stay focused on your main idea. Make sure it's clear to your reader how your examples relate to your thesis. Do not create fictional examples and try to pass them off as factual. It is OK to use hypothetical situations in your discussion if that is appropriate. Just be sure to let your readers in on the fact that the situations are hypothetical.

The Response Format

Don't feel that you must develop a complete, traditional five-paragraph essay to succeed on this task. Remember: Everything in your essay should work to strengthen your argument. That includes the essay's structure. If you have the time and ability to write a strong five-paragraph essay, go right ahead. However, a solid three-paragraph essay is often sufficient. In fact, a very solid, effective strategy is to write just three paragraphs. The first paragraph would contain your thesis, and by extension, the position that you are arguing *for*. The second would address the position that you are arguing *against*. The third would be an effective concluding paragraph. Whatever form you choose, you should use relevant examples to support your argument.

Be sure to explain the connection between the examples that you use and your conclusion. Don't assume that the reader will agree with your viewpoint regarding the significance of a given fact. For instance, in a situation in which you suggest that private education is relevant to a given issue, a statement in your essay such as ". . . merely a public school . . ." would reveal prejudices held by the writer and might or might not actually contribute to a convincing essay. A safer course of action would be to go out of your way to adopt a neutral, convincing tone and try not to reveal very much at all about any personal axes that you might have to grind.

The four categories of information that should be included in an Issue essay are as follows:

1. Positive for your position.
2. Negative for your position.
3. Positive for the other side.
4. Negative for the other side.

While an effective essay uses facts from all four categories, you should not give all four categories equal time. Consider the solid three-paragraph construction mentioned above: Most of the first paragraph should focus on a positive for your position, followed by a "weak" negative. The second paragraph should be a "weak" positive for the other side, followed by a longer, answering negative. Write a strong concluding paragraph to tie everything together.

You can think of your side as "correct" and the other side as "incorrect." When you write a paragraph that is focused on the "correct" side of the issue, you should mention at least one aspect of your choice that might be seen as a negative by some people. Your essay will be much more persuasive if you do not ignore potential problems with your side of the debate. The negative can be obvious, but it should be weak enough that you can easily explain why it doesn't destroy your argument. In other words, you should be sure to mention plenty of positive information to overcome the potential down side that you are admitting to.

The Counterargument

The previous technique can be applied to the part of your essay in which you discuss the opposition's position. You should admit that the other side of the debate has at least one good point. Then, follow up with enough discussion of the pitfalls associated with the other side of the argument that your side still ends up looking like the clear winner. This is known as dealing with counterarguments, and it is the most effective way of presenting a written argument. Remember: The goal is not to be fair; it's to be persuasive.

An effective counterargument requires certain transition words to guide the reader through your pros and cons. Following are four basic categories of transition words, along with some examples of effective transition words and phrases:

Contrast: But, however, on the other hand, conversely, although

Similarity: Likewise, similarly

Evidence: Since, because, in light of, first, second, third

Conclusion: Therefore, thus, as a result, so, it follows that, in conclusion

> **NOTE**
>
> See Chapter 6, "Introduction to GRE Logic," for more examples of structural signal words.

Your Tone

Avoid being too familiar, or colloquial, in your response. Just as you can't assume your reader will agree with you about a given issue, you also can't assume he or she will share your sense of humor. Also, do not take any chances with vocabulary. If you are at all unsure of the meaning of a word, *do not* use it in your essay. If you are wrong, you'll end up sounding foolish or even offensive to your readers. While the GRE rewards sophisticated language, it's better to use simple vocabulary correctly than to misuse a fancy word.

> **NOTE**
>
> See Chapter 11, "Verbal Review," for help with common mistakes in vocabulary and grammar.

Now let's take a look at some sample Issue essays.

Sample Essay Prompt 1: Present Your Perspective on an Issue

Following is a sample prompt, similar to the prompts you will encounter on the GRE. Carefully read the directions and write your essay using the strategies outlined previously. After you have written your essay, read the graded sample essays that follow. You can compare your essay to the samples to get a sense of how your essay stacks up. You should also compare the samples to one another to understand better what the GRE readers are looking for. Finally, try to show your essay to an English professor or other qualified person for an evaluation. Remember that many different essays can earn high scores.

<u>Directions:</u> You have 45 minutes to plan and compose a response that presents your perspective on the topic in the prompt below. You may accept, reject, or qualify the claim made in the prompt, as long as the ideas you present are relevant to the topic. A response to any other topic will earn a score of zero.

Use a word processor with the spell-checker and grammar checker turned off. You may cut, copy, and paste parts of your essay. Take a few minutes to plan your response and write an outline before you begin your essay. Be sure to develop your ideas fully and organize them coherently. Leave time to proofread your essay and make any revisions you think are necessary.

> "In raising a child, love is important, but discipline is most important of all."
> Write an essay in which you take a position on the statement above. In developing and supporting your position, you should consider ways in which the statement might or might not hold true.

Issue Task Sample Essay: Score of 6

The following essay received a score of 6 because it is well organized and focused, uses language effectively, and provides an insightful in-depth analysis of a complex issue.

> *The issue of proper child rearing is an important, yet rarely debated, social issue, with implications affecting both children and adults. One of the most important variables in a child-rearing philosophy is whether the philosophy values discipline or love more highly. A philosophy that values discipline above love is one in which love may be denied for the purpose of promoting discipline, particularly through withheld affection or through corporal punishment. Most of today's leading authorities recommend that discipline be valued above love for raising children, especially boys. However, most of these commentators, such as James Dobson, base their child-rearing philosophies not on sound research studying the happiness and social success of the children, but on one particular interpretation of religious texts. Studies have shown that these ideas about*

child-rearing, far from producing happy, competent adults, in fact do serious harm to children raised under their influence. Indeed, a child-rearing philosophy that values discipline above love fails both a philosophical and a pragmatic test.

From a practical perspective, a child-rearing technique can be considered successful if the child has generally positive memories of childhood, and goes on to be a valuable member of society, as measured through such traits as honesty, compassion, and initiative. Most discipline-based child-rearing philosophies fail on precisely these grounds. It needs little argument that most children do not have happy memories of physical discipline, but the denial of affection can also be a powerfully traumatic act: children who are told that they run the risk of losing a parent's love also grow up to be nervous, clingy adults, prone to pretending that problems do not exist, in lieu of risking the alienation of affection. Further, child-rearing research has come down strongly on the side of a care-based parenting method. Studies show that, <u>contra</u> Dobson et al, harsh punishment for disobedience does not create a powerful sense of self-discipline; instead, it promotes adults who are guided by punishment rather than conscience. To the contrary, children who are raised with compassion and love (though not without a due measure of discipline) tend to behave towards others in a compassionate and loving manner.

Philosophically, the discipline-based child-rearing philosophy also comes up short. Physical coercion as a valid means of achieving one's objectives is never a good lesson to teach. Moreover, some would argue that it is simply morally wrong to harm a child, whether it is with the intent of promoting discipline or not; since such behavior would not be tolerated in a non-discipline context, there is no reason to believe it acceptable in a discipline context, especially when there is no solid evidence that it has any beneficial effects. It is also unsatisfactory that strict-discipline parenting methodology presupposes the need to be even more strict and firm with male children than with female children. Without evidence for substantial behavioral differences between male and female prepubescent children, there is no reason to believe that their development would require radically different parenting strategies.

I do not wish to argue that discipline should be avoided. Completely lax parenting is just as bad as domineering parenting. However, parental discipline must always come second to love; parents must meet the physical and emotional needs of their children, even disobedient ones, under all circumstances. The good parent, having set boundaries, can make sure that the child is free to explore within them, and to deal adequately with the challenges beyond the home, simply by setting the positive example of treating the child with affection, care, and respect.

Issue Task Sample Essay: Score of 4

The following essay received a score of 4 because, although the ideas were supported with relevant examples, the essay lacks focus and includes errors that reduce its overall clarity.

I believe that love and discipline are both important, but discipline has to be more important. Too many children these days are raised without discipline. They do whatever they want, and don't pay attention to the effect they have on society. For a child to really grow up right, you have to set limits and make sure the child follows them, because otherwise they won't think that there ever are any limits. Nowadays we hear all kinds of stories from the media—in the papers, on television—about the things that kids do when they grow up unsupervised. All these things could have been prevented by a bit of discipline when that child was growing up.

Kids who grow up without discipline always wind up getting into trouble. Whether it's disrespecting their parents or their employers, to having no goals for themselves, to violent and unrestrained behavior, not having discipline leads to problems. Sometimes undisciplined children grow into violent adults, for instance, Lyle and Erik Menendez, who killed their parents solely to get the insurance money, clearly showed a profound lack of discipline. Their desire for material goods was not restrained by a proper sense of discipline that would have led them to work hard to get it. Thus, these two wild children did the unthinkable: they killed their parents in their undisciplined search for greater material happiness.

Another person who showed a remarkable lack of discipline in her life was Janet Jackson. Her crazy antics at the Super Bowl showed a remarkable lack of discipline, while it may be fun to flaunt yourself, someone with the proper upbringing that emphasizes the importance of discipline will know better than to expose herself on national television. She just wanted to jump-start her career without putting in the work. What she needed was more discipline.

In short, discipline is extremely important. A person who does not have will not go far in life, whether because of the mistakes they make or because they will lack ambition to achieve his or her goals, and if a person does not learn discipline in childhood, then when will they learn it? Therefore, the most important thing when raising a child is discipline, to prevent those kinds of mistakes in adulthood.

Issue Task Sample Essay: Score of 2

The following essay received a score of 2 because it lacks any serious development of the stimulus, and contains frequent errors that either distract from or obscure the author's intended meaning.

Give a kid nothing but love all the time will turn them into spoiled brats. They'll think they never have to face any consequences for their actions and that they can get away with anything they want.

The Bible says to spare the rod and spoil the child and I agree. My aunt raised my two cousins and never spanked them or hit them and they are both spoiled and mean. Every time I see them growing up, they take my toys and hit me and the other kids and they never get punished. My aunt always takes their side and blamed other kids for fights and problems.

I'm not saying people should beat there kids, just that kids need discipline. It doesn't have to be spankings, it could be grounding them or taking away toys or something. But they need to know they can't just do anything they want.

Sample Essay Prompt 2: Present Your Perspective on an Issue

Following is a sample prompt, similar to the prompts you will encounter on the GRE. Carefully read the directions and write your essay using the strategies outlined previously. After you have written your essay, read the graded sample essays that follow. You can compare your essay to the samples to get a sense of how your essay stacks up. You should also compare the samples to one another to understand better what the GRE readers are looking for. Finally, try to show your essay to an English professor or other qualified person for an evaluation. Remember that many different essays can earn high scores.

<u>Directions:</u> You have 45 minutes to plan and compose a response that presents your perspective on the topic in the prompt below. You may accept, reject, or qualify the claim made in the prompt, as long as the ideas you present are relevant to the topic. A response to any other topic will earn a score of zero.

Use a word processor with the spell-checker and grammar checker turned off. You may cut, copy, and paste parts of your essay. Take a few minutes to plan your response and write an outline before you begin your essay. Be sure to develop your ideas fully and organize them coherently. Leave time to proofread your essay and make any revisions you think are necessary.

> "Health care in the United States should be free for all citizens, fully financed by the government."
> Write an essay in which you take a position on the statement above. In developing and supporting your position, you should consider ways in which the statement might or might not hold true.

Issue Task Sample Essay: Score of 6

The following essay received a score of 6 because it is well organized and focused, uses language effectively, and provides an insightful in-depth analysis of a complex issue.

> *In the United States today an atmosphere of entitlement exists that could cause one to believe that free health care for all citizens is the best course of action. Government subsidized programs such as welfare and Medicaid continue to perpetuate the myth that all people, regardless of their actual need, should be entitled to unlimited government assistance simply by virtue of being born in America. While I agree that American citizens who evidence a legitimate need should receive help for such things as emergency health care, I do not believe that health care in the United States should be free for all citizens, fully financed by the government.*

History is replete with examples of failed states, which failed, for the most part, because they subverted the market and created a command economy, thus limiting the role of individual choice. The most recent example is the collapse of the Soviet Union, which proved that allocation of resources by a government bureaucracy is so inherently inefficient as to be literally fatal to a government and many of its individual citizens.

While I recognize that the proposal is limited to government-provided health care, it must be noted that the health care segment represents an overwhelmingly large portion of the total economy of the United States. Furthermore, the same weaknesses inherent in any centrally controlled economy will be found in a national system of health care.

It is a fundamental fact that human desires are limitless while resources are limited. When the market allocates resources via innumerable individual human decisions, it is likely that the highest overall satisfaction will be achieved. The proper role of government is to enforce procedural fairness so that no individual member of society gains an unfair advantage in bargaining. Once government steps into the process of actually allocating scarce resources, such as medicine, it must introduce a decision-making process that, by its nature, must be inefficient. Simply put, someone must decide who has access to which medicine, doctors, equipment, etc. If the government were to take over a system of payment, it would then take over such decisions.

I believe that such a government system would be disastrous. To paraphrase a political candidate from recent history: "It would combine the compassion of the Internal Revenue Service with the efficiency of the Department of Motor Vehicles."

Furthermore, the concept of health care is poorly defined. Would this free service be limited to "basic" health care or include sophisticated diagnostic services such as CAT scans and MRI's? Where would the lines be drawn? The opportunities for ridiculous waste are nearly limitless, as are the possibilities for abuse: Should the government health care system pay for multiple attempts at rehabilitation for unrepentant drug abusers?

There is also the potential slippery slope to consider. If government takes over payment for all health care, then it is conceivable that the government would be interested in limiting dangerous behaviors: for example, certain high-risk sports and activities such as motorcycle riding, as well as more mundane activities such as overeating. Could government health care regulations end up requiring a state-issued permit to consume a cheeseburger and a beer? Perhaps.

Because the unintended consequences would probably be far-reaching and overwhelmingly negative, I do not support the idea that health care should be government funded and free to all citizens.

Issue Task Sample Essay: Score of 4

The following essay received a score of 4 because, although the ideas were supported with relevant examples, the essay lacks focus and includes errors that reduce its overall clarity.

In light of the current national debt situation, I disagree with the statement that health care in the United States should be free for all citizens, and that the government should finance health care. Many other countries around the world have government financed health care programs; the United States should see that these programs are not always very successful.

For example, in a country like Canada, where health care is free to all citizens, the risk of heart disease is on the rise. Even though every citizen has access to free health care, it is not being taken advantage of. Studies show that people are not any healthier in a country, such as Canada, where health care is fully financed by the government. Many people think that if health care was free, the general population would be healthier. However, based on the previous example, it is not the case.

In addition, government funded health care would put a financial strain on the government. We are already paying too much taxes, and that is the only place for the government to get the extra money it would need to pay for free health care. This, again, shows that each citizen should be responsible for their own health care, and not rely on the government to provide it. If we rely on the government for too much help, we learn, as a society, not to take care of ourselves, which may reduce our current status among the other countries of the world.

Although some people may disagree, government financed health care is not the best action for the United States. As free citizens, we should be responsible for our own well-being.

Issue Task Sample Essay: Score of 2

The following essay received a score of 2 because it seriously lacks any development of the stimulus and contains frequent errors that either distract from or obscure the author's intended meaning.

If helth care in the US was free, then everyone could take advantage of it and Americans would be more healthy. There are many health problems that we face in the US, namely heart disease and obesity, that could be helped by free health care. Many other programs financed by the government are quite helpful. They should be available to all Americans, just like health care. Paying for programs for it's citizens is the job of the goverment.

I think that the US government should pay for health care for all Americans because things like health care should be free for all Americans. Why do we live in America anyway? If programs aren't free for all? To me, that's what America is all about. We deserve the right to free health care; because we pay taxes. Other countries have free health care, and we, as the US, should do the same.

Argument Task

GRE Tip

If you haven't yet mastered the material in Chapter 6, "Introduction to GRE Logic," you should attempt to do so before tackling the rest of this chapter. Pay close attention to the sections on assumptions and fallacies.

As with the Issue Task, the topic presented in the Argument Task is usually of general public interest. You are expected to think clearly and critically about the topic and create a logical analysis of the flaws in its presentation. To this purpose, you should read the prompt in the Argument Task even more carefully than you read the prompts in the Issue Task. You are being asked to critique an argument, not to present your own views on the subject. On the Argument Task, you are given only one argument. You are expected to analyze and critique how well its evidence supports its conclusion. It's important to remember that you must critique the argument as it's presented, as opposed to creating your own argument as you must on the Issue Task.

The Time Limit

The 30-minute time limit starts running from the moment that the argument is revealed to you on the computer screen. Use the scratch paper you are given to take notes about the argument's logical development.

The Argument

The arguments are carefully chosen so that they aren't biased toward any one college major or profession. And you don't have to be a logic major to analyze an argument effectively. However, if you happen to be presented with a topic that you know something about, you will probably feel more comfortable in writing about it. In these situations, be careful not to focus too much on facts themselves. Your job is to criticize the way the facts are organized and presented. For example, you may disagree with your prompt, and think that public libraries are an excellent use of public funds. This is not the time to make that argument. Instead, focus on the ways the author has failed to be convincing. No matter what the topic, the argument will always have multiple flaws.

Your Response

As you've probably noticed, Argument Task essays are fundamentally different from most of the essays you have written as an undergraduate. Therefore, your mental approach must also be fundamentally different. First, *read* the prompt carefully. Make sure you understand exactly what the writer is saying, not what you might expect him to say. Next, *analyze* the structure of the argument, especially how the writer puts forth claims (i.e., evidence) and conclusions, and any assumptions that might link them. Then *consider the content*; you want to come up with alternative explanations and counterexamples. Would additional evidence strengthen or weaken the argument? What kind? Finally, you should also give some thought to the *implications* of the argument. That is, what would probably follow if the conclusion of the argument is accepted at face value?

When reading the Argument prompt, pay special attention to the structural signal words that indicate *evidence*, *conclusion*, *contrast*, and *continuation*. These terms usually blend into the background as you read. However, because structure is part of what you are analyzing and critiquing, you need to notice them. Take advantage of the printed format of the practice tests and circle the words as you read them. They'll provide handy signposts to understanding the argument. This habit will be useful on the actual exam.

Following are four basic categories of transition words, along with some examples of effective transition words and phrases:

Evidence: Since, because, in light of, first, second, third

Conclusion: Therefore, thus, as a result, so, it follows that, in conclusion

Contrast: But, however, on the other hand, conversely, although

Continuation: Similarly, next

> **NOTE**
>
> See Chapter 6, "Introduction to GRE Logic," for more examples of structural signal words.

The Response Format

GRE Tip

One handy technique is to circle key function words as you read the prompt. Obviously, you won't be able to do this during the actual test, but it will train your mind to focus on structure while you practice your essays.

Between assumptions and fallacies, an argument can have many different types of flaws. Keeping in mind your time constraints, you are free to focus on any or all of them. Thus, there are many possible responses to any Argument prompt. As with the Issue Task, don't feel the need to restrict yourself to a five-paragraph format. Remember: Everything in your essay should work to strengthen your argument. That includes the essay's structure. Many writers start a new paragraph for each new criticism. Others will group the criticisms by type of flaw. Whatever form you choose, explain clearly how each of your examples functions as a logical flaw. Don't assume your reader will make the connection without your help.

However you choose to structure your argument, your thesis statement should give your reader an overview of your criticism. To refer to our library example, you could say that while using public funds to support public libraries may be desirable in most cases, the given argument is fundamentally flawed for the following reasons. The rest of your essay would then develop those reasons. You should certainly use at least one criticism to support your position. You may choose to use more than one criticism, which is fine as long as the examples you select are relevant and you stay focused on your main idea. Make sure it's clear to your reader how your examples illustrate a flaw in the argument.

You don't need to know a lot of specialized logic vocabulary, although the concepts themselves are invaluable. Still, the GRE does reward the use and understanding of some terminology, including:

- **Argument:** an orderly process of supporting a conclusion with evidence
- **Analysis:** the process of breaking an argument down to its component parts in order to understand how they work together
- **Evidence:** the information that supports a conclusion
- **Conclusion:** the main point of an argument
- **Assumption:** unstated, or *assumed*, evidence
- **Alternative explanation:** competing evidence that also leads to the conclusion of the stated argument, but that has been ignored or omitted by the writer.
- **Counterexample:** an example, real or hypothetical, which disproves evidence used in an argument

Review Chapter 6, "Introduction to GRE Logic," if these terms aren't entirely familiar to you. You should also review the different types of logical flaws. You won't need to name the flaws in your essay, but being able to spot them quickly will be very handy on test day.

Your Tone

Despite the inherently negative content in an Argument essay, it's still important to adopt a neutral, convincing tone. Your reader should never get the impression that your criticism is personal.

Avoid being too familiar, or colloquial, in your response. Just as you can't assume your reader will agree with you about a given issue, you also can't assume he or she will share your sense of humor. Finally, do not take any chances with vocabulary. If you are at all unsure of the meaning of a word, *do not* use it in your essay. If you are wrong, you'll end up sounding foolish or even offensive to your readers.

> **NOTE**
>
> See Chapter 11, "Verbal Review," for help with common mistakes in vocabulary and grammar.

Now, let's take a look at some sample Argument essays.

Sample Essay Prompt 1: Analyze an Argument

Following is a sample prompt, similar to the prompts you will encounter on the GRE. Carefully read the directions and write your essay using the strategies outlined previously. After you have written your essay, read the graded sample essays that follow. You can compare your essay to the samples to get a sense of how your essay stacks up. You should also compare the samples to one another to understand better what the GRE readers are looking for. Finally, try to show your essay to an English professor or other qualified person for an evaluation. Remember that many different essays can earn high scores.

<u>Directions</u>: You have 30 minutes to read the prompt below and write an evaluation of the argument. An evaluation of any other topic will earn a score of zero.

In your assessment, analyze the line of reasoning used in the argument. Consider what, if any, questionable assumptions underlie the reasoning and how well any evidence given supports the conclusion. You can also discuss what sort of additional evidence would strengthen or refute the argument, what changes would make the conclusion more logically sound, and what additional information might be needed to better evaluate the argument. *Note that you are NOT being asked to present your views on the subject.*

Use a word processor with the spell-checker and grammar checker turned off. You may cut, copy, and paste parts of your essay. Take a few minutes to plan your response and write an outline before you begin your essay.

"Funding for space exploration and colonization needs to be greatly expanded. At present, Earth is the only planet known to support life. A cataclysmic event could result in the extinction not only of human life, but of all life in the known universe. Moreover, as human society continues to progress, it will seek new frontiers to expand to and to gather resources from. For both of these reasons, we must ensure that humanity establishes a foothold on other worlds."

Write a response in which you examine the argument's unstated assumptions, making sure to explain how the argument depends on the assumptions and what the implications are if the assumptions prove unwarranted.

Argument Task Sample Essay: Score of 6

The following essay received a score of 6 because it correctly identifies and supports its position, discusses the structure of the argument, and contains compelling logic and persuasive examples. Any errors are minor and do not affect the logic of the essay.

The argument presented, while interesting, makes several errors in reasoning that undermine its effectiveness. For this argument to be considered valid, it must state all of its premises more clearly. Further, it recommends a course of action based upon a chain of cause and effect, which is not internally supported. Last, it contains self-contradictory reasoning, which needs to be untangled before the argument will be truly convincing.

The most striking feature of this argument is its sweeping assumptions. The author of the argument attempts to argue that funding for space colonization must be increased, because of the possibility of a cataclysmic event wiping out all life on Earth. However, the author does not indicate why the continued survival of life in the general sense—or, more to the point, a relatively small group of individuals—would be important to the general masses presently on Earth, if life on this planet were to be wiped out. The author assumes that the need to spread and preserve life on a small scale is self-evident, when it is not. The author also assumes that human intervention would increase the chance of life surviving in the universe as a whole, without considering the possibility that Earth-bound life might have negative effects on what extraterrestrial life may already exist. And the author assumes that the probability of a cataclysmic event destroying life on earth is significant. The fossil record shows that life on earth has survived at least six cataclysmic events in the past; the argument does not specify the magnitude of future risks, nor does it estimate the extent to which those risks would be reduced.

Many of the more significant assumptions made in this argument are those which assume the effectiveness of the prescribed course of action. Supposing it is granted that Earth-bound life, particularly human life, needs to be spread to other planets; it does not follow that it is within our power to colonize other worlds, nor that increased funding for space exploration and colonization would let us achieve that goal. It is possible that current funding is sufficient; it is also possible that no amount of money would be enough to achieve an impossible goal. The funding could well be money wasted chasing a worthwhile cause, and without the author mentioning specific uses for the money, we cannot say otherwise. If the premise is that we need to preserve some form of terrestrial life in general, then it does not follow that humanity needs to establish a foothold on other worlds. It could easily be concluded that we should ensure some hardy form of terrestrial life, such as bacteria, be sent elsewhere.

Finally, one additional weakness bears consideration: the argument mentions the human need for more resources and more frontiers. However, the argument does not consider that catering to this aspect of human nature might well undermine the goal of the survival of Earth-bound life. One commonly-mentioned cataclysmic scenario is environmental destruction as a result of human activity; while spreading humanity to other planets might provide a reprieve from this scenario, there is no reason to think it would reduce the risk of further self-destruction. This is a conflict between the two premises that needs to be resolved. Were the argument to state all these assumptions directly as premises, and to use more specific examples, it would be more compelling. As it is, the chain of reasoning is hampered by generalities and by skipped steps that detract from its intellectual force.

Argument Task Sample Essay: Score of 4

The following essay received a score of 4 because it shows an adequate grasp of the argument and is reasonably clear. However, it includes some errors in logic and construction that reduce its overall clarity.

The argument presented above is generally a good one. However, there are some ways it could be improved. The author doesn't talk about where the money for space exploration will come from, and doesn't indicate how that money should be spent to ensure that humans can colonize space. Moreover, the argument is not convincing until we know how we will be able to get the resources gathered from other worlds to our own Earth.

While the author's argument is well-formed, he is a little lacking on the details. He rightly indicates that funding for space exploration needs to be increased. But who is going to pay for it? For this kind of colonization effort to work, we need to know there are practical sources for the money. Is every country going to pay? If poor countries pay less, do they get less? And whose going to spend the money? The author assumes that everything will go smoothly, but does not propose any way to monitor things to be sure.

In a similar vain, this argument would be much more convincing if the author detailed ways that the money could be spent to improve our current efforts to colonize space. While more money certainly couldn't hurt, we would be more inclined to believe the author if he gave us some practical examples of exactly how the money would be used to advance our goals of space exploration.

Last, the author mentions using colonies to provide resources for Earth society and to provide a new frontier for people to explore. These are great ideas, but will not have their full force unless the author explains how we can get large numbers of people to colonize other planets, and how we can bring those resources back to Earth to improve the standard of living of the people still here, a plan without specifics is not very effective when it comes to convincing an audience.

In short, this is a good start, but the author needs to provide more details of how the plan will work before it can be put into action. Until the specifics of how the money will be used, how the project will be overseen, and how space colonization will work, are provided, this proposal will not be as convincing as it otherwise could be.

Argument Task Sample Essay: Score of 2

The following essay received a score of 2 because it lacks analysis of the argument, is vague, and contains pervasive structural and grammatical errors.

This argument is just stupid. First, the author assumes we've just got all this money sitting around for space exploration. That's not true. And even if we did have alot of money, why not just use it to repare the damage they've done to our own planet. We could use the money for other energy and resources and then we wouldnt' need to look at space to meet our needs.

I think we should just start buying hibrid cares and stop using coal and stuff like that. Then no bodied need to go into space. I mean, man has walked on the moon for over 30 years and what have we gotten out of it? Like I said, this argument is just stupid.

Sample Essay Prompt 2: Analyze an Argument

Following is a sample prompt, similar to the prompts you will encounter on the GRE. Carefully read the directions and write your essay using the strategies outlined previously. After you have written your essay, read the graded sample essays that follow. You can compare your essay to the samples to get a sense of how your essay stacks up. You should also compare the samples to one another to understand better what the GRE readers are looking for. Finally, try to show your essay to an English professor or other qualified person for an evaluation. Remember that many different essays can earn high scores.

<u>Directions</u>: You have 30 minutes to read the prompt below and write an evaluation of the argument. An evaluation of any other topic will earn a score of zero.

In your assessment, analyze the line of reasoning used in the argument. Consider what, if any, questionable assumptions underlie the reasoning and how well any evidence given supports the conclusion. You can also discuss what sort of additional evidence would strengthen or refute the argument, what changes would make the conclusion more logically sound, and what additional information might be needed to better evaluate the argument. *Note that you are NOT being asked to present your views on the subject.*

Use a word processor with the spell-checker and grammar checker turned off. You may cut, copy, and paste parts of your essay. Take a few minutes to plan your response and write an outline before you begin your essay.

"The following appeared in a letter to the editor of a local newspaper: 'Too much emphasis is placed on the development of math skills in high school. Many students who are discouraged by the difficulty of the content turn away from schoolwork merely because they lack basic math skills. But practice questions and content review on the Internet provide an important alternative for students at this crucial stage in their education, an alternative that the school board should not reject merely because of the expense involved. After all, many studies attest to the value of using Internet-based math review. Thus, allowing students to practice basic math skills and review relevant math content on the Internet can only make students more eager to study and learn math. Therefore, the school board should encourage schools to purchase computers and permit high school students to access the Internet.'"

Argument Task Sample Essay: Score of 6

The following essay received a score of 6 because it correctly identifies and supports its position, discusses the structure of the argument, and contains compelling logic and persuasive examples. Any errors are minor and do not affect the logic of the essay.

The argument is not persuasive for several reasons. It contains unexamined assumptions, fails to sufficiently address the issue of cost, and fails to consider potentially negative unintended consequences.

The argument begins by stating that, "Too much emphasis is placed on the development of math skills in high school." It then goes on to discuss a major expenditure that could only serve to place emphasis on math skills as educators seek to justify the expense of new equipment by focusing more energy and time on math. Furthermore, the author of the argument must be assuming that the students at this particular school will have access to the same Internet-based math review that was included in the studies that were cited. Additionally, the studies refer to "review" which may or may not be synonymous with "basic skill" acquisition.

In addition, the argument fails to make a valid comparison between the current methods of math instruction and the Internet method that is proposed. The argument states only that the Internet is an "important alternative" and neglects to provide any level of description of current methods.

Because the argument absolutely lacks even the most rudimentary cost-benefit analysis, it should not be considered valid. The expenditure should be justified by increased levels of achievement by students, or by increased efficiency, or both. There is simply insufficient evidence upon which the reader can base a decision.

The argument also ignores the fact that there are many distractions on the Internet as well as a large volume of content, including math review content, that may be unedited, unfiltered, and incorrect. The distractions alone should give one pause. At best, Internet access in the schools would provide a whole new level of supervision challenges for the faculty and staff. Students could easily be spending time communicating with each other, playing games, or viewing material that is completely irrelevant and perhaps even harmful to their development process.

All in all, the argument lacks merit due to its lack of completeness and its failure to provide a strong connection between the evidence provided and its conclusion.

Argument Task Sample Essay: Score of 4

The following essay received a score of 4 because it shows an adequate grasp of the argument and is reasonably clear. However, it includes some errors in logic and construction that reduce its overall clarity.

The argument presented lacks any serious support, and fails to consider some problems that might come up if high school students use the Internet in school. The argument does not address any financial issues that might arise from encouraging schools to purchase more computers.

First, because the argument doesn't say whether the Internet use would be monitored in any way, it is likely that students would abuse the privilege. Teenagers have too much access to the Internet in the home and would most likely just use the Internet at school to chat with friends and look at information that is not appropriate, like games or movies. This would not help a student to learn anything about math.

Also, the argument does not cover the additional cost of putting computers in the schools. Although computers are relatively inexpensive these days, a high school would probably need to install many computers in order to give students access to the Internet. There is no evidence provided to support any additional cost to the schools. Many schools are facing budget crunches right now, and may not be able to afford computers or be able to pay for the cost of Internet access.

Finally, if high school students had access to the Internet in school, it might take away from their other studies. There is no gurantee that students would learn the right math skills or if they would be able to spend enough time away from the computer to focus on other classes. Therefore, I believe that the argument is not sufficient and does not completely answer all of the questions necessary to make a good decision.

Argument Task Sample Essay: Score of 2

The following essay received a score of 2 because it lacks analysis of the argument, is vague, and contains pervasive structural and grammatical errors.

I support the argument that the Internet should be available to high schoolers, especially math students. Despite that putting computers into high schools will be expensive, it is a good investment. Not enough high school students focus on math, and being able to access the Internet and be exposed to different learning tools and practice tests will be a good thing.

Also, the school board should encourage schools to purchase computers, because many students don't have computers at home. So, they can't get online and learn important math skills. If they could access the Internet at school, in the classroom even, there time would be spent more effectively learning. Because math is an important skill to have—even if some people would disagree - being able to learn more math more easily should be supported.

The argument is a good one that the school board should encourage high schools to purchase computers and permit high schoolers to access the Internet. There are many good reasons for it.

Practice Writing Prompts

Use the following set of prompts to practice your analysis and writing skills. Limit your time to 45 minuets for the Issue Task and 30 minutes for the Argument Task. Use scratch paper to plan your response before you begin to write.

Because you have virtually unlimited space in which to type your answer on the computer version of the GRE General Test, we have not included any lined pages here. Using regular lined paper, practice writing a complete, well-supported essay in the time allotted. You may also type your responses using a word processor with the spell and grammar check functions turned off.

Issue Task Practice

Plan and compose a response that represents your perspective on the following topic. Support your views with reasons and examples drawn from personal experience, reading, observations, or academic studies. Take a few minutes to think about the issue and plan a response. Organize and fully develop your ideas; be sure to leave time to evaluate your response and revise as necessary.

Sample Prompt

"When high-profile celebrities speak out in favor of a certain politician, that politician's reputation is generally damaged."

Argument Task Practice

Plan and write a critique of the argument presented. Analyze the line of reasoning in the argument and consider any questionable assumptions that underlie the thinking. Discuss the evidence provided and whether there might be evidence that strengthens or weakens the argument, as well as what changes would make the argument more logically sound. You are not being asked to present your views on the subject.

Sample Prompt

"Sadly, widespread negative images of teenagers have been created in large part by popular movies. Consider the fact that, although they make up a mere 15 percent of the characters in dramatic roles in movies, teenagers are responsible for about one-fifth of all the crimes committed in dramatic films. In fact, in a recent survey of movie producers, only 35 percent of the movie roles for teenagers were viewed as positive ones."

What's Next?

Each of the practice tests in Part IV of this book includes an Issue Task and an Argument Task. Continue to practice your writing under timed conditions.

The remaining chapters in this section provide a comprehensive review of the GRE Quantitative and Verbal sections.

8

GRE Quantitative

CHAPTER GOALS

- Review the three types of GRE quantitative questions: Discrete Problem Solving, Quantitative Comparison, and Numeric Entry.
- Study examples of each quantitative question type.
- Learn specific strategies for answering each quantitative question type.
- Practice answering sample GRE quantitative questions.

The GRE Quantitative section is designed to test your ability to reason mathematically, to understand basic math terminology, and to recall basic mathematic formulas and principles. You should be able to solve problems and apply relevant mathematics concepts in arithmetic, algebra, geometry, and data analysis. Keep in mind, though, that the GRE is primarily a critical thinking test, so your ability to apply reason and logic to solving the quantitative questions is more important than your ability to recall mathematic formulas and principles.

The GRE Quantitative sections include Discrete Problem Solving questions, each with five answer choices (A–E), Quantitative Comparison questions, each with four possible answers (A–D), and Numeric Entry questions, for which you must come up with an answer on your own. Numeric Entry questions are new to the GRE, and you will most likely see only one of them on your test.

As with all sections on the computer adaptive GRE, you must answer each quantitative question before you can move on to the next question.

In this chapter, we will discuss the format of each question type and provide you with specific strategies for successfully answering the GRE quantitative questions. Chapter 10, "Basic GRE Math Review," provides an overview of the mathematical content tested on the GRE, so be sure to read that chapter to fill any gaps in your knowledge.

GRE Tip

Be sure to practice the strategies and techniques covered in this chapter on the simulated exams found in Part IV of this book.

Discrete Problem Solving Questions

The Discrete Problem Solving questions on the GRE might involve straightforward calculations, analysis of given data, or evaluation of a word problem in a real-life setting. You cannot use a calculator in this section, which means that you will not be required to perform elaborate calculations. However, you will be provided with scratch paper on which to solve the problems.

Anatomy of a GRE Discrete Problem Solving Question

Before you learn the strategies, you should understand what a Discrete Problem Solving question looks like. Consider the following:

If $5x - 6 = 14$, then $8x =$

(A) $\frac{8}{5}$

(B) 4

(C) $\frac{64}{5}$

(D) 20

(E) 32

As you can see, you will be presented with a question and be asked to select from among five answer choices. This example is a basic algebra question that requires you to solve for a variable, which is a fairly common multiple-choice question type.

Additionally, Discrete Problem Solving questions will include answer choices in the Roman numeral format. Roman numeral questions typically include three to five statements identified by Roman numerals. You must evaluate each of the statements to decide whether each one is true or false, based on the question asked. The answer choices will contain various combinations of the Roman numerals.

Consider the following example:

If x and y are both positive even integers, which of the following must be even?

I. x^y

II. $(x + 1)^y$

III. $x^{(y + 1)}$

(A) I only

(B) II only

(C) I and II only

(D) I and III only

(E) II and III only

> **NOTE**
>
> Always take each Roman numeral as a true or false statement: Does it answer the question or not? As you evaluate each of the Roman numeral questions, eliminate answer choices based on whether the answer choices include the Roman numeral. This process might allow you to arrive at the correct answer without looking at every Roman numeral statement. Roman numeral questions are also found in the Reading Comprehension section of the GRE.

General Strategies for Discrete Problem Solving Questions

Remember the following general strategies when approaching GRE Discrete Problem Solving questions. Note that these strategies might also be helpful in answering the other question types.

Draw Pictures

Visualize the problem by creating a figure or diagram. This strategy should not take a lot of time, and can prevent careless errors. Sometimes, you are given a figure or a table that you can work with; sometimes, you just have to make your own. Consider the following examples:

The greatest number of diagonals that can be drawn from one vertex of a regular 8-sided polygon is

(A) 1

(B) 2

(C) 3

(D) 4

(E) 5

The correct answer is E. To solve this problem, draw a diagram such as the one that follows:

(Vertex)

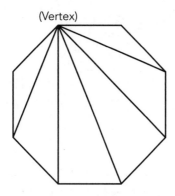

As you can see, if you draw a regular octagon (8-sided polygon), you can make only five diagonals from one vertex.

A square is inscribed in a circle. If the area of the inscribed square is 50, then the area of the circle is

(A) 5π

(B) $5\pi\sqrt{2}$

(C) 10π

(D) 25π

(E) 50π

The correct answer is D. To solve this problem, draw a diagram such as the one that follows:

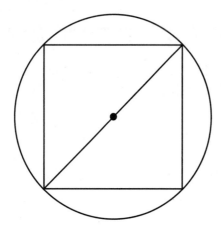

If the area of the square is 50, then one side of the square is $\sqrt{50}$, which is equivalent to $(\sqrt{25})(\sqrt{2})$, or $5\sqrt{2}$. The diagonal of an inscribed square is equal to the diameter of the circle. The diagonal creates two isosceles right triangles. Use the Pythagorean theorem: $(5\sqrt{2})^2 + (5\sqrt{2})^2 = c^2$. Simplify the equation to get $(50) + (50) = c^2$, and $c = 10$. If the diameter (d) is 10, then the radius (r) is 5. Since the area of a circle is πr^2, the area of this circle is 25π.

Apply Logic

Remember, you cannot use a calculator on the GRE, so most of the actual calculations are fairly simple. In fact, the GRE test writers are just as likely to test your logical reasoning ability or your ability to follow directions as they are to test your ability to plug numbers into an equation. Consider the following examples:

If $b - c = 2$, and $a + c = 16$, then $a + b =$

(A) 8

(B) 14

(C) 16

(D) 18

(E) 32

The correct answer is D. To solve this problem, first recognize that $(b - c) + (a + c) = a + b$. This is true because the c values cancel each other out, leaving you with $b + a$, which is equivalent to $a + b$. Therefore, $a + b$ must equal $2 + 16$, or 18.

Which of the following equations correctly translates this statement: "Three less than twice a number is the same as eight more than half the number"?

(A) $3 - 2x = 8 + \frac{x}{2}$

(B) $2 - 3x = x - 4$

(C) $2x - 3 = 4 - x$

(D) $3x - 2 = \frac{1}{2}x + 8$

(E) $2x - 3 = \frac{1}{2}x + 8$

The correct answer is E. The first step in solving this problem is to recognize that "three less than" means to subtract 3 from some other quantity. Quickly review the answer choices to see that you only need to consider answer choices C and E. Likewise, the statement "eight more than" means to add 8 to some other quantity. Only answer choice E meets both of these criteria. The expression "three less than twice a number" is expressed mathematically as $2x - 3$, and "eight more than half the number" is expressed mathematically as $\frac{1}{2}x + 8$.

Answer the Question Asked

If the problem requires three steps to reach a solution and you only completed two of the steps, then it is likely that the answer you arrived at will be one of the choices. However, it will not be the correct choice! Consider the following examples:

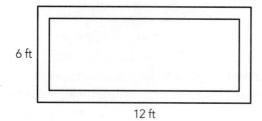

6 ft

12 ft

The rectangular garden shown in the figure above has a stone border 2 feet in width on all sides. What is the area, in square feet, of that portion of the garden that excludes the border?

(A) 4

(B) 16

(C) 40

(D) 56

(E) 72

The correct answer is B. This problem asks for the area of the *middle* portion of the garden. To solve this problem, perform the following calculations, and remember that the border goes around the entire garden. First, subtract the border width from the length of the garden:

$$12 - 2(2) = 8$$

Next, subtract the border width from the width of the garden:

$$6 - 2(2) = 2$$

The area (length × width) of the portion of the garden that excludes the border is 8 × 2, or 16.

If you only accounted for the border along one length and one width of the garden, you would have gotten answer choice C. Answer choice D is the area of the border around the garden. Answer choice E is the area of the entire garden, including the stone border.

Which of the following is the slope of a line that is perpendicular to the line $3x + 5y = 10$?

(A) -3

(B) $-\dfrac{5}{3}$

(C) $-\dfrac{3}{5}$

(D) $\dfrac{3}{5}$

(E) $\dfrac{5}{3}$

The correct answer is E. The first step in solving this problem is to put the equation in the standard form $y = mx + b$, where m is the slope:

$$3x + 5y = 10$$
$$5y = -3x + 10$$
$$y = -\frac{3}{5}x + 2$$

The slope of the given line is $-\frac{3}{5}$. However, you are asked for the slope of a line that is *perpendicular* to the given line. Perpendicular lines have negative reciprocal slopes, so the correct answer is $\frac{5}{3}$.

Don't Quit Early

Reason your way through the problem so that it makes sense. Keep in mind, though, that these questions do not usually involve intensive calculations or complicated manipulations. Consider the following examples:

If $0 < pr < 1$, then which of the following CANNOT be true?

(A) $p < 0$ and $r < 0$

(B) $p < -1$ and $r < 0$

(C) $p < -1$ and $r < -1$

(D) $p < 1$ and $r < 1$

(E) $p < 1$ and $r > 0$

The correct answer is C. At first glance, you might think that you don't have enough information to solve this problem. However, if you recognize that pr must be a positive fraction because it lies between 0 and 1, you can work your way through the answer choices and eliminate those that could be true:

Answer choice A: If both p and r were less than 0, then their product would be positive. It's possible for pr to be a positive fraction because both p and r could be negative fractions, so eliminate answer choice A.

Answer choice B: If p was less than -1 and r was less than zero, then their product would be positive because a negative times a negative yields a positive. It's possible for pr to be a positive fraction, so eliminate answer choice B.

Answer choice C: If both p and r were less than -1, then pr would be greater than 1, so this statement cannot be true, and answer choice C is correct.

At this point, you can select your answer and move on to the next question. We've included an expanded explanation to cover the remaining answer choices.

Answer choice D: If both p and r were less than 1 but greater than 0, then their product could be positive. It's possible for pr to be a positive fraction because either p or r could be a fraction, so eliminate answer choice D.

Answer choice E: If p were less than 1 but greater than 0, p could be a positive fraction. If r were greater than 0, it would be a positive number; therefore, it's possible for pr to be a positive fraction, so eliminate answer choice E.

For which values of x is the following function undefined?

$$f(x) = \frac{x^2 - 9}{x^2 - 49}$$

(A) 3

(B) 3, 7

(C) 7

(D) 7, −7

(E) 3, −3

The correct answer is D. Don't let the term *function* scare you; this is not really a function question at all. To solve this problem, first recall that a fraction is undefined when the denominator is 0. This is true because you cannot divide a number by 0. Therefore, the correct answer will include the values of x for which $x^2 = 49$. Eliminate answer choices A, B, and E. Because both 7^2 and $-7^2 = 49$, answer choice D is correct.

Check the Choices

Take a quick look at the answer choices as you read the problem for the first time. They can provide valuable clues about how to proceed. For example, many answer choices will be in either ascending or descending order. If the question asks you for the least possible value, try the smallest answer choice first. If it does not correctly answer the question, work through the rest of the answer choices from smallest to largest. Remember that one of them is the correct choice. Consider the following examples:

If x is an integer and $y = 7x + 11$, what is the greatest value of x for which y is less than 50?

(A) 7

(B) 6

(C) 5

(D) 4

(E) 3

The correct answer is C. Because the question asks for the greatest value of x, evaluate answer choice A first because it is the greatest value among the answer choices:

Answer choice A: $y = 7(7) + 11 = 60$. This is not less than 50, so eliminate answer choice A, and look at answer choice B.

Answer choice B: $y = 7(6) + 11 = 53$. This is not less than 50, so eliminate answer choice B, and look at answer choice C.

Answer choice C: $y = 7(5) + 11 = 46$. Because 5 is the greatest of the remaining answer choices and the result is less than 50, answer choice C must be correct.

Noah's Ark Fish Store sold 80 guppies and 48 bala sharks on Saturday. Which of the choices below could represent the ratio of bala sharks to guppies sold on Saturday?

(A) $\frac{12}{20}$

(B) 5:3

(C) $\frac{6}{5}$

(D) 25 to 15

(E) $\frac{20}{35}$

The correct answer is A. The first step in solving this problem is to note that the ratio is bala sharks to guppies, which can be expressed mathematically in the following ways: 48 to 80, 48:80, and $\frac{48}{80}$. Therefore, the correct answer must include a factor of 48 in the first position. Eliminate answer choices B, D, and E because 5, 25, and 20 are not factors of 48. Answer choice C cannot be correct because, although 6 is a factor of 48 and 5 is a factor of 80, the fraction $\frac{48}{80}$ is less than the fraction $\frac{6}{5}$ (note that the numerator is larger than the denominator in the second fraction). Therefore, the correct answer must be A; $\frac{12}{20} = \frac{48}{80}$.

Pick Numbers for the Variables

You can sometimes simplify your work on a given problem by using actual numbers as "stand-ins" for variables. This strategy works when you have variables in the question and the same variables in the answer choices. You can simplify the answer choices by substituting actual numbers for the variables. Pick numbers that are easy to work with and that meet the parameters of the information given in the question. If you use this strategy, remember that numbers on the GRE can be either positive or negative and are sometimes whole numbers and sometimes fractions. You should also be careful not to use 1 or 0 as your "stand-ins" because they can create "identities," which can lead to more than one seemingly correct answer choice. The word identity refers to an equality that remains true regardless of the values of any variables that appear within the equality. For example, any number multiplied by 0 is always 0.

In addition, it is sometimes necessary to try more than one number to see if the result always correctly responds to the question. If the numbers that you pick work for more than one answer choice, pick different numbers and try again, focusing on the remaining answer choices. Consider the following examples:

If x and y are both positive even integers, which of the following must be even?

  I. x^y

 II. $(x + 1)^y$

III. $x^{(y + 1)}$

(A) I only

(B) II only

(C) I and II only

(D) I and III only

(E) II and III only

The correct answer is D. The question states that both x and y are positive even integers. Therefore, you can pick any positive even integer and substitute that value for x and y in each of the Roman numeral choices, as follows:

Roman numeral I: $2^2 = 4$, which is even; $4^2 = 16$, which is also even. Any positive even integer raised to another positive even integer will result in an even number; therefore, Roman numeral I correctly answers the question. At this point, you could safely eliminate any answer choices that do not contain Roman numeral I.

Roman numeral II: $(2 + 1)^2 = 3^2 = 9$, which is odd; $(4 + 1)^2 = 5^2 = 25$, which is also odd. When you add 1 to a positive even integer and raise the sum to a positive even integer, the result will be odd; therefore, Roman numeral II does not correctly answer the question. At this point, you could safely eliminate any remaining answer choices that contain Roman numeral II.

Note that, if you were short on time, you could now guess between answer choices A and D, improving your odds to 50 percent.

Roman numeral III: $2^{(2 + 1)} = 2^3 = 8$, which is even; $4^{(2 + 1)} = 4^3 = 64$, which is also even. Any positive even integer raised to an odd power will result in an even number; therefore, Roman numeral III correctly answers the question, and you can eliminate any remaining answer choices that do not contain Roman numeral III, which leaves you with the correct answer.

If a and b are positive consecutive odd integers, where $b > a$, which of the following is equal to $b^2 - a^2$?

(A) $2a$

(B) $4a$

(C) $2a + 2$

(D) $2a + 4$

(E) $4a + 4$

The correct answer is E. You are given that both a and b are positive consecutive odd integers, and that b is greater than a. Pick two numbers that fit the criteria: $a = 3$ and $b = 5$. Now substitute these numbers into $b^2 - a^2$, as follows:

$5^2 = 25$ and $3^2 = 9$; therefore, $b^2 - a^2 = 25 - 9$, or 16

Now substitute the value that you selected for a into the answer choices until one of them yields 16, as follows:

$2(3) = 6$; eliminate answer choice A.

$4(3) = 12$; eliminate answer choice B.

$2(3) + 2 = 8$; eliminate answer choice C.

$2(3) + 4 = 10$; eliminate answer choice D.

$4(3) + 4 = 16$; answer choice E is correct.

Read the Questions Carefully

Sometimes the questions include irrelevant data, so be sure you're working with the correct numbers! Also, it helps to write down key words and phrases in the question. When you are looking at ratio problems, for example, note whether the question is giving a part-to-part ratio or a part-to-whole ratio. The ratio of girls to boys in a class is a part-to-part ratio. The ratio of girls to students in a class is a part-to-whole ratio. Focusing on the right information will help you to quickly answer the question. Consider the following examples:

The ratio of two quantities is 4 to 5. If each of the quantities is increased by 3, what is the ratio of these two new quantities?

(A) $\frac{1}{2}$

(B) $\frac{4}{5}$

(C) $\frac{7}{8}$

(D) $\frac{17}{18}$

(E) It cannot be determined from the information given.

The correct answer is E. To understand this problem, realize that, although the ratio of two quantities is 4 to 5, the actual values of the quantities might be very different. Because the quantities are unknown, increasing each by 3 will have an indeterminate effect on the ratio of the quantities. For instance, if the quantities were 4 and 5, increasing them both by 3 would result in a ratio of 7 to 8. However, if the quantities were 20 and 25 (a ratio of 4 to 5), increasing both quantities by 3 would result in a new ratio of 23 to 28, which is not the same as a ratio of 7 to 8.

What percent of 5 is 7?

(A) 35%

(B) 57%

(C) 71%

(D) 140%

(E) 157%

The correct answer is D. To solve this problem, note that 7 is greater than 5, which means that the correct answer must be greater than 100%; eliminate answer choices A, B, and C. To find what percent of 5 the number 7 is, you can simply divide 7 by 5 and multiply by 100%, as follows:

$$\frac{7}{5} = 1.4$$

$$(1.4)(100) = 140\%$$

Discrete Problem Solving Multiple-Choice Practice Questions

1. Jim's Hardware store normally sells bulk nails at $1.09 a pound. There is a sale of 3 pounds of nails for $2.19. How much can be saved by purchasing 9 pounds of nails at the sale price?

(A) $1.89

(B) $3.24

(C) $4.29

(D) $5.34

(E) $9.90

2. In $\triangle ABC$, $AB \cong AC$ and the measure of $\angle B$ is 34°. What is the measure of $\angle A$?

(A) 34°

(B) 56°

(C) 68°

(D) 73°

(E) 112°

3. If $7y + 9$ represents an odd integer, which of the following represents the next smaller odd integer?

   (A) $7(y + 1)$

   (B) $7(y - 2)$

   (C) $7(y + 3)$

   (D) $7(y + 2)$

   (E) $7(y - 2) + 1$

4. What is the largest integer value of t that satisfies the inequality $\frac{24}{30} > \frac{t}{24}$?

   (A) 8

   (B) 10

   (C) 18

   (D) 19

   (E) 30

5. The larger of two numbers exceeds twice the smaller number by 9. The sum of twice the larger and 5 times the smaller number is 74. If a is the smaller number, which equation below determines the correct value of a?

   (A) $5(2a + 9) + 2a = 74$

   (B) $5(2a - 9) + 2a = 74$

   (C) $(4a + 9) + 5a = 74$

   (D) $2(2a + 9) + 5a = 74$

   (E) $2(2a - 9) + 5a = 74$

6. If $W = XYZ$, then which of the following is an expression for Z in terms of W, X, and Y?

   (A) $\frac{XY}{W}$

   (B) $\frac{W}{XY}$

   (C) WXY

   (D) $W - XY$

   (E) $W + XY$

7. What is $\frac{1}{5}$ of 16% of $24,000?

   (A) $160

   (B) $768

   (C) $3,840

   (D) $4,032

   (E) $7,500

8. If $x = -3$ and $y = 2$, then $x^3y + xy^3 =$

   (A) 78

   (B) 30

   (C) -6

   (D) -30

   (E) -78

9. What is the least common multiple of 3, $4a$, $5b$, and $6ab$?

   (A) $15ab$

   (B) $60ab$

   (C) $60a^2b$

   (D) $120ab$

   (E) $120a^2b$

10. A hot dog and a soda at a basketball game's concession stand costs $3.40. A family purchases three hot dogs and two sodas, and the total cost is $9.10. What is the cost of a soda?

    (A) $1.00

    (B) $1.10

    (C) $1.15

    (D) $1.20

    (E) $1.40

Answers and Explanations

1. **The correct answer is B.** The first step in solving this problem is to calculate the cost of 9 pounds of nails at the regular price:

    9 ($1.09) = $9.81

    Next, calculate the cost of 9 pounds of nails at the sale price:

    3($2.19) = $6.57

    Finally, subtract $6.57 from $9.81 to get a savings of $3.24.

2. **The correct answer is E.** A good way to solve this problem is to sketch triangle *ABC*, as shown below:

    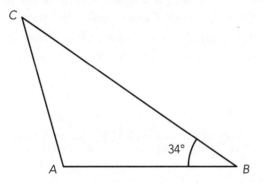

    You are given that *AB* is congruent to *AC*, and that the measure of angle *B* is 34°. This means that the measure of angle *C* is also 34°, and the measure of angle *A* is 180° − 34° − 34° = 112°.

3. **The correct answer is A.** To answer this question, note that odd numbers are every other number: 1, 3, 5, 7, . . . , etc. So an odd number plus or minus 2 would create another odd number. Therefore, $7y + 7$ would be the next *smaller* odd integer. Factor out a 7 to get $7(y + 1)$.

4. **The correct answer is D.** One way to solve this problem is to recognize that, in order for $\frac{24}{30}$ to be greater than $\frac{t}{24}$, t must be less than 24. This is true because any fraction with a denominator larger than or equal to its numerator will always be *less* than a fraction whose numerator is larger than or equal to its denominator. So, $\frac{t}{24}$ is only less than $\frac{24}{30}$ when t is less than 24. Because you are asked for the largest integer value of t and you know that t must be less than 24, the correct answer must be 19. You could also set the values equal to each other, cross-multiply and solve for t, as follows:

    $$\frac{24}{30} = \frac{t}{24}$$

    $$30t = 576$$

    $$t = 19.2$$

    The integer value that makes $\frac{24}{30}$ greater than $\frac{t}{24}$, therefore, is 19.

5. **The correct answer is D.** To solve this problem, first convert the information given into its mathematical equivalent, as follows (use *b* to represent the larger number):

   The larger of two numbers exceeds twice the smaller number by 9:
   $$b = 2a + 9$$

   The sum of twice the larger and five times the smaller number is 74:
   $$2b + 5a = 74$$

   Now, simply substitute the value of *b* into the second equation in order to solve for *a*:

   $$2(2a + 9) + 5a = 74$$

6. **The correct answer is B.** Don't let the fact that there are no numbers in this math problem confuse you! Simply remember that W, X, Y, and Z each represent some number, and perform the correct mathematical operations to isolate Z on one side of the equation, as follows:

   $$W = XYZ$$
   $$\frac{W}{XY} = Z$$

7. **The correct answer is B.** To solve this problem, first calculate 16% of 24,000, as follows:

   $$24,000 \times .16 = 3,840$$

   Next, calculate $\frac{1}{5}$ of 3,840, as follows:

   $$3,840 \times \frac{1}{5}$$
   $$= 3,840 \div 5 = 768$$

8. **The correct answer is E.** To solve this problem, simply substitute -3 for x and 2 for y in the equation, as follows (carefully track the negative sign!):

   $$x^3y + xy^3 = (-3)^3(2) + (-3)(2)^3$$
   $$= (-27)(2) + (-3)(8)$$
   $$= -54 - 24$$
   $$= -78$$

9. **The correct answer is B.** Each of the numbers in the values given must divide evenly into the least common multiple. Therefore, you can quickly eliminate answer choice A because 4 does not divide evenly into 15. Next, notice that each of the number values divides evenly into 60, which is less than 120, so eliminate answer choices D and E. Because ab is a smaller multiple than a^2b, and ab divides evenly into the product of all of the given values, answer choice B is the least common multiple of the given values.

10. **The correct answer is B.** This problem can be solved by using two simultaneous equations, as follows:

    Equation 1: s(soda) + d(hot dogs) = 3.40

    Equation 2: $3s + 2d = 9.10$

    Doubling the first equation and subtracting it from the second gives the result that s (the cost of a soda) is \$1.10. You could also have solved the first equation for d to get $d = 3.40 - s$, then substituted that value for d in the second equation to solve for s.

Quantitative Comparison Questions

Quantitative Comparison questions ask you to compare the quantities in two columns and determine whether one is larger than the other, if the quantities are equal, or if there is not enough information to determine a relationship between the two quantities. Some questions include additional information that is centered above the two columns that concerns one or both of the quantities. Quantitative Comparison questions generally require more logic skills than math skills, so refer to Chapter 6, "GRE Logic," for additional help.

You will be asked to select from answer choices A through D. If you decide that the quantity in Column A is greater than the quantity in Column B, select answer choice A. If you decide that the quantity in Column B is greater than the quantity in Column A, select answer choice B. If you decide that the quantities are equal, select answer choice C. If there is not enough information to determine a relationship between the two quantities, select answer choice D.

GRE Tip

Memorize the answer choices to Quantitative Comparison questions to save on time:

A = Quantity A is greater

B = Quantity B is greater

C = Quantities are equal

D = Not enough information

NOTE

Quantitative Comparison figures might not be drawn to scale. Rely on the information given, not on the appearance of the figures, to answer the questions.

The best way to handle the Quantitative Comparison questions is to simply determine the value of the quantities in each column. It is often better to estimate values because you are really just trying to decide if one value is greater than the other. After you have calculated the values, you can easily determine the relationship, if one exists.

If one column is sometimes greater than or sometimes less than the other column, the relationship cannot be determined from the information. You should select answer choice D if *no one* can determine the relationship between the two values.

Anatomy of a GRE Quantitative Comparison Question

Before moving on to strategies, you should understand what a Quantitative Comparison question looks like. Consider the following example:

<u>Column A</u>	<u>Column B</u>
$-(3)^4$	$(-3)^4$

General Strategies for Quantitative Comparison Questions

Most of the strategies that apply to the Discrete Problem Solving questions will work for the Quantitative Comparison questions, too. Use the following additional strategies when tackling more difficult Quantitative Comparison questions.

Memorize the Answer Choices

Don't spend time on test day trying to determine what A, B, C, and D mean. Remember that if Column A is greater, choose A; if Column B is greater, choose B; if the columns are equal, choose C; if you can't determine a relationship, choose D. Take the time now to commit the answer choices to memory.

Simplify

You generally will not have to perform all of the calculations necessary to reach a definitive answer. You need to manipulate the quantities only until you know the relationship between them. Stop as soon as you know whether one is always greater than the other, or whether the quantities will always be equivalent. Consider the following example:

Column A	Column B

x is an integer less than 0.

3^{2x}	4^x

The correct answer is B. You are given that *x* is an integer, which means that it is a whole number. You also know that *x* is less than zero, which means it is a negative number. Choose several values for *x* that meet the previous criteria, and substitute those values into the quantities in each column:

When $x = -1$, the quantity in Column A is 3^{-2}, which is equivalent to $\frac{1}{32}$, or $\frac{1}{9}$.

When $x = -1$, the quantity in Column B is 4^{-1}, which is equivalent to $\frac{1}{4}$. Therefore, the quantity in Column B is greater than the quantity in Column A.

When $x = -2$, the quantity in Column A is 3^{-4}, which is equivalent to $\frac{1}{3^4}$, or $\frac{1}{81}$.

When $x = -2$, the quantity in Column B is 4^{-2}, which is equivalent to $\frac{1}{4^2}$, or $\frac{1}{16}$, and the quantity in Column B is still greater than the quantity in Column A.

In fact, because you will always multiply *x* by 2 in Column A, the denominator in Column A will always be greater than the denominator in Column B, and the quantity in Column B will always be greater than the quantity in Column A.

Use What You Know

You can often apply common sense to solving Quantitative Comparison problems. For example, if you are asked to compare the quantity $(399)^2$ to the quantity $(299)^3$, you can simply recognize that 399 is almost 400, and 400 squared is 1,600. Likewise, 299 is almost 300, and 300 cubed is 2,700. You don't actually have to perform the calculations in the question.

Be sure to read and evaluate the information (if any) that is given above the quantities to be compared. Sometimes you will only have to substitute values into equations in the column to reach an answer.

Consider the following example:

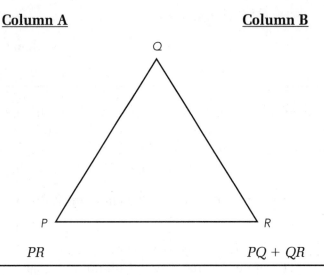

Column A

Column B

PR $PQ + QR$

The correct answer is B. Any side of a triangle must be greater than the difference and less than the sum of the other two sides. Otherwise, you have either a triangle that falls in on itself, or two lines that lie on top of each other. Therefore, the quantity in Column B, which is the sum of two sides of the triangle, is greater than the quantity in Column A, which is the length of one side.

> **NOTE**
>
> Logical approximations are rewarded on the GRE; the test makers realize that you will not have time to perform detailed calculations for most of the questions.

Quantitative Comparison Practice Questions

Column A	**Column B**
1. The cost of p pens at a cost of $r + 29$ cents each	The cost of 7 notebooks at a cost of $(p + r)$ cents each

$$7x - 4 = 16 - 3x$$

	Column A	**Column B**
2.	x	4
3.	$(-3)^7$	$(-3)^6$

$$x + y = 27$$
$$y + 12 = 23$$

	Column A	**Column B**
4.	x	y

A windmill makes one revolution every 8 seconds.

5.	23	The number of revolutions made in 3 minutes.

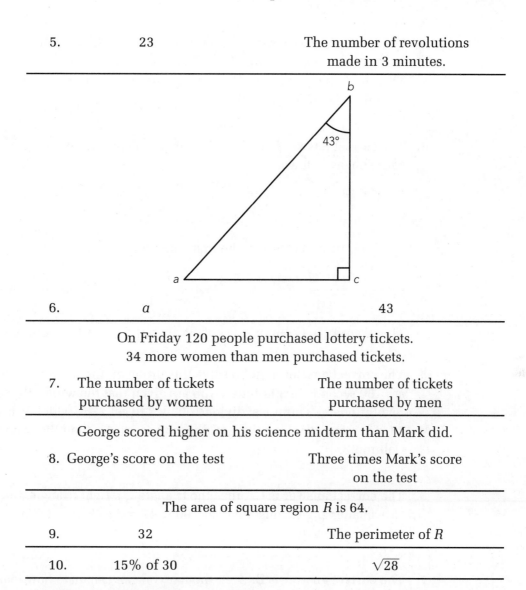

6.	a	43

On Friday 120 people purchased lottery tickets.
34 more women than men purchased tickets.

7.	The number of tickets purchased by women	The number of tickets purchased by men

George scored higher on his science midterm than Mark did.

8.	George's score on the test	Three times Mark's score on the test

The area of square region R is 64.

9.	32	The perimeter of R

10.	15% of 30	$\sqrt{28}$

Answers and Explanations

1. **The correct answer is D.** The values of p and r are not given, so you cannot determine the relationship between Column A and Column B.

2. **The correct answer is B.** To solve this problem, simplify the equation:

$$10x = 20$$

$$x = 2$$

The quantity in Column B is greater than the quantity in Column A.

3. **The correct answer is B.** A negative number raised to an odd power is negative. A negative number raised to an even power is positive. Therefore, the quantity in Column A is negative and the quantity in Column B is positive.

4. **The correct answer is A.** To solve this problem, simplify the second equation, as follows:

   $$y + 12 = 23$$

   $$y = 11$$

   Now substitute 11 for y in the first equation:

   $$x + 11 = 27$$

   $$x = 16$$

   The quantity in Column A is greater than the quantity in Column B.

5. **The correct answer is A.** To solve this problem, first determine that there are 180 seconds in 3 minutes. You are given that the windmill makes 8 revolutions in 3 minutes; divide 180 by 8 to get 22.5, which is less than 23. Therefore, the quantity in Column A is greater than the quantity in Column B.

6. **The correct answer is C.** Since the triangle is a right triangle, the two smaller angles must total 90°. 90 − 47 = 43. So $a = 43$, and the quantities are equal.

7. **The correct answer is D.** Even though you can calculate how many women and men purchased tickets, you have no information about how many tickets each individual purchased. Therefore, you do not have enough information to determine the relationship between the quantities.

8. **The correct answer is D.** You are not given the relationship between the scores. For example, if George scored an 88 and Mark scored an 87, then the quantity in Column B would be greater. However, if George scored a 90 and Mark scored a 30, then the two quantities would be equal. Therefore, the relationship cannot be determined from the information given.

9. **The correct answer is C.** You are given that the area of the square is 64, which means that each side must be $\sqrt{64}$, or 8 (remember, the area of a square is equal to s^2). Therefore, the perimeter of the square is 8×4, or 32, making the quantities equal.

10. **The correct answer is B.** To calculate 15% of 30, multiply 30 by .15:

$$30 \times .15 = 4.5$$

You can use logic to determine that the quantity in Column B is greater: $\sqrt{25} = 5$, so $\sqrt{28}$ must be greater than 5.

Numeric Entry Questions

This is a new question type that was added to the GRE Computer Adaptive Test in November 2007. Questions of this type require you to enter your answer as an integer in a single answer box or as a fraction in two separate answer boxes. You will use the computer mouse and keyboard to make your entry.

Once you've calculated your answer using scratch paper, click on the answer box(es) to activate, then type your answer. To erase, simply backspace. For a negative sign, type a hyphen, and for a decimal point, type a period. You should apply the standard rules of rounding if the question asks for an approximate answer; otherwise, type in the exact answer. It is not necessary to reduce fractions to their lowest terms.

> **NOTE**
>
> As of the writing of this book, the POWERPREP® software does not include Numeric Entry questions. However, in addition to the samples you will find in this book, there are practice questions at www.gre.org. Keep in mind that there will be only one Numeric Entry question on your GRE.

Anatomy of a GRE Numeric Entry Question

Before moving on to strategies, you should understand what a Numeric Entry question looks like. Consider the following example:

Solve the equation for x: $2(x - 3) + 9 = 4x - 7$

$x =$ ☐

General Strategies for Numeric Entry Questions

You can apply many of the strategies discussed for Discrete Problem Solving questions to Numeric Entry questions. In addition, keep the following in mind when answering this new question type:

- Read the questions carefully and be sure to provide the type of answer indicated. For example, if you are asked to type an answer to the nearest tenth, don't round your answer to the nearest whole number.

- If you are not asked to round or estimate your answer, type in an exact value. Make the necessary computations on your scratch paper—set up equations, draw pictures, and so on—to avoid making careless errors.

- You will not have any answer choices to guide you, so check your answer and make sure it is logical based on the information provided in the question.

Numeric Entry Practice Questions

1. If $3x + 4y = 17$ and $5x + 2y = 23$, what is the value of $x - y$?

2. If $-7 \leq x \leq 5$ and $-3 \leq y \leq 4$, what is the greatest possible value of $(y - x)(x + y)$?

3. A salesperson made a profit of $50 on the sale of a bicycle that cost the salesperson $180. What is the profit expressed as a percent of the salesperson's cost? Give your answer to the nearest tenth of a percent.

4. A rope 55 feet long is cut into two pieces. If one piece is 23 feet longer than the other, what is the length, in feet, of the shorter piece?

5. An integer from 10 through 99, inclusive, is to be chosen at random. What is the probability that the number chosen will have 0 as at least one digit? Give your answer as a fraction.

Answers and Explanations

1. **The correct answer is 3.** In order to solve this system of equations, subtract the first equation from the second. The result is $2x - 2y = 6$. Factor out 2 to get $2(x - y) = 6$. Divide both sides by 2 to get $x - y = 3$.

2. **The correct answer is 99.** Because you are looking for the greatest value of $(y - x)(x + y)$, your goal is to make $x + y$ as big as possible and $y - x$ as big as possible. Therefore, use $x = 5$ and $y = 4$ to get $x + y = 9$, and $x = -7$ and $y = 4$ to get $y - x = 11$. The greatest value of $(y - x)(x + y)$ is $(9)(11) = 99$.

3. **The correct answer is 27.8.** One way to solve this problem is to set up a proportion, as follows:

   $50 is to $180 as x is to 100%

   $$\frac{50}{180} = \frac{x}{100}$$

   $$180x = 5{,}000$$

   $x = 27.777$, which should be rounded to 27.8, as per the instructions in the question.

4. **The correct answer is 16.** To solve this problem, set up an equation to determine the length of the shorter piece, substituting x for the unknown, shorter length:

   $$x + (x + 23) = 55$$
   $$2x + 23 = 55$$
   $$2x = 32$$
   $$x = 16$$

5. **The correct answer is $\frac{1}{10}$.** The first step in solving this problem is to determine how many integers between 10 and 99, inclusive, will have 0 as at least one digit, as follows:

   10, 20, 30, 40, 50, 60, 70, 80, 90

   There are 9 integers that will have 0 as at least one digit. Next, because there is a total of 90 numbers in the given range, the probability of choosing one of those 9 numbers is $\frac{9}{90}$, which simplifies to $\frac{1}{10}$.

What's Next?

If you require a review of the basic math concepts tested on the GRE, be sure to read Chapter 10, "Basic GRE Math Review," before you tackle the practice tests in Part IV.

9

GRE Verbal

CHAPTER GOALS

- Review the five types of GRE verbal questions: Antonym, Analogy, Sentence Completion, Reading Comprehension, and Text Completion with Two or Three Blanks.
- Study examples of each verbal question type.
- Learn specific strategies for answering each verbal question type.
- Practice answering sample GRE verbal questions.

The GRE Verbal section is designed to measure the skills required to carefully read and understand sentences and passages in standard written English. A GRE Verbal section includes 30 questions of the following five question types: Antonym, Analogy, Sentence Completion, Reading Comprehension, and Text Completion with Two or Three Blanks (this is a new question type and you will likely see only one of them on your GRE).

The questions appear in random order, which means that you might first be given a Sentence Completion question, followed by two Analogy questions, followed by a passage and several Reading Comprehension questions, followed by three Antonym questions, and so on.

This chapter provides you with useful strategies and techniques, an overview of the question types, and a breakdown of the critical reading skills that will be tested. This chapter also includes some sample practice questions with explanations.

GRE Tip

Remember that you must answer all the questions in the order in which they are presented. The computer adaptive test will ask you to select and confirm your answer to each question.

Antonym Questions

The Antonym questions on the GRE Verbal section are designed to test not only the strength of your vocabulary, but also your ability to reason from one concept to an opposite concept. You should be able to answer many questions with only a general knowledge of a vocabulary word; however, some challenging questions might require you to make distinctions between more subtle meanings.

Questions in this section are composed of a word in all capital letters, followed by five answer choices. You will be required to determine the answer choice that is the antonym of, or is most nearly opposite to, the definition of the given word.

In general, the words that appear in the antonym questions are limited to nouns, adjectives, and verbs. Answer choices will be either a single word or a short phrase. Some of the answer choices might be very similar to one another. Your job is to select the best choice from the five options.

> **NOTE**
>
> Antonyms require your brain to take an additional step in logic. By including synonyms among the answer choices, the GRE can test your ability to consistently make the logical choice.

Anatomy of a GRE Antonym Question

Before moving on to the strategies that will help you to approach these questions with confidence, you should understand what a GRE Antonym question looks like. Consider the following:

Stem Word	CREDULOUS
Answer Choices	(A) skeptical
	(B) naive
	(C) spontaneous
	(D) sensitive
	(E) discrete

General Strategies for Antonym Questions

The following are some general strategies that will help you to answer GRE Antonym questions correctly:

- Clearly define the stem word.
- Use the correct part of speech.
- Beware of homonyms.
- Use prefixes, suffixes, roots, and cognates.
- Use connotations.
- Use the given word in a sentence.

- Predict an answer choice.
- Use the process of elimination.

Clearly Define the Stem Word

Because you are looking for an antonym of the stem, or given word, it's important that you first determine the meaning of the given word. If you are only somewhat familiar with the given word, it might help to use the word in a sentence or recall a quotation that includes the word. In addition, pay attention to the next few strategies to help you correctly and clearly define the stem word.

Use the Correct Part of Speech

Make sure that you recognize whether the word is a noun, adjective, or verb. The best answer will use the same part of speech. The answer choices might help you to make this determination. If all of the answer choices are adjectives, for example, the given word will also be an adjective.

It is important to remember that a single word can often be used interchangeably as a verb and a noun, or a noun and an adjective, or might simply have multiple definitions.

For example, the word *bore* can be:

A verb, as in "to cause a loss of interest."

A verb, as in "to drill a hole."

A verb, as in the past tense of "to bear," which means to "support," "carry," or "have" something.

A noun, as in "a dull or boring person or thing."

The key to successfully answering a GRE Antonym question will often be your ability to quickly switch between possible meanings and select a correct answer based on your reactions to the answer choices.

Beware of Homonyms

Generally, *homonyms* are words that are pronounced the same, but have different spellings and different meanings. Be sure that you are defining the correct word. For example, the words *course* and *coarse* are pronounced exactly the same, but have very different meanings. If you mistakenly define *course* as "common or rough," you will have a hard time finding an antonym among the answer choices. Consider the following example of a question similar to those found on the GRE:

ASSENT:

(A) indifference

(B) disagreement

(C) carelessness

(D) stability

(E) significance

The best answer is B. The word *assent* refers to "agreement," so the correct answer is B, *disagreement*. If you had defined *assent* as "the act of climbing" (*ascent*), you would most likely have struggled to find an antonym from among the answer choices.

Use Prefixes, Suffixes, Roots, and Cognates

If you have never seen the word before, use your knowledge of *prefixes*, *suffixes*, and *roots* to help you to determine the meaning of the word.

Prefix refers to a letter or letters attached to the front of a word to produce a derivative of that word. For example, the prefix *multi-* means "many," as in *multilingual*, which means "many languages."

A *suffix*, on the other hand, is a letter or series of letters added to the end of a word, serving to form a new word or functioning as an inflectional ending. For example, the suffix *-less* means "without," as in *careless*.

Learn to recognize *roots*, or stems, that some words have in common. The root provides the basis from which certain words are derived. For example, the Latin root *gen* means "birth, class, or kin," as in *congenital*, which refers to a condition that is present at birth.

In addition, look for *cognates* from French, Spanish, or Italian (the modern versions of Latin) if you recognize them. A cognate is a word that means the same or nearly the same thing in more than one language. For example, the word *amigo*, which means "friend" in Spanish, the word *ami*, which means "friend" in French, and the word *amicable*, which means "friendly" in English, all come from the Latin root word for "friend," *amicus*. These words are considered *cognates*.

Following is an example of how to use a prefix to select the correct answer:

INVARIABLE:

(A) overstated

(B) sufficient

(C) erratic

(D) reasonable

(E) intact

The best answer is C. The prefix *in-* can mean "not" or "without". Therefore, something that is *invariable* is "not variable." *Erratic* means "irregular, unpredictable, or subject to change," which is most nearly opposite to *invariable*.

Use Connotations

Each word in the English language expresses two things: a *definition* and a *connotation*. A definition conveys the meaning of the word. A connotation is a positive, negative, or neutral feeling or emotion that is suggested by or associated with a word. For example, the noun *happiness* implies a positive connotation. Using connotations might help you to determine the correct answer or at least eliminate a few wrong answers.

> **GRE Tip**
>
> Keep in mind that GRE test writers rarely use exact opposites. In fact, you should not expect to find a perfect antonym among the answer choices. Remind yourself to look for the word that is "most nearly opposite."

Here is an example of how to use a connotation to help you to select the correct answer:

FALLACY:

(A) tentative disagreement

(B) personal philosophy

(C) simple hypothesis

(D) legitimate claim

(E) indirect statement

The best answer is D. The word *fallacy* has a negative connotation because it relates to something that has errors or flaws or is false. It comes from the Latin word *fallere*, which means "to deceive." Therefore, the best answer will have an opposite, or positive connotation. Answer choice A is slightly negative, answer choice B is neutral, answer choice C is neutral, answer choice D is positive, and answer choice E is neutral but slightly negative. The connotations of the given word and the answer choices should lead you to answer choice D, "legitimate claim."

Use the Given Word in a Sentence

Unfortunately, you cannot guess the meaning of an unfamiliar word from the context in GRE Antonym questions. The good news is that you have probably seen or heard the unfamiliar word, or some version of it, at some point in your life. Create a sentence that uses the word in a familiar way, and use the sentence to help you establish the definition of the word. Substitute the answer choices for the word in the sentence; the choice that successfully reverses the meaning or tone of the sentence is the best choice. Consider the following example:

DORMANCY:

(A) remaining active

(B) creating confusion

(C) lurking about

(D) hibernation

(E) opposition

The best answer is A. You probably have heard the word *dormant*, which means "inactive." *Dormancy*, then, refers to the "state of being dormant, or inactive." Use the word in a sentence: "The bear awoke after several months of dormancy." Now, insert the answer choices; the one that changes the meaning of the sentence the most will be the correct answer. When you insert answer choice A, the sentence becomes, "The bear awoke after several months of remaining active."

This sentence contradicts the meaning of the original sentence. Therefore, answer choice A is best. Answer choices B and C are nonsensical, answer choice D is a synonym of *dormancy*, and answer choice E means "being in conflict," which is not an antonym of *dormancy*.

Predict an Answer Choice

Before you look at the answer choices, try to predict an antonym on your own. Remember that experts create incorrect answers to distract you. If you predict an answer before you look at the answer choices, you can begin to eliminate words and are less likely to get caught up in these confusing, incorrect answers. If your antonym matches one of the answer choices, it is most likely correct. The following examples and detailed explanations show you how predicting an answer can help you to eliminate obviously incorrect answer choices:

1. LOCAL:

    (A) regional

    (B) lofty

    (C) global

    (D) unusual

    (E) durable

The best answer is C. Because *local* generally refers to a specific place on Earth, an antonym would most likely involve the entire Earth. *Global* is a word that could easily be predicted and is the correct answer. Note that the first distracter is a synonym for the stem word.

2. RANDOM:

    (A) rational

    (B) aimless

    (C) systematic

    (D) deliberate

    (E) genuine

The best answer is C. You might have predicted *regular* or *orderly* as antonyms of *random*. Both are correct, but neither appears as an answer choice. However, *systematic* is a synonym of both of your predicted answers, so answer choice C is correct. Answer choice D, *deliberate*, might have been tempting, but *systematic* is more opposite because it implies a sense of order. Be sure to look at all of the answer choices before you select a final answer, even if your predicted antonym is among the choices. Eliminate clearly incorrect answers as you work through the choices.

Use the Process of Elimination

This strategy is useful if you are unable to find the correct answer using any of the previously mentioned strategies. Look at each answer choice, determine whether you know something about each word or phrase, and use that information to eliminate answer choices that are clearly incorrect. For example, if you find several answer choices that have similar meanings, those choices can usually be eliminated. The process of elimination can be time consuming, so it should generally be saved for last-ditch efforts in selecting the correct answer. You will probably employ this strategy in conjunction with the others mentioned, eliminating answer choices that do not fit logically into the sentence that you created, for example.

Practice Antonym Questions

Following are simulated GRE Antonym questions with explanations.

<u>Directions:</u> Each question below contains a word in capital letters and five answer choices. Each answer choice contains a word or phrase. Select the word or phrase that best expresses a meaning *opposite* to the word in capital letters.

1. RECEIVE:

    (A) decline

    (B) organize

    (C) deliver

    (D) locate

    (E) absorb

2. APEX:

    (A) lowest point

    (B) greatest length

    (C) furthest distance

    (D) shortest height

    (E) smallest curve

3. INSIPID:

    (A) bland

    (B) inventive

    (C) interesting

    (D) prosaic

    (E) insubordinate

4. SOLICITOUS:

   (A) attentive

   (B) sequential

   (C) precise

   (D) sophisticated

   (E) negligent

5. VENAL:

   (A) eclectic

   (B) extant

   (C) ethical

   (D) esoteric

   (E) exigent

6. RECONDITE:

   (A) perplexing

   (B) straightforward

   (C) anxious

   (D) translucent

   (E) apprehensive

7. COGENT:

   (A) keen

   (B) convincing

   (C) dense

   (D) implausible

   (E) systematic

8. PROFLIGATE:

   (A) profuse

   (B) permanent

   (C) altruistic

   (D) eternal

   (E) miserly

9. DEBILITATE:

   (A) masticate

   (B) fortify

   (C) annotate

   (D) impair

   (E) elucidate

10. BLITHE:

    (A) jovial

    (B) nonchalant

    (C) satisfied

    (D) melancholy

    (E) vehement

Answers and Explanations

1. **The best answer is C.** The word that has a meaning most opposite to *receive* is *deliver*.

2. **The best answer is A.** The *apex* is the "highest point," so the phrase with the most opposite meaning is "lowest point."

3. **The best answer is C.** The word *insipid* means "dull" or "lacking interest." Therefore, the word with the most opposite meaning is *interesting*.

4. **The best answer is E.** Someone who is *solicitous* is generally "caring and concerned," whereas someone who is *negligent* exhibits "little care or concern." Therefore, *negligent* is most opposite in meaning to *solicitous*.

5. **The best answer is C.** The word *venal* generally refers to someone who is "corrupt," or "open to bribery," whereas an *ethical* person is "moral" and would not likely be "corrupt." Therefore, *ethical* has a meaning most opposite to that of *venal*.

6. **The best answer is B.** The word *recondite* means "difficult to understand," so *straightforward* is most nearly opposite in meaning to *recondite*.

7. **The best answer is D.** The word *cogent* means "to be convincing and reasonable," whereas the word *implausible* means "to be too extraordinary or improbable to believe." Therefore, the word *incredible* is most nearly opposite in meaning to the word *cogent*.

8. **The best answer is E.** The word *profligate* means "recklessly wasteful," whereas to be *miserly* means to be "stingy." Therefore, *miserly* is most nearly opposite in meaning to the *profligate*.

9. **The best answer is B.** To *debilitate* means "to weaken or impair," whereas to *fortify* means to "secure or strengthen." Therefore, *fortify* is most nearly opposite in meaning to the word *debilitate*.

10. **The best answer is D.** The word *blithe* means "carefree or joyous," whereas the word *melancholy* means "sorrowful." Therefore, *melancholy* is most nearly opposite in meaning to the word *blithe*.

Analogy Questions

An *analogy* is a comparison of two things that seem unrelated, but are actually related or similar to each other in some respect. The Analogy questions on the GRE Verbal section are designed to test your ability to recognize these relationships between words and successfully identify parallel relationships.

These questions are composed of a pair of words in all capital letters, followed by five lettered pairs of words. You will be required to identify the answer choice that expresses a relationship most similar to that expressed in the original pair.

Anatomy of a GRE Analogy Question

Before moving on to strategies, you should understand what a GRE Analogy question looks like. Consider the following related word pair and answer choices:

Related Word Pair   APPRENTICE : PLUMBER ::

Answer Choices   (A) player : coach

(B) child : parent

(C) student : teacher

(D) author : publisher

(E) intern : doctor

General Strategies for Analogy Questions

Several strategies can help you to correctly answer GRE Analogy questions. Following is a description of those strategies that have proven most helpful:

- Establish the relationship.
- Create a general sentence.
- Use the correct part of speech.
- Be aware of homonyms.
- Recognize common relationship types.
- Use the process of elimination.
- Select the best answer.

Establish the Relationship

Before you look at any of the answer choices, attempt to express the relationship between the original pair in your own words. If you can establish a precise connection between the words, you will most likely select the best answer choice.

Create a General Sentence

One successful technique is to create a sentence that expresses a specific relationship between the stem words, and then replace the original words from your sentence with the words in the answer choices. You should look for the simplest relationship first. If more than one answer choice expresses the same relationship, you might have to revise your original sentence to indicate a more explicit connection between the words. For example:

MUSICIAN : ORCHESTRA ::

(A) mechanic : car

(B) songwriter : lyrics

(C) desk : office

(D) player : team

(E) actor : screen

The best answer is D. Ask yourself what a *musician* has to do with an *orchestra*. A musician plays in an orchestra. Or more specifically, a musician plays an instrument as one part of an orchestra as a whole. Your general sentence becomes "A -------- does something as one part of a -------- as a whole." A player participates as one part of a team as a whole. Although answer choice B includes words related to music, the exact relationship is not the same as the relationship in the question stem; a *songwriter* does not participate as one part of *lyrics* as a whole. Likewise, the remaining answer choices do not fit logically into

> **GRE Tip**
> The GRE uses only logically strong relationships. If you find yourself saying things such as "this could be true" or "sometimes this happens," the relationship, and thus your answer, is probably incorrect. Try for a relationship that must be true or is true all of the time.

the general sentence that you created. A *mechanic* does not do something as one part of a *car* as a whole. Although a *desk* might be considered one part of an *office*, a *desk* is an inanimate object, so it does not do something as one part of an *office* as a whole. An *actor* is portrayed on the *screen*, but an *actor* does not do something as one part of a *screen* as a whole.

Use the Correct Part of Speech

Don't forget about other possible, secondary meanings of words. If you are having trouble creating a sentence, you might be thinking of the wrong definition or part of speech. The questions will always ask you to compare the same parts of speech. For example, if one of the words in the original pair can be used as either a noun or a verb, all of the corresponding words in the answer choices will be either nouns or verbs, but not both. You can let the answer choices guide you in this way. Consider the following example:

CORRAL : LIVESTOCK ::

(A) fence : posts

(B) capture : thieves

(C) nest : birds

(D) devise : plans

(E) fire : employees

The best answer is B. At first glance, you might have created a general sentence such as "A *corral* is an enclosure for *livestock*." However, none of the answer choices fits logically into that sentence. Because *corral* is also a verb that means "to take control or possession of," you must now consider this secondary meaning. A closer look at the answer choices shows you that the first word in the pair is either a verb, or a word that can be used as a verb *or* a noun. Create another sentence using *corral* as a verb: "The rancher was unable to *corral* his *livestock* after they escaped." Manipulate the sentence slightly, as follows: "The police officer was unable to *capture* the *thieves* after they escaped." The remaining answer choices do not fit logically into this general sentence.

Be Aware of Homonyms

Be aware of *homonyms*, which are words that sound alike but have different meanings. For example, *mettle* is a noun meaning "courage or fortitude," whereas *meddle* is a verb meaning "to interfere." As in the earlier discussion regarding parts of speech, let the answer choices help you to determine the meaning of the words in the original pair. It is likely that you will know the meaning of some of the words in the answer choices and be able to establish a relationship between some of the word pairs listed. Use this knowledge to eliminate answer choices in which the word pairs do not have a clear connection, as well as to identify the correct meaning of the words in the original pair.

Recognize Common Relationship Types

GRE Analogy questions require you to consider many different possible relationships. After you are able to determine a specific relationship for the original pair, select the answer choice that expresses a relationship in the same way. Most GRE questions tend to fall into one of several common categories of relationships. The following sections describe many of the common analogy relationships tested on the GRE.

Definition/Evidence

One word in a pair helps to define the other word; or, one word in a pair is a defining characteristic of the other word.

> **Example:**
>
> PARAGON : EXCELLENCE ::

A *paragon*, by definition, is a "model or example of *excellence*."

> CRATER : CONCAVE ::

A *crater* is *concave*; therefore, being *concave* is a defining characteristic of a *crater*.

Synonym/Antonym

One word in a pair is a *synonym* or *antonym* of the other word.

> **Example:**
>
> FASCINATION : INTEREST ::

The nouns *fascination* and *interest* have a similar meaning. They are synonyms.

> STINGY : GENEROUS ::

The adjective *stingy* is the opposite of the adjective *generous*. They are antonyms.
    Note that synonyms and antonyms do not have to come from the same parts of speech.

> **Example:**
>
> CONTRARY : OPPOSE ::

To be *contrary*, which is an adjective, is to *oppose*, which is a verb. These words have similar meanings, even though the parts of speech are not the same.

> SKEPTICAL : BELIEVE ::

Skeptical, an adjective, means that you do *not* believe, which is the opposite of the verb *believe*. These words are opposite in meaning, even though the parts of speech are not the same.

Type/Kind

One word in a pair is a type or example of the other word.

> **Example:**
> FRENCH : LANGUAGE ::

French is a type of *language*.

Degree/Intensity

Both words in a pair are similar in concept, but vary in intensity. In other words, one word in the pair is stronger, harsher, or more intense. Words can also vary spatially, by size, weight, and so on.

> **Example:**
> PHOBIA : FEAR ::

A *phobia* is a "disabling, exaggerated fear," which is far more extreme than a typical *fear*.

Purpose/Function

One word in a pair describes the purpose or function of the other word.

> **Example:**
> NEEDLE : STITCH ::

The purpose or function of a *needle* is to *stitch*.

Note that *stitch* can be used as either a noun or a verb. You could also say that a *needle* is used to create a *stitch*.

Component/Part

One word in a pair represents one part of the other word, which represents a whole; or one word is simply a component of the other.

> **Example:**
> ACTOR : CAST ::

An *actor* is one member of an entire *cast* of actors.

>   FLOUR : BREAD ::

Flour is a component of *bread*.

Cause and Effect

One word leads to or results in the other word.

>   **Example:**
>   PREPARATION : SUCCESS ::

Preparation will most likely lead to *success*.

>   ANTIBODIES : PROTECTION ::

The presence of *antibodies* results in *protection* against infection.

> **NOTE**
>
> A correct answer will never contain a relationship that has been reversed. For example, if the analogy given is TOUCH : TACTILE, the answer cannot be AUDIBLE : HEARING. Even though the relationship is the same, the order of the relationship is reversed. The correct answer will always mirror the parts of speech in the original word pair.

Use the Process of Elimination

This strategy is useful if you are unable to find the correct answer using any of the previously mentioned strategies. Look at each answer choice and determine whether you know something about each word in the pair, and use that information to eliminate answer choices that are clearly incorrect. The process of elimination can be time consuming, so it should generally be saved for last-ditch efforts in selecting the correct answer. You will probably employ this strategy in conjunction with the others mentioned, eliminating answer choices that do not fit logically into the sentence that you created.

Select the Best Answer

Remember that the test experts create incorrect answers to distract you; if you establish a relationship beforehand, you will be less likely to get caught up in any confusing, incorrect answers that the test writers have set up. If your relationship matches a relationship expressed in *one* of the answer choices, it is most likely correct.

It might be difficult to determine an answer choice without eliminating a few incorrect answers first. Beware of obvious answer choices. At first glance, several choices might appear to express a similar relationship to the original pair.

The correct relationship will be paralleled in only one of the answer choices; you might have to dig a little deeper to discover the true relationship. For example:

PASSENGERS : AIRPLANE ::

(A) audience : theater

(B) birds : nest

(C) sailors : submarine

(D) freight : warehouse

(E) students : classroom

The best answer is C. One possible relationship between *passengers* and *airplane* is that passengers are in an airplane. At first glance, several answer choices appear to have the same relationship as the words in the question stem: A *theater* holds an *audience*, *freight* is in a *warehouse*, and so on. There cannot be more than one correct answer, so you should look for a more specific relationship. Create a sentence using the words in the question stem: "An *airplane* transports *passengers* from one place to another." Only the words in answer choice C can be logically inserted into this sentence.

Be sure to consider all of the answer choices before you select a final answer, even if you think you have already found the correct one. If you are struggling to find just one correct answer, make your relationship statement more specific or, if you must, adjust the relationship entirely.

Practice Analogy Questions

Following are simulated GRE Analogy questions with explanations.

<u>Directions:</u> Each question below contains a pair of words in capital letters and five answer choices. Each answer choice contains a pair of words. Select the pair that best expresses the relationship expressed by the pair in all capital letters.

1. VOCAL : CHORUS ::

   (A) musical : harmony

   (B) instrumental : band

   (C) honorable : student

   (D) fanatical : athlete

   (E) fearful : discord

2. REMEDIATION : DEFICIENCY ::

   (A) reparation : misfortune

   (B) discrimination : poverty

   (C) repudiation : duty

   (D) speculation : proof

   (E) cancellation : appointment

3. PLUNGE : FLOAT ::

   (A) dive : swim

   (B) throw : catch

   (C) wait : hurry

   (D) drive : park

   (E) gallop : stroll

4. ANNOTATE : ESSAY ::

   (A) elevate : level

   (B) research : theory

   (C) abridge : chapter

   (D) elaborate : plan

   (E) mitigate : damage

5. OBSTINATE : YIELDING ::

   (A) dogmatic : principled

   (B) serene : tranquil

   (C) bilious : irritable

   (D) cryptic : obvious

   (E) stark : austere

6. INTEGRAL : UNNECESSARY ::

    (A) fatuous : smug

    (B) insular : liberal

    (C) feckless : careless

    (D) florid : colorful

    (E) formidable : scary

7. ENIGMATIC : EXPLAINABLE ::

    (A) inscrutable : obscure

    (B) dubious : sure

    (C) insipid : dull

    (D) integral : common

    (E) spurious : isolated

8. OSTRACIZE : INCLUDE ::

    (A) mollify : soften

    (B) mar : blemish

    (C) placate : excite

    (D) obviate : make

    (E) eliminate : objectify

9. SOIL : CROP ::

    (A) womb : embryo

    (B) root : tree

    (C) liquid : nutrient

    (D) bacteria : germ

    (E) ocean : sand

10. VINDICTIVE : REVENGE

   (A) thirsty : water

   (B) angry : peace

   (C) scholarly : books

   (D) tranquil : irony

   (E) mercenary : money

Answers and Explanations

1. **The best answer is B.** A *chorus* is a *vocal* group, and a *band* is an *instrumental* group. In fact, a good test sentence in which to insert the answer choices is: "A -------- is a -------- group." Answer choice A also refers to music, but the word pair does not have the same relationship as *vocal* and *chorus*. Likewise, none of the other answer choices make sense in the test sentence.

2. **The best answer is A.** The relationship that exists between *remediation* and *deficiency* can be expressed with the following sentence: "A *deficiency* can be corrected through *remediation*." *Remediation* means "the act of correcting a fault or deficiency." A *misfortune* can be corrected through *reparation*, which means "the act or process of making amends," so this choice best expresses the relationship that exists between the words in the question.

3. **The best answer is E.** To **plunge** is to "fall quickly," whereas to *float* is to "fall slowly." The words in the question stem have relatively opposite meanings. The word pair that has the most similar relationship is *gallop*, which means to "run quickly," and *stroll*, which means to "walk slowly." The other word pairs are related, but not in the same way as *plunge* and *float*.

4. **The best answer is D.** The verb *annotate* means to "provide extra information." A general sentence that can be used to describe the analogy is: "A person will -------- in order to add something extra and enhance a/an --------." Answer choice D is correct because a person might *elaborate* on a *plan* in order to provide more detail or add something extra.

5. **The best answer is D.** The word *obstinate* means "stubborn," or "difficult to manage." The word *yielding* means "inclined to give way to." Therefore, someone who is *obstinate* is not *yielding*. Likewise, someone who is *cryptic*, or "secretive," is not *obvious*. The other word pairs are synonyms.

6. **The best answer is B.** The relationship that exists between *integral* and *unnecessary* can be expressed with the following sentence: "Something that is *integral* is not *unnecessary*; in fact, just the opposite is true." *Insular* is an antonym for *liberal*, so this choice best expresses the relationship that exists between the words in the question stem.

7. **The best answer is B.** The word *enigmatic* means "perplexing or mysterious." Therefore, it is an antonym of *explainable*. *Dubious* is the opposite of *sure*, so this choice best expresses the relationship that exists between the words in the question stem.

8. **The best answer is C.** To *ostracize* is to "exclude," so the words in the question stem are antonyms. To *placate* means to "calm," so this choice best expresses the relationship that exists between the words in the question.

9. **The best answer is A.** The relationship that exists between *soil* and *crop* can be expressed with the following sentence: "A crop grows in the *soil*." Because an *embryo* grows in the *womb*, this pair best expresses the relationship that exists between the words in the question.

10. **The best answer is E.** Someone who is *vindictive* necessarily seeks *revenge*, and someone who is *mercenary* necessarily seeks *money*. The other word pairs are related, but not in the same way as *vindictive* and *revenge*.

Sentence Completion Questions

The Sentence Completion questions on the GRE Verbal section are designed to measure your ability to understand the intended meaning of a sentence. Each question requires you to analyze the context of a sentence and determine which word or words best complete that sentence. The GRE includes both vocabulary-in-context and logic-based Sentence Completion questions that are designed to test your grasp of the English language.

Questions in this section consist of an incomplete sentence that includes one or two blanks, followed by five answer choices. You should be able to determine which answer choice best fills the blank(s) of the given sentence. Keep in mind that a complete sentence is clear and concise, conveys a logical meaning, and is uniform in grammar and style.

Anatomy of a GRE Sentence Completion Question

Before we get to the strategies, we want you to understand what a GRE Sentence Completion question looks like. Consider the following example:

Sentence	Despite Jordan's -------- efforts, the team still suffered a -------- loss.
Answer Choices	(A) complicated . . modest
	(B) daring . . beneficial
	(C) generous . . constructive
	(D) heroic . . devastating
	(E) selfish . . desperate

General Strategies for Sentence Completion Questions

Every sentence contains hints that will help you select the correct answer. Each of the following strategies will help you decipher those hints, but remember that any given question might require you to use more than one approach:

- Understand the context.
- Use context, prefixes, suffixes, and cognates to define unfamiliar words.
- Identify "clue" words and phrases.
- Use connotation.
- Watch for idiom.
- Select an answer.
- Pay attention to questions with two blanks.

Understand the Context

GRE Tip

Let the context of the sentences guide you. Make sure that you understand what is going on in the sentence, and pay attention to introductory and transition words and phrases in each sentence that might suggest a continuation, contrast, or comparison.

GRE Sentence Completion questions usually test the standard meaning of a word. Pay attention to the logic and context of the sentence. Try to predict a word to insert in the blank or blanks as you read the sentence, and then look for your word or a *synonym* of your word among the answer choices. A synonym is a word with the same or a similar meaning. You should also look for *antonyms*, which are words that have the opposite meaning of your predicted word. If you locate any words among the answer choices that have a meaning opposite to the word that you would like to insert in the blank, eliminate those answer choices.

You should immediately begin to pick up on the idea the sentence is trying to convey, as well as any suggestions of tone or mood. Understanding the general meaning and nature of the sentence will help you to choose the most logical and stylistically appropriate answer. Examples of transition words and phrases are given in Figure 9.1, later in this chapter.

Use Context, Prefixes, Suffixes, and Cognates to Define Unfamiliar Words

Understanding the context of a sentence also helps to determine the meaning of any unfamiliar words you might encounter. Consider the following example:

Although the fossils were well preserved, paleontologists were unable to -------- the identity of the mammal species.

(A) display

(B) ascertain

(C) violate

(D) embellish

(E) exploit

The best answer is B. You might not have heard the word *paleontologists* before, but you can deduce from the context of the sentence that they are most likely the scientists who study fossils. Another hint provided by the context is the word *although*, which suggests a contrast between the condition of the fossils and the ability of the paleontologists to identify the species. Now, you can insert the words in the answer choices into the sentence to see which one best fits the context. It does not make sense that scientists would *display* or *violate* the identity of a mammal species, so eliminate answer choices A and C. Likewise, scientists might *embellish* or *exploit* certain findings, but these words do not accurately describe what the scientists might do with the identity of a mammal species. If you did not know the meaning of *ascertain*, you could arrive at it as the correct choice by using the context of the sentence to help you eliminate incorrect answer choices.

Also, if you have trouble establishing the meaning of an unfamiliar word from the context of the sentence, you can use your knowledge of prefixes and suffixes to help you. For example, the prefix *multi-* means "many," as in *multinational*, and the suffix *-less* means "without," as in *careless*.

Last, look for any recognizable *cognates* from French, Spanish, or Italian (the modern versions of Latin) in words that you are not familiar with. A *cognate* is a word that means the same or nearly the same thing in more than one language. For example, the word *amigo*, which means "friend" in Spanish, the word *ami*, which means "friend" in French, and the word *amicable*, which means "friendly" in English, all come from the Latin root word for "friend," *amicus*.

Identify "Clue" Words and Phrases

When reading, pay attention to words or phrases in the structure of the sentence that indicate a relationship between ideas or tell you where the sentence is going. Consider the following examples:

> Due to recent studies touting the health benefits of regular exercise, health club memberships have increased dramatically in the past year.

The phrase "due to" implies a cause of action, or suggests that one thing provides evidence for another: *Recent studies promoting the health benefits of regular exercise have led to a dramatic increase in health club memberships.*

> Just as Traci's excellent grade in physics is a result of her diligent study habits, so too is her medal-winning performance at the track meet proof of her adherence to a difficult training regime.

The phrase "just as" indicates a comparison between the first part of the sentence and the last part of the sentence: *Traci received a good grade in physics because she studied hard, and she won a medal at the track meet because she trained hard.*

The GRE might have left a blank for "adherence to," and asked you to select that phrase from among the answer choices.

Transitional words often lead you to the correct answer. Even if you cannot immediately determine the best answer using "clues," you can still use the words to help you establish the nature and meaning of the sentence.

GRE Tip

As with Analogy and Antonym questions, Sentence Completion questions can be more easily answered if your vocabulary is strong. Review Appendix A, "GRE Vocabulary List," to strengthen your GRE-specific vocabulary.

Figure 9.1 contains tables of commonly used introductory and transitional words and phrases.

WORDS OR PHRASES THAT SUGGEST CONTINUATION
Furthermore
Moreover
In addition

WORDS OR PHRASES THAT SUGGEST CONCLUSION
Therefore
Thus
In other words

WORDS OR PHRASES THAT SUGGEST COMPARISON
Likewise
Similarly
Just as
Like

WORDS OR PHRASES THAT SUGGEST CONTRAST
But
Whereas
Although
Despite
However

WORDS OR PHRASES THAT SUGGEST EVIDENCE
Because
Since
As a result of
Due to

Figure 9.1 Common introductory and transitional words and phrases.

Use Connotation

Each word expresses two things: a *definition* and a *connotation*. A connotation is a positive, negative, or neutral feeling that is implied by or associated with a word. Although context is the part of a sentence that surrounds a particular word or passage and determines its meaning, *connotation* refers to the emotion that is suggested by the word itself.

For example, the adjective *thrifty* implies a positive connotation, whereas the adjective *cheap* implies a negative connotation. Both words have similar definitions, but very different connotations. Using connotations can help you to determine the correct answer or at least eliminate a few wrong answers.

Here is an example of how to use connotation to select the correct answer:

Because of his --------, Max's guests felt very welcome and comfortable staying at his house for the weekend.

(A) animosity

(B) hospitality

(C) determination

(D) wittiness

(E) severity

The best answer is B. The sentence has a positive connotation—Max's guests feel welcome and comfortable. In addition, the transition word *because* indicates that something that belongs to Max has caused his guests to feel welcome and comfortable. *Animosity* and *severity* have a negative connotation and *determination* has a neutral connotation. *Hospitality* and *wittiness* both have positive connotations, but *hospitality* best fits the context of the sentence.

Watch for Idiom

Idiom refers to the common or everyday usage of a word or phrase. Learn to recognize idiomatic words and phrases, as they might provide additional clues regarding the intended meaning of the sentence. Idiom is part of standard written English, and must be considered when answering this type of GRE question. Ask yourself if the completed sentence "sounds" correct, and make sure that the sentence effectively combines words into phrases that express a logical idea. If any portion of the sentence becomes unclear, wordy, or awkward after you insert an answer choice, eliminate that choice.

Select an Answer

Before you look at the answer choices, try to predict an answer. If your predicted word or words matches one of the answer choices, it is most likely the correct choice. Remember that the test writers create incorrect answers in an attempt to distract you—if you predict an answer you are less likely to get caught up on these confusing incorrect answers.

> **NOTE**
>
> Be careful to consider all of the choices before you confirm your answer, even if your predicted answer is among the choices. The difference between the best answer and the second-best answer is sometimes very subtle. When you think that you have the correct answer, read the entire sentence to yourself, using your choice(s) in the blank(s). If it makes sense, mark your answer on the computer screen and move on to the next question.

Pay Attention to Questions with Two Blanks

If a sentence has two blanks, you can quickly eliminate incorrect answer choices if any word alone does not fit into the blank. When you select an answer choice for a two-blank question, always ensure that *both* the words make sense in the sentence, both logically and stylistically. It helps to focus on one blank at a time. You can start with either the first or the second blank. Remember that if one word in the answer choice doesn't fit within the context of the sentence, you can eliminate the entire answer choice. Work on both blanks together only if you have not been able to eliminate all of the incorrect answers.

Practice Sentence Completion Questions

Following are simulated GRE Sentence Completion questions with explanations.

> **GRE Tip**
>
> Answer choices for questions with two blanks are commonly structured to trick you into selecting an answer just because one of the words fits perfectly. To avoid making this mistake, choose an answer that effectively uses *both* words to complete the sentence.

Directions: The following sentences each contain one or two blanks, indicating that something has been left out of the sentence. Each answer choice contains one word or a set of words. Select the word or set of words, that, when inserted in the blank(s), best fits the context of the sentence.

1. As the employee's motives were found to be --------, no disciplinary action will be taken against him for the mistake.

   (A) absurd

   (B) gratuitous

   (C) improvised

   (D) benign

   (E) intentional

2. Jennifer loves roses for the -------- appeal of their petals and leaves, but I am most -------- by their olfactory properties.

   (A) aesthetic . . enthralled

   (B) acrid . . interested

   (C) nurturing . . persuaded

   (D) visual . . displeased

   (E) tacit . . disenchanted

3. His -------- for learning history should prove to be -------- during his studies to become a history teacher.

   (A) disdain . . useful

   (B) penchant . . practical

   (C) dislike . . exceptional

   (D) affinity . . futile

   (E) appreciation . . gratuitous

4. We felt -------- once the committee issued its report that -------- our actions.

   (A) angered . . supported

   (B) abused . . endorsed

   (C) vindicated . . authenticated

   (D) helpless . . applauded

   (E) ignorant . . dignified

5. The air in a room that contains several houseplants can be more --------
   oxygen than a room that contains no plants.

   (A) enjoyed for

   (B) exhausted with

   (C) obscured to

   (D) saturated with

   (E) complicated by

6. Before eating the main courses at a buffet, my mother likes to -------- her
   appetite with a garden salad.

   (A) discern

   (B) obscure

   (C) whet

   (D) obviate

   (E) clear

7. Earth sheltering, the practice of using packed earth or soil to cover and
   insulate homes, is sometimes regarded with -------- by eccentrics, though
   practical considerations often -------- this original enchantment.

   (A) disdain . . capture

   (B) curiosity . . increase

   (C) apathy . . jeopardize

   (D) agitation . . diminish

   (E) fascination . . temper

8. During a time of protracted economic duress, the wealthy can become
   poor, -------- both income from high-paying jobs and dividends earned on
   investments.

   (A) losing

   (B) regaining

   (C) denying

   (D) insuring

   (E) pursuing

9. The presence of oxygen is an essential -------- for all animal life on Earth.

   (A) luxury

   (B) condition

   (C) choice

   (D) position

   (E) option

10. The elementary school students have a -------- understanding of fractions; some days they comprehend the math concepts, and other days they seem not to grasp them at all.

   (A) formidable

   (B) conducive

   (C) inadvertent

   (D) tenuous

   (E) peripatetic

Answers and Explanations

1. **The best answer is D.** The context of the sentence indicates that the employee will not be disciplined as a result of his mistake, which suggests that the error was not intentional, and that the employee meant no harm. The word *benign* means "harmless," so it is the best choice based on the context of the sentence.

2. **The best answer is A.** Because the sentence indicates that Jennifer "loves roses," the word that best fits in the first blank should have a positive connotation. The first word in answer choice B has a negative connotation, and the first words in both answer choices D and E have neutral connotations, so none of those choices will be best. *Aesthetic* refers to "the appreciation of beauty," which makes the most sense in this sentence. Likewise, *enthralled*, which means "captivated," works well in the second blank.

3. **The best answer is B.** To have a *penchant* for something means to have a fondness for it. A fondness for history would be practical or helpful for future studies in the field. Answer choices A and C are incorrect because anyone having *disdain* (hate) or *dislike* for history would certainly not study to become a history teacher.

4. **The best answer is C.** *Vindicated* means "cleared of suspicion or doubt," and *authenticated* means "proved to be genuine." The rest of the answer choices are contradictory in nature and do not fit the context of the sentence.

5. **The best answer is D.** The word *saturated* most accurately indicates the density of the oxygen in the room. The other answer choices do not fit the context of the sentence, nor are they all idiomatic.

6. **The best answer is C.** The word *whet* means to "sharpen or stimulate," so it is the best choice based on the context. None of the other answer choices can reasonably be applied when describing someone's appetite.

7. **The best answer is E.** The sentence refers to "original enchantment," so the word for the first blank should be a synonym of *enchantment*. Answer choices B and E could work, but *fascination* is more closely synonymous with *enchantment*. Likewise, *temper*, which means to "moderate," best fits in the second blank

8. **The best answer is A.** It makes sense that the wealthy would become poor by *losing* both income and dividends. None of the other answer choices fits the context of the sentence.

9. **The best answer is B.** The sentence indicates that oxygen is *essential*, so eliminate answer choices A, C, and E, which contradict *essential*. A *condition* refers to something that is "required," which makes the most sense here.

10. **The best answer is D.** The word that best fits in the blank is defined by the information the follows the semicolon. *Tenuous* means "unsubstantial or vague," so it is the best choice.

Reading Comprehension Questions

The GRE Reading Comprehension questions are designed to measure your ability to read, understand, and analyze a written passage. Correctly answering a question requires you to recognize both what is stated and what is implied within the passage, and to establish the relationships and ideas expressed in the passage.

The computer adaptive (CAT) GRE includes a balance of reading passages across different subject matter areas, such as humanities, social sciences, and natural sciences. Each passage ranges from approximately 150 to 500 words in length, and will be followed by two to five questions, each with five answer choices. You should select the best possible answer for each question.

Anatomy of a GRE Reading Comprehension Question

Before you learn about strategies, you should understand what a GRE Reading Comprehension question looks like. Consider the following:

Passage
Scientists know very little about the eating habits of our ancestors who lived over 2.5 million years ago. To solve this problem, scientists have started examining chimpanzees' hunting behavior and diet to find clues
(5) about our own prehistoric past. It is not difficult to determine why studying chimpanzees might be beneficial. Modern humans and chimpanzees are actually very closely related. Experts believe that chimpanzees share about 98.5 percent of our DNA sequence. If this is true,
(10) humans are more closely related to chimpanzees than they are to any other animal species.

Question Stem 1. The main purpose of the passage is to

Answer Choices

(A) explore biological and physiological similarities between humans and chimpanzees

(B) examine the hunting behavior and diet of chimpanzees and compare them to human activity

(C) discuss the health benefits of eating and hunting meat while simultaneously predicting the effect of this behavior on chimpanzee offspring

(D) bring attention to the pioneering research of Dr. Jane Goodall in Tanzania

(E) educate the pubic on the impact that tool use had in early human societies

General Strategies for Reading Comprehension Questions

Probably the biggest mistake that you could make is to read these passages as though you are studying for a college exam. The "open-book" aspect of the passage-based Reading Comprehension sections means that you should read in a way that helps your brain to work through the information efficiently. You should *not* read slowly and carefully as though you will have to remember the information for a long period of time. You should read loosely and dwell only on information that you are sure is important because you need it to answer a question. This type of reading should be very goal oriented; if the information you are looking at does not help to answer a question that the test writers find important, you should not linger over it.

Each of the passages has numbered lines. Some of the questions will refer to a particular line or lines. When you read a question that contains a line reference, locate those lines in the passage and make a note on your scratch paper so that you know where to find the answer to the question. Be sure to read a line or two before and after the referenced text.

Students who possess two key skills—paraphrasing and skimming—usually earn the best scores on this section. These skills, along with techniques on how to determine the main idea, read and answer the questions, and use the process of elimination, are discussed in more detail in the following sections.

> **GRE Tip**
>
> The CAT includes highlighted lines of text in place of using line references on some reading passages. You can use the same skill-set (locating information in the text) to answer questions that refer to highlighted text.

> **NOTE**
>
> The following strategies should almost always be applied to the long reading passages. However, it might be easier to simply read the short passages straightaway and then answer the two questions.

Paraphrase the Questions and Predict an Answer

After you have found the information in the passage that will provide the answer that you are looking for, try to answer the question in your mind. Put the question in your own words so that it makes more sense to you. Try to predict an answer for the question, and then skim the choices presented and look for your answer. You might have to be a little flexible to recognize it. If you can recognize a paraphrase of your predicted answer, select it. Developing this skill will help you to become more time efficient and will lead you to the correct answer more often than not.

Skim the Passage

Don't use context clues to help you determine the meaning of any unfamiliar terms the first time that you skim through a passage. When you come to a word or phrase that is unfamiliar, just read past it. There is a strong chance that you won't need to determine exactly what that one word or phrase means to answer the bulk of the questions that accompany the passage. If you waste some of your precious time, you'll never get it back. With perseverance and practice, you will start to get comfortable with a less-than-perfect understanding of the passage.

While reading through paragraphs, follow these tips to help you gather information more effectively:

- Try to determine the subtopic for each paragraph quickly.
- Focus on the general content of each paragraph.
- Determine the purpose of each paragraph.

> **NOTE**
>
> The first sentence is not always the topic sentence. Don't believe those people who say that you can read the first and last sentence of each paragraph and skip the rest of the sentences completely. You are better off skimming over all of the words even if you end up forgetting most of what you read almost immediately.

Be sure to read actively. That is, think about things such as the tone and the purpose of the passage. This technique will help you to stay focused on the material, and, ultimately, will allow you to select the best answer to the questions.

The goal at this stage is to get a general understanding of the structure of the passage so that you can find what you are looking for when you refer to the passage. Keep moving through the material.

Determine the Main Idea

As you begin to read a passage, your first step should be determining the main idea. This technique will help you to answer the "big picture" questions, and assist you in locating information necessary to answer other question types. The main idea has three components:

- *Topic* ("What is the passage about?")
- *Scope* ("What aspect of the topic does the passage focus on?")
- *Purpose* ("Why did the author write the passage?")

If you can answer these three questions, you understand the main idea. Consider the following scenarios:

1. The world's tropical rain forests are being decimated at an alarming rate. Each day, thousands of acres of trees are destroyed in both developing and industrial countries. Nearly half of the world's species of plants and animals will be eliminated or severely threatened over the next 25 years due to this rapid deforestation. Clearly, it is imperative that something be done to curtail this rampant destruction of the rain forests.

2. Tropical rain forests are crucial to the health and welfare of the planet. Experts indicate that over 20 percent of the world's oxygen is produced by the Amazon rain forest alone. In addition, more than half of the world's estimated 10 million species of plants, animals, and insects live in the tropical rain forests. These plants and animals of the rain forest provide us with food, fuel wood, shelter, jobs, and medicines. Indigenous humans also inhabit the tropical rain forests.

The *topic* of both passages is tropical rain forests. However, the *scope* of each passage is very different. The first passage discusses destruction of the tropical rain forests, whereas the second passage introduces the diversity of the rain

GRE Tip

Too often, test-takers confuse *topic* with *main idea*. The topic of a passage only answers the question "What is the passage about?" If that is all that you notice, you are missing some very important information.

forests and indicates why the rain forests are important. The *purpose* of the first passage is a call to action, while the second passage is primarily informative.

The introductory paragraph often indicates the topic or topics being discussed, the author's point of view, and exactly what the author is trying to prove. So, read a little more slowly at the beginning until you get a grip on the three components of the main idea and then you can shift to a higher gear and skim the rest of the passage.

As you read the passage for the main idea, and particularly the author's purpose, avoid arguing with the author. If you disagree with any viewpoints expressed in a passage, do not let your personal opinions interfere with your selection of answer choices. In addition, you should not rely on any prior knowledge you might have about a particular topic. The questions will ask about information that is stated or implied in the passage, not information that you might recall about the topic being discussed.

The Reading Comprehension questions are not meant to test your knowledge about a particular subject. You should answer questions based only on the information presented in the passage, and not on any prior knowledge that you might have of the subject. You might be asked to draw a conclusion or make an inference, but you should do so based only on what the writer's words actually state or imply.

Read and Answer the Questions

Follow these tips as you read and answer the questions in the GRE Reading Comprehension section:

- Read the question and make sure that you understand it, paraphrasing if you need to. Use the structure of the passage to lead you to the correct answer. Go back to the part of the passage that relates to the question, and that part will probably contain the answer to your question.

- After you read the questions, take a moment to mentally summarize the main idea and the structure of the passage.

- Some of the questions on the GRE ask you to draw conclusions based on the information that you read. However, even these questions should be answered based on the information in the passage. There are always some strong hints or evidence that will lead you to an answer.

- Some of the questions contain references to specific lines of the passage. The trick for these question types is to read a little before and a little after the specific line that is mentioned. Remember that you must answer the questions based on the context of the passage, so be sure that you fully understand what that context is. At a minimum, read the entire sentence that contains the line that is referenced.

- Some of the questions might not tell you where to look for the answer, or they might question the passage as a whole. In situations like this, think about what you learned about the passage overall while you were skimming it. Note the subtopics for the paragraphs and let them guide you to the part of the passage that contains the information that you are looking for.

- One of the important skills rewarded by the GRE is the ability to sift through text and find the word or concept that you are looking for. This skill improves with practice.

NOTE

It is possible for an answer choice to be both true and wrong. The answer that you choose must respond correctly to the question being asked. Simply being true is not enough to make an answer correct. The best answer is always supported by details, inference, or tone.

Apply Logic

It is important that you know the difference between information that is stated directly in the passage, and inferences and assumptions. You might be asked questions based on factual information found in the reading passages. The reading passages might also include information about which you will be asked to make an inference.

GRE Tip

Refer to Chapter 6, "Introduction to GRE Logic," for a more thorough overview of inference and assumption.

Inference: An inference is a conclusion based on what is stated in the passage. You can infer something about a person, place, or thing by reasoning through the descriptive language contained in the reading passage. In other words, the author's language *implies* that something is probably true.

Assumption: An assumption, conversely, is unstated evidence. It is the missing link in an author's argument.

Use the Process of Elimination

Elimination is the process most test-takers use when answering exam questions. It is reliable, but slow. However, it is still useful as a backup strategy for questions for which you cannot predict an answer or for which you find that your prediction is not a choice.

The process of elimination is a good tool, but it shouldn't be the only tool in your box. It can be hard to break the habit of always applying the process of elimination. You have likely developed this habit because on past exams you have been given too much time to answer questions. On the GRE, you will need to be more time efficient, which is why you should use the process of elimination only when other strategies fail to yield an answer.

Eliminate any answer choices that are clearly incorrect, including answer choices that are outside the scope of the passage. Answer choices that fall outside the scope of the passage are very common in this section. For example, an answer choice might be too specific, too general, or have no relation to the content of the passage itself or for the question being asked.

Finally, always consider all of the choices before you confirm your answer, even if your predicted answer is among the choices. The difference between the best answer and the second-best answer is sometimes very subtle.

Reading Comprehension Question Types

The following subsections discuss the types of Reading Comprehension questions you are likely to encounter on the GRE. Specific approaches to each question type are also included. You will begin to recognize the different question types as you work through the sample questions and practice exams. The most common question types include the following:

- Main idea/primary purpose
- Specific detail
- Purpose of detail
- Conclusion/inference
- Extrapolation
- Structure
- Weakening
- EXCEPT

Main Idea/Primary Purpose

These questions can ask about the main idea of the whole passage or of a specific paragraph. They also often ask about the author's point of view or perspective and the intended audience. These questions might also ask you to determine the best title for the passage.

Questions that begin "The author of the passage would be most likely to agree with which of the following?" or "The primary purpose of the passage is to" are main idea/primary purpose questions.

> **Strategy:** Answer these questions according to your understanding of the three components of the main idea, which are mentioned previously (topic, scope, and purpose). It is also worth noting that the incorrect choices are usually either too broad or too narrow. You should eliminate the answer choices that focus on a specific part of the passage and also eliminate the answer choices that are too general and could describe other passages besides the one on which you are working.

Specific Detail

These questions can be as basic as asking you about some fact that is easily found in the passage. Some questions even provide specific line references or text from the passage.

Questions that begin "According to the author" or "According to the passage" might be specific detail questions.

> **Strategy:** When you skim the passage, make sure that you establish the structure of the passage and the purpose of each paragraph. If you have a clear idea of how the passage is organized, you should be able to refer quickly to the portion of the passage that contains the answer. Otherwise, use the line or paragraph references in the questions, if they are given. Sometimes the answer choices are paraphrased, so don't just select the answers that contain words that appear in the passage. Make sure that the choice you select is responsive to the question being asked.

Purpose of Detail

These questions ask you to determine the author's purpose in mentioning certain details, as well as how details contained within the passage might support the main idea.

Questions that begin "The author mentions -------- probably in order to" are most likely purpose of detail questions.

> **Strategy:** Making a connection between the supporting details and the main idea of the passage helps you to answer these questions correctly. Think of the details as the building blocks of the author's thesis. This should provide you with some insight into why the author included these details in the passage. Refer specifically to any line references given in the questions.

Conclusion/Inference

These questions require you to put together information in the passage and use it as evidence for a conclusion. You have to find language in the passage that leads you to arrive at the inference that the question demands.

Questions that begin "According to the author" or "It can be inferred from the passage" might require you to locate clues or evidence that lead you to the answer.

> **Strategy:** Understanding the main idea of the passage or paragraph, and particularly the author's tone, is key for these types of questions. Although you have to do a bit of thinking for these questions, you should be able to find very strong evidence for your answers. If you find yourself creating a long chain of reasoning and including information from outside the passage, stop and reconsider your selection.

Extrapolation

These questions ask you to go beyond the passage itself and find answers that are *probably* true based on what you know from the passage. They can be based on the author's tone or on detailed information in the passage. You are often required to reason by analogy or to discern relationships between a situation presented in the passage and other situations that might parallel those in the passage.

These questions might begin with "The author anticipates" or "Which of the following best exemplifies -------- as it is presented in the passage."

> **Strategy:** You need to be sensitive to any clues about the author's tone or attitude and any clues about how the characters in the passage feel. Eliminate any choices that are outside the scope of the passage. As with the inference questions, the GRE rewards short, strong connections between the passage and the correct answers.

Structure

These questions might ask you to describe the structure of the passage or how a particular detail or paragraph functions within the passage as a whole.

Questions such as "The last paragraph performs which function?" or "Which of the following describes the organization of the passage?" are structure questions.

> **Strategy:** You need to recognize the author's purpose in writing the passage and determine how the author develops the main thesis or argument. If the passage is purely informational, for example, the author might simply make a statement followed by some supporting details. Conversely, the author might offer comparisons between two different theories in order to persuade the reader that one theory is better. Pay attention to both the language and the connotation.

Weaken

These questions require you to select the answer choice that weakens the author's argument. Weakening does not necessarily mean to disprove completely; it merely means to make the conclusion of the argument somewhat less likely.

These questions take the form of "Which of the following, if true, would most weaken the author's argument in lines . . ."

> **Strategy:** The best approach to answering these questions correctly is to first make sure that you understand the author's argument or main point. To weaken the author's argument, you should usually attack the author's assumptions (unstated evidence). In some cases, the correct answer actually contradicts a statement made in the passage.

EXCEPT

Questions that require you to *eliminate* all of the correct or possible answer choices fall into this category.

These questions are often phrased as follows: "The author probably believes all of the following EXCEPT," or "All of the following are listed in the passage as examples of biodiversity EXCEPT."

Strategy: The best answer in these instances includes information that is *not* directly stated in the passage or *cannot* be inferred from information stated in the passage. In addition, in the first sample question—"The author probably believes all of the following EXCEPT"—the incorrect answer choices would all be something that the passage would suggest that the author *does* believe. Likewise, in the second sample question— "All of the following are listed in the passage as examples of biodiversity EXCEPT"—the incorrect answer choices would likely be stated explicitly in the passage as examples of biodiversity.

> **NOTE**
>
> The process of elimination is a good strategy for EXCEPT questions.

Practice Reading Comprehension Questions

Following are two simulated GRE Reading Comprehension passages with questions and explanations.

<u>Directions:</u> The passage below is followed by several questions. The questions correspond to information that is stated or implied in the passage. Read the passage and choose the best answer for each question.

According to many scholars, Johan Gutenberg's mid-15th century invention of the movable-type printing press fueled the scientific and cultural revolution today known as the European Renaissance. With their unique combination of easy and accurate reproduction, printed books quickly became the repository of
(5) Western knowledge, replacing laboriously produced, handwritten manuscripts. Early works, known as *incunabula*, often married the two traditions. Texts could be printed with spaces left for scribes and illustrators to add the illuminated capitals and intricate artwork expected by wealthy patrons. Often religious texts, these volumes were designed to move believers with rich colors, florid
(10) imagery, and precious materials. Indeed, the resultant product was very much like its predecessor, the illuminated manuscript, a book whose text was adorned with painted initials, borders, and illustrations. Today, a few treasured 15th-century *incunabula* survive in libraries and museums, a testament to their robust construction and the care bestowed on them by their owners.
(15)   Despite the luxury exhibited in some *incunabula* texts, movable-type print can be argued to have been a powerful democratizing force. While running the press was not without its own expense and toil, a work printed on paper could be made available for one-fifth that of a scribal text on vellum or parchment. The availability of scientific, political, and religious texts simply exploded.
(20) Nevertheless, many historians would quickly point out that Renaissance Europe was not the resplendent cultural and scientific center of the world envisioned in

(25)

(30)

modern populist media. While exact rates of literacy are extremely controversial, it is generally agreed that the vast majority of Europeans in the 15th century were uneducated and wholly disenfranchised. The lofty realms of philosophy, science, and the arts were the preoccupation of society's elite. Hence, the printed word frequently reflected the aspirations of the aristocracy or the interests of affluent landowners and merchants, all of whom were still the primary market for books. In this way, the perspective of the common citizen, what we may term the "working class," is all but absent in the profusion of communication that is the Renaissance.

(35)

(40)

Swiss historian Jacob Burckhardt, to whom the word *Renaissance* is attributed, makes no claim for increased equity in the authorship, publication, or ownership of printed manuscripts in 15th-century Europe. He asserts, however, that in the Italian Renaissance—an intellectual movement begun a full century before the invention of the printing press—was the fall of the notion of birthright: "And as time went on, the greater the influence of humanism on the Italian mind, the firmer and more widespread became the conviction that birth decides nothing as to the goodness or badness of a man." While the idea of social fairness may have taken hold in the Renaissance, spread by the proliferation of ideas and texts, real economic justice was slower to develop. Just as *incunabula* bridged the transition from handwritten manuscript to fully printed text, the Renaissance revolution held a middle ground between medieval feudalism and Enlightenment democracy.

1. The author is primarily concerned with

   (A) describing how movable-print type revolutionized production of the written word

   (B) explaining how Johan Gutenberg's invention of the printing press revolutionized the production of written texts, laying the groundwork for social democracy

   (C) arguing that printed books were shoddy replacements for resplendent illuminated manuscripts

   (D) examining how the European Renaissance resulted in significantly increased social equity due to the invention of the printing press

   (E) denying that social justice always precedes economic justice in the evolution of human civilization

2. Which one of the following most accurately describes the author's attitude toward "social fairness" (line 38)?

   (A) "Social fairness" is a false academic construction and is impossible to achieve in "real-world" conditions.

   (B) "Social fairness" is a by-product of the medieval period carried over to the Enlightenment.

   (C) "Social fairness" is a modern term and, therefore, irrelevant to any discussion of the Renaissance.

   (D) "Social fairness" is the ultimate goal of the human condition and is a necessary component of modern civilization.

   (E) "Social fairness" is a desirable human condition that began to be realized in 15th-century Europe as a product of the Renaissance.

3. According to the author, which of the following would be the most accurate description of the *incunabula*?

   (A) The intricate artwork added to printed books in order to make them more appealing to the masses

   (B) Public funds dedicated to publishing scientific books

   (C) Imaginary demons supposed to descend upon sleeping persons

   (D) Cheap Renaissance paperbacks

   (E) Early printed works that often combined printing with elements of illuminated manuscripts

4. According to the passage, the statement made in line 24 ("uneducated and wholly disenfranchised") regarding most 15th-century Europeans serves to

   (A) preview the rise of Rousseauesque pedagogic techniques in the Enlightenment

   (B) reveal the prejudices of late-15th-century book dealers

   (C) reinforce the idea that the Renaissance was primarily an intellectual movement of and for the upper classes

   (D) counter the descriptions usually given by academics

   (E) explain why *incunabula* were frequently less expensive than handwritten manuscripts

5. Which of the following, if true, would most weaken the argument that the printing press enabled a Renaissance strictly for the upper classes?

   (A) Most printed Bibles (the most commonly printed book) were purchased by working-class people.

   (B) Johan Gutenberg frequently refused to print cookbooks or herbals.

   (C) The advent of paper books lead to a serious reduction in the price of vellum.

   (D) The cheapest printed books often cost as much as a year's salary for a day laborer, which is clearly too much.

   (E) William Caxton, a prolific English printer, often printed historical texts.

Answers and Explanations

1. **The best answer is B.** Only answer choice B covers the full scope of the passage. Although answer choice A states a point clearly made in the passage, it does not include the social and political concerns of the author. The other choices are either too broad or are inaccurate.

2. **The best answer is E.** Although academic, the author's tone in the passage is mildly argumentative and favorable toward social reform, as indicated in answer choice E. Although the author promotes the idea of "social fairness," the tone in answer choice D is too strong and the language too absolute. Likewise, the other answer choices are not supported by the passage.

3. **The best answer is E.** As defined in the first paragraph, *incunabula* are early printed works that often combined printing with elements of illuminated manuscripts. They are not the artwork added to the texts, so answer choice A is incorrect. Answer choice C is incorrect because it defines an *incubus*.

4. **The best answer is C.** Despite the introduction of mass-produced books, the book market was still primarily composed of the upper classes. The lower classes are implied to lack the academic and political education—not to mention cash—to take advantage of the newly available books. Answer choice D is incorrect because the statement counters the descriptions ascribed to "populist media," not to academics.

5. **The best answer is A.** If working-class people were discovered to have owned large numbers of printed books, it would suggest that book ownership was more equitable than the author believes, and that Renaissance ideals were, in fact, reaching the masses. The other choices either strengthen the argument or are irrelevant.

Directions: The passage below is followed by two questions. The questions correspond to information that is stated or implied in the passage. Read the passage and choose the best answer for each question.

Defined biologically, hair is primarily composed of keratin, a protein, which
Line grows out through the skin from follicles deep within the dermis. This definition holds for all mammals. The difference for humans is not in the hair, but in the follicle. Under the microscope, an individual human's hair follicles are
(5) anatomically indistinguishable, meaning that a hair follicle on your head is visually identical to one on your upper arm. Physiologically, however, the two follicles behave very differently. The first type produces *terminal* hair, the longer, darker, thicker hair generally found on the scalp, eyebrows, and eyelashes. The second type produces the fine, unpigmented *vellus* hair found on most places of
(10) the body, including the face and back. Vellus hair is usually very short and the follicles are not connected to sebaceous glands.

1. It can be inferred from the passage that

(A) mammals do not have sebaceous glands

(B) animals such as monkeys cannot grow terminal hair

(C) the hair of a horse is composed mainly of keratin

(D) scientists cannot distinguish human hair from the hair of other mammals

(E) terminal hair grows much faster than vellus hair

2. The main purpose of the passage is to

(A) introduce the idea that human hair is different from the hair of other mammals

(B) explain how terminal hair follicles change into vellus hair follicles

(C) describe the similarities between two types of human hair follicles

(D) compare the anatomy of human hair follicles with that of other types of hair follicles

(E) demonstrate that human hair growth contradicts the commonly held definition of biology

Answers and Explanations

1. **The best answer is C.** According to the passage, "hair is primarily composed of keratin, a protein, which grows out through the skin from follicles deep within the dermis. This definition holds for all mammals." Therefore, a horse has hair that is mainly composed of keratin. The other answer choices are not supported by the passage.

2. **The best answer is A.** The main purpose of this short passage is simply to introduce the idea that human hair is different from the hair of other mammals. Answer choices B, C, and D are too specific and beyond the scope of the passage. Answer choice E is not supported by information in the passage.

Text Completion with Two or Three Blanks Questions

The GRE has introduced a new question type that includes a short passage, usually one or two sentences in length, containing two or three numbered blanks. The blanks indicate that something has been omitted from the text. You are required to select words or phrases from corresponding columns of choices to fill all the blanks in a way that best completes the text.

You will be given a choice of three answers per blank, each of which functions independently. Selecting an answer choice for one blank does not affect your choice for the second or third blanks. A correct answer must include one choice for each blank. You will *not* be given partial credit.

> **NOTE**
>
> As of the writing of this book, the POWERPREP® software does not include Text Completion with Two or Three Blanks questions. However, in addition to the samples you will find in this book, there are practice questions at www.gre.org. Keep in mind that there will be only one Text Completion question on your GRE.

Anatomy of a GRE Text Completion Question

Before moving on to strategies, you should understand what a Text Completion question looks like. Consider the following example:

Experts believe that humans have 10 trillion cells in their bodies that (i) _____ any number of essential genetic elements; scientists often marvel at what incredible (ii) _____ would ensue should the cells become jumbled or misunderstand their purpose.

Blank (i)	Blank (ii)
govern	order
organize	method
dislocate	chaos

General Strategies for Text Completion Questions

You can apply many of the strategies discussed for the other question types to Text Completion questions, particularly the strategies for Sentence Completion questions. In addition, keep the following things in mind when answering this new question type:

- The text is generally only a few sentences, so read through it once to get a sense of the context.

- Pay attention to "clue" words in the text, such as transition words, that will help you to identify the structure of the text.

- Predict a word or phrase for the blanks based on the context clues.

- You do not have to complete the blanks in order; start with the blank that seems the most simple to fill, and then work on the others.

- Once you've made your selections, check the text for logic and grammar. Review Chapter 6, "Introduction to GRE Logic," Chapter 11, "Verbal Review," and Appendix A, "GRE Vocabulary List," for additional help.

Practice Text Completion Questions

Following are simulated GRE Text Completion questions with explanations.

<u>Directions:</u> The following passages each contain two or three blanks, indicating that something has been left out of the passage. Select one entry for each blank from the corresponding column of choices. Fill all of the blanks in the way that best completes the text.

1. Built over 50 years by two private companies and one city-owned corporation, the New York subway suffers from certain problems (i) _____ infrastructure, which has evolved over time rather than being (ii) _____ planned from the beginning.

Blank (i)	Blank (ii)
predictive of	querulously
relegated to	conscientiously
endemic to	sporadically

2. Primarily a fantasy writer, Ursula K. LeGuin is also a (i) _____ literary critic and philosophical commentator. Her fiction (ii) _____ this: Her stories are woven through with a wide range of complex themes, such as the importance of naming, the nature of identity, and courage in the face of the self, which draw from such (iii) _____ sources as the work of Carl Jung and the *Tao Te Ching*.

Blank (i)	Blank (ii)	Blank (iii)
conventional	stymies	relevant
recondite	pinpoints	eclectic
profound	underscores	vapid

3. Foucault turned the world of ideas on its head by boldly charging in to explore the subjects of prisons and sexuality, about which previous writers had done little more than (i) _____ But the *tour de force* of this exploration was his habit of using these fields to draw (ii) _____ parallels to safe, sanitized everyday life.

Blank (i)	Blank (ii)
ruminate	trenchant
equivocate	presumptuous
politicize	probative

4. Computer technology has made checking dictionaries written in Chinese a much more (i) _____ task. Since the Chinese languages did not traditionally use a phonetic alphabet, looking up a word in a traditional dictionary could be incredibly (ii) _____. Computers have decreased that time remarkably.

Blank (i)	Blank (ii)
reliable	noisome
specious	noxious
accessible	vexatious

5. Sometimes the combination of several (i) _____ improvements creates an overall improvement much greater than would be predicted by merely adding the individual contributions together. For instance, Oliver Cromwell's New Model Army revealed the (ii) _____ relationship that could be achieved through organized discipline, regular pay, meritocracy, and, of course, (iii) _____ devotion to a Puritan cause.

Blank (i)	Blank (ii)	Blank (iii)
lackluster	salutary	sanctimonious
incremental	meretricious	saturnine
picayune	minatory	fervid

Answers and Explanations

1. **The best answers are *endemic to* and *conscientiously*.** Problems "endemic to" a certain situation are particularly characteristic of and commonly found within that situation. In this case, the infrastructure predates the problems, so they are not "predictive of" it, nor are they "relegated to," or placed into a minor role relating to, it. Good infrastructure systems are *conscientiously*, or thoroughly, planned from the beginning.

2. **The best answers are *profound*, *underscores*, and *eclectic*.** The point of the paragraph is that this author is an insightful thinker, and that her fiction reflects it, being inspired by diverse intellectual sources. *Profound* reflects the idea of insight. *Conventional* would not demonstrate insight, while *recondite* means "obscure," and is usually applied to things, rather than people. The second blank shows how her fiction illustrates, emphasizes, or *underscores* her insight; *stymies* means "bogs down," which does not apply, and *pinpoints* means "locates": The

fiction is not used to locate her insight, it merely reflects it. The final blank should reflect the wide array of interesting intellectual works that share her themes: These are a broad selection, and therefore *eclectic*. *Relevant* would not work in the context of the sentence (relevant to what?), and vapid indicates a lack of substance, which one hopes does not apply to recognized philosophical works.

3. **The best answers are *equivocate* and *trenchant*.** The word *equivocate* means to "hesitate or dodge an issue, or to avoid discussion." *Trenchant* observations are insightful ones, precisely the sort that would make people uncomfortable with Foucault's comparisons. *Presumptuous* comparisons might be shocking, but would not constitute a *tour de force*.

4. **The best answers are *accessible* and *vexatious*.** The first sentence seems to be describing an improvement in the ease of use of Chinese dictionaries, while the second sentence states that formerly, these books were not easy to use. *Accessible*, or "convenient," is a fair way to describe a greatly simplified task, and *vexatious* or "vexing" is an apt description of a troublesome one.

5. **The best answers are *incremental*, *salutary*, and *fervid*.** The improvements themselves are all minor and build upon one another; in other words, they are *incremental*. However, together they create synergy, a healthful, or *salutary*, effect. Part of this effect was grounded on the troops' fanatical, *fervid*, devotion to their religious cause. *Lackluster* means "unimpressive," and *picayune* means "tiny"; both are a bit harsh for the kind of improvement referenced here. *Meretricious* means "vulgar or gaudy," and *minatory* means "threatening"; neither one describes the generally positive relationship. While the Puritans were not *saturnine*, or "gloomy," they may have seemed *sanctimonious*, or "morally fussy"; however, the real function of the sentence is to stress their fanatical, *fervid* devotion to their cause.

What's Next?

If you require a review of the rules that govern standard written English, be sure to read Chapter 11, "Basic GRE Verbal Review," before you tackle the practice tests in Part IV.

PART III

Content Area Review

10

Basic GRE Math Review

CHAPTER GOALS

- Review the math concepts tested on the GRE: numbers and operations, algebra and functions, geometry, word problems, and data analysis.
- Solve practice problems to test your mastery of each concept.

The GRE Quantitative questions are designed to measure your basic mathematical skills, as well as your ability to reason mathematically. You should be able to solve problems and apply relevant mathematics concepts in arithmetic, algebra, geometry, and data analysis. As you've already seen, the GRE Quantitative Section includes both Discrete Problem Solving and Quantitative Comparison multiple-choice questions, as well as Numeric Entry questions. Each question type was covered previously in Chapter 8, "GRE Quantitative."

This chapter serves as a review of the mathematical concepts tested on the GRE. Familiarize yourself with the basic mathematical concepts included here and be able to apply them to a variety of math problems. Remember that you cannot use a calculator on the Quantitative section, so you will not be required to perform any elaborate computations. However, you should be able to recognize the underlying math concept being tested.

NOTE

The GRE is rarely a test of pure mathematics calculations; rather, it involves seeing relationships and patterns—a skill broadly applicable across all disciplines.

Following is a review of the arithmetic concepts generally tested on the GRE.

Numbers and Operations

The GRE Quantitative section requires you to add, subtract, multiply, and divide whole numbers, fractions, and decimals. When performing these operations, be sure to keep track of negative signs and line up decimal points to eliminate careless mistakes. These questions might involve basic arithmetic operations, operations involving decimals, factoring, percents, ratios, proportions, sequences, number sets, number lines, absolute value, and prime numbers.

The Properties of Integers

The following are properties of integers commonly tested on the GRE:

- Integers include both positive and negative whole numbers.
- Zero is considered an integer.
- Consecutive integers follow one another and differ by 1. For example, 6, 7, 8, and 9 are consecutive integers.
- The value of a number does not change when multiplied by 1. For example, $13 \times 1 = 13$.

Real Numbers

The following are properties of real numbers commonly tested on the GRE:

- All real numbers correspond to points on the number line, as shown below:

Figure 10.1 Number line.

- All real numbers except zero are either positive or negative. On a number line such as that shown above, numbers that correspond to points to the right of 0 are positive, and numbers that correspond to points to the left of 0 are negative.
- For any two numbers on the number line, the number to the left is always less than the number to the right.
- *Ordering* is the process of arranging numbers from smallest to greatest or from greatest to smallest. The symbol $>$ is used to represent "greater than," and the symbol $<$ is used to represent "less than." To represent "greater than or equal to," use the symbol $\geq$; to represent "less than or equal to," use the symbol $\leq$.

- If any number n lies between 0 and any positive number x on the number line, then $0 < n < x$; in other words, n is greater than 0 but less than x. If n is any number on the number line between 0 and any positive number x, including 0 and x, then $0 \leq n \leq x$. This means that n is greater than or equal to 0, or less than or equal to x.

- If any number n lies between 0 and any negative number x on the number line, then $-x < n < 0$; in other words, n is greater than $-x$ but less than 0. If n is any number on the number line between 0 and any negative number x, including 0 and $-x$, then $-x \leq n \leq 0$. This means that n is greater than or equal to $-x$, or less than or equal to 0.

Order of Operations (PEMDAS)

Following is a description of the correct order in which to perform mathematical operations. The acronym PEMDAS stands for Parentheses, Exponents, Multiplication, Division, Addition, Subtraction. It should help you to remember to do the operations in the correct order, as follows:

P—First, do the operations within the *parentheses*, if any.

E—Next, do the *exponents*, if any.

M/D—Next, do the *multiplication and/or division*, in order from left to right.

A/S—Next, do the *addition and/or subtraction*, in order from left to right.

For example, $\dfrac{2(4 + 1)^2 \times 3}{5} - 7$ would be solved in the following order:

$$= \frac{2(5)^2 \times 3}{5} - 7$$

$$= \frac{2(25) \times 3}{5} - 7$$

$$= \frac{50 \times 3}{5} - 7$$

$$= \frac{150}{5} - 7$$

$$= 30 - 7 = 23$$

Decimals

The following are properties of decimals that are commonly tested on the GRE:

- *Place value* refers to the value of a digit in a number relative to its position. Starting from the left of the decimal point, the values of the digits are ones, tens, hundreds, and so on. Starting to the right of the decimal point, the values of the digits are tenths, hundredths, thousandths, and so on.

- When *adding and subtracting decimals*, be sure to line up the decimal points.

  For example,
  $$
  \begin{array}{r}
  236.78 \\
  +113.21 \\
  \hline
  349.99
  \end{array}
  \qquad
  \begin{array}{r}
  78.90 \\
  -23.42 \\
  \hline
  55.48
  \end{array}
  $$

- When *multiplying decimals*, it is not necessary to line up the decimal points. Simply multiply the numbers, then count the total number of places to the right of the decimal points in the numbers being multiplied to determine placement of the decimal point in the product.

  For example,
  $$
  \begin{array}{r}
  173.248 \\
  \times \quad 0.35 \\
  \hline
  60.63680
  \end{array}
  $$

- When *dividing decimals*, first move the decimal point in the divisor to the right until the divisor becomes an integer. Then move the decimal point in the dividend the same number of places.

  For example, $58.345 \div 3.21 = 5834.5 \div 321$. (The decimal point was moved two places to the right, in order to make the divisor an integer.)

- You can then perform the long division with the decimal point in the correct place in the quotient, as shown below:

$$
\begin{array}{r}
18.17 \\
321\overline{)5834.50} \\
-321 \\
\hline
2624 \\
-2568 \\
\hline
565 \\
-321 \\
\hline
2440 \\
-2247 \\
\hline
193
\end{array}
$$

and so on

Fractions and Rational Numbers

The following are properties of fractions and rational numbers that are commonly tested on the GRE:

- The *reciprocal* of any number, n, is expressed as $\frac{1}{n}$. The product of a number and its reciprocal is always 1. For example, the reciprocal of 3 is $\frac{1}{3}$, and $3 \times \frac{1}{3} = \frac{3}{3}$, which is equivalent to 1. By the same token, the reciprocal of $\frac{1}{3}$ is $\frac{3}{1}$, or 3.

- To *change any fraction to a decimal*, divide the numerator by the denominator. For example, $\frac{3}{4}$ is equivalent to $3 \div 4$, or 0.75.

- Multiplying and dividing both the numerator and the denominator of a fraction by the same non-zero number will result in an *equivalent fraction*. For example, $\frac{1}{4} \times \frac{3}{3} = \frac{3}{12}$, which can be reduced to $\frac{1}{4}$. This is true because whenever the numerator and the denominator are the same, the value of the fraction is 1; $\frac{3}{3} = 1$.

- When *adding and subtracting like fractions*, add or subtract the numerators and write the sum or difference over the denominator. So, $\frac{1}{8} + \frac{2}{8} = \frac{3}{8}$, and $\frac{4}{7} - \frac{2}{7} = \frac{2}{7}$.

- To *simplify a fraction*, find a common factor of both the numerator and the denominator. For example, $\frac{12}{15}$ can be simplified into $\frac{4}{5}$ by dividing both the numerator and the denominator by the common factor 3.

- To *convert a mixed number to an improper fraction* (a fraction that includes both a whole number and a fraction, such as $3\frac{2}{5}$), multiply the whole number by the denominator in the fraction, add the result to the numerator, and place that value over the original denominator. For example, $3\frac{2}{5}$ is equivalent to $(3 \times 5) + 2$ over 5, or $\frac{17}{5}$.

- When *multiplying fractions*, multiply the numerators to get the numerator of the product, and multiply the denominators to get the denominator of the product. For example, $\frac{3}{5} \times \frac{7}{8} = \frac{21}{40}$.

- When *dividing fractions*, multiply the first fraction by the reciprocal of the second fraction. For example, $\frac{1}{3} \div \frac{1}{4} = \frac{1}{3} \times \frac{4}{1}$, which equals $\frac{4}{3}$, or $1\frac{1}{3}$.

- A *rational number* is a fraction whose numerator and denominator are both integers, and the denominator does not equal 0. Note that when the denominator is 0, the fraction is undefined; you cannot divide an integer by 0.

Squares and Square Roots

The following are properties of squares and square roots that are commonly tested on the GRE:

- When a number is multiplied by itself, the product is called the *square* of the number. A square will always be a positive number. However, square roots can be negative; for example, when $x^2 = 25$, $x = 5$ or -5, because a negative times a negative yields a positive. The *principal square root* is the positive square root of any number.

- The principal square root of a number, n, is written as $\sqrt{n}$, or the non-negative value a that fulfills the expression $a^2 = n$. For example, "the principle square root of 5" is expressed as $\sqrt{5}$, and $(\sqrt{5})^2 = 5$.

- A number is considered a *perfect square* when the square root of that number is a whole number. For example, 25 is a perfect square because its principal square root is 5.

Exponents

The following are properties of exponents that are commonly tested on the GRE:

$$a^m \times a^n = a^{(m + n)}$$

- When multiplying the same base number raised to any power, add the exponents. For example, $3^2 \times 3^4 = 3^6$. Likewise, $3^6 = 3^2 \times 3^4$; $3^6 = 3^1 \times 3^5$; and $3^6 = 3^3 \times 3^3$.

$$(a^m)^n = a^{mn}$$

- When raising an exponential expression to a power, multiply the exponent and power. For example, $(3^2)^4 = 3^8$. Likewise, $3^8 = (3^2)^4$; $3^8 = (3^4)^2$; $3^8 = (3^1)^8$; and $3^8 = (3^8)^1$.

$$(ab)^m = a^m \times b^m$$

- When multiplying two different base numbers and raising the product to a power, the product is equivalent to raising each number to the power, and multiplying the exponential expressions. For example, $(3 \times 2)^2 = 3^2 \times 2^2$, which equals 9×4, or 36. Likewise, $3^2 \times 2^2 = (3 \times 2)^2$, or 6^2, which equals 36.

$$\left(\frac{a}{b}\right)^m = \frac{a^m}{b^m}$$

- When dividing two different base numbers and raising the quotient to a power, the quotient is equivalent to raising each number to the power, and dividing the exponential expressions. For example, $\left(\frac{2}{3}\right)^2 = \frac{2^2}{3^2}$, or $\frac{4}{9}$.

$$a^0 = 1, \text{ when } a \neq 0$$

- When you raise any number to the power of 0, the result is always 1.

$$a^{-m} = \frac{1}{a^m}, \text{ when } a \neq 0$$

- When you raise a number to a negative power, the result is equivalent to 1 over the number raised to the same positive power. For example, $3^{-2} = \frac{1}{3^2}$, or $\frac{1}{9}$.

Scientific Notation

When numbers are very large or very small, they are often expressed using *scientific notation*. To write a number in scientific notation, express it as a decimal greater than or equal to 1 but less than 10, multiplied by 10 raised to a power. The power depends on the number of places to the left or right that the decimal was moved.

For example, 667,000,000 written in scientific notation would be 6.67×10^8 because the decimal was moved 8 places to the left. The number 0.0000000298 written in scientific notation would be 2.98×10^{-8} because the decimal was moved 8 places to the right.

Mean, Median, and Mode

The following are properties of mean, median, and mode that are commonly tested on the GRE:

- The *arithmetic mean* is equivalent to the average of a series of numbers. Calculate the average by dividing the sum of all of the numbers in the series by the total count of numbers in the series. For example, a student received scores of 80%, 85%, and 90% on 3 math tests. The average score received by the student on those tests is 80 + 85 + 90 divided by 3, or 255 ÷ 3, which is 85%.

- The *median* is the middle value of a series of numbers when those numbers are in either ascending or descending order. In the series (2, 4, 6, 8, 10) the median is 6. To find the median in a data set with an even number of items, find the average of the middle two numbers. In the series (3, 4, 5, 6) the median is 4.5.

- The *mode* is the number that appears most frequently in a series of numbers. In the series (2, 3, 4, 5, 6, 3, 7) the mode is 3, because 3 appears twice in the series and the other numbers each appear only once in the series.

Ratio, Proportion, and Percent

The following are properties of ratios, proportions, and percents that are commonly tested on the GRE:

- A *ratio* expresses a mathematical comparison between two quantities. A ratio of 1 to 5, for example, is written as either $\frac{1}{5}$ or 1:5.

- When working with ratios, be sure to differentiate between part-to-part and part-to-whole ratios. In a part-to-part ratio, the elements being compared are parts of the whole. For example, if two components of a recipe are being compared to each other, it is a part-to-part ratio (2 cups of flour : 1 cup of sugar). Conversely, if one group of students is being compared to the entire class, it is a part-to-whole ratio (13 girls : 27 students).

- A *proportion* indicates that one ratio is equal to another ratio. For example, $\frac{1}{5} = \frac{x}{20}$ is a proportion. Consider the following example:

  If a 20% deposit that has been paid toward the purchase of a certain product is $150, how much more remains to be paid? If a 20% deposit equals $150, then 20% of the price of the product is $150. Calculate the price of the product, x, by setting up a proportion, as follows:

  $150 is to $x, as 20% is to 100%

  $$\frac{150}{x} = \frac{1}{2000}; \text{ solve for } x$$

  $20x = 15{,}000$

  $x = 750$

  The total price of the product is $750, so $750 − $150, or $600, remains to be paid.

- A *percent* is a fraction whose denominator is 100. The fraction $\frac{25}{100}$ is equal to 25%, which can also be expressed as 0.25. To calculate the percent that one number is of another number, set up a ratio, as shown next:

  What percent of 40 is 5?

  5 is to 40 as x is to 100

  $$\frac{5}{40} = \frac{x}{100}$$

  Cross-multiply and solve for x:

  $$40x = 500$$

  $$x = \frac{500}{40} = 12.5$$

  5 is 12.5% of 40

- If a price is discounted by p percent, then the discounted price is $(100 - p)$ percent of the original price.

Absolute Value

Absolute value describes the distance of a number on the number line from 0, without considering which direction from 0 the number lies. Therefore, absolute value is always positive. For example, consider the distance from −10 to 0 on the number line and the distance from 0 to 10 on the number line; both distances equal 10 units.

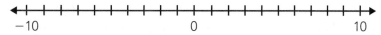

Figure 10.2 Absolute value.

The absolute value is indicated by enclosing a number within two vertical lines, as follows:

$$|-3| = 3 \text{ and } |3| = 3$$

Simple Probability and Outcomes

Following are properties of probability and outcomes that are commonly tested on the GRE:

- *Probability* refers to the likelihood that an event will occur. For example, Jeff has three striped and four solid ties in his closet; therefore, he has a total of seven ties in his closet. He has three chances to grab a striped tie out of the seven total ties, because he has three striped ties. So, the probability that Jeff will grab a striped tie is 3 out of 7, which can also be expressed as 3:7 or $\frac{3}{7}$.

- Two specific events are considered independent if the *outcome* of one event has no effect on the outcome of the other event. For example, if you toss a coin, there is a 1 in 2, or $\frac{1}{2}$, chance that it will land on either heads or tails. If you toss the coin again, the outcome will be the same. To find the probability of two or more independent events occurring together, multiply the outcomes of the individual events. For example, the probability that both coin tosses will result in heads is $\frac{1}{2} \times \frac{1}{2}$, or $\frac{1}{4}$.

Factors and Multiples

The following are properties of factors and multiples that are commonly tested on the GRE:

- A *prime number* is any number that can be divided only by itself and 1. That is, 1 and the number itself are the only factors of a prime number. For example, 2, 3, 5, 7, and 11 are prime numbers. (Note that 2 is the only even prime number, since all other even numbers can be divided by 2.)

- *Factors* are all of the numbers that will divide evenly into one number. For example, 1, 2, 4, and 8 are all factors of 8.

- *Common factors* include all of the factors that two or more numbers share. For example, 1, 2, 4, and 8 are all factors of 8, and 1, 2, 3, and 6 are all factors of 6. Therefore, 8 and 6 have common factors of 1 and 2.

- *The Greatest Common Factor* (GCF) is the largest number that will divide evenly into any 2 or more numbers. For example, 1, 2, 4, and 8 are all factors of 8, and 1, 2, 3, and 6 are all factors of 6. Therefore, the Greatest Common Factor of 8 and 6 is 2.

- A number is a *multiple* of another number if it can be expressed as the product of that number and a second number. For example, $2 \times 3 = 6$, so 6 is a multiple of both 2 and 3.

- *Common multiples* include all of the multiples that two or more numbers share. For example,

    Multiples of 3 include $3 \times 4 = 12$; $3 \times 8 = 24$; $3 \times 12 = 36$.

    Multiples of 4 include $4 \times 3 = 12$; $4 \times 6 = 24$; $4 \times 9 = 36$.

    Therefore, 12, 24, and 36 are all common multiples of both 3 and 4.

- The *Least Common Multiple* (LCM) is the smallest number that any two or more numbers will divide evenly into. For example, the common multiples of 3 and 4 include 12, 24, and 36; 12 is the smallest multiple, and is, therefore, the Least Common Multiple of 3 and 4.

- The *Commutative Property of Multiplication* is expressed as $a \times b = b \times a$, or $ab = ba$. For example, $2 \times 3 = 3 \times 2$.

- The *Distributive Property of Multiplication* is expressed as $a(b + c) = ab + ac$. For example, $x(x + 3) = x^2 + 3x$.

- The *Associative Property of Multiplication* can be expressed as $(a \times b) \times c = a \times (b \times c)$. For example, $(2 \times 3) \times 4 = 2 \times (3 \times 4)$; they both equal 24.

Exercises: Numbers and Operations

These exercises are designed to help you apply the mathematics concepts just covered. They are not in GRE format, but should help you to identify your areas of strength and weakness.

Basic Operations

These questions will test your knowledge of operations using integers, real numbers, fractions, and decimals.

Insert the correct operator in the blanks below.

1. 108 _____ $9 = 12$

2. 7 _____ $2 = 3.5$

3. $\frac{1}{4}$ _____ $\frac{3}{8} = \frac{5}{8}$

Answer the following questions.

4. When 5 consecutive odd integers, each greater than 34 are added, what is the smallest possible sum?

5. What is the Lowest Common Denominator of $\frac{5}{8}$ and $\frac{3}{4}$?

Solve the following equations.

6. $\dfrac{(96 - 21)}{15} + 11 =$ _____

7. $3(27 + 2 - 3) =$ _____

8. $\frac{1}{3} + \frac{3}{7} =$ _____

9. $231.2 - 198.7 =$ _____

10. $0.25 \times \frac{1}{5} =$ _____

Squares and Square Roots

These questions will test your knowledge of operations using square roots.

Solve the following problems.

1. $7^2 =$ _____

2. $\sqrt{36} \div \sqrt{4} =$ _____

3. Express 3×3 as a square: _____

4. $7^2 - 3^2 =$ _____

5. $\sqrt{64} \times 2^2 =$ _____

Exponents

These questions will test your knowledge of operations using exponents.

Fill in the blanks below with the correct number.

1. 2 raised to the power of _____ = 8

2. 3^3 = _____

3. $2^2 + 2^3$ = _____

4. 125 = 5 _____

5. $(2^4)2$ = _____

Scientific Notation

These questions will test your knowledge of operations using scientific notation.

Fill in the blanks below with the correct number.

1. 423,700,000 = 4.237 × 10 to the power of _____

2. $3.76 × 10^5$ = _____

3. $(2.50 × 10^4) ÷ (1.25 × 10^3)$ = _____

4. $6.47 × 10^{-5}$ = _____

5. $9.832 × 10^4$ = _____

Mean, Median, and Mode

These questions will test your knowledge of operations involving mean, median, and mode.

Fill in the blanks below with the correct number.

1. Ann scored 88, 93, 84, and 99 on 4 tests. What is her mean test score?

2. What is the mode of the data given below?

    7, 3, 6, 7, 5, 8, 9, 7

3. What is the median of the data given below?

     8, 13, 9, 8, 15, 14, 10

4. Jordan had 3 hits in his first 4 baseball games and 4 hits in his next 4 games. What is the average number of hits Jordan had in all of his games?

5. What is the median of the data given below?

     80, 27, 19, 82, 15, 72, 3

Ratio, Proportion, and Percent

These questions will test your knowledge of operations involving ratio, proportion, and percent.

Answer the following questions.

1. _____ is 30% of 20.

2. $\frac{x}{6} = \frac{39}{78}$ What is the value of x?

3. As an analyst for the Department of Natural Resources, you analyze samples of river water. A 2-liter sample of water contained about 24 of a particular organism and a 4-liter sample of water contained about 48 such organisms. At this rate, how many of the organisms would you expect to find in a 10-liter sample of water from the same river?

4. If 20% of x equals 16, then $x =$ _____

5. Jim scored 95 points in 5 basketball games for his school. At this rate, how many points will he have scored by the end of the 12-game season?

Absolute Value

These questions will test your knowledge of operations involving absolute value.

Solve the following equations.

1. If $x = -8$, what is the value of $|x - 6|$?

2. Solve $|4x - 6| = 10$ for x.

3. $|-15| \times |6| =$ _____

4.   Solve $|6x + 8| = |3x - 7|$ for x.

5. $\dfrac{-32}{|-8|} =$ _____

Simple Probability and Outcomes

These questions will test your knowledge of operations involving simple probability and outcomes.

Answer the following questions.

1.   If you roll a single 6-sided die, what is the probability that you will roll an odd number?

2.   A company knows that 2.5% of the CD players it makes are defective. If the company produces 300,000 CD players, how many will be defective?

3.   When flipping a coin, what is the probability that it will land on tails four times in a row?

4.   If the probability that Dave will go to class is 0.7, what is the probability that he will not go to class?

5.   A bowl contains 20 marbles (8 blue, 6 red, 3 green, 2 yellow, and 1 orange). If you reach in and choose one marble at random, what is the probability that it will be red?

Factors and Multiples

These questions will test your knowledge of operations involving factors and multiples.

Answer the following questions.

1.   A certain integer n is a multiple of both 5 and 9. Must n be a multiple of 15?

2.   What are the common factors of 7 and 42?

3.   What is the Greatest Common Factor of 48 and 72?

4.   What is the Least Common Multiple of 4 and 6?

5.   What is the greatest positive integer x such that 2^x is a factor of 12^{10}?

Answers and Explanations

Basic Operations

1. In order for 12 to be the result of this operation, you must divide 108 by 9. Insert the ÷ symbol in the blank.

2. To reach an answer of 3.5, you must divide 7 by 2. Insert the ÷ symbol in the blank.

3. One way to solve this problem is to look for the Lowest Common Denominator (LCD). The smallest number that both 4 and 8 divide evenly into is 8, so the fraction $\frac{3}{8}$ does not need to be changed. The fraction $\frac{1}{4}$ is equivalent to $\frac{2}{8}$; $\frac{2}{8}$ plus $\frac{3}{8}$ equals $\frac{5}{8}$, so insert the + symbol in the blank.

4. To find the smallest possible sum, take the 5 consecutive odd integers that are the closest to 34 (remember, they all must be greater than 34). These numbers would be: 35, 37, 39, 41, and 43. Add them together: $35 + 37 + 39 + 41 + 43 = 195$.

5. The Lowest Common Denominator (LCD) is the smallest number into which all of the denominators will divide evenly. For this problem, you must find the smallest number into which 8 and 4 will divide evenly. Since 4 will divide evenly into 8 ($\frac{8}{4} = 2$), 8 is the LCD.

6. You must first complete the math within the parentheses ($96 - 21 = 75$). Next, do any multiplication or division in the problem, from left to right: $\frac{75}{15} = 5$. Finally, do any addition or subtraction in the problem, from left to right: $5 + 11 = 16$.

7. You must first do the operations within the parentheses ($27 + 2 - 3 = 26$). Now multiply the value from the parentheses by 3: $3 \times 26 = 78$.

8. You must first find the Lowest Common Denominator (LCD) for the two fractions involved. The denominators are 3 and 7. The smallest number into which both of these numbers can divide evenly is 21. Convert each denominator to 21 by multiplying $\frac{1}{3}$ by $\frac{7}{7}$ and $\frac{3}{7}$ by $\frac{3}{3}$. This gives you $\frac{7}{21} + \frac{9}{21}$, which equals $\frac{16}{21}$.

9. This is a simple subtraction problem. To solve this without a calculator, line up the decimal points and subtract (remembering to "borrow" and "carry"), as follows:

$$\begin{array}{r} 231.2 \\ -198.7 \\ \hline 32.5 \end{array}$$

10. First convert $\frac{1}{5}$ to its decimal equivalent, which is .2. Then multiply .25 by .2 to get .05. Another way to solve is to first convert .25 to its equivalent fraction, which is $\frac{1}{4}$. When multiplying the two fractions, you first multiply the numerators, and then the denominators, giving you $\frac{1}{20}$. Because this is equivalent to .05, either answer will be correct.

Squares and Square Roots

1. 7^2 simply means 7 times 7, which is 49.

2. Find the square roots before you do the division. The square root of 36 is 6, and the square root of 4 is 2. You then divide 6 by 2, which equals 3.

3. Three times 3 can be stated as "3 squared." The proper way to write this is 3^2.

4. Both numbers are raised to the power of 2 (they are squared.) You must first find these squares before you do your subtraction; 7 squared is 49, and 3 squared is 9. So, the answer is $49 - 9$, which equals 40.

5. This problem requires you to find a square root of a number as well as a number squared. The square root of 64 is 8 (64 is called a "perfect square" because its square root is a whole number), and 2 squared equals 4. The answer is 8 times 4, which is 32.

Exponents

1. The power that a number is raised to is equivalent to the number of times you multiply that number by itself: $2 \times 2 \times 2$ is equal to 8, so the answer is 2 raised to the power of 3 (2^3).

2. 3^3, or 3 to the third power, means you must multiply $3 \times 3 \times 3$, which equals 27.

3. Remember to add the exponents when multiplying exponential values with the same base: $2^2 \times 2^3 = 2^5 = 32$.

4. $5^3 = 5 \times 5 \times 5$, which gives you 125.

5. When raising an exponent to another power, multiply the exponents ($4 \times 2 = 8$). So, the answer is 2^8, or 256.

Scientific Notation

1. When dealing with scientific notation, the power that 10 is raised to gives you the number of spaces you must move the decimal place, either to the right (for a positive value), or to the left (for a negative value). To turn 4.237 into 423,700,000, you must move the decimal place 8 spaces to the right. Therefore, 10 needs to be raised to the power of 8 (10^8).

2. To solve this problem, you must simply move the decimal point the number of times indicated by the power to which 10 is raised. Since you are given 10^5, you know that you must move the decimal point 5 spaces to the right, because the exponent is a positive number. This gives an answer of 376,000.

3. This problem can be set up as $\left(\frac{2.50}{1.25}\right) \times \left(\frac{10^4}{10^3}\right)$; $\frac{2.50}{1.25} = 2$. When dividing like bases, you subtract your exponents, so $10^4 \div 10^3 = 10^1$. You are left with 2×10^1. Since 10 to the first power is 10, the correct answer is 20.

4. You are given a negative value for the power to which 10 is raised (-5). This means that you must move the decimal point 5 spaces to the left to get the answer, which is .0000647.

5. Because 10 is raised to the fourth power, move the decimal point 4 places to the right to get 98,320.

Mean, Median, and Mode

1. The mean is the average, so simply add the test scores and divide by 4 (the total number of tests):

    $$88 + 93 + 84 + 99 = 364$$
    $$364 \div 4 = 91$$

2. The mode is the number that appears most frequently in a series of numbers. In this case, the mode is 7.

3. The median is the middle value in an ordered set of values. Therefore, the first step is to put the numbers in order, as follows:

     8, 8, 9, 10, 13, 14, 15

   As you can see, 10 is the middle value.

4. To calculate Jordan's average number of hits, first find his total number of hits:

     $3 \times 4 = 12$ and $4 \times 4 = 16$

     $12 + 16 = 28$

   Next, find the average:

     $28 \div 8 = 3.5$

5. The median is the middle value in an ordered set of values. Therefore, the first step is to put the numbers in order, as follows:

     3, 15, 19, 72, 80, 82

   Because the set includes an even number of values, take the average of the middle values:

     $19 + 72 = 91$

     $91 \div 2 = 45.5$

Ratio, Proportion, and Percent

1. To solve this problem, set up a proportion. You are looking for a number that is 30% of 20. The proportion will be $\frac{x}{20} = \frac{30}{100}$, because the unknown number is 30% of the whole (20). To solve, cross-multiply, leaving you with $100x = 600$. Divide both sides by 100, and you get the final answer: $x = 6$.

2. You are given a proportion to solve. To find the answer, cross-multiply, giving you $78x = 234$. Dividing both sides by 78 will give you the answer: $x = 3$.

3. To answer this question you must determine the ratio of organisms to liters of river water. The problem states that a 2-liter sample of water contained about 24 organisms and a 4-liter sample of water contained about 48 organisms. Upon closer examination of this information you will see that the ratio of organisms to water is the same in each sample. Therefore, you can set up a ratio using one sample:

     2 liters of water yields 24 organisms.

This can be expressed as 2 to 24, or 2:24, which can be reduced to 1:12. For every 1 liter of water you will see 12 organisms. Therefore, 10 liters of water will contain 120 organisms.

4. Set up a proportion. You are given that 20% of x is equal to 16, and you want to find the value of x. The proportion will look like this:

$$\frac{16}{x} = \frac{20}{100}$$

After cross-multiplying, you are left with $20x = 1,600$. After dividing both sides by 20, you have the answer: $x = 80$.

5. Use a proportion to solve this problem. You know that Jim scored 95 points in 5 games, and you want to find out how many points he will score in a total of 12 games. The proportion will look like this:

$$\frac{95}{5} = \frac{x}{12}$$

Cross-Multiply to get $5x = 1,140$. Divide both sides by 5, and you get the answer: $x = 228$. If Jim continues to score at this rate, he will score a total of 228 points by the end of the season (12 games).

Absolute Value

1. First, substitute -8 for x and do the subtraction within the absolute value lines ($-8 - 6 = -14$.) Absolute value is the numerical value of a real number without regard to its sign. Therefore, the absolute value of -14 is 14.

2. To solve this problem, set up two equations because x has two values:

   $4x - 6 = 10$, and $4x - 6 = -10$.

   Solve both for x.

   $4x = 16$, and $4x = -4$

   $x = 4$, and $x = -1$

3. In order to perform the multiplication in this problem, first find the absolute value of both numbers. The absolute values of -15 and 6 are 15 and 6, respectively. The answer is $15 \times 6 = 90$.

4. To find the possible answers for x in this problem, set up two equations:

$$6x + 8 = 3x - 7, \text{ and } 6x + 8 = -(3x - 7).$$

First, distribute the minus sign in the second equation, giving you $6x + 8 = -3x + 7$. Then solve both for x:

$$3x = -15, \text{ and } 9x = -1$$

$$x = -5, \text{ and } x = -\frac{1}{9}$$

5. First find the absolute value of the denominator. The absolute value of -8 is 8. Now perform the division: $-32 \div 8 = -4$.

Simple Probability and Outcomes

1. On a 6-sided die, there are 3 even numbers, and 3 odd numbers. Therefore, the probability that you will roll an odd number is 3 out of 6, or $\frac{3}{6}$. This can be reduced to $\frac{1}{2}$, or 0.5.

2. If 2.5% of the CD players produced by this company are defective, then the number of defective devices out of 300,000 can be determined by multiplication, as follows:

$$0.025 \times 300,000 = 7,500$$

3. When flipping a coin, there are only two possible outcomes: heads or tails. Therefore, each side has a probability of $\frac{1}{2}$, or .5, of landing facing up. The chances of the coin landing on tails four times in a row can be expressed as $\frac{1}{2} \times \frac{1}{2} \times \frac{1}{2} \times \frac{1}{2}$, or $\frac{1}{2^4} = \frac{1}{16}$.

4. The probability that Dave will go to class is 0.7, or 70%. Therefore, the probability that he will NOT go to class is 100% − 70%, or 30%, which is equivalent to 0.3, so either answer will be correct.

5. There is a total of 20 marbles in the bowl, 6 of which are red. If one marble is selected at random, the probability that it will be red is $\frac{6}{20} \left(\frac{\text{the number of red marbles}}{\text{the total number of marbles}} \right)$. This can be reduced to $\frac{3}{10}$.

Factors and Multiples

1. The first step in solving this problem is to find the Least Common Multiple (LCM) of 5 and 9. Because a multiple of 5 must have either a 5 or a 0 in the digits place, and 9×5 is the first multiple of 9 with a 5 in the digits place, $9 \times 5 = 45$ must be the LCM. Therefore, n must be a multiple of 15, since 45 (one possible value of n) is a multiple of 15.

2. Remember that common factors are all of the factors that two or more numbers share. The factors of 7 are 1 and 7 because 7 is a prime number. The factors of 42 include 1 ($42 \times 1 = 42$) and 7 ($6 \times 7 = 42$), so the common factors of 7 and 42 are 1 and 7.

3. The Greatest Common Factor (GCF) is the largest number that divides evenly into any two or more numbers. List the factors of 48 and 72, then select the largest factor that they have in common:

48	72
1	1
2	2
3	3
4	4
6	6
8	8
12	9
16	12
24	18
48	**24**
	36
	72

Based on this list, the GCF is 24.

4. The Least Common Multiple is the smallest number that any two or more numbers can divide evenly into. One way to solve this problem is to determine the multiples of 30, stopping at the first one that is also a multiple of 40:

$$30 \times 1 = 30$$
$$30 \times 2 = 60$$
$$30 \times 3 = 90$$
$$30 \times 4 = 120$$

Because 40 divides evenly into 120, 120 it is the Least Common Multiple of 30 and 40.

5. To reach an answer, you first must find the smallest factors of 12, as follows:

$$12^{10} = (3 \times 2 \times 2)^{10}$$

Remember that the exponent applies to every value within the parentheses; thus, $(3 \times 2 \times 2)^{10} = 3^{10} \times 2^{10} \times 2^{10}$. When multiplying powers with the same base, you add the exponents:

$$3^{10} \times 2^{(10 + 10)} = (3^{10})(2^{20}); 2^{20} \text{ is a factor of } 12^{10}$$

Algebra and Functions

These questions might involve solving linear equations with one variable, polynomial equations and inequalities, factoring, and working with functions.

Linear Equations with One Variable

In a *linear equation with one variable*, the variable cannot have an exponent or be in the denominator of a fraction. An example of a linear equation is $2x + 13 = 43$. The GRE will most likely require you to solve for x in that equation. Do this by isolating x on the left side of the equation, as follows:

$$2x + 13 = 43$$
$$2x = 43 - 13$$
$$2x = 30$$
$$x = \frac{30}{2}, \text{ or } 15$$

Polynomial Operations and Factoring Simple Quadratic Expressions

Following are properties of polynomial operations and factoring simple quadratic expressions that are commonly tested on the GRE:

- A *polynomial* is the sum or difference of expressions such as $2x^2$ and $14x$. The most common polynomial takes the form of a simple quadratic expression, such as $2x^2 + 14x + 8$, with the terms in decreasing order. The standard form of a simple quadratic expression is $ax^2 + bx + c$, where a, b, and c are whole numbers. When the terms include both a number and a variable, such as x, the number is called the *coefficient*. For example, in the expression $2x$, 2 is the coefficient of x.

- The GRE will often require you to evaluate, or solve a polynomial, by substituting a given value for the variable, as follows:

  For $x = -2$, $2x^2 + 14x + 8 = ?$

Substitute -2 for x and solve:

$$2(-2)^2 + 14(-2) + 8$$
$$= 2(4) + (-28) + 8$$
$$= 8 - 28 + 8 = -12$$

- You will also be required to add, subtract, multiply, and divide polynomials. To *add or subtract polynomials*, simply combine like terms, as in the following examples:

1. $(2x^2 + 14x + 8) + (3x^2 + 5x + 32)$

    $= 5x^2 + 19x + 40$

and

2. $(8x^2 + 11x + 23) - (7x^2 + 3x + 13)$

    $= x^2 + 8x + 10$

- To *multiply polynomials*, use the distributive property to multiply each term of one polynomial by each term of the other polynomial. Following are some examples:

1. $(3x)(x^2 + 4x - 2)$

    $= (3x^3 + 12x^2 - 6x)$

and

2. $(2x^2 + 5x)(x - 3)$

Remember the *FOIL* Method whenever you see the type of multiplication in Example 2: multiply the *F*irst terms, then the *O*utside terms, then the *I*nside terms, then the *L*ast terms.

$(2x^2 + 5x)(x - 3) =$

*F*irst terms: $(2x^2)(x) = 2x^3$

*O*utside terms: $(2x^2)(-3) = -6x^2$

*I*nside terms: $(5x)(x) = 5x^2$

*L*ast terms: $(5x)(-3) = -15x$

Now put the terms in decreasing order:

$2x^3 + (-6x^2) + 5x^2 + (-15x)$

$= 2x^3 - x^2 - 15x$

Systems of Equations

The GRE will include questions that contain two equations and two unknowns. To solve a *system of equations* like this, follow the steps below:

$4x + 5y = 21$

$5x + 10y = 30$

If you multiply the top equation by -2, you will get:

$-8x - 10y = -42$

$5x + 10y = 30$

Now, you can add the two equations together.

$-8x - 10y + 5x + 10y = -42 + 30$

$-3x = -12$

Notice that the two y-terms cancel each other out. Solving for x, you get $x = 4$. Now, choose one of the original two equations, substitute 4 for x, and solve for y:

$$4(4) + 5y = 21$$
$$16 + 5y = 21$$
$$5y = 5$$
$$y = 1$$

Inequalities

Inequalities can usually be solved in much the same way equations are solved. For example, to solve for x in the inequality $2x > 8$, simply divide both sides by 2 to get $x > 4$.

When an inequality is multiplied by a negative number you must switch the sign. For example, follow these steps to solve for x in the inequality $-2x + 2 < 6$:

$$-2x + 2 < 6$$
$$-2x < 4$$
$$-x < 2$$
$$x > -2$$

Functions

A *function* is a set of ordered pairs in which no two of the ordered pairs have the same x-value. In a function, each input (x-value) has exactly one output (y-value). An example of this relationship would be $y = x^2$. Here, y is a function of x because for any value of x, there is exactly one value of y. However, x is not a function of y because for certain values of y, there is more than one value of x (if $y = 25$, then $x = 5$ and $x = -5$).

The *domain* of a function refers to the x-values, while the *range* of a function refers to the y-values. If the values in the domain correspond to more than one value in the range, the relation is not a function.

Consider the following example:

For the function $f(x) = x^2 - 3x$, what is the value of $f(5)$?

Solve this problem by substituting 5 for x wherever x appears in the function:

$$f(x) = x^2 - 3x$$
$$f(5) = (5)^2 - (3)(5)$$
$$f(5) = 25 - 15$$
$$f(5) = 10$$

Exercises: Algebra and Functions

These exercises are designed to help you apply the mathematics concepts just covered. They are not in GRE format, but should help you to identify your areas of strength and weakness.

Linear Equations with One Variable

These questions will test your knowledge of linear equations involving one variable.

Solve the following equations.

1. $3x - 17 = 46$. Solve for x.

2. $\frac{x}{4} = -6$. Solve for x.

3. If $x = 15$, then $4x - \underline{\hspace{1cm}} = 42$

4. Two trains running on parallel tracks are 600 miles apart. One train is moving east at a speed of 90 mph, while the other is moving west at 75 mph. How long will it take for the two trains to pass each other?

5. $3(x - 4) = 5x - 20$. Solve for x.

Polynomial Operations and Factoring Simple Quadratic Equations

These questions will test your knowledge of operations involving polynomial operations and factoring simple quadratic equations.

Solve the following equations.

1. For $x = 4$, $3x^2 - 5x + 9 = \underline{\hspace{1cm}}$

2. $(5x^3 + 3x - 12) - (2x^3 - 6x + 17) = \underline{\hspace{1cm}}$

3. $(4x^2 + 2x)(x - 6) = \underline{\hspace{1cm}}$

Answer the following questions.

4. What are the solution sets for $x^2 + 2x - 48$?

5. $(x - 4)$ and $(2x + 3)$ are the solution sets for what equation?

Systems of Equations

These questions will test your knowledge of operations involving systems of equations.

Solve the following systems of equations.

1. $x - 2y = 14$
   $x - 4y = -8$

2. $4x - 2y = 6$
   $-6x + 5y = 7$

3. $3x - y = 18$
   $4x = 24 - 6y$

4. $8(y + x) = 12$
   $4x - 3y = -22$

5. $4x - y = 63$
   $3y + x = 6$

Linear Inequalities with One Variable

These questions will test your knowledge of operations involving linear inequalities with one variable.

Answer the following questions.

1. For $-5 \le x < 15$, $x =$ _____

2. For which values of x is $6x - 3 > 4x + 5$?

3. If $x = 7$, then is $3x + 7$ greater than or less than $5x - 6$?

4. For which values of x is $2x - 5 < -3x + 20$?

5. Solve for x: $-4 \le x + 3 < 18$

Functions

These questions will test your knowledge of operations involving functions.

Answer the following questions.

1. For the function $f(x) = x^2 - 4x + 8$, what is the value of $f(6)$?

2. If $f(x) = x^2$, find $f(x + 1)$.

3. If the function $f(x) = x + 2$, and the function $g(x) = 3x$, what is the function $g(f(x))$?

4. For the function $f(x) = \dfrac{x^4 - 3x}{2}$, what is the value of $f(2)$?

5. For the function $f(x) = x^2 - x$, what is the value of $f(-5)$?

Answers and Explanations

Linear Equations with One Variable

1. To solve this problem, first isolate the unknown number on one side. To do this, add 17 to both sides to get $3x = 63$. Next, divide both sides by 3 to isolate the x on the left side: $x = 21$.

2. To solve this problem, multiply both sides by 4 to get rid of the fraction and isolate the x on the left side: $x = -24$.

3. You are given the value of x, and asked to calculate a missing number in the equation. Because $x = 15$, then $4x = 60$. The equation is now $60 -$ (some number) $= 42$. The difference between 60 and 42 is 18.

4. This is a standard Rate $\times$ Time $=$ Distance problem. Since the two trains start 600 miles apart, the combined distance traveled by both trains must equal 600. Using the $R \times T = D$ formula, you know that (Rate of Train 1 $\times$ Time of Train 1) + (Rate of Train 2 $\times$ Time of Train 2) $= 600$. You are given that the rate of travel is 90 mph for the first train and 75 mph for the second train, and the distance traveled is 600 miles; therefore, you must solve for T, as follows:

$$90T + 75T = 600$$

$$165T = 600$$

$$T = \text{(approximately) } 3.64 \text{ hours}$$

5. To solve this problem, first do the multiplication on the left side of the equation to get $3x - 12 = 5x - 20$. Next, put the like terms together. To do this, subtract $3x$ from both sides, and add 20 to both sides to get $8 = 2x$. Divide both sides by 2 to get $x = 4$.

Polynomial Operations and Factoring Simple Quadratic Equations

1. To solve the equation, substitute 4 for x:

    $$3(4^2) - 5(4) + 9 =$$
    $$3(16) - 20 + 9 =$$
    $$48 - 20 + 9 = 37$$

2. To add or subtract polynomials, combine like terms (remember to keep track of the negative signs!):

    $$(5x^3 + 3x - 12) - (2x^3 - 6x + 17)$$
    $$(5x^3 - 2x^3) + (3x + 6x) - (17 - 12)$$
    $$3x^3 + 9x - 29$$

3. Use the Distributive Property to multiply each term of one polynomial by each term of the other (remember to use the FOIL method).

    $$(4x^2 + 2x)(x - 6)$$

    First terms: $(4x^2)(x) = 4x^3$

    Outside terms: $(4x^2)(-6) = -24x^2$

    Inside terms: $(2x)(x) = 2x^2$

    Last terms: $(2x)(-6) = -12x$

    Now place the terms in decreasing order:

    $$4x^3 - 22x^2 - 12x$$

4. Find two numbers whose product is -48 and sum is 2. 8 and -6 are the only possible numbers. Therefore, the solution sets are $(x - 6)$ and $(x + 8)$.

5. The solution sets are given, so multiply the two sets together to find the original equation, using the FOIL method:

    $$(x - 4)(2x + 3)$$
    $$= 2x^2 + 3x - 8x - 12$$
    $$= 2x^2 - 5x - 12$$

Systems of Equations

1. When solving systems of equations, the best thing to do first is to isolate one of the variables. In this problem, you can do so by changing the sign on the bottom equation:

$$x - 2y = 14$$
$$-x + 4y = 8$$

Add the two equations together (note that the x terms cancel out):

$$2y = 22$$
$$y = 11$$

Choose one of the original equations and substitute 11 in for y. Solve for x:

$$x - 2(11) = 14$$
$$x - 22 = 14$$
$$x = 36$$

It is a good idea to test your answers by substituting x and y values into both of the original equations.

2. This problem is a little trickier than the first, as you cannot simply change the sign of one of the equations to isolate one of the variables. In this situation, you have to make the coefficients the same through multiplication. Since you know that 4 and 6 both go into 12, use the x term. Multiply the top equation by 3, and the bottom by 2:

$$12x - 6y = 18$$
$$-12x + 10y = 14$$

Add the two equations together (note that the x terms cancel out):

$$4y = 32$$
$$y = 8$$

Finally, choose one of the original equations, substitute 8 for y, and solve for x.

$$4x - 2(8) = 6$$
$$4x - 16 = 6$$
$$4x = 22$$
$$x = \frac{22}{4}, \text{ or } \frac{11}{2}$$

3. The first step is rearranging the equations to align like terms:

$$3x - y = 18$$
$$4x + 6y = 24$$

Multiply the top equation by 6 and add the equations:

$$18x - 6y = 108$$
$$\underline{4x + 6y = 24}$$
$$22x = 132$$
$$x = 6$$

Now choose one of the original equations, substitute 6 in for x, and solve for y:

$$3(6) - y = 18$$
$$18 - y = 18$$
$$-y = 0$$
$$y = 0$$

4. First, distribute the 8 to get $8y + 8x = 12$. You can then multiply the second equation by -2 to isolate one of the variables, and rearrange the equations to line up the like terms:

$$8x + 8y = 12$$
$$-8x + 6y = 44$$

Add the equations together (note that the x terms cancel out):

$$14y = 56$$
$$y = 4$$

Now choose one of the original equations, substitute 4 for y, and solve for x.

$$8x + 8(4) = 12$$
$$8x + 32 = 12$$
$$8x = -20$$
$$x = -\frac{20}{8}$$
$$x = -\frac{5}{2}$$

5. First distribute the 4 in the first equation to get $4x - y = 63$. Then line up the like terms in both equations:

$$4x - y = 63$$
$$x + 3y = 6$$

Multiply the top equation by 3 and add the equations:

$$12x - 3y = 189$$
$$x + 3y = 6$$

Note that the y terms cancel out:

$$13x = 195$$
$$x = 15$$

Now substitute 15 for x in one of the equations.

$$x + 3y = 6$$
$$15 + 3y = 6$$
$$3y = -9$$
$$y = -3$$

Linear Inequalities with One Variable

1. The inequality states that x must be greater than or equal to -5 AND less than 15($\leq$ means "greater than or equal to" and $<$ means "less than"). Therefore, x could be any number between and including -5 and 15.

2. Solve this problem algebraically, as follows:

$$6x - 4x > 5 - (-3)$$
$$2x > 8$$
$$x > 4$$

x must be greater than 4 for this inequality to be true.

3. The value of x is given, so substitute 7 for x and calculate the value of both sides:

$$3(7) + 7 = 28 \text{ and } 5(7) - 6 = 29$$

The less than sign ($<$) is used because $28 < 29$.

4. The first step in solving this problem is to isolate the variable on one side of the inequality:

$$-5 - 20 < -3x - 2x$$
$$-25 < -5x$$
$$5 > x$$

It is important to remember that when dealing with inequalities, multiplying or dividing by a negative number involves reversing the sign. In this case, both sides were divided by -5, so the sign changes from $<$ to $>$.

5. To solve this problem, subtract the 3 from both sides of the inequality:

$$-4 - 3 \le x < 18 - 3$$
$$-7 \le x < 15$$

x is greater than or equal to -7, and it is less than 15.

Functions

1. To solve, substitute 6 for x in the function:

$$f(6) = 6^2 - 4(6) + 8$$
$$f(6) = 36 - 24 + 8$$
$$f(6) = 20$$

2. To solve, substitute $(x + 1)$ for x in the function:

$$f(x + 1) = (x + 1)^2$$
$$(x + 1)(x + 1)$$
$$x^2 + x + x + 1$$
$$x^2 + 2x + 1$$

3. The problem gives $g(x) = 3x$ and $f(x) = x + 2$ and asks for $g(f(x))$. The function $g(f(x))$ means that all of the x values in $g(x)$ are replaced with $f(x)$, as follows:

$$g(f(x)) = 3(f(x))$$
$$g(f(x)) = 3(x + 2)$$
$$g(f(x)) = 3x + 6$$

4. To solve, substitute 2 for x in the function:

$$f(2) = \frac{2^4 - 3(2)}{2}$$
$$f(2) = \frac{16 - 6}{2}$$
$$f(2) = \frac{10}{2}$$
$$f(2) = 5$$

5. To solve, substitute -5 for x in the function:

$$f(-5) = (-5)^2 + (-5)$$
$$f(-5) = 25 - 5$$
$$f(-5) = 20$$

Geometry

These questions might involve coordinate geometry; parallel and perpendicular lines; triangles, rectangles, and other polygons; circles; area, perimeter, volume, and angle measure in degrees.

Coordinate Geometry

The following are properties of coordinate geometry that are commonly tested on the GRE:

- The (*x,y*) *coordinate plane* is defined by two axes at right angles to each other. The horizontal axis is the *x*-axis, and the vertical axis is the *y*-axis.

- The *origin* is the point (0,0), where the two axes intersect, as shown in the following figure:

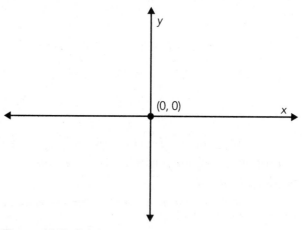

Figure 10.3 Origin.

- The *slope* of a line is calculated by taking the change in *y*-coordinates divided by the change in *x*-coordinates from two given points on a line. The formula for slope is $m = \dfrac{(y_2 - y_1)}{(x_2 - x_1)}$ where m is the slope and (x_1,y_1) and (x_2,y_2) are the two given points. For example, the slope of a line that contains the points (3,6) and (2,5) is equivalent to $\dfrac{(6-5)}{(3-2)}$, or $\dfrac{1}{1}$, which equals 1.

- A positive slope means that the graph of the line will go up and to the right. A negative slope means that the graph of the line will go down and to the right. A horizontal line has slope 0, while a vertical line has an undefined slope, because it never crosses the *y*-axis. The figure shown next illustrates the possible slopes of line *l*:

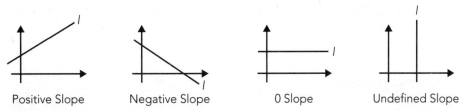

Positive Slope   Negative Slope   0 Slope   Undefined Slope

Figure 10.4 Different slopes.

> **NOTE**
>
> The slope of a vertical line is undefined because there is no change in the x-coordinate of any of the points on the line. This will make the denominator 0 in the formula for determining slope.

- The *slope-intercept (standard) form* of the equation of a line is $y = mx + b$, where m is the slope of the line and b is the y-intercept (that is, the point at which the graph of the line crosses the y-axis).

- Two lines are *parallel* if and only if they have the same slope. For example, the two lines with equations $2y = 6x + 7$ and $y = 3x - 14$ have the same slope (3).

- Two lines are *perpendicular* if and only if the slope of one of the lines is the negative reciprocal of the slope of the other line. In other words, if line a has a slope of 2, and line b has a slope of $-\frac{1}{2}$, the two lines are perpendicular.

- To find the distance between two points in the (x,y) coordinate plane, use the Distance Formula $\sqrt{([x_2 - x_1]^2 + [y_2 - y_1]^2)}$, where (x_1,y_1) and (x_2,y_2) are the two given points. For example, if you are given the points (2,3) and (4,5), you would set up the following equation to determine the distance between the two points:

$$\sqrt{(4 - 2) + (5 - 3)}$$
$$= \sqrt{2 + 2}$$
$$= \sqrt{4} = 2$$

- To find the midpoint of a line given two points on the line, use the *Midpoint Formula* $\left(\frac{[x_1 + x_2]}{2}, \frac{[y_1 + y_2]}{2}\right)$. For example, you would set up the following equation to determine the midpoint of the line between the two points (2,3) and (4,5):

$$\frac{(2 + 4)}{2}$$

$$= \frac{6}{2} = 3;$$ the x-value of the midpoint is 3

$$\frac{(3 + 5)}{2}$$

$$= \frac{8}{2} = 4;$$ the y-value of the midpoint is 4

Therefore, the midpoint of the line between the points (2,3) and (4,5) is (3,4).

Triangles

The following are properties of triangles that are commonly tested on the GRE:

- In an *equilateral* triangle, all three sides have the same length, and each interior angle measures 60 degrees.

- In an *isosceles* triangle, two sides have the same length, and the angles opposite those sides are congruent.

- In a *right* triangle, one of the angles measures 90 degrees. The side opposite the right angle is the hypotenuse, and it is always the longest side.

- The sum of the interior angles in any triangle is always 180 degrees.

- The *perimeter* (P) *of a triangle* is the sum of the lengths of the sides.

- The *area* (A) *of a triangle* is equivalent to $\frac{1}{2}$(base)(height). The height is equal to the perpendicular distance from an angle to a side. Following are examples of the height of a given triangle:

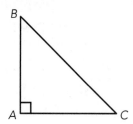

In right triangle *ABC*, the height is simply the distance from *A* to *B*.

Figure 10.5 Triangle height (right triangle).

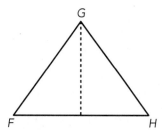

In triangle *FGH*, the height is the perpendicular line drawn from angle *G* to the midpoint of side *FH*. The height is **not** the distance from *F* to *G* or from *G* to *H*.

Figure 10.6 Triangle height.

- The *Pythagorean theorem* states that $c^2 = a^2 + b^2$, where c is the hypotenuse (the side opposite the right angle) of a right triangle and a and b are the two other sides of the triangle.

- The following are angle measures and side lengths for *Special Right Triangles*:

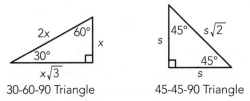

30-60-90 Triangle   45-45-90 Triangle

Figure 10.7 Special right triangles.

Quadrilaterals, Lines, Angles

The following are properties of quadrilaterals, lines, and angles that are commonly tested on the GRE:

- A *quadrilateral* is any four-sided object.

- In a *parallelogram*, the opposite sides are of equal length, and the opposite angles are equal, as shown below:

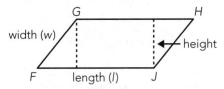

Figure 10.8 Parallelogram.

You can write the following equations for the parallelogram above:

$$GH = FJ$$

$$GF = HJ$$

$$\angle F = \angle H$$

$$\angle G = \angle J$$

- The *area* (A) *of a parallelogram* is equivalent to (base)(height). The *height* is equal to the perpendicular distance from an angle to a side. In the parallelogram shown above, the height is the distance from angle *G* to the bottom side, or base, or the distance from angle *J* to the top side, or base. The height is **not** the distance from *G* to *F* or the distance from *H* to *J*.

- A *rectangle* is a polygon, or multisided figure, with four sides (two sets of congruent, or equal sides) and four right angles, as shown below. All rectangles are parallelograms.

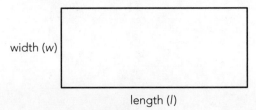

length (*l*)

Figure 10.9 A rectangle.

- The sum of the angles in a rectangle is always 360 degrees, because a rectangle contains four 90-degree angles.
- The *perimeter* (P) *of both a parallelogram and a rectangle* is equivalent to $2l + 2w$, where *l* is the length and *w* is the width.
- The *area* (A) *of a rectangle* is equivalent to $(l)(w)$.
- The lengths of the diagonals of a rectangle are congruent, or equal in length. A *diagonal* is a straight line between opposite angles, as shown below:

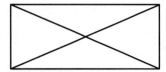

Figure 10.10 Diagonals of a rectangle.

- A *square* is a special rectangle where all four sides are of equal length. All squares are rectangles.
- The length of each diagonal of a square is equivalent to the length of one side times $\sqrt{2}$. For example, a square with a side length of x would have diagonals equal to $x\sqrt{2}$.
- A *line* is generally understood to be a straight line.
- A *line segment* is the part of a line that lies between two points on the line.
- Two distinct lines are said to be *parallel* if they lie in the same plane and do not intersect.
- Two distinct lines are said to be *perpendicular* if their intersection creates right angles.
- When two parallel lines are cut by a *transversal*, each parallel line has four angles surrounding the intersection that are matched in measure and position with a counterpart at the other parallel line. The vertical (opposite) angles are congruent, and the adjacent angles are *supplementary* (they total 180°). See the figure below.

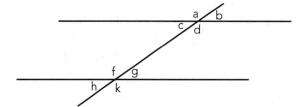

Figure 10.11 Parallel lines cut by a transversal.

- You can write the following equations regarding the parallel lines cut by a transversal shown:

  Vertical angles: $a = d = f = k$

  Vertical angles: $b = c = g = h$

  Supplementary angles: $a + b = 180°$

  Supplementary angles: $c + d = 180°$

  Supplementary angles: $f + g = 180°$

  Supplementary angles: $h + k = 180°$

- An *acute angle* is any angle less than 90 degrees.

- An *obtuse angle* is any angle that is greater than 90 degrees and less than 180 degrees.

- A *right angle* is an angle that measures exactly 90 degrees.

- Two angles are *complementary* if the sum of their measures is 90 degrees.

Some Other Polygons

The following are properties of other polygons (multisided objects) that are commonly tested on the GRE:

- A *pentagon* is a five-sided figure, as shown below.

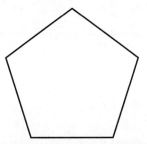

Figure 10.12 A pentagon.

- The sum of the interior angles of a pentagon is $(5 − 2)(180°)$, or $540°$.

- A *hexagon* is a six-sided figure, as shown below.

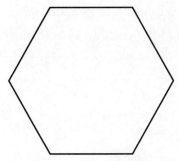

Figure 10.13 A hexagon.

- The sum of the interior angles of a hexagon is (6 − 2)(180°), or 720°.
- An *octagon* is an eight-sided figure, as shown below.

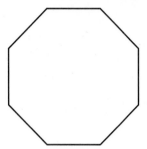

Figure 10.14 An octagon.

- The sum of the interior angles of an octagon is (8 − 2)(180°), or 1,080°.

Circles

The following are properties of circles that are commonly tested on the GRE:

- The *radius (r) of a circle* is the distance from the center of the circle to any point on the circle.
- The *diameter (d) of a circle* is twice the radius.

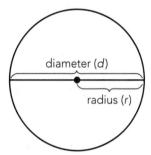

Figure 10.15 A circle.

- The *area* (A) *of a circle* is equivalent to πr^2. So, the area of a circle with a radius of 3 is $3^2\pi$, or 9π.
- The *circumference* (C) *of a circle* is equivalent to $2\pi r$ or πd. So, the circumference of a circle with a radius of 3 is $2\pi 3$, or 6π.
- The *equation of a circle* centered at the point (*h,k*) is $(x - h)^2 + (y - k)^2 = r^2$, where *r* is the radius of the circle.
- The complete *arc* of a circle has 360°.

Three-Dimensional Figures

The following are properties of three-dimensional figures that are commonly tested on the GRE:

- The formula for the *volume* (V) of a rectangular solid is V = *lwh*, where *l* = length, *w* = width, and *h* = height, as shown in the following figure:

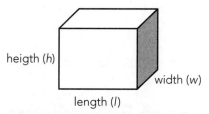

heigth (*h*)

width (*w*)

length (*l*)

Figure 10.16 A rectangular solid.

- The *surface area* of a rectangular solid is the sum of the area (*l* × *w*) of each of the six faces of the solid. Think of each face as a square or a rectangle.

Exercises: Geometry

These exercises are designed to help you apply the mathematics concepts just covered. They are not in GRE format, but should help you to identify your areas of strength and weakness.

Coordinate Geometry

These questions will test your knowledge of operations involving the equation and the slope of a line and distance and midpoint formulas.

Answer the following questions.

1. What is the *y*-intercept of the line with the equation $2y = 4x + 6$?

2. What is the slope of the line with the equation $3y = -2x + 5$?

3. What is the slope of the line $x = 4$?

4. What is the equation of a line parallel to $y = 4x - 12$ that crosses the *y*-axis at 3?

5. What is the equation of a line perpendicular to $3x = 2 - y$ with the *y*-intercept 8?

6. What is the distance between the points $(3, -4)$ and $(9, 4)$?

7. Solve for *y* if the distance between the two points $(2, 8)$ and $(-6, y)$ is 17.

8. What is the midpoint between (12,5) and (10,−7)?

9. Solve for x if the midpoint between the two points $(x,1)$ and $(−2, −3)$ is $(5,−1)$.

10. What is the distance between the points (0,5) and (5,0)?

Properties and Relations of Plane Figures

These questions will test your knowledge of operations involving plane figures.

Answer the following questions.

1. What is the hypotenuse of a right triangle with a base of 9 cm and an area of 54 cm²?

2. What is the area of a circle with a circumference of 14π inches?

3. If one of the angles of a parallelogram measures 35°, what is the sum of the remaining angles?

4. A trapezoid has one base of 8 ft, a height of 3 ft, and an area of 30 ft². What is the length of the other base?

5. A polygon with four sides and four right angles has one side of 6 mm. If the area of the polygon is 42 mm², would the polygon be considered a square or a rectangle?

Angles, Parallel Lines, and Perpendicular Lines

These questions will test your knowledge of operations involving angles, parallel lines, and perpendicular lines.

Answer the following questions.

1. What is the measure of the angle that is supplementary to a 40° angle?

2. What is the measure of the angle that is complementary to a 25° angle?

3. In the figure below, line n is parallel to line m, and line p is parallel to line o. What is the measure of angle θ?

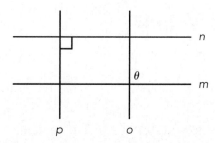

4. In the figure below, line *x* is parallel to line *y*. What is the measure of angle *a*?

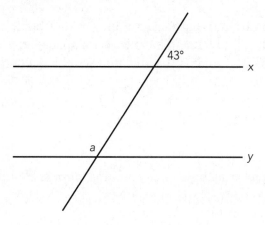

5. In the figure below, line *t* is parallel to line *u*, and line *v* is perpendicular to line *u*. What is the measure of angle *a*?

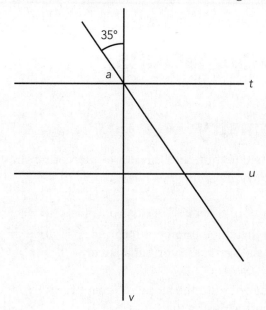

Perimeter, Area, and Volume

These questions will test your knowledge of operations involving perimeter, area, and volume.

Answer the following questions.

1. You are applying fertilizer to your backyard. The rectangular yard measures 40 feet wide and 70 feet long. You use 6 pounds of fertilizer to treat 700 square feet. The fertilizer comes in 8-pound bags. How many bags of fertilizer will you need to complete the job?

2. John is building a circular fence around his circular pool. The pool is 26 feet in diameter. If John wants to have 4 feet of space between the edge of the pool and the fence, what is the area that will be encompassed by the fence? ($\pi = 3.14$)

3. Tiffany inflates a beach ball. If the diameter of the ball is 0.6 m, what is its volume?

4. A cylindrical can of pineapple juice contains 350π cm³ of liquid. If the can is $\frac{14}{\pi}$ cm tall, what is its diameter?

5. If a square prism has an edge of 5 inches, what is the volume of the square?

Answers and Explanations

Coordinate Geometry

1. First, rearrange the equation into the slope-intercept form by isolating y on the left side; divide both sides by 2:

   $$y = 2x + 3$$

   You know that in the slope intercept formula, $y = mx + b$, b is the y-intercept. Because $b = 3$, the correct answer is 3.

2. Rearrange the equation into the slope intercept form by isolating y on the left side; divide both sides by 3:

   $$y = -\frac{2}{3x} + \frac{5}{3}$$

You know that in the slope intercept formula, $y = mx + b$, m is the slope. Because $m = -\frac{2}{3}$, the correct answer is $-\frac{2}{3}$.

3. This equation represents a vertical line; the y-intercept is 0, so the line is parallel to the y-axis. A vertical line has an undefined slope, because the denominator is 0.

4. For two lines to be parallel, their slopes must be equal; therefore, in the standard equation $y = mx + b$, $m = 4$. You are given that the line crosses the y-axis at 3, so the y-intercept (b) must be 3. If you substitute 4 for m and 3 for b in the standard equation, you get $y = 4x + 3$.

5. First, rearrange the equation into slope-intercept form, by subtracting $3x$ and $-y$ from both sides:

$$y = -3x + 2$$

For two lines to be perpendicular, their slopes must be negative reciprocals. The negative reciprocal of -3 is $\frac{1}{3}$. The problem also states that the perpendicular line has a y-intercept of 8. If you substitute $\frac{1}{3}$ for m and 8 for b in the standard equation, you get $y = \frac{1}{3}x + 8$.

6. Use the Distance Formula to solve this problem. Substitute the given values of x and y into the formula to solve for the distance, as follows:

$$\text{Distance} = \sqrt{(3 - 9)^2 + (-4 - 4)^2}$$
$$\text{Distance} = \sqrt{(6)^2 + (8)^2}$$
$$\text{Distance} = \sqrt{36 + 64}$$
$$\text{Distance} = \sqrt{100}$$
$$\text{Distance} = 10$$

7. Use the Distance Formula to solve this problem. Because you are given the distance between the points, your equation will look like this:

$$17 = \sqrt{(-6 - 2)^2 + (y_2 - 8)^2}$$

Square both sides and solve for y_2:

$$289 = (-8)^2 + (y_2 - 8)^2$$
$$289 = (64) + (y_2 - 8)^2$$
$$225 = (y_2 - 8)^2$$
$$15 = y_2 - 8$$
$$23 = y_2$$

8. Use the midpoint equation to solve this problem. First solve for the x-coordinate, which is half the distance between 12 and 10:

$$x_m = \frac{(x_2 + x_1)}{2}$$

$$x_m = \frac{(10 + 12)}{2}$$

$$x_m = \frac{22}{2}$$

$$x_m = 11$$

Do the same for y_m, which is half the distance between 5 and -7:

$$y_m = \frac{(y_2 + y_1)}{2}$$

$$y_m = \frac{(5 + -7)}{2}$$

$$y_m = \frac{-2}{2}$$

$$y_m = -1$$

Therefore, the midpoint is $(11, -1)$

9. You only have to solve for the x-coordinate because you are given the y-coordinate:

$$x_m = \frac{(x_2 + x_1)}{2}$$

$$5 = \frac{(-2 + x_1)}{2}$$

$$10 = -2 + x_1$$

$$12 = x_1$$

10. Use the Distance Formula to solve this problem. Substitute the given values of x and y into the formula to solve for the distance, as follows:

$$\text{Distance} = \sqrt{(x_2 - x_1)^2 + (y_2 - y_1)^2}$$

$$\text{Distance} = \sqrt{(5 - 0)^2 + (0 - 5)^2}$$

$$\text{Distance} = \sqrt{(5)^2 + (5)^2}$$

$$\text{Distance} = \sqrt{(25 + 25)}$$

$$\text{Distance} = \sqrt{50}, \text{ which can be reduced to } 5\sqrt{2}$$

Properties and Relations of Plane Figures

1. The area of a triangle and the length of one of the legs of a right triangle are given. However, you need the length of both legs to use the Pythagorean theorem to determine the hypotenuse. Since you have the

area, start there. For a triangle, $A = \frac{1}{2}$ (base) $\times$ (height). You are given the base and area, so solve for the height:

$$54 = \frac{1}{2} (9) \times (\text{height})$$
$$\text{height} = 12$$

Now you know the lengths of the two legs of the right triangle and can use the Pythagorean theorem ($a^2 + b^2 = c^2$) to determine the hypotenuse:

$$9^2 + 12^2 = c^2$$
$$81 + 144 = c^2$$
$$225 = c^2$$
$$15 = c. \text{ The hypotenuse is 15 cm.}$$

2. The equation for the area of a circle is $A = \pi r^2$. The equation for the circumference of a circle is $C = 2\pi r$. Since you are given the circumference, you can use that to find the radius, r, and then use the radius to find the area:

$$14\pi = 2\pi r$$
$$14 = 2r$$
$$r = 7$$

Now substitute r into the equation for area:

$$\text{Area} = \pi(7^2)$$
$$\text{Area} = 49\pi.$$

3. A parallelogram's angles add up to 360°. So simply subtract 35° from 360°: $360° - 35° = 325°$.

4. The equation for the area of a trapezoid is $A = \frac{1}{2}$ (base$_1$ + base$_2$) (height). Substitute the given variables into the equation and solve for the missing base:

$$30 = \frac{1}{2}(8 + \text{base}_2) (3)$$
$$20 = (8 + \text{base}_2)$$
$$\text{base}_2 = 12 \text{ ft}$$

5. A square is a special kind of rectangle. All of its sides are equal in length. Since the area of a rectangle is area $= l \times w$, the area of a square would be area $= s^2$ (side squared) because length and width are equal. For this problem, the given side is 6 mm. If the figure were a square, the area would be 36 mm². However, the area is said to be 42 mm². Therefore the shape is a rectangle and not a square.

Angles, Parallel Lines, and Perpendicular Lines

1. Supplementary angles add together to total 180°. Therefore, the supplementary angle to a 40° angle is a 140° angle.

2. Complementary angles add together to total 90°. Therefore, the complementary angle to a 25° angle is a 65° angle.

3. The answer is 90°. You are given that the angle formed by the intersection of line p and line n is a right angle, which is 90°. Since line o is parallel to line p, it will make the same angles as any line crossing line p. The same rule applies for line m and line n. Therefore, all of the angles on the diagram are equal to 90°.

4. The answer is 137°. The transversal crosses two parallel lines, so the angles made at the intersections will be identical. 43° corresponds to the complementary angle of a on line y. Since 43° and a are complementary angles, they must add up to 180°. Therefore, the answer is 137°.

5. The answer is 55°. Since line v is perpendicular to line t, it forms four right angles. Another line, which is unnamed in the diagram, dissects one of the right angles. Angle a is one side and 35° is the given measurement for the other side. These two angles are complementary because they must add up to 90°: 35° + 55° = 90°.

Perimeter, Area, and Volume

1. The question asks you to determine the number of bags of fertilizer that will cover your rectangular backyard. According to information in the problem, 6 pounds of fertilizer can cover 700 square feet. Calculate the area of the backyard. The area of a rectangle is determined by multiplying the length (70 feet) by the width (40 feet):

   $$70 \times 40 = 2,800$$

   The area of the backyard is 2,800 square feet. The problem states that 6 pounds of fertilizer can cover 700 square feet. Calculate the number of times that 700 will go into 2,800:

   $$2,800 \div 700 = 4$$

   You will need 4 times 6 pounds of fertilizer to treat 2,800 square feet:

   $$4 \times 6 = 24$$

Since you will need a total of 24 pounds of fertilizer to treat the backyard, and each bag of fertilizer weighs 8 pounds, divide 24 by 8 to find the number of bags of fertilizer you will need:

$$24 \div 8 = 3$$

You will need 3 bags of fertilizer to treat a backyard that measures 2,800 square feet.

2. If the pool has a diameter of 26 feet, and the fence needs to be two feet away from the edge of the pool, the diameter of the area enclosed by the fence would be 26 + 2 + 2 = 30 feet. Draw a picture to help visualize the problem:

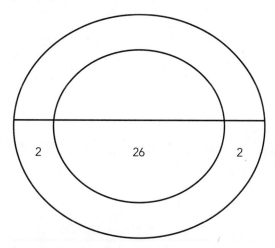

The area of a circle is πr^2. The radius is half of the diameter, so $r = 15$. Substitute 15 for r and 3.14 for π and solve:

Area = $(3.14)(15)^2$

Area = 706.5 ft^2

3. A beach ball is a sphere, and the equation for the volume of a sphere is $\left(\frac{4}{3}\right)\pi r^3$. The diameter is given as 0.6 m, so the radius is half of that, 0.3 m. Substitute that value into the equation and solve:

Volume = $\left(\frac{4}{3}\right)\pi(0.3^3)$

Volume = $\left(\frac{4}{3}\right)\pi(0.027)$

Volume = 0.036π m^3 or approximately 0.113 m^3

4. The equation for the volume of a cylinder is $\pi r^2 h$. The question is asking for diameter, so first solve for r, then double it.

    $$350 = \pi r^2\left(\frac{14}{\pi}\right)$$

    $$r^2 = 25 \text{ cm}$$

    $$r = 5 \text{ cm}$$

    Since the radius is 5 cm, the diameter is 10 cm.

5. The equation for the volume of a square prism is s^3. Since you are given a side (s) of 5, simply substitute 5 for s. The answer is 125 in^3.

Word Problems and Data Analysis

The GRE might test any of the previous concepts as word problems or data analysis questions. This section will give you some strategies for approaching these questions.

Word Problems

The following are concepts that are commonly tested in word problems (story problems) on the GRE:

- When solving word problems, translate the verbal statements into algebraic expressions. For example:

  "greater than," "more than," and "sum of" means addition (+)

  "less than," "fewer than," and "difference" means subtraction (−)

  "of" and "by" means multiplication (×)

  "per" means division (÷)

- Rate = Distance × Time. So, if you know that Jordan travels 50 miles per hour (Rate), you can calculate how long (Time) it would take him to travel 100 miles (Distance) as follows:

  $$100 = 50 \times \text{Time}$$

  $$\frac{100}{50} = \text{Time}$$

  $$2 = \text{Time}$$

- To calculate simple annual interest, multiply the principal × interest rate × time. For example, if you invest $10,000 at 6.0% for 1 year, you would earn $10,000 × 0.06 × 1, or $600 in interest during that year.

- If interest is compounded, interest must be computed on the principal as well as on interest that has already been earned.

- Apply logic and critical thinking to more easily solve word problems.

Data Analysis

Some of the information presented on the GRE will be in the form of charts, tables, and graphs.

Carefully read the labels on the tables, charts, or graphs. Make sure that you understand the relationships between the data represented in the tables, charts, or graphs before you answer the question.

For example, in the pie graph shown next, you should recognize that Miscellaneous funding, $x\%$, is less than 50% and less than 20% of the Total funding. A question might ask you to calculate the value of x as a percentage, and you might be able to quickly eliminate some incorrect answer choices. You should also remember that there are 360 degrees in a circle, because a question might ask you to calculate the value of *x* as the number of degrees it represents on the graph.

SOURCES OF SCHOOL FUNDING, 1997

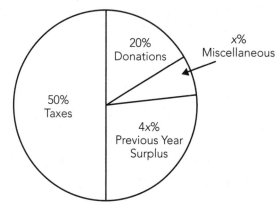

Figure 10.17 Sample pie graph.

Frequency distribution is often a more convenient way to express a set of measurements. A frequency distribution table or graph shows the frequency of occurrence of each value in the set. Following is an example of a frequency distribution table:

Rank	Degree of Agreement	Number of Students
1	Strongly agree	23
2	Somewhat agree	31
3	Somewhat disagree	12
4	Strongly disagree	7

Exercises: Word Problems and Data Analysis

These exercises are designed to help you apply the mathematics concepts just covered. They are not in GRE format, but should help you to identify your areas of strength and weakness in these areas.

Translating Word Problems

These questions will test your ability to locate relevant mathematical information in word problems.

Place an X next to the correct expression in the questions below.

1. Tom had 6 books. He gave 2 to his sister and then purchased 3 more books at the bookstore. Which of the following mathematical expressions is equivalent to the number of books that Tom now has?

    _____ $6 - 2 + 3$

    _____ $6 + 2 - 3$

    _____ $6(2 + 3)$

    _____ $6(2 - 3)$

2. Juan walked 3 more miles than Rebecca. Rebecca walked 4 times as far as William. William walked 2 miles. Which of the following mathematical expressions is equivalent to the number of miles Juan walked?

    _____ $3 \times 4 \times 2$

    _____ $(2 + 4) \times 3$

    _____ $4(2) + 3$

    _____ $4 + 3 + 2$

3. Tina goes to the store to purchase some CDs and DVDs. CDs cost $15 and DVDs cost $18. Which of the following expressions gives the total amount of money, in dollars, Tina will pay for purchasing 2 of the CDs and D of the DVDs?

    _____ $15 + D$

    _____ $30 + 18D$

    _____ $18 + D + 30$

    _____ $D(18 + 15)$

4. Mark is older than Frank, but younger than David. If m, f, and d represent the ages, in years, of Mark, Frank, and David, respectively, which of the following is true?

    _____ $d < f < m$

    _____ $f < m < d$

    _____ $d < m < f$

    _____ $f < d < m$

5. Kathy was twice as old as Jim 2 years ago. Today, Jim is j years old. In terms of j, how old was Kathy 2 years ago?

_____ $2(j - 2)$

_____ $2j - 2$

_____ $2(j + 2)$

_____ $j(2 + 2)$

Data Analysis

These questions will test your ability to interpret and analyze data presented in charts, tables, and graphs.

Answer the following questions.

Medals awarded to the 10 highest-ranked countries in the Winter Olympics in Torino, Italy, in 2006 were as shown:

Country	Gold Medals	Silver Medals	Bronze Medals
Germany	11	12	6
United States	9	9	7
Austria	9	7	7
Russian Federation	8	6	8
Canada	7	10	7
Sweden	7	2	5
Korea	6	3	2
Switzerland	5	4	5
Italy	5	0	6
France	3	2	4

1. How many more medals did Germany win than Korea?

2. What is the ratio of bronze to gold medals earned by Italy and France combined?

3. What percentage of all of the medals earned by the top 5 of these countries were silver medals (rounded to the nearest percent)?

Answers and Explanations

Word Problems

1. You are given that Tom started out with 6 books. After he gave 2 books to his sister he was left with 6 − 2 books. He then purchased 3 more books, so he now has 6 − 2 + 3 books.

2. To solve this problem, start with William and work backward. William walked 2 miles, and Rebecca walked 4 times as far as William. Therefore, Rebecca walked 4(2) miles. Juan walked 3 more miles than Rebecca, so Juan walked 4(2) + 3 miles.

3. The first step is to calculate the total cost of the CDs: 2(15) = 30. You are given that, in addition to the 2 CDs, Tina also purchases D of the DVDs, each of which cost $18. Therefore, her cost for the DVDs was 18D. Now simply add the terms together to get 30 + 18D.

4. You are given that Mark, m, is older than Frank, f. Therefore, $f < m$. You are also given that Mark, m, is younger than David, d. Therefore, $d > m$. Mark's age is between Frank and David's ages, so $f < m < d$

5. You are given that Jim is j years old today; therefore, 2 years ago Jim would have been $j − 2$ years old. At that time, Kathy was twice as old as Jim, or $2(j − 2)$.

Data Analysis

1. Germany won a total of 29 medals, while Korea won a total of 11 medals. Therefore, Germany won 18 (29 − 11) more medals than Korea.

2. In total, Italy and France earned 10 bronze and 8 gold medals. Therefore, the ratio of bronze medals to gold medals is 10:8, which simplifies to 5:4.

3. The top 5 countries were awarded 123 medals in all, 44 of which were silver medals. Therefore, the percentage of silver medals is $\frac{44}{123}$, or approximately 36%.

What's Next?

In our experience, those test-takers who internalize the basic math concepts will perform better on the GRE. When you can quickly recognize the concept being tested with a particular question, you can approach the question with confidence. Work through the simulated tests in Part IV and refer to this chapter as needed to review any math concepts with which you continue to struggle.

Basic GRE Verbal Review

The GRE Essay tasks—both the Issue and Argument tasks discussed in Chapter 7—require effective writing skills. In addition, each of the question types in the Verbal section—Reading Comprehension, Analogy, Antonym, Sentence Completion, and Text Completions with Two or Three Blanks—requires a basic understanding of the rules that govern standard written English. This chapter provides an overview of the rules of grammar and punctuation that you should understand for success on the GRE.

Grammar Rules

You should have a firm grasp of the following concepts:

- Subject/Verb Agreement
- Nouns and Pronouns
- Verbs and Verb Forms
- Sentence Construction

Subject/Verb Agreement

A well-constructed sentence contains a subject and a verb and expresses a complete thought. The *subject* indicates who or what the sentence is about. The *verb* tells you what is happening with the subject or the state of the subject.

Subjects and verbs are linked and must agree, meaning that they must match in form, according to person (first, second, or third) and number (singular or plural). Some complex sentences on the GRE try to conceal the subject, making identification of proper subject/verb agreement more of a challenge.

Person. A main verb must agree with the subject in person:

> *First Person*—**I am** eating lunch. **We left** the movie early.
>
> *Second Person*—**You are** eating lunch.
>
> *Third Person*—**She is** eating lunch. **He mowed** the lawn Tuesday. **It snows** often here in winter. **Someone is** paying for this mistake.

Number. A singular subject requires a singular verb.

> **Earth is** round.
>
> **One** of the boys **has** a dog.
>
> **Everyone thinks** that I will win.

A plural subject requires a plural verb.

> The **girls are** waiting for the bus.
>
> **Patricia and Janet enjoy** suspense novels.
>
> **Do football players like** classical music?

Voice. Voice defines whether the subject performs the action of the verb or receives the action of the verb. The active voice is usually the preferred mode of writing.

Active voice means that the subject is acting, as in the following sentence:

> The **dog licked** my brother.

Passive voice means that the subject is being acted upon, as in the following sentence:

> My brother **was licked** by the dog.

> **NOTE**
>
> Passive voice often appears as a present or past form of the verb *to be* (*am, are, is, was, were*) + past participle (*shot, laughed [at], interviewed, impressed*).

Tense. Verb *tense* provides you with information about when the action took place. Actions take place in the present, in the past, or in the future, as shown below:

Simple Present: The action takes place continuously or regularly (this tense has the sense that that action has taken place in the past and will continue taking place in the future): Robin **works** at the mall after school.

Present Perfect: The action began in the past and is ongoing: Robin **has worked** at the mall for the last two years.

Present Progressive: The action is ongoing *or* the action will take place in the near future: Robin **is working** today until six o'clock. Robin **is working** for her father this summer.

Simple Past: The action happened in the past: Robin **worked** at the mall last year.

Past Perfect: The action took place before another specified action: Robin **had worked** at the mall before taking a job at the theater.

Past Progressive: The action was ongoing in the past (and was interrupted): Robin **was working** when the tornado hit.

Future Tense: The action will take place in the future: Robin **will work** Tuesdays and Thursdays next semester.

Future Perfect: The action takes place in the past relative to a time in the future: Robin **will have worked** at the mall for two years as of next week.

Future Progressive: The action is ongoing relative to a time in the future: Robin **will be working** 40 hours per week by the end of the summer.

Nouns and Pronouns

English nouns can be categorized as *proper nouns*, which name specific people, places, objects, or ideas, or *common nouns*, which name nonspecific people, places, objects, or ideas. Proper nouns begin with an uppercase letter, and common nouns do not.

Pronouns take the place of either a proper or a common noun. Generally, a pronoun begins with an uppercase letter only if the pronoun begins a sentence. (The exception is *I*, which is always capitalized.) You should be able to determine and correctly apply pronoun case, as follows:

Nominative Case (renames the subject): *I, you, he, she, it, they, we*

Mandy recently graduated from college; **she** now has a degree in nursing.

NOTE

Use the *nominative* case of a personal pronoun with a compound subject. If the subject consists of one or more nouns it is a compound subject.

Alan and **I** worked together on the project.

She and Pamela have been friends for a long time.

Use the *nominative* case for a pronoun that is the subject of an incomplete clause. Completing the clause will lead you to the correct pronoun case.

No one in the classroom was as surprised as **I** (was).

He worked longer today than **she** (worked).

Possessive Case (shows possession): mine, ours, yours, his/hers, theirs

That one is John's plane ticket, and this one is **mine**.

NOTE

English possessive determiners (*my, our, your, his/her/its, their*—sometimes called possessive adjectives) must match the person and number of the possessor and not the noun phrase to which they are linked:

Richard likes **his** hot dogs with lots of relish. (The word *his* is third-person singular to match with Richard, NOT third-person plural [*their*] to match with hot dogs.)

Use a *possessive* determiner before a gerund. A *gerund* is a verb ending in *–ing* that can function as a noun.

Her singing has often been admired.

His studying for the exam shocked the class.

Objective Case (renames the object of a verb or preposition): me, us, you, him, her, it, them

The monkey made faces at **him** through the bars of the cage.

NOTE

Use the *objective* case when the pronoun is the object of a verb.

A large dog chased **me** down the road. (What/who was chased? Me.)

The teacher gave **him** and **her** passing grades. (To what/whom did the teacher give passing grades? To him and her.)

Use the *objective* case when the pronoun is the object of a preposition. A *preposition* is a word such as *from* or *before* that establishes a relationship between an object and some other part of the sentence, often expressing a location in place or time.

Matt received the greatest support from **you** and **me**.

The paper fluttered to the ground before **him**.

Relative Pronouns are used to identify people, places, and objects in general. The relative pronouns **who, whom,** and **whose** refer to people. The relative pronouns **which, what, that,** and **whose** refer to places and objects.

Indefinite Pronouns are used to represent an indefinite number of persons, places, or things. Indefinite pronouns are treated as singular pronouns. Following are some examples of indefinite pronouns:

Everyone gather around the campfire!

There will be a prize for **each** of the children.

One of my sisters always volunteers to drive me to school.

Some are friendlier than others.

Be sure to maintain consistency in pronoun person and number. It is not grammatically correct to use the plural pronoun *their* to represent neutral gender. This is an example of a major difference between standard written English and the English that we ordinarily use when speaking.

A **small child** should always be with **his or her** parent or guardian.

NOT A small child should always be with **their** parent or guardian.

Ambiguous or Misleading Pronouns

The noun that a pronoun renames or to which it refers is called its *antecedent*. If the antecedent is not clear, the pronoun can be ambiguous or misleading. To make the meaning clear, you may need to substitute the noun that the pronoun replaced. See the following examples:

Ambiguous Pronoun: Matt asked Phil if **he** could play first base.

- Who is going to play first base, Matt or Phil?

Correct Sentence: Matt asked Phil if **Phil** could play first base.

Ambiguous Pronoun: When Leanne hit the car door with her bicycle, she badly damaged **it**.

- In this sentence, it is unclear what was damaged, the car door or the bicycle.

Correct Sentence: When Leanne hit the car door with her bicycle, she badly damaged the **car door**.

Every pronoun must have a clear antecedent. A pronoun that lacks an antecedent can be confusing. To make the meaning clear, you may need to supply an antecedent. Here is an example:

Pronoun Lacking Antecedent: The two species are somehow related, but the nature of **it** has been a subject of intense debate.

- What is the antecedent of *it*? To make the meaning clear, you need to provide an antecedent.

Correct Sentence: The two species are somehow related, but the nature of **the relationship** has been a subject of intense debate.

Verbs and Verb Forms

A *verb* describes the action that is taking place in the sentence. All verbs have five principle forms:

Bare Form: I like to **write**. (In this sentence, tense is carried on *like*.)

Simple Present: I **write**.

Simple Past: I **wrote**.

Gerund: I am **writing**. (In this sentence, tense is carried on *am*.)

Past Participle: I have **written**. (In this sentence, tense is carried on *have*.)

Simple Past versus Past Participle. The *simple past* and *past participle* forms of verbs can sometimes be confusing. Most past participles are formed by adding *–ed* to the word, as shown in the examples below:

Simple Present Tense: We **move** often.

Past Participle Tense: We have **moved** again this year.

Remember that there are many irregular past participles in English—for example, *written, eaten, come, gone,* and so on.

Some verbs have *irregular simple past-tense* forms, as shown in the examples below:

Simple Present Tense: I **see** my best friend every day.

Simple Past Tense: I **saw** my best friend yesterday.

Simple Present Tense: My little sister **eats** her breakfast quickly.

Simple Past Tense: My little sister **ate** her breakfast quickly.

Remember that the perfect and progressive tenses include so-called helping or *auxiliary* verbs, as shown in the examples below:

Present Perfect: They **have** already **passed** Calculus II.

Past Perfect: I **had seen** my best friend the day before.

Present Progressive: My little sister **is eating** her breakfast quickly.

Past Progressive: The winds **were howling** loudly as the vinyl siding began flying off the house.

Sentence Construction

A well-written sentence is clear, balanced, and properly punctuated. Refer to the next sections for more information on how to construct a sentence.

Parallel Construction

Parallel construction, or *parallelism*, allows a writer to show order and clarity in a sentence or a paragraph by putting grammatical elements that have the same function in the same form. Parallelism creates a recognizable pattern within a sentence and adds unity, force, clarity, and balance to writing. All words, phrases, and clauses used in parallel construction must share the same grammatical form. We have included some examples of sentences that include faulty parallelism, followed by revised versions of each sentence:

Non-Parallel Construction: Patricia enjoyed **running** and **to ride** her bike.

- In this sentence, the verb forms do not match. The first of the two verbs is a gerund (*running*), and the second verb is in the infinitive form (*to ride*), which is composed of the particle *to* and the bare form of the verb.

Correct Sentence: Patricia enjoyed **running** and **riding** her bike.

Non-Parallel Construction: **The distance** from Los Angeles to Detroit is greater than Detroit to New York City.

- In this sentence, "The distance" links only with the first portion of the comparative construction "from Los Angeles to Detroit."

Correct Sentence: **The distance** from Los Angeles to Detroit is greater than **the distance** from Detroit to New York City.

Run-On Sentences

A *run-on sentence* is a sentence that is composed of more than one main idea, and does not use proper punctuation or connectors. Following are examples of run-on sentences along with suggested corrections:

Run-On Sentence: Janet is an actress **she** often appears in major network television shows.

Correct Sentence: Janet is an actress **who** often appears in major network television shows.

Run-On Sentence: My nephew loves to play **football, you** can find him on the practice field almost every day.

Correct Sentence: My nephew loves to play **football. You** can find him on the practice field almost every day.

Run-On sentences are often created by substituting a comma for a semicolon or a period. This is called a *comma splice*, and it is incorrect.

Sentence Fragments/Incomplete Sentences

A *sentence fragment* has end punctuation (so it appears as a sentence) but lacks one or more crucial features of a sentence (subject, verb, or predicate). Following are examples of sentence fragments along with suggested corrections:

Sentence Fragment: My car is difficult to start in the winter. Because of the cold weather.

Correct Sentence: My car is difficult to start in the winter because of the cold weather.

Sentence Fragment: John is a heavy eater. Two hot dogs for lunch and four for dinner.

Correct Sentence: John is a heavy eater who normally consumes two hot dogs for lunch and four for dinner.

Sentence fragments may lack a verb, as shown in the examples below:

Incomplete Sentence: Yesterday, the **winning** float in the parade.

- The sentence as it is written is incomplete; there is no main verb. The sentence should be revised so that the **winning float** either performs an action or has an action performed upon it.

Revised Sentence: Yesterday, the **winning float** in the parade **received** its prize.

Incomplete Sentence: **Releasing** personal information by many school districts to third parties.

- The sentence as it is written is incomplete; the gerund **releasing** is being used as a noun in this sentence. Add a verb with tense.

Revised Sentence: Many school districts **prohibit releasing** personal information to third parties.

Misplaced Modifiers

A sentence must contain at least one main clause. A complex sentence may contain more than one main clause, as well as one or more *relative clauses.* *Relative clauses* follow the nouns that they modify. In order to maintain clarity within a sentence, it is important to place a relative clause near the object that it modifies. A *modifier* is a word, phrase, or clause that modifies, or changes, the meaning of another word or part of the sentence. Often, a modifier helps explain or describe who, when, where, why, how, and to what extent. Misplaced modifiers can inadvertently change the meaning of the sentence. We have included some examples of sentences that contain misplaced modifiers, followed by revised versions of each sentence:

Misplaced Modifier: Cassie had trouble deciding which college to attend **at first.**

- The meaning of this sentence is obscured by the placement of the modifying clause **at first.** It is unlikely that the writer intended to suggest that Cassie was considering attending more than one college.

Correct Sentence: **At first**, Cassie had trouble deciding which college to attend.

Misplaced Modifier: **As a teacher**, the school board hired Mrs. Smith to coach our team.

- This sentence as it is written suggests that the school board, and not Mrs. Smith, is a teacher.

Correct Sentence: The school board hired Mrs. Smith, **a teacher**, to coach our team.

> **GRE Tip**
> Make sure that each sentence is clear so that you know exactly "who" is doing "what," "how" something happens, and so on.

Punctuation Rules

A properly punctuated sentence helps the reader understand the organization of the writer's ideas. You should be able to identify and correct errors involving the following punctuation marks:

- Commas [,]
- Apostrophes [']
- Colons [:] and Semicolons [;]
- Parentheses [( )] and Dashes [—]
- Periods [.], Question Marks [?], and Exclamation Points [!]

Commas

A comma is used to indicate a separation of ideas or of elements within a sentence.

Use a comma with a coordinating conjunction to separate independent clauses within a sentence. There are seven basic coordinating conjunctions in English:

1. Jenny sings in the choir, **and** she plays the guitar in a rock band.

2. Amanda enjoys her job, **but** she is looking forward to her vacation.

3. Either I will study mathematics, **or** I will study chemistry.

4. His mother doesn't eat meat, **nor** does she eat dairy products.

5. Jordan will be playing football this year, **for** he made the team.

6. Frank earned a promotion, **so** we decided to celebrate.

7. I just completed my workout, **yet** I'm not tired.

Use a comma to separate elements that introduce and modify a sentence.

Yesterday, I painted the entire garage.

Before deciding on a major at college, Rana discussed her options with her parents.

Use commas before and after a parenthetical expression. A parenthetical expression is a phrase that is inserted into the writer's train of thought. Parenthetical expressions are most often set off using commas.

Stephanie's decision, **in my opinion,** was not in her best interest.

The new park, **of course,** is a popular tourist destination.

Use a comma to separate an appositive from a clause. An appositive is a noun or phrase that renames the noun that precedes it.

My brother, **a well-respected scientist,** made an important discovery.

Mr. Smith, **the fifth grade math teacher,** was a favorite among the students.

Use commas to set off interjections.

Well, it's about time that you got here.

Say, did you pass your history test?

Use commas to separate coordinate adjectives. If two adjectives modify a noun in the same way, they are called coordinate adjectives. Coordinate adjectives can also be joined with the coordinating conjunction *and.*

We walked the **long, dusty** road to the abandoned farm.

OR We walked the **long and dusty** road to the abandoned farm.

Cows are **gentle, friendly** creatures.

OR Cows are **gentle and friendly** creatures.

Use commas to set off nonrestrictive phrases and clauses. A nonrestrictive phrase can be omitted from a clause without changing the meaning of the clause. Nonrestrictive clauses are useful because they can modify the nouns that they follow.

My sister's dog, **a brown and white terrier,** barks at me whenever I visit.

Katie celebrated her birthday, **which was in June,** with a party and a chocolate cake.

Use a comma to separate elements in a list or series.

Jill decided to purchase a **leash, a collar, and a water dish** for her dog.

Skippy **packed his suitcase, put on his jacket, and left the house.**

Use commas in dates, addresses, place names, numbers, and quotations.

Mary is leaving for Jamaica on **Monday, February 19, 2009**.

The Library of Congress is located at **101 Independence Avenue,**

Washington, D.C, U.S.A.

Forecasted annual earnings are currently **$42,521,000**.

"My sister is a nurse," Becky said proudly.

John replied, **"So where are we exactly?"**

"You'll soon regret this," Luc cautioned under his breath, **"for things are not as they seem."**

*Do **not** use a comma:*
  to separate a subject from a verb;

My cousin Mary walked down to the corner.

NOT My cousin **Mary, walked** down to the corner.

to separate an adjective from the word it modifies;

The pretty girl sat in front of me on the bus.

NOT The **pretty, girl** sat in front of me on the bus.

to separate two independent clauses; this is known as a comma splice.

I plan to attend a liberal arts college. My parents want me to get a well-rounded education.

NOT I plan to attend a liberal arts **college, my** parents want me to get a well-rounded education.

This sentence could be fixed by adding a conjunction, for example: "I plan to attend a liberal arts college, *as* my parents want me to get a well-rounded education."

Apostrophes

An apostrophe is used to form the possessive in nouns, to show the omission of letters in contractions, and to indicate plurals of letters and (as a matter of preference) numerals.

*Use an apostrophe with **s** to form the possessive of singular nouns, plural nouns that do not end in **s**, or indefinite pronouns that do not end in **s**.*

My **friend's** house is at the end of the street.

The **Women's** Society meets every Thursday at the high school.

Someone's bicycle is leaning against the building.

Use an apostrophe to form the possessive of plural nouns ending in s.

The **horses'** stalls were filled with straw.

I did not enjoy the **brothers'** rendition of my favorite song.

Use an apostrophe with the last noun in a series to indicate joint possession.

Frank and **Ruth's** anniversary is in September.

Roger, Clark, and **Mike's** proposal will certainly beat any other trio's (proposal).

Add an apostrophe to all nouns to indicate individual possession.

Brian's, Jason's, and Michael's computers were stolen.

Add an apostrophe to indicate contractions.

It's raining outside again. (It's = It is)

We're running against each other in the election. (We're = We are)

If **you're** going to the movie with me we should leave now. (you're = you are)

My cousin **should've** taken the bus. (should've = should have)

Didn't Kevin know that classes had begun? (Didn't = Did not)

Regrettably, I **won't** be able to attend the party. (won't = will not)

That'll break his heart! (That'll = That will)

Add an apostrophe to form the plural of letters and numbers.

Did you dot your *i's* and cross your *t's*?

There are a total of four **7's** in my phone number.

*Do **not** use apostrophes with possessive pronouns.*

The car with the flat tire is **ours**.

NOT The car with the flat tire is **our's**.

Yours is the dog that barks all night.

NOT **Your's** is the dog that barks all night.

My car has a dent in **its** door.

NOT my car has a dent in **it's** door.

Colons and Semicolons

A *colon* is used before a list or after an independent clause that is followed by information that directly modifies or adds to the clause. An independent clause can stand alone as a complete sentence. A *semicolon* is used to join closely related independent clauses when a coordinate conjunction is not used, with conjunctive adverbs to join main clauses, to separate items in a series that contains commas, and to separate coordinate clauses when they are joined by transitional words or phrases.

Use a colon before a list.

> We are required to bring the following items to camp: a sleeping bag, a pillow, an alarm clock, clothes, and personal care items.

Use a colon after an independent clause that is followed by information that directly modifies or adds to the clause.

> Jennifer encountered a problem that she had not anticipated: a power outage.
>
> My sister suggested a great location: the park down the street from our house.

Colons can be used before direct quotations, after salutations in business correspondence, and between titles and subtitles.

> Captain John Paul Jones said: "I have not yet begun to fight."
>
> Dear Mr. Smith:
>
> *Blaze: A Story of Courage*

Use a semicolon to join closely related independent clauses when a coordinate conjunction is not used.

> Jane starts a new job today; she is very excited.
>
> I don't understand the directions; my teacher must explain them to me.

Use a semicolon with conjunctive adverbs to join independent clauses.

> Martha is interested in taking the class; **however,** it does not suit her schedule.
>
> My brother is very tall; **in fact,** he is the tallest person in our family.

Use semicolons in a series to separate elements containing commas.

> The art museum contained some fragile, old oil paintings; bronze, plaster, and marble statues; and recently completed modern art pieces.
>
> My first meal at college consisted of cold, dry toast; runny, undercooked eggs; and very strong, acidic coffee.

Use a semicolon to separate coordinate clauses when they are joined by transitional words or phrases. When a sentence contains more than one clause, each of which is considered to be equally as important as the other, the clauses are called coordinate clauses. They are typically joined by a coordinating conjunction. When the coordinating conjunction is not used, a semicolon should be.

> My sister and I enjoyed the play; **afterward,** we stopped for an ice cream cone.

OR My sister and I enjoyed the play, **and afterward,** we stopped for an ice cream cone.

Betty often misplaces her keys; **perhaps** she should get a key locator.

OR Betty often misplaces her keys, **so perhaps** she should get a key locator.

Parentheses and Dashes

Parentheses are used to enclose supplemental information that is not essential to the meaning of the sentence. *Dashes* are used to place special emphasis on a word or phrase within a sentence.

Use parentheses to enclose explanatory or secondary supporting details.

In addition to serving as Class Treasurer (**a challenging job**), she was also a National Merit Scholar.

Alan visited the Football Hall of Fame (**after years of begging his parents**) during his summer vacation.

Use dashes in place of parentheses to place special emphasis on certain words or phrases.

Dr. Evans—**a noted scientist and educator**—spoke at our commencement ceremony.

The homecoming float—**a cobbled mess of wire and nails**—meandered dangerously down the street.

End Punctuation

Periods, *question marks*, and *exclamation points* are considered end punctuation, which means that they should be used at the end of a sentence.

Use a period to end most sentences.

Scott enrolled in classes at the university.

Mary wanted to know what John made for dinner.

Use a question mark to end a direct question.

Do you think it will rain today?

What is the shortest route to the stadium?

Use an exclamation point to end an emphatic statement.

Please don't leave your vehicle unattended!

Wow! What a huge trout!

Rhetoric

Rhetoric refers to the effective and persuasive use of language. Rhetorical skills, then, refer to your ability to make choices about the effectiveness and clarity of a word, phrase, sentence, or paragraph. Good writing involves effective word choice as well as clear and unambiguous expression. The best-written sentences are relevant based on the context of the paragraph, avoid redundancy, and clearly and simply express the intended idea.

Commonly Misused Words

Following is a list of some of the words that are commonly misused in writing, along with definitions and examples of the proper use of each word. When practicing your essay-writing skills, remember that appropriate word choice will garner more points.

Accept, Except

Accept is a verb that means "to agree to receive something."

Example: I could not pay for my purchases with a credit card because the store would only *accept* cash.

Except is either a preposition that means "other than, or but," or a verb meaning "to omit or leave out."

Example: *Except* for a B+ in history, Kate received all A's on her report card.

Affect, Effect

Affect is usually a verb meaning "to influence."

Example: Fortunately, Kylie's sore ankle did not *affect* her performance in the game.

Effect is usually a noun that "indicates or achieves a result." Effect is also sometimes used as a transitive verb meaning "to bring into existence," but it is generally not used in this way on the GRE.

Example: Studies have shown that too much exercise can have a negative *effect* on a person's health.

Among, Between

Among is used with more than two items.

Example: Jackie's performance last night was the best *among* all of the actors in the play.

Between is usually used with two items.

Example: Simon could not decide *between* the two puppies at the pound, so he adopted them both.

Assure, Insure, Ensure

Assure means "to convince" or "to guarantee" and usually takes a direct object.

Example: If we leave two hours early, I *assure* you that we will arrive at the concert on time.

Insure means "to guard against loss."

Example: Before he could leave for his trip, Steve had to *insure* his car against theft.

Ensure means "to make certain."

Example: Our company goes to great lengths to *ensure* that every product that leaves the warehouse is of the highest quality.

Because, Since

Because means "for the reason that."

Example: My sister was late for school *because* she missed the bus.

Since implies "time," either continuous or not, in addition to "reason."

Example: *Since* he lost the election, he has remained sequestered in his home.

It is important to note that in your writing, you should be aware of the subtle difference in meaning.

Compare to, Compare with

Compare to means "assert a likeness."

Example: The only way to describe her eyes is to *compare* them *to* the color of the sky.

Compare with means "analyze for similarities and differences."

Example: For her final project, Susan had to *compare* bike riding *with* other aerobic activities and report her findings.

Complement, Compliment

A *complement* is "something that completes or adds to" something else. *Complement* can also be used as a verb meaning "to complete."

Example: My favorite place to dine is on the terrace; the breathtaking views are the ideal *complement* to a romantic dinner.

A *compliment* is "flattery or praise." *Compliment* can also be used as a verb.

Example: Larry was thrilled when the award-winning author *complimented* him on his writing style.

Farther, Further

Farther refers to distance.

Example: At baseball camp, Jack learned that with the correct stance and technique, he could throw the ball *farther* this year than he could last year.

Further indicates "additional degree, time, or quantity." It can also be used as a verb.

Example: I enjoyed the book to a certain degree, but I felt that the author should have provided *further* details about the characters.

Example: Kim *furthered* her education by taking summer classes.

Fewer, Less

Fewer refers to units or individuals that can be counted.

Example: Trish received all the credit, even though she worked *fewer* hours on the project than did the other members of the group.

Less refers to mass or bulk that can't be counted.

Example: When it comes to reading, Mike is *less* inclined to read for pleasure than is Stephanie.

Imply, Infer

Imply means "to suggest."

Example: His sister did not mean to *imply* that he was incorrect.

Infer means "to deduce," "to guess," or "to conclude."

Example: She *inferred* from the professor's remarks that he admired Russian novels.

Its, It's

Its is the possessive form of "it."

Example: In the summer, my family enjoys drinking white tea for *its* refreshing, light flavor.

It's is the contraction of "it is."

Example: Fortunately for the runners, *it's* a sunny day.

Lay, Lie

Lay means "to put" or "to place," and requires a direct object to complete its meaning.

Example: To protect your floor or carpet, you should always *lay* newspaper or a sheet on the ground before you begin to paint a room.

Lie means "to recline, rest, or stay," or "to take a position of rest." This verb cannot take a direct object. The past tense of *lie* is *lay*, so use extra caution if you see these words on the GRE.

Example: On sunny days, our lazy cat will *lie* on the porch and bask in the warmth of the sunlight.

Example: Yesterday, our lazy cat *lay* in the sun for most of the afternoon.

Like, Such As

Like indicates similarity.

Example: Kate and Allie were very close, *like* two peas in a pod.

Such as indicates an example or examples.

Example: Composers *such as* Mozart and Bach are among my favorites.

Number, Amount

Number is used when the items can be counted.

Example: The *number* of students enrolled at Valley College has increased during the last 5 years.

Amount denotes quantity.

Example: A small *amount* of rain has fallen so far this year.

Precede, Proceed

Precede means "to go before."

Example: When I go to an expensive restaurant, I expect a salad course to *precede* the main course.

Proceed means "to move forward."

Example: As a result of failed negotiations, the labor union announced its plan to *proceed* with a nationwide strike.

Principal, Principle

Principal is a noun meaning "the head of a school or an organization."

Example: A high school *principal* is responsible not only for the educational progress of his students, but also for their emotional well-being.

Principal can also mean "a sum of money."

Example: I hope to see a 30 percent return on my invested *principal* within the first two years.

Principal can also be used as an adjective to mean "first" or "leading."

Example: Our *principal* concern is the welfare of our customers, not the generation of profits.

Principle is a noun meaning "a basic truth or law."

Example: A study of basic physics will include Newton's *principle* that every action has an opposite and equal reaction.

Set, Sit

The verb *set* takes an object.

Example: I *set* the bowl of pretzels in the middle of the table so that everyone could reach it.

The verb *sit* does not take an object.

Example: When I dine alone, I always *sit* by the window so that I can watch all the people who pass by the restaurant.

Than, Then

Than is a conjunction used in comparison.

Example: Rana made fewer mistakes during her presentation *than* she thought she would make.

Then is an adverb denoting time.

Example: Mandy updated her resume and *then* applied for the job.

That, Which

That is used to introduce an essential clause in a sentence. Commas are not required before the word "that."

Example: I usually take the long route because the main highway *that* runs through town is always so busy.

Which is best used to introduce a clause containing nonessential and descriptive information. A comma is required before *which* if is used in this way. *Which* can also be used to introduce an essential clause in order to avoid repeating the word *that* in the sentence.

Example: The purpose of the Civil Rights Act of 1991, *which* amended the original Civil Rights Act of 1964, was to strengthen and improve federal civil rights laws.

Example: I gave Mandy that book *which* I thought she might like.

There, Their, They're

There is an adverb specifying location.

Example: Many people love to visit a big city, but few of them could ever live *there*.

Their is a possessive pronoun.

Example: More employers are offering new benefits to *their* employees, such as day-care services and flexible scheduling.

They're is a contraction of "they are."

Example: *They're* hoping to reach a decision by the end of the day.

To, Too, Two

To has many different uses in the English language, including the indication of direction and comparison. It is also used as an infinitive in verb phrases.

Example: Mary is driving *to* the beach tomorrow.

Example: Jill's painting is superior *to* Alan's painting.

Example: I try *to* run three miles every day.

Too generally means "in addition," or "more than enough."

Example: It is important that we consider Kara's opinion, *too*.

Example: Yesterday, I ran *too* far and injured my foot.

Two is a number.

Whether, If

Whether should be used when listing alternatives.

Example: Traci could not decide *whether* to order to fish or the chicken.

If should be used when referring to a future possibility.

Example: *If* Traci orders the fish, she will be served more quickly.

Your, You're

Your is a possessive pronoun.

Example: Sunscreen protects *your* skin from sun damage.

You're is a contraction of "you are."

Example: When *you're* at the beach, always remember to wear sunscreen.

What's Next?

Now that you have reviewed the grammar rules included in this chapter, you might decide to focus on improving your own speaking and writing where applicable. We've found that the GRE test-takers who do the best on the GRE Verbal and Writing sections are those who have internalized the rules and can simply recognize correct English by its "sound." You should practice using proper English in your daily life to supplement the practice testing that you'll do; this will pay off in ways far beyond an improved GRE score.

PART IV

Practicing for the GRE General Test

12

GRE Practice Test 1

CHAPTER GOALS

- Take a simulated full-length GRE under actual test conditions.
- Check your results using the Answer Key.
- Review the explanations for each question, focusing particularly on questions you answered incorrectly or did not answer at all.
- Build your test-taking confidence.

The simulated GRE in this chapter contains 58 multiple-choice questions and two essay tasks, divided into four main sections. You should allow approximately 2 hours and 30 minutes to complete the test.

Each of the test sections should be completed in the time indicated at the beginning of the sections, and in the order in which they appear.

There are several different types of questions within each section. Make sure that you read and understand all directions before you begin. To achieve the best results, time yourself strictly on each section.

You should answer each question before you move on to the next question to make this simulated test as much like the actual CAT as possible. Remember to circle your answers on the test so that you can compare your answers to the correct answers listed in the Answer Key on page 301. Carefully review the explanations for any question that you answered incorrectly.

We suggest that you make this practice test as much like the real test as possible. Find a quiet location, free from distractions, and make sure that you have pencils and a timepiece.

Review the Scoring Guidelines on page 302, but remember that your score on the actual GRE will be dependent on many factors, including your level of preparedness and your fatigue level on test day.

SECTION 1—ISSUE TASK

45 Minutes

1 Question

You will have 45 minutes to select one topic, organize your thoughts, and compose a response that represents your point of view on the topic that you choose. Do not respond to any topic other than the one you select; a response to any other topic will receive a score of 0.

You will be given a choice between two general issues on a broad range of topics. You will be required to discuss your perspective on one of the issues, using examples and reasons drawn from your own experiences and observations.

Use scratch paper to organize your response before you begin writing. Write your response on the pages provided, or type your response using a word processor with the spell and grammar check functions turned off.

<u>Directions:</u> Present your viewpoint on *one* of the claims made below. Use relevant reasons and examples to support your point of view.

Topic 1

"Leaders should focus more on the needs of the majority than on the needs of the minority."

Topic 2

"The study of mathematics has value only to the extent that it is relevant in our daily lives."

SECTION 2—ARGUMENT TASK

30 Minutes

1 Question

You will have 30 minutes to organize your thoughts and compose a response that critiques the given argument. Do not respond to any topic other than the one given; a response to any other topic will receive a score of 0.

You are not being asked to discuss your point of view on the statement. You should identify and analyze the central elements of the argument, the underlying assumptions that are being made, and any supporting information that is given. Your critique can also discuss other information that would strengthen or weaken the argument or make it more logical.

Use scratch paper to organize your response before you begin writing. Write your response on the pages provided, or type your response using a word processor with the spell and grammar check functions turned off.

<u>Directions:</u> Critique the reasoning used in the following argument.

The following appeared as part of an article in a health and fitness magazine.

"Several volunteers participated in a study of consumer responses to the new Exer-Core exercise machine. Every day for a month, they worked out on the machine for 30 minutes in addition to maintaining their normal fitness regime. At the end of that month, most of the volunteers reported a significant improvement in both their stamina and muscle condition. Therefore, it appears that the Exer-Core exercise machine is truly effective in improving a person's overall general health and fitness."

SECTION 3—VERBAL

30 Minutes

30 Questions

This section consists of five different types of questions: Sentence Completion, Analogy, Antonym, Text Completion with Two or Three Blanks (this is a new question type; you will typically see only one of these questions on your GRE), and Reading Comprehension. To answer the questions, select the best answer from the answer choices given. Circle the letter or word(s) of your choice.

Directions for Sentence Completion Questions: The following sentences each contain one or two blanks, indicating that something has been left out of the sentence. Each answer choice contains one word or a set of words. Select the word or set of words that, when inserted in the blank(s), best fits the context of the sentence.

Example: Because of his --------, Brian's guests felt very welcome and comfortable staying at his house for the weekend.

    (A) animosity

    (B) hospitality

    (C) determination

    (D) wittiness

    (E) severity

Directions for Analogy Questions: The following questions contain a set of related words in capital letters and five answer choices. Each answer choice also contains a set of words. Select the set of words that represents a relationship similar to the original set of words.

Example: APPRENTICE : PLUMBER ::

    (A) player : coach

    (B) child : parent

    (C) student : teacher

    (D) author : publisher

    (E) intern : doctor

<u>Directions for Antonym Questions:</u> The following questions contain a word in capital letters and five answer choices. Each answer choice contains a word or phrase. Select the word or phrase that best expresses a meaning opposite to the word in capital letters.

Example: CREDULOUS:

(A) skeptical

(B) naive

(C) spontaneous

(D) sensitive

(E) discrete

<u>Directions for Text Completion with Two or Three Blanks Questions:</u> These questions consist of a short passage with two or three numbered blanks, indicating that something has been left out of the text. Select the word or set of words that, when inserted in the blanks, best completes the text.

Example: Experts believe that humans have ten trillion cells in their bodies that (i) _____ any number of essential genetic elements; scientists often marvel at what incredible (ii) _____ would ensue should the cells become jumbled or misunderstand their purpose.

Blank (i)	Blank (ii)
govern	order
organize	method
dislocate	chaos

<u>Directions for Reading Comprehension Questions:</u> The passages in this section are followed by several questions. The questions correspond to information that is stated or implied in the passage. Read the passage and choose the best answer for each question.

Answer the questions in the order presented.

The Verbal section questions begin on the next page.

1. MEDICINE : DOSE ::

    (A) surgeon : scalpel

    (B) paper : ream

    (C) treatment : hospital

    (D) ocean : water

    (E) office : decor

2. ACCEPT : DEMUR ::

    (A) enact : revoke

    (B) deny : repel

    (C) mute : dispel

    (D) despise : annoy

    (E) reject : disdain

3. In addition to advising the school newspaper staff, Mr. Mathison also regularly -------- the junior class regarding community service opportunities.

    (A) rallied against

    (B) counseled

    (C) argued with

    (D) suppressed

    (E) emulated

4. I could barely follow the -------- story line; the numerous twists and turns in the plot made it extremely hard to comprehend.

    (A) convoluted

    (B) unambiguous

    (C) conventional

    (D) resolute

    (E) dependable

5. GLACIER : ICE ::

    (A) beach : sand

    (B) mountain : clouds

    (C) ship : harbor

    (D) hammer : chisel

    (E) novel : characters

6. CAPRICIOUS:

    (A) dogmatic

    (B) eccentric

    (C) steadfast

    (D) poignant

    (E) raucous

7. GLIB:

    (A) pugnacious

    (B) gleeful

    (C) guileless

    (D) punctilious

    (E) flippant

8. COLLUSION : FRAUD ::

    (A) dissident : friend

    (B) eccentricity : normalcy

    (C) enigma : mistake

    (D) diatribe : insult

    (E) surplus : debit

9. INSULAR:

   (A) insolvent

   (B) cosmopolitan

   (C) ominous

   (D) biased

   (E) perceptible

10. PLETHORA:

   (A) rhetoric

   (B) presumption

   (C) mutiny

   (D) deficiency

   (E) figment

11. MALEVOLENT:

   (A) marred

   (B) meticulous

   (C) magnanimous

   (D) malcontent

   (E) malignant

12. DISCONCERTED:

   (A) composed

   (B) miserly

   (C) relentless

   (D) sheepish

   (E) perturbed

13. REVIVE : EXHAUSTED ::

   (A) reward : superior

   (B) refer : adjacent

   (C) replace : lost

   (D) rejuvenate : drained

   (E) resume : interrupted

14. Some teachers complained that the school board was --------, focusing on short-term goals while ignoring the long-term benefits of classroom reorganization.

   (A) ambiguous

   (B) myopic

   (C) perceptive

   (D) discerning

   (E) replete

15. The apparent rigidity of military discipline often (i) _____ the surprising level of independent thinking expected of the modern officer. Combat situations often (ii) _____ spur-of-the-moment decisions.

Blank (i)	Blank (ii)
belies	defy
impinges	discourage
supplants	mandate
negates	banish
mitigates	emulate

16. Certain members of my family continued to lead -------- lives, often indulging in wild and -------- behavior.

   (A) chaotic . . impulsive

   (B) temperate . . frenzied

   (C) moderate . . destructive

   (D) arbitrary . . leisurely

   (E) boisterous . . unpretentious

Questions 17 and 18 are based on the following passage.

The Lincoln Memorial, located on the National Mall in Washington, D.C., is one of the most profound symbols of American democracy in the world. Dedicated in 1922, it won the prestigious Gold Medal of the American Institute of Architects for its architect, Henry Bacon. The physical presence of the memorial is awe inspiring. There are a total of 36 Doric columns around the building, each representing one of the 36 states of the union at the time of Lincoln's death in 1865. Stones from various states were used in the construction of the memorial. The names of the 48 states in the Union at the time of the memorial's completion are carved on the outside walls. The north wall of the Lincoln Memorial boasts the sixteenth president's second inaugural address, while on the south wall, the Gettysburg Address is proudly carved. Above the statue of Abraham Lincoln are these words: "In this Temple, as in the hearts of the people for whom he saved the Union, the memory of Abraham Lincoln is enshrined forever."

17. The word *boasts* (line 9) most nearly means

   (A) to possess

   (B) to construct

   (C) to brag

   (D) to dedicate

   (E) to inaugurate

18. The passage suggests that the author would be most likely to agree with which of the following statements?

   (A) The Lincoln Memorial was constructed at a time when little was known about architecture.

   (B) The true meaning of the Lincoln Memorial is obscured by its architecture.

   (C) Most people who visit the Lincoln Memorial are unaware of its importance.

   (D) Since the completion of the Lincoln Memorial, few other memorials have been built that match its quality.

   (E) The size and significance of the Lincoln Memorial are equally impressive.

19. TACIT : EXPLICIT ::

    (A) lucid : muddled

    (B) negligible : obedient

    (C) odious : intact

    (D) pedantic : curious

    (E) wily : expert

20. Her disheveled clothing and -------- hair surprised me; Amanda's appearance is normally very polished and chic.

    (A) orderly

    (B) capacious

    (C) unkempt

    (D) formal

    (E) striking

Questions 21–24 are based on the following passage.

Human reliance on information technology today is quickly becoming global. The
Line technological developments in the areas of computing, networking, and software
engineering have aided the transitions from paper to paperless transactions, and
text and data media to multimedia. Today, speed, efficiency, and accuracy in the
(5) exchange of information have become primary tools for increasing productivity
and innovation. Activities as diverse as health care, education, and manufacturing
have come to depend on the generation, storage, and transmission of electronic
information. Computers are not only used extensively to perform the industrial and
economic functions of society but are also used to provide many services upon which
(10) human life depends. Medical treatment, air traffic control, and national security are
a few examples. Even a small glitch in the operation of these systems can put human
lives in danger. Computers are also used to store confidential data of a political,
social, economic, or personal nature. This fairly recent and progressive dependence
on computer technology signals a real danger for the human race.
(15)   Current computer systems offer new opportunities for lawbreaking and
the potential to commit traditional types of crimes in nontraditional ways. For
example, the threat of identity theft is magnified by our reliance on computers to
assist us in everyday activities such as shopping and paying bills. Identity theft
refers to all types of crime in which someone wrongfully obtains and uses another
(20) person's personal data by way of fraud or deception, typically for economic gain.
By making personal and credit information available on the Internet, people open
themselves up to the possibility of a criminal obtaining this information and
using it for nefarious purposes. This is but one instance of the negative impact
that overreliance on computer technology can have on society.

(25)   As humans continue to make technological advances, so too do they rely more heavily upon those innovations. This is a dangerous progression that must be tempered with common sense and self-restraint. We cannot allow computer technology to control too many aspects of our lives, lest we become victims of our own ingenuity.

21. The primary purpose of the passage is to

    (A) challenge a commonly held belief regarding identity fraud

    (B) discuss some potentially devastating effects of our dependence on computers

    (C) suggest ways in which the human race can reduce its dependence on technology

    (D) evaluate the pros and cons of computer technology

    (E) defend a controversial perspective on the transmission of electronic data

22. The author most likely uses the phrase "a small glitch" (line 11) in order to

    (A) acknowledge the fact that human reliance on computer technology is completely safe

    (B) emphasize the idea that it is dangerous for humans to rely so heavily on computer technology

    (C) cast doubt on the accuracy of any personal data collected on the Internet by criminals

    (D) criticize human technological advances in the areas of education, medicine, and national security

    (E) disprove the theory that computer technology is unnecessary for human advancement

23. The passage suggests that the author would be most likely to agree with which of the following statements?

   (A) Human dependence on computer technology has never been known to advance the species.

   (B) Human dependence on computer technology should never be allowed under any circumstances.

   (C) Human dependence on computer technology is a key component in the advancement of the species.

   (D) Human dependence on computer technology cannot be accurately measured.

   (E) Human dependence on computer technology can sometimes have a negative impact on society.

24. Each of the following is mentioned in the passage as a potential danger resulting from greater reliance on computer technology EXCEPT:

       I. The transmission of electronic data
       II. Increased opportunity for criminal activity
       III. A drastic reduction in national security

   (A) I only

   (B) I and II only

   (C) I and III only

   (D) II and III only

   (E) I, II, and III

Questions 25 and 26 are based on the following passage.

This passage is adapted from *The American Republic: Constitution, Tendencies, and Destiny* by O. A. Brownson, © 1866.

Line
(5)
(10)

The ancients summed up the whole of human wisdom in the maxim "Know Thyself," and certainly there is for an individual no more important and no more difficult knowledge, than knowledge of himself. Nations are only individuals on a larger scale. They have a life, an individuality, a reason, a conscience, and instincts of their own, and have the same general laws of development and growth, and, perhaps, of decay, as the individual man. Equally important, and no less difficult than for the individual, is it for a nation to know itself, understand its own existence, its own powers and faculties, rights and duties, constitution, instincts, tendencies, and destiny. A nation has a spiritual as well as a material existence, a moral as well as a physical existence, and is subjected to internal as well as external conditions of health and virtue, greatness and grandeur, which it must in some measure understand and observe, or become lethargic and infirm, stunted in its growth, and end in premature decay and death.

Among nations, no one has more need of full knowledge of itself than the United States, and no one has, to this point, had less. It has hardly had a distinct
(15) consciousness of its own national existence, and has lived the naive life of the child, with no severe trial, till the recent civil war, to throw it back on itself and compel it to reflect on its own constitution, its own separate existence, individuality, tendencies, and end. The defection of the slaveholding States, and the fearful struggle that has followed for national unity and integrity, have
(20) brought the United States at once to a distinct recognition of itself, and forced it to pass from thoughtless, careless, heedless, reckless adolescence to grave and reflecting manhood. The nation has been suddenly compelled to study itself, and from now on must act from reflection, understanding, science, and statesmanship, not from instinct, impulse, passion, or caprice, knowing well what it does, and
(25) why it does it. The change that four years of civil war have wrought in the nation is great, and is sure to give it the seriousness, the gravity, and the dignity it has so far lacked.

25. Which of the following statements best summarizes the main point of the first paragraph?

   (A) Understanding one's own strengths and weaknesses is a difficult yet important task, not only for individuals, but for nations as a whole.

   (B) The spirituality of individuals should be dictated by the nation's government.

   (C) The comparing of a nation to a person is inaccurate and leads only to confusion and misrepresentation.

   (D) The United States was founded upon a principle of law that originated from the ancient world.

   (E) A nation's moral existence is governed by external conditions only.

26. The author's argument is developed primarily by the use of

   (A) an example of one nation's success

   (B) an analogy between man and nation

   (C) a critique of the United States Constitution

   (D) a warning against civil war

   (E) a personal account of self-realization

27. The editors of the magazine are often criticized for the -------- of their opinion column, which frequently -------- from one side of an issue to the other.

    (A) monotony . . continues

    (B) ingenuity . . settles

    (C) unpredictability . . scuttles

    (D) inconsistency . . vacillates

    (E) rigidity . . dithers

28. DEPLORABLE:

    (A) eligible

    (B) acceptable

    (C) irreproachable

    (D) reprehensible

    (E) intractable

29. CIRCUMSPECT:

    (A) intricate

    (B) reckless

    (C) dissonant

    (D) formative

    (E) prudent

30. RESERVOIR : LAKE ::

    (A) dam : river

    (B) hub : wheel

    (C) canal : waterway

    (D) bank : stream

    (E) window : door

END OF SECTION 3

SECTION 4—QUANTITATIVE

30 Minutes

28 Questions

This section includes three types of questions: Quantitative Comparison, Discrete Problem Solving, and Numeric Entry. For each question, circle the letter of your choice or write your answer as instructed.

General Information:

Numbers: All of the numbers used in this section are real numbers.

Figures: Assume that the position of all points, angles, etc., are in the order shown and the measures of angles are positive.

Straight lines can be assumed to be straight.

All figures lie in a plane unless otherwise stated.

The figures given for each question provide information to solve the problem. The figures are not drawn to scale unless otherwise stated. To solve the problems, use your knowledge of mathematics; do not estimate lengths and sizes of the figures to answer questions.

Directions for Quantitative Comparison Questions: Some of the following questions give you two quantities, one in Column A and one in Column B. Compare the two quantities and choose one of the following answer choices:

A if the quantity in Column A is greater;

B if the quantity in Column B is greater;

C if the two quantities are equal;

D if you cannot determine the relationship based on the given information.

Do not mark answer choice E, as there are only four choices from which to choose.

Note: Information and/or figures pertaining to one or both of the quantities may appear above the two columns. Any information that appears in both columns has the same meaning in Column A and in Column B.

Example: | **Column A** | **Column B**
| $-(3)^4$ | $(-3)^4$

Directions for Discrete Problem Solving Questions: Select the best answer for the remaining multiple-choice questions.

Example: If $y = 5x$ and $z = 3y$, then in terms of x, $x + y + z =$

       (A) $21x$

       (B) $16x$

       (C) $15x$

       (D) $9x$

       (E) $8x$

Directions for Numeric Entry Questions: Enter your answer in the box below the question.

Example: Solve the equation for x: $2(x - 3) + 9 = 4x - 7$

$x = $ ☐

Answer the questions in the order presented.

The Quantitative section questions begin on the next page.

<u>Column A</u>	<u>Column B</u>

An entire 5-pound bag of flour is to
be divided equally among 3 students
in a home economics class.

1.	$\dfrac{11}{2}$	The number of pounds of flour that each of the students will receive.

$a > 0$

2.	$(\sqrt{a})^2$	$\sqrt{a^2}$

x is an integer greater than 1.

3.	$\dfrac{1}{x} - \dfrac{1}{2}$	$\dfrac{1}{2}$

4.	The increase in the area of a circle C when its radius is increased by 1 inch.	The increase in the area of a circle R when its radius is increased by 1 inch.

5. If Jason traveled 30 miles in 6 hours and Katie traveled three times as far in half the time, what was Katie's average speed, in miles per hour?

    (A) 5

    (B) 15

    (C) 30

    (D) 45

    (E) 90

6. If $r = -2$ and $p < 0$, which of the following has the least value?

    (A) $4pr^2$

    (B) $2pr^3$

    (C) $-2pr^4$

    (D) $-4pr^5$

    (E) $-6pr^6$

Column A	**Column B**

$$2a + 15 = 4a - 1$$

7. $2a$ 14

$$(x + 2)(x - 3) < 0$$

8. 3 x

Andrew has d dollars in a savings account.

$$d > 0$$

9. Twice the number of 200d
dollars that Andrew has
in his account.

10. Rectangle *PQRS* lies in the *xy*-coordinate plane so that its sides are *not* parallel to the axes. What is the product of the slopes of all four sides of rectangle *PQRS*?

(A) −2

(B) −1

(C) 0

(D) 1

(E) 2

Column A	**Column B**

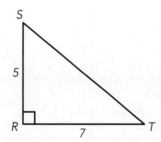

11. The length of *ST* 9

12. All numbers divisible by both 3 and 8 are also divisible by which one of the following numbers?

   (A) 5

   (B) 6

   (C) 9

   (D) 21

   (E) 38

Column A	**Column B**

When the square of $2a$ is multiplied by 2, the result is n.

13. $\dfrac{n}{4a}$ a

Refer to the following graphs for Questions 14 and 15.

14. Each of the following is a valid conclusion that can be drawn from the information in the graphs EXCEPT:

   (A) from 1970 to 1980, the number of stores increased by approximately 200

   (B) from 1970 to 2000, the number of stores approximately doubled

   (C) from 1980 to 2000, the average number of employees increased by approximately 50%

   (D) In 2000, there were about 75,000 employees

   (E) from 1970 to 2000, the number of employees increased each decade

15. According to the graphs, which of the following is the best estimate of the total number of employees in 1990?

    (A) 75,000

    (B) 62,000

    (C) 57,000

    (D) 50,000

    (E) 48,000

	<u>**Column A**</u>	<u>**Column B**</u>

s and *t* are different prime numbers.

16.	The number of positive integer divisors of s^3.	The number of positive integer divisors of *st*.

$$x - y = 1$$

17.	$3y - 1$	$2x$

18. What is the area of the triangle in the figure below?

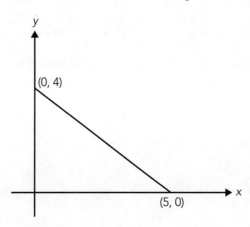

    (A) 4.5

    (B) 9.0

    (C) 10.0

    (D) 12.5

    (E) 20.0

19. The average of x and y is 16 and the average of x, y, and z is 22. What is the value of z?

    (A) 16

    (B) 22

    (C) 34

    (D) 45

    (E) 66

Refer to the following graph for Questions 20 and 21.

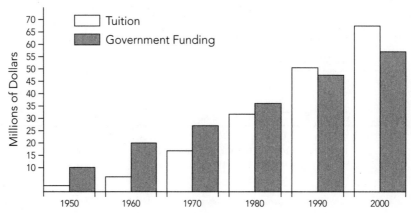

University Revenues from Government and Tuition

20. According to the graph, which of the following is the best estimate of the total revenue from government funding in 1990?

    (A) $60 million

    (B) $55 million

    (C) $45 million

    (D) $35 million

    (E) $30 million

21. Each of the following is a valid conclusion that can be drawn from the information in the graph EXCEPT:

    (A) the total revenue from tuition and government funding in 2000 was $120 million

    (B) between 1980 and 1990, the proportion of total revenue from government funding increased

    (C) revenue from government funding increased every year from 1950 to 2000

    (D) revenue from tuition increased every year from 1960 to 1990

    (E) revenue from tuition increased at a greater rate than did revenue from government funding

22. The length of a rectangular kitchen floor is 3 feet more than its width. If the length of the floor is 12 feet, what is the area of the floor in square feet?

    (A) 9

    (B) 15

    (C) 42

    (D) 108

    (E) 144

	Column A	**Column B**
	$4 < a < b < 5$	
23.	25% of a	20% of b
	x is two times y. y is $\frac{1}{2}$ of z.	
24.	x	z
	$r > 0$	
25.	$\dfrac{(r + r)}{r}$	r

26. A colored marble is to be chosen at random from a bag of marbles. The probability that the marble chosen will be green is $\frac{4}{9}$. Which of the following could NOT be the total number of marbles in the bag?

    (A) 36

    (B) 64

    (C) 72

    (D) 81

    (E) 108

27. What is the surface area of a right rectangular solid with dimensions 4 by 7 by 5 inches?

28. In the right triangle below, if $x = 9$, what is the value of y?

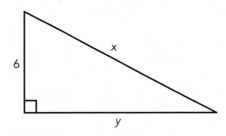

    (A) 3

    (B) $\sqrt{45}$

    (C) $\sqrt{55}$

    (D) $\sqrt{65}$

    (E) 15

END OF SECTION 4

GRE Practice Test 1 Answer Key

<table>
<tr><td colspan="4" align="center">**Section 3**</td></tr>
<tr><td>1. B</td><td>16. A</td></tr>
<tr><td>2. C</td><td>17. A</td></tr>
<tr><td>3. B</td><td>18. E</td></tr>
<tr><td>4. A</td><td>19. A</td></tr>
<tr><td>5. A</td><td>20. C</td></tr>
<tr><td>6. C</td><td>21. B</td></tr>
<tr><td>7. C</td><td>22. B</td></tr>
<tr><td>8. D</td><td>23. E</td></tr>
<tr><td>9. B</td><td>24. A</td></tr>
<tr><td>10. D</td><td>25. A</td></tr>
<tr><td>11. C</td><td>26. B</td></tr>
<tr><td>12. A</td><td>27. D</td></tr>
<tr><td>13. D</td><td>28. B</td></tr>
<tr><td>14. B</td><td>29. B</td></tr>
<tr><td>15. belies, mandate</td><td>30. C</td></tr>
</table>

Section 3

1. B
2. C
3. B
4. A
5. A
6. C
7. C
8. D
9. B
10. D
11. C
12. A
13. D
14. B
15. belies, mandate
16. A
17. A
18. E
19. A
20. C
21. B
22. B
23. E
24. A
25. A
26. B
27. D
28. B
29. B
30. C

Section 4

1. B
2. C
3. B
4. D
5. C
6. D
7. A
8. A
9. B
10. D
11. B
12. B
13. D
14. E
15. C
16. C
17. D
18. C
19. C
20. C
21. B
22. D
23. A
24. C
25. D
26. B
27. 166
28. B

Scoring Guidelines

To calculate your approximate Scaled Score, count the number of questions that you answered correctly on the Verbal and Quantitative sections. This is your Raw Score, which can then be converted to a Scaled Score for each section using the table on the facing page. Remember that this is just an *approximation* of what you might expect to score on the GRE if you took the test today!

SCORE CONVERSION TABLE FOR GRE GENERAL TEST

Raw Score	Scaled Score	
	Verbal	Quantitative
30	800	
29	780	
28	750	800
27	730	780
26	710	750
25	690	720
24	660	700
23	640	680
22	620	650
21	600	630
20	580	610
19	570	600
18	550	590
17	520	570
16	490	540
15	470	500
14	450	480
13	440	460
12	400	430
11	380	400
10	360	390

Continued on Next Page

9	320	370
8	240	320
7	200	290
6	200	240
5	200	200
4	200	200
0–3	200	200

NOTE: Your actual scaled GRE score may vary by as many as 60 points.

GRE Practice Test 1 Answers and Explanations

Sections 1 and 2—Analytical Writing

Because grading the essays is subjective, we've chosen not to include any "graded" essays here. Your best bet is to have someone you trust, such as your personal tutor, read your essays and give you an honest critique. Make the grading criteria mentioned in Chapter 7, "GRE Analytical Writing Assessment," available to whoever grades your essays. If you plan on grading your own essays, review the grading criteria and be as honest as possible regarding the structure, development, organization, technique, and appropriateness of your writing. Focus on your weak areas and continue to practice in order to improve your writing skills.

Section 3—Verbal

1. **The best answer is B.** A *dose of medicine* is a specific quantity of medicine. Likewise, a *ream* of *paper* is a specific quantity of paper. Although answer choice A includes words that are related to medicine, they do not have the same relationship as do the words in the question stem.

2. **The best answer is A.** The words in the question stem are antonyms; they have opposite meanings; *demur* means to "oppose or delay." Therefore, the correct answer will include a pair of antonyms. *Accept* and *revoke* are the only antonyms among the answer choices.

3. **The best answer is B.** To answer this question, you must understand the context of the sentence. The introductory phrase "in addition" indicates that the sentence will provide you with more than one example of what Mr. Mathison does to help students. The sentence implies that Mr. Mathison "advised" or "informed" the students about community service opportunities. *Counseled* is similar to *advised* or *informed*, making answer choice B the best selection.

4. **The best answer is A.** The information following the semicolon is a definition of the word that should go in the blank. The word that best fits the definition of "numerous twists and turns" is *convoluted*, which means "intricate and complicated." Answer choices B, C, D, and E are words that could be used to describe a story line, but they do not fit the context of the sentence.

5. **The best answer is A.** A *glacier* is made up of *ice*. Likewise, a *beach* is made up of *sand*. None of the other answer choices have this relationship.

6. **The best answer is C.** The word *capricious* means "impulsive or unpredictable," whereas *steadfast* means "solid and predictable." Therefore, *steadfast* is most opposite in meaning to *capricious*.

7. **The best answer is C.** The word *glib* means "doing something with ease and slickness, but lacking sincerity." The word *guileless* means "without cunning," which is most opposite in meaning to *glib*.

8. **The best answer is D.** The word *collusion* refers to a secret agreement, usually to commit *fraud*. A *diatribe* is a statement usually meant to cause *insult*. Therefore, a good general sentence describing the relationship would be: A "--------" is made in order to commit "--------." None of the other answer choices make sense when inserted into the blanks in this sentence.

9. **The best answer is B.** The word *insular* refers to being "isolated," whereas the word *cosmopolitan* refers to being "common to the whole world." Therefore, *cosmopolitan* has the meaning that is most opposite to *insular*.

10. **The best answer is D.** The word *plethora* refers to having a "great abundance," whereas *deficiency* suggests a "lack" or a "reduced quantity." Therefore, *deficiency* is most opposite in meaning to *plethora*.

11. **The best answer is C.** The word *malevolent* means "having an evil influence," whereas the word *magnanimous* means "having a generous and kind nature." Therefore, *magnanimous* is most opposite in meaning to *malevolent*.

12. **The best answer is A.** If someone is *disconcerted*, he or she is "frustrated, or out of sorts." A person who is *composed*, on the other hand, is "free from agitation." Therefore, *composed* is most opposite in meaning to *disconcerted*.

13. **The best answer is D.** When someone is *exhausted*, that person must be *revived* in order to regain his or her strength. While several of the answer choices seem to have the same relationship—*replace* and *lost*, *rejuvenate* and *drained*, and *resume* and *interrupted*— *exhausted* refers to a particular state of being. Only *drained* also refers to a particular state of being—someone who is *drained* must be *rejuvenated* in order to regain his or her strength.

14. **The best answer is B.** The information following the blank helps to define the word that should go in the blank. The word *myopic* means "short-sighted or near-sighted." Both *perceptive* and *discerning* have meanings that are opposite to *myopic*, so answer choices C and D should be eliminated.

15. **The best answer is *belies*; *mandate*.** The apparently rigid discipline mentioned in the beginning of the sentence provides a false impression: In fact, the modern officer needs the ability to think independently. *Belies* indicates that the apparent rigidity is false. The second through fourth choices all imply that discipline is antithetical to independent thinking, while the last choice, *mitigates*, suggests that discipline is a refreshing alternative from independent thought, which does not fit in the context of the sentence. The best word for the second blank will support the statements made in the previous sentence; "independent thinking" suggests that soldiers will engage in making "spur-of-the-moment decisions." *Mandate* means "to order or require," which is the best choice from among the words listed.

16. **The best answer is A.** The information following the first blank helps to define the word that should go in the blank. People who indulge in wild behavior could lead either *chaotic* or *boisterous* lives. *Temperate* and *moderate* do not describe such people, so eliminate answer choices B and C. Now look at the second blank, which should be filled with a word that has a meaning similar to *wild*. Neither *leisurely* nor *unpretentious* will work in the second blank, so eliminate answer choices D and E.

17. **The best answer is A.** As it is used in the passage, the word *boasts* means "possesses." The north wall of the Lincoln Memorial "possesses" Lincoln's inaugural address; the words are carved into the wall. Each of the remaining answer choices are either alternate meanings of the word *boasts* or are other words stated in the passage that do not mean *boasts*.

18. **The best answer is E.** The passage states, "The physical presence of the memorial is awe inspiring," and also uses phrases such as "proudly carved" and "profound symbols" to reflect the meaning behind the monument. This best supports answer choice E. None of the other answer choices is supported by the passage.

19. **The best answer is A.** Something that is *tacit* is not *explicit*. In fact, *tacit* refers to something that is "implied, not expressed." Therefore, the words in the question stem are antonyms, and the correct answer will include a pair of antonyms. Something that is *lucid* is clear, which means it is not *muddled*. None of the other answer choices include antonyms.

20. **The best answer is C.** The information following the semicolon provides a clue to which word best fits in the blank. Because Amanda is normally very polished and chic, but today her appearance would suggest otherwise, look for a word that has a meaning opposite to "polished" or "chic." The word *unkempt* means "disorderly" and is often used to describe hair, so it is the best choice for the blank.

21. **The best answer is B.** The passage describes several potentially devastating effects of overreliance on computers. The general tone of the passage is one of warning. Although the passage indicates that we should look for ways to reduce our dependence on technology, the passage does not offer any suggestions, so answer choice C is incorrect. Likewise, the other answer choices are not supported by the passage.

22. **The best answer is B.** The author states, "Even a small glitch in the operation of these systems can put human lives in danger." This statement indicates the potential danger of overreliance on computer technology, especially regarding services that are essential to survival. Answer choices A, C, D, and E are not supported by the passage.

23. **The best answer is E.** The main idea of the passage is that, although computer technology has contributed to the advancement of the human race, our dependence on this technology can be dangerous. Statements and phrases such as ". . . dependence on computer technology signals a real danger for the human race," and ". . . dangerous progression . . ." best support answer choice E.

24. **The best answer is A.** The passage indicates that the transmission of electronic data is one way in which humans are taking advantage of computer technology, but the passage does not necessarily suggest that this is a danger. However, the passage explicitly states that both increased opportunity for criminal activity (identity theft) and a reduction in national security are potential dangers.

25. **The best answer is A.** The first paragraph states, in response to the introduction of the maxim of "Know Thyself," "there is for an individual no more important and no more difficult knowledge, than knowledge of himself. Nations are only individuals on a larger scale." The paragraph goes on to say that a nation's failure to understand its existence will lead to its ultimate undoing. This best supports answer choice A.

26. **The best answer is B.** The passage states, "Nations are only individuals on a larger scale," which is a direct comparison of nations to man. The other answer choices are not supported by the passage.

27. **The best answer is D.** The context of this sentence indicates that there is something about the column that is often criticized. Look at each answer choice and fill in the blanks in the sentence. The words in answer choice A do not fit the context of the sentence. *Ingenuity* is not usually criticized and does not make sense with *settles*. *Unpredictability* could very well be criticized, but *scuttles* does not logically define an opinion. *Rigidity* could very well be criticized, but something that is *rigid*, or inflexible, does not usually *dither*, which describes something uncertain or undecided. Therefore, answer choice D is best: The column is criticized for *inconsistency* (the opinions disagree or are not predictable) because the opinions stated often *vacillate* (vary between two opposing beliefs).

28. **The best answer is B.** The word *deplorable* is used to describe something that is bad or "worthy of reproach." Therefore, something that is *deplorable* would most likely not be *acceptable*.

29. **The best answer is B.** The word *circumspect* refers to someone who is "mindful" or "prudent." A *reckless* person, on the other hand, is generally not very "prudent," or "careful." Therefore, *reckless* is most opposite in meaning to *circumspect*.

30. **The best answer is C.** A *reservoir* is a man-made *lake*. Likewise, a *canal* is a man-made *waterway*. None of the other answer choices have the same relationship.

Section 4—Quantitative

1. **The correct answer is B.** To solve this problem, first calculate the amount of flour each student will receive if 5 pounds is shared equally among 3 students. Each student will receive $\frac{5}{3}$ pounds. To compare the quantities, conversion to decimal might be helpful. The quantity $1\frac{1}{2} = 1.5$ while the quantity $\frac{5}{3} \approx 1.667$. Thus the quantity in Column B ($\frac{5}{3}$) is greater than the quantity in Column A ($\frac{11}{2}$).

2. **The correct answer is C.** To solve this problem, recall that $\sqrt{a} = a^{\frac{1}{2}}$. The quantity in Column A, $(\sqrt{a})^2$, can be written as $(a^{\frac{1}{2}})^2$. Using the rules of exponents $(a^{\frac{1}{2}})^2 = a^{(\frac{1}{2})(2)} = a^1 = a$. Likewise, the quantity in Column B, $\sqrt{a^2}$, can be written as $(a^2)^{\frac{1}{2}} = a^{(2)(\frac{1}{2})} = a^1 = a$. Thus the quantities are equal.

3. **The correct answer is B.** To solve this problem, recognize that because x is an integer greater than 1 (that is, x can equal 2, 3, 4, 5, and so on), the quantity $\frac{1}{x}$ is less than or equal to $\frac{1}{2}$ ($\frac{1}{x}$ can be $\frac{1}{2}, \frac{1}{3}, \frac{1}{4}, \frac{1}{5}$, and so on). Therefore, the quantity in Column A, $\frac{1}{x} - \frac{1}{2}$, must be less than or equal to zero. The quantity in Column B is $\frac{1}{2}$. Thus the quantity in Column B is greater than the quantity in Column A.

4. **The correct answer is D.** The formula for the area of a circle is πr^2, where r is the radius. Because the area is dependent on the square of the radius, it is not apparent what increasing the radius by 1 will do to the area. The quantities in neither column specify the original radii, so the increases in areas cannot be calculated; the relationship cannot be determined from the given information.

5. **The correct answer is C.** You are given that Jason traveled 30 miles in 6 hours and that Katie traveled three times as far in half the time; Katie traveled 30×3, or 90 miles, in $6 \times \frac{1}{2}$, or 3 hours. Therefore, Katie traveled $\frac{90}{3}$, or 30 miles per hour.

6. **The correct answer is D.** You are given that $r = -2$. Therefore, the best approach to solving this problem is to replace r with -2 in each of the answer choices, as follows:

   Answer choice A: $4pr^2 = 4p(-2)^2$, which equals $(4)(4)p$, or $16p$.

   Answer choice B: $2pr^3 = 2p(-2)^3$, which equals $(2)(-8)p$, or $-16p$.

   Answer choice C: $-2pr^4 = -2p(-2)^4$, which equals $(-2)(16)p$, or $-32p$.

   Answer choice D: $-4pr^5 = -4p(-2)^5$, which equals $(-4)(-32)p$, or $128p$.

   Answer choice E: $-6pr^6 = -6p(-2)^6$, which equals $(-6)(64)p$, or $-384p$.

   The question asks for the least value. You are given that $p < 0$, which means that p is a negative number. If you substitute any negative number into the results obtained above, only answer choices A and D will yield a negative value. Therefore, you can eliminate answer choices B, C, and E, because they will all be larger than either answer choice A or D. When $p < 0$, $128p$ will always be less than $16p$, so answer choice D is correct.

   Alternatively, if you recognize that a negative number raised to an odd number remains negative, then only answer choice D will yield a negative number: $-4 \times p$ (another negative number) $\times r^5$ (another negative number) = a negative number. All of the other answer choices would yield a positive number, so answer choice D must have the least value.

7. **The correct answer is A.** To solve this problem, first find the value of $2a$. To do so, take the equation $2a + 15 = 4a - 1$, and solve for $2a$ by adding 1 and $-2a$ to both sides of the equation. The result is $2a = 16$. Thus the quantity in Column A (16) is greater than the quantity in Column B (14).

8. **The correct answer is A.** To solve this problem, it will be helpful to test intervals of x to see if they satisfy the inequality $(x + 2)(x - 3) < 0$. Logical intervals would be $x < -2$, $-2 < x < 3$, and $x > 3$ because $x = -2$ or $x = 3$ would make the expression $(x + 2)(x - 3)$ equal to 0. For the intervals $x < -2$ and $x > 3$, the expression $(x + 2)(x - 3)$ is positive, which is not what the question is looking for. For the interval $-2 < x < 3$, however, the expression $(x + 2)(x - 3)$ is negative. Thus because the acceptable values for x are between -2 and 3, not inclusive, x must be less than 3. Therefore the quantity in Column A is greater than the quantity in Column B.

9. **The correct answer is B.** Because Andrew has d dollars in his account, twice the number of dollars in his account would equal $2d$. Because $d > 0$, $200d$ is always greater than $2d$. Thus the quantity in Column B is greater than the quantity in Column A.

10. **The correct answer is D.** Because the figure is a rectangle, the adjacent sides are perpendicular. Perpendicular lines have slopes that are negative reciprocals of each other, meaning that the product of their slopes is -1. Because there are four lines and four perpendicular angles, the product of the slopes is $(-1)(1)(-1)(1)$, or 1.

11. **The correct answer is B.** To solve this problem, calculate the length of ST using the Pythagorean theorem. Because RST is a right triangle, $5^2 + 7^2 = ST^2$; $25 + 49 = 74$, which is equal to ST^2. Because $9 > \sqrt{74}$, the quantity in Column B is greater than the quantity in Column A.

12. **The correct answer is B.** The best approach to solving this problem is to find one number that is divisible by both 3 and 8, and then determine which of the answer choices also goes into that number. When you multiply 3 times 8, you get 24, which means that 24 is one number that is divisible by both 3 and 8. Of the answer choices, only 6 also goes into 24, so answer choice B must be correct. None of the other answer choices is a divisor of 24.

13. **The correct answer is D.** To solve this problem, transform the phrase "When the square of $2a$ is multiplied by 2, the result is n" into its mathematical equivalent, as follows:

$$n = 2(2a)^2$$
$$2(4a^2) = 8a^2$$

The quantity $\frac{n}{4a}$ can be put in terms of a by substituting $8a^2$ for n and simplifying as follows:

$$\frac{(8a^2)}{4a} = 2a$$

However, without information about whether a is positive or negative, it is impossible to determine which quantity is greater.

14. **The correct answer is E.** According to the graph, the slope of the line segment between the number of employees in 1970 and the number of employees in 1980 is negative (slopes down). Thus the number of employees decreased between 1970 and 1980; the statement "From 1970 to 2000, the number of employees increased each decade" is therefore false.

15. **The correct answer is C.** According to the graph, the number of employees in 1990 is slightly below the line representing 60,000 employees. Thus 57,000 is the logical answer choice.

16. **The correct answer is C.** To solve this problem, it might be helpful to use test numbers in place of s and t (try the prime numbers 2 and 3, for instance). In the general case, s^3 has divisors 1, s, and s^2; st has divisors 1, s, and t. Thus the quantities in Column A and B are equal.

17. **The correct answer is D.** To determine which quantity is greater, solve the equation $x - y = 1$ for y by subtracting x from both sides, and then multiplying the entire equation by -1 to get $y = x - 1$. Substituting $x - 1$ for y in the expression $3y - 1$ yields $3(x - 1) - 1$, or $3x - 4$. The quantities being compared are then $3x - 4$ and $2x$. However, the greater quantity cannot be determined because the sign of x is unknown.

18. **The correct answer is C.** To correctly answer this question, remember that the area of a triangle is calculated using the formula $A = \frac{1}{2}(bh)$, where b is the base of the triangle and h is the height of the triangle. The base of the triangle extends from the origin in the (x,y) coordinate plane, $(0,0)$ to the point $(5,0)$. This means that the base is 5. The height of the triangle extends from the origin in the (x,y) coordinate plane, $(0,0)$ to $(0,4)$. The height of the triangle is 4. Plug these values into the formula:

$$A = \frac{1}{2}(bh)$$

$$A = \frac{1}{2}(5 \times 4)$$

$$A = \frac{1}{2}(20)$$

$$A = 10$$

19. **The correct answer is C.** You are given that the average of x and y is 16. Therefore, $(x + y) \div 2 = 16$, which means that $x + y = 32$. It is not important to know what x and y equal individually, only to know that their sum is 32. Given that the average of x, y, and z is 22, then $(x + y + z) \div 3 = 22$, and $x + y + z = 66$. Since $x + y = 32$, then $32 + z = 66$, and $z = 34$.

20. **The correct answer is C.** According to the graph, the bar that represents the revenue from government funding in 1990 is slightly below the line representing $45 million. Thus $44 million is the logical answer choice.

21. **The correct answer is B.** According to the graph, it is apparent that revenue from government funding increased between 1980 and 1990. However, in 1980, revenue from government funding was greater than revenue from tuition, but in 1990 revenue from government funding was less than revenue from tuition. Thus, between 1980 and 1990, the proportion of total revenue that came from government funding *decreased*.

22. **The correct answer is B.** You are given that the length of the floor is 12 feet, and that the length is 3 more than the width. Set the width equal to w, and set up an equation to find the width.

$$3 + w = 12$$

$$w = 9$$

To calculate the area, multiply the length by the width.

$$12 \times 9 = 108$$

The area of the kitchen floor is 108 square feet.

23. **The correct answer is A.** To solve this problem, find maximum or minimum values for the percentages, given that $4 < a < b < 5$. The quantity 25% of a must be greater than 1 because it is given that $4 < a$, and 25% of 4 is 1. The quantity 20% of b must be less than 1 because it is given that $b < 5$, and 20% of 5 is 1. Therefore the quantity in Column A is greater than the quantity in Column B.

24. **The correct answer is C.** To solve this problem, convert the written English into mathematical symbols. If "x is two times y," then $x = 2y$. Similarly, if y is $\frac{1}{2}$ of z, then $y = \frac{z}{2}$. To determine which quantity is greater, substitute $\frac{z}{2}$ for y into $x = 2y$ to get $x = 2(\frac{z}{2}) = z$. Therefore, the quantities in Column A and B are equal.

25. **The correct answer is D.** To solve this problem, simplify the quantity in Column A and compare it to Column B. It is given that $r > 0$, so the quantity $\frac{(r + r)}{r} = \frac{2r}{r} = 2$. However, you know only that r is greater than 0, so r could be less than, equal to, or greater than 2. Thus it is impossible to determine which quantity is greater based on the given information.

26. **The correct answer is B.** You are given that the probability of drawing a green marble is $\frac{4}{9}$ or 4 out of 9. This means that the total number of marbles in the bag must be a multiple of 9. The question asks for the answer choice that cannot be the number of marbles in the bag. Therefore, the answer choice that is not a multiple of 9 will be the correct answer. Only 64 is not a multiple of 9.

27. **The correct answer is 166.** Surface area is the total area of each face of a rectangular solid. In this case, the figure is a six-sided box, as shown below:

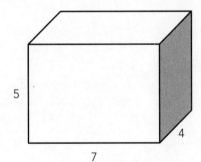

It will have three pairs of two matching sides: Two will be 5 by 7 inches, two will be 5 by 4 inches, and two will be 7 by 4 inches. Calculate the surface area as follows:

$$2(5 \times 7) + 2(5 \times 4) + 2(7 \times 4)$$
$$= 2(35) + 2(20) + 2(28)$$
$$= 70 + 40 + 56 = 166$$

28. **The correct answer is B.** To solve this problem, use the Pythagorean theorem, which states that $(a^2 + b^2 = c^2)$:

$$6^2 + y^2 = 9^2$$
$$36 + y^2 = 81$$
$$y^2 = 81 - 36$$
$$y^2 = 45$$
$$y = \sqrt{45}$$

13

GRE Practice Test 2

CHAPTER GOALS

- Take a simulated full-length GRE under actual test conditions.
- Check your results using the Answer Key.
- Review the explanations for each question, focusing particularly on questions you answered incorrectly or did not answer at all.
- Build your test-taking confidence.

The simulated GRE in this chapter contains 58 multiple-choice questions and two essay tasks, divided into four main sections. Please allow approximately 2 hours and 30 minutes to complete the following test.

Each of the test sections should be completed in the time indicated at the beginning of the sections, and in the order in which they appear on this test.

There are several different types of questions within each section. Make sure that you read and understand all directions before you begin. To achieve the best results, time yourself strictly on each section.

You should answer each question before you move on to the next question to make this simulated test as much like the actual CAT as possible. Remember to circle your answers on the test so that you can compare your answers to the correct answers listed on the Answer Key on page 345. Carefully review the explanations for any question that you answered incorrectly.

We suggest that you make this practice test as much like the real test as possible. Find a quiet location, free from distractions, and make sure that you have pencils and a timepiece.

Review the Scoring Guidelines on page 346, but remember that your score on the actual GRE will be dependent on many factors, including your level of preparedness and your fatigue level on test day.

SECTION 1—ISSUE TASK

45 Minutes

1 Question

You will have 45 minutes to select one topic, organize your thoughts, and compose a response that represents your point of view on the topic that you choose. Do not respond to any topic other than the one you select; a response to any other topic will receive a score of 0.

You will be given a choice between two general issues on a broad range of topics. You will be required to discuss your perspective on one of the issues, using examples and reasons drawn from your own experiences and observations.

Use scratch paper to organize your response before you begin writing. Write your response on the pages provided, or type your response using a word processor with the spell and grammar check functions turned off.

<u>Directions:</u> Present your viewpoint on *one* of the claims made below. Use relevant reasons and examples to support your point of view.

Topic 1

"Progress is accomplished only through trial and error."

Topic 2

"Communication through technology should replace all other forms of communication in contemporary society."

SECTION 2—ARGUMENT TASK

30 Minutes

1 Question

You will have 30 minutes to organize your thoughts and compose a response that critiques the given argument. Do not respond to any topic other than the one given; a response to any other topic will receive a score of 0.

You are not being asked to discuss your point of view on the statement. You should identify and analyze the central elements of the argument, the underlying assumptions that are being made, and any supporting information that is given. Your critique can also discuss other information that would strengthen or weaken the argument or make it more logical.

Use scratch paper to organize your response before you begin writing. Write your response on the pages provided, or type your response using a word processor with the spell and grammar check functions turned off.

<u>Directions:</u> Critique the reasoning used in the following argument.

"The state of Lexiana, which imposes a mandatory deposit of 5 cents on all soft drink containers, has very few problems with littering along public highways. This strongly suggests that for the neighboring state of Indiansin, the best way to prevent any increase in littering is to collect a deposit on all disposable containers. By collecting this deposit money, Indiansin will be moving to preserve the unspoiled scenery along its public thoroughfares."

SECTION 3—VERBAL

30 Minutes

30 Questions

This section consists of five different types of questions: Sentence Completion, Analogy, Antonym, and Text Completion with Two or Three Blanks (this is a new question type; you will typically see only one of these questions on your GRE), and Reading Comprehension. To answer the questions, select the best answer from the answer choices given. Circle the letter or word(s) of your choice.

Directions for Sentence Completion Questions: The following sentences each contain one or two blanks, indicating that something has been left out of the sentence. Each answer choice contains one word or a set of words. Select the word or set of words that, when inserted in the blank(s), best fits the context of the sentence.

Example: Because of his --------, Brian's guests felt very welcome and comfortable staying at his house for the weekend.

(A) animosity

(B) hospitality

(C) determination

(D) wittiness

(E) severity

Directions for Analogy Questions: The following questions contain a set of related words in capital letters and five answer choices. Each answer choice also contains a set of words. Select the set of words that represents a relationship similar to the original set of words.

Example: APPRENTICE : PLUMBER ::

(A) player : coach

(B) child : parent

(C) student : teacher

(D) author : publisher

(E) intern : doctor

<u>Directions for Antonym Questions:</u> The following questions contain a word in capital letters and five answer choices. Each answer choice contains a word or phrase. Select the word or phrase that best expresses a meaning opposite to the word in capital letters.

Example: CREDULOUS:

(A) skeptical

(B) naive

(C) spontaneous

(D) sensitive

(E) discrete

<u>Directions for Text Completion with Two or Three Blanks Questions:</u> These questions consist of a short passage with two or three numbered blanks, indicating that something has been left out of the text. Select the word or set of words that, when inserted in the blanks, best completes the text.

Example: Experts believe that humans have ten trillion cells in their bodies that (i) _____ any number of essential genetic elements; scientists often marvel at what incredible (ii) _____ would ensue should the cells become jumbled or misunderstand their purpose.

Blank (i)	Blank (ii)
govern	order
organize	method
dislocate	chaos

<u>Directions for Reading Comprehension Questions:</u> The passages in this section are followed by several questions. The questions correspond to information that is stated or implied in the passage. Read the passage and choose the best answer for each question.

Answer the questions in the order presented.

The Verbal section questions begin on the next page.

1. ZENITH : PEAK ::

    (A) urbanity : refinement

    (B) accretion : decrease

    (C) musician : artist

    (D) debate : candidate

    (E) coach : athlete

2. ODIOUS : HATRED ::

    (A) nascent : love

    (B) negligent : care

    (C) culpable : blame

    (D) noxious : harm

    (E) obdurate : frustration

3. Winning the party's nomination for president signaled the -------- of the senator's political career; he had reached his ultimate goal.

    (A) collection

    (B) aberration

    (C) descent

    (D) pinnacle

    (E) metamorphosis

4. The principal's -------- speech caused the students to begin whispering to each other and fidgeting in their seats.

    (A) minuscule

    (B) cognitive

    (C) empirical

    (D) gregarious

    (E) interminable

5. WILY : SLY ::

   (A) boring : different

   (B) acute : slow

   (C) profuse : abundant

   (D) virtual : constant

   (E) ambiguous : correct

6. IMMEASURABLE:

   (A) finite

   (B) deflated

   (C) profound

   (D) bereaved

   (E) thorough

7. MAGNANIMOUS:

   (A) avaricious

   (B) philanthropic

   (C) grandiose

   (D) rancid

   (E) unpretentious

8. WHET : SHARPEN ::

   (A) protract : prolong

   (B) cut : paste

   (C) assert : demonstrate

   (D) create : assimilate

   (E) increase : denounce

9. OBDURATE:

   (A) inflexible

   (B) yielding

   (C) obsolete

   (D) facile

   (E) methodical

10. ASSUAGE:

    (A) abate

    (B) obviate

    (C) mollify

    (D) restrain

    (E) exacerbate

11. GARRULOUS:

    (A) articulate

    (B) taciturn

    (C) pompous

    (D) enlightening

    (E) verbose

12. LAUDABLE:

    (A) dubious

    (B) tranquil

    (C) contemptible

    (D) praiseworthy

    (E) plausible

13. VEHEMENT : FORCEFUL ::

    (A) culpable : deserving

    (B) cryptic : strange

    (C) cordial : honest

    (D) credulous : easy

    (E) unstinting : generous

14. Because modern art is neither completely accepted nor rejected by critics, their ultimate evaluations of it remain --------.

    (A) unrelenting

    (B) arbitrary

    (C) diminished

    (D) equivocal

    (E) passive

15. KEEN:

    (A) opaque

    (B) precise

    (C) lucid

    (D) remedial

    (E) dull

16. The new teacher ------- between adhering strictly to her lesson plans and taking advantage of a teachable moment.

    (A) incinerated

    (B) vacillated

    (C) coalesced

    (D) enumerated

    (E) immigrated

Questions 17 and 18 are based on the following passage.

Around the world, the bicycle is a favorite method of transportation, especially
Line in China. With its large urban population, China ranks first in the world in
bicycle production and use. In fact, China is responsible for half of the world's
bike ownership, with 10 million bicycles found in Beijing alone. This amounts
(5) to about one bicycle for every two residents, and makes cycling the most popular
form of transportation in the capital.

However, as economic prosperity has increased, individual car ownership
has also risen. This shift has contributed to already serious problems with urban
pollution and traffic congestion. As a result, the government has encouraged even
(10) more bicycle use. Bike lanes have been added to city streets, and more bicycle
parking lots have been created throughout Beijing. Still, critics point out that cars
are much more convenient for many daily activities in a large city. Only time will
tell if government measures will ensure that bicycles remain the favorite method
of transportation.

17. The author of the passage is primarily concerned with

   (A) promoting the use of bicycles in urban areas

   (B) documenting the rise of car ownership in modern China

   (C) illustrating the importance of bike lanes in promoting bicycle usage

   (D) describing the various sources of air pollution in modern China

   (E) describing the importance of bicycles for transportation in urban
       China

18. The author implies that car ownership in China is on the rise because

   (A) bicycles are seen as old-fashioned

   (B) Beijing air pollution makes cycling too difficult

   (C) there are now more wealthy Chinese able to purchase cars

   (D) bicycles are easier to maneuver on busy streets

   (E) government measures to increase bicycle use have been largely
       unsuccessful

19. VILIFY : MALIGN ::

   (A) cite : prove

   (B) banish : force

   (C) trail : pursue

   (D) bolster : cooperate

   (E) coerce : understand

20. Honesty is not a -------- human attribute, but rather a central virtue,
    whose existence is unreasoningly being -------- by selfish desires.

   (A) superficial .. undermined

   (B) trivial .. enhanced

   (C) pervasive .. threatened

   (D) worthless .. supported

   (E) resilient .. forestalled

Questions 21–24 are based on the following passage.

All mammals require sleep; it is an essential part of life. For giraffes, two hours a
day is enough. For bats, that number is closer to twenty. The average adult human
needs between seven and nine hours of sleep every day. Despite these differences,
mammals all have one thing in common: If they do not get enough sleep, they can
(5) suffer serious mental and physical consequences.

The most extensive sleep research has been conducted on people. Through
these studies, scientists have identified two broad categories of sleep, which can
be further divided into five stages with distinct physiological functions. Taken
together, they form a complete sleep cycle. The first four stages are marked by a
(10) lack of rapid eye movement (REM). Therefore, they are referred to as non-REM
sleep. While people are engaged in non-REM sleep, several things are occurring.
Researchers have discovered that during this early sleep, the human body
releases a series of hormones responsible for the proper functioning of certain
body systems. Disrupted sleep can cause these hormones to fall out of balance.
(15) The results can contribute to disorders such as diabetes, depression, infertility,
or even cancer. Lack of sleep, especially in stages 3 and 4, can literally stunt the
growth of children and may increase rates of obesity in adults.

Stage 5 sleep is defined by the occurrence of rapid eye movement, otherwise
known as dreaming. Note that, while REM sleep is the final stage in a sleep cycle,
(20) a complete cycle generally lasts only about 95 minutes. A person will experience
four to six cycles in one sleep session, with REM sleep taking up a larger portion
of the cycle as the night continues. Scientists have advanced several theories
about why humans need REM sleep. One view is that dreaming aids in memory

Line

consolidation. Under this theory, during REM sleep the brain not only strengthens
(25)   memory of important actions or events, but it weakens memory of unimportant
things. Another view is that dreaming is necessary for proper central nervous
system development. Yet another theory suggests that REM sleep involves the
repair of monoamine receptors. The theories are not necessarily exclusive; in fact,
they all reach the conclusion that REM sleep deprivation can result in death.

21. The author of the passage is primarily concerned with

(A) promoting mammalian sleep research

(B) documenting the importance of non-REM sleep in hormone
regulation

(C) describing the role of sleep in human behavior and development

(D) arguing that humans need more sleep to function optimally

(E) illustrating the importance of REM sleep to brain function

22. The author implies that disrupted sleep can cause disorders such as
diabetes (line 15) because

(A) diabetes is linked to obesity

(B) sufficient sleep is not crucial to good health

(C) diabetes is a serious physical consequence of poor sleep

(D) the disorders are probably a result of unbalanced hormone
production

(E) non-REM sleep is more important than REM sleep

23. The passage suggests that the author would be most likely to agree with
which of the following statements?

(A) A typical person needs more than six sleep cycles to maintain
optimal health.

(B) REM sleep is more important than non-REM sleep.

(C) A typical person experiences more REM sleep at the end of the
night.

(D) Lack of sleep can stunt the growth of adults.

(E) The majority of sleep disorders occur in children.

24. The author's argument is developed primarily by the use of

    (A) an attack on poorly constructed sleep research studies

    (B) a critique of recent scientific studies on REM-sleep

    (C) a warning against getting too little sleep

    (D) an analogy between human and non-human sleep processes

    (E) an overview of specific processes that may occur during different stages of sleep in humans

Questions 25 and 26 are based on the following passage.

While forensic scientists commonly rely on fingerprints to help identify a
person, it is not possible to use the same kind of technology with other species
of mammals. Recently, however, a group of researchers from Tokyo developed a
device that allows them to identify individuals of the endangered Ganges River
(5)   dolphin species. This underwater acoustic device measures the clicking sounds
produced by the creatures and helps with identification and tracking, since each
sound is as completely unique as a fingerprint.
   Ganges River dolphins are rare in that, unlike the majority of their
counterparts, they live in rivers and lakes rather than oceans. The species is blind
(10)   and uses clicks to send out sonar pulses for guidance and to find food. In the past
few decades, their numbers have decreased by 50 percent, because of fishing net
entanglement, human predation, pollution, construction, or a combination of
these factors. With this new acoustic technology, scientists hope to get a better
idea of how many of these dolphins still exist, as well as their migration patterns
(15)   and feeding habits. In turn, this information may help scientists protect and
conserve this unique species.

25. The author mentions that the Ganges River dolphin species is blind and uses clicks to send out sonar pulses for guidance and to find food (lines 9–10) most probably in order to

    (A) support the claim that an underwater acoustic device is helpful in identifying and tracking the Ganges River dolphin

    (B) suggest that, because of this blindness, the Ganges River dolphin survives only in rivers and lakes

    (C) challenge the claim that the species' decline in numbers is due to fishing net entanglement, human predation, pollution, or construction

    (D) refute the claim that the Ganges River dolphin can in fact be identified and tracked by underwater acoustic devices

    (E) lend credibility to the claim that the Ganges River dolphin is a rare species

26. The passage supplies information for answering which of the following questions?

    (A) How do the remaining Ganges River dolphins still exist?

    (B) What is the primary use of the new underwater acoustic technology?

    (C) Why do Ganges River dolphins make their homes in rivers and lakes?

    (D) How does the underwater acoustic technology work?

    (E) Can the new underwater acoustic technology be used in identifying and tracking other species of dolphins?

27. The emu, far from being endangered, has actually been (i) _____; it is one of the few Australian animals that has found the effects of farm life (ii) _____.

Blank (i)	Blank (ii)
terminated	palliative
domesticated	nugatory
exported	sanguine
decimated	salubrious
eradicated	splenetic

28. AVERSION:

    (A) prejudice

    (B) predilection

    (C) diversion

    (D) disdain

    (E) bias

29. VERITABLE:

    (A) genuine

    (B) bogus

    (C) substantiated

    (D) ample

    (E) authoritative

30. VERACITY : DECEPTION ::

   (A) renunciation : acceptance

   (B) countenance : face

   (C) tenacity : weakness

   (D) climax : estimation

   (E) consternation : incompetence

END OF SECTION 3

SECTION 4—QUANTITATIVE

30 Minutes

28 Questions

This section includes three types of questions: Quantitative Comparison, Discrete Problem Solving, and Numeric Entry. For each question, circle the letter of your choice or write your answer as instructed.

General Information:

Numbers: All of the numbers used in this section are real numbers.

Figures: Assume that the position of all points, angles, etc., are in the order shown and the measures of angles are positive.

Straight lines can be assumed to be straight.

All figures lie in a plane unless otherwise stated.

The figures given for each question provide information to solve the problem. The figures are not drawn to scale unless otherwise stated. To solve the problems, use your knowledge of mathematics; do not estimate lengths and sizes of the figures to answer questions.

Directions for Quantitative Comparison Questions: Some of the following questions give you two quantities, one in Column A and one in Column B. Compare the two quantities and choose one of the following answer choices:

A if the quantity in Column A is greater;

B if the quantity in Column B is greater;

C if the two quantities are equal;

D if you cannot determine the relationship based on the given information.

Do not mark answer choice E, as there are only four choices from which to choose.

Note: Information and/or figures pertaining to one or both of the quantities may appear above the two columns. Any information that appears in both columns has the same meaning in Column A and in Column B.

Example: | <u>Column A</u> | <u>Column B</u> |
|---|---|
| $-(3)^4$ | $(-3)^4$ |

<u>Directions for Discrete Problem Solving Questions:</u> Select the best answer for the remaining multiple-choice questions.

Example: If $y = 5x$ and $z = 3y$, then in terms of x, $x + y + z =$

    (A) $21x$

    (B) $16x$

    (C) $15x$

    (D) $9x$

    (E) $8x$

<u>Directions for Numeric Entry Questions:</u> Enter your answer in the box below the question.

Example: Solve the equation for x: $2(x - 3) + 9 = 4x - 7$

$x =$

Answer the questions in the order presented.

The Quantitative section questions begin on the next page.

	Column A	**Column B**

1.   The perimeter of a   The perimeter of an
       rectangle whose width   equilateral triangle in
       is 6 cm and whose   which one side length
       diagonal is 10 cm.   is 10 cm.

$$y^2 = x^2 + 1$$
$$x \neq 0$$

2. $y^4 - 1$ x^4

Part of a $15,000 inheritance is invested
at 5%, and the remainder is invested at 6%.
The total simple annual interest earned on
the $15,000 at the end of 1 year is $800.

3.   Amount invested at 5%   Amount invested at 6%

4. $4\frac{1}{8} \div \frac{1}{2}$ $16\frac{1}{2} \div 2$

5. A ball has been rolling at the constant rate x cm/min. How many centimeters has it rolled in the last y seconds?

   (A) $\dfrac{xy}{60}$

   (B) $\dfrac{60x}{y}$

   (C) $\dfrac{x}{60y}$

   (D) $\dfrac{60}{xy}$

   (E) $60xy$

6. A membership list of 720 people shows that 36 have first and last names that begin with the same letter. If a person is selected at random, what is the probability that his or her first and last name does NOT begin with the same letter?

   (A) 0.05

   (B) 0.25

   (C) 0.50

   (D) 0.75

   (E) 0.95

	Column A	**Column B**

The average of a, b, and 5 is 4.

7. $\dfrac{(a + b)}{3}$ 2

___

8.   The greatest prime   The greatest prime
      factor of 4^5.   factor of 5^4.

___

9. Solve the equation for x: $3(x + 4) - 8 = 2x + 7$

$x =$ [   ]

10. A receptionist typed 8 memos, each either 1 or 2 pages long. If the receptionist typed 12 pages in all, how many of the memos had 2 pages?

(A) 1

(B) 2

(C) 3

(D) 4

(E) 5

	Column A	**Column B**

$8x^2 = 24$

11. x 2

___

12. If the assets of a stock drop by \$4.03 billion to \$74.02 billion, what was the percent decrease in the stock's assets?

(A) 0.4

(B) 4.0

(C) 5.0

(D) 25.0

(E) 40.0

<u>**Column A**</u>   <u>**Column B**</u>

Lilly randomly selects 1 of 18 beads in
a container of 3 red, 6 purple, and 9 blue beads.

13.   The probability that Lilly   The probability that Lilly selects
       selects a blue bead.   either a red or purple bead.

Refer to the following graph for Questions 14 and 15.

Hours Per Day Spent by Typical Teenagers on Certain Activities

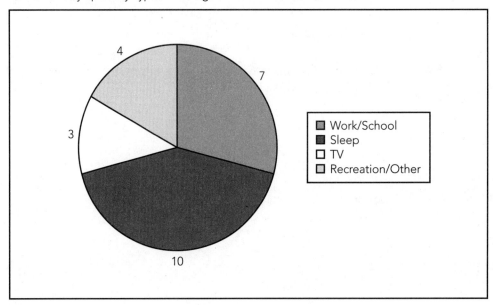

14. According to the survey data, on average, how many hours will a typical
    teenager spend watching television and sleeping in one year?

    (A) 1,460 hours

    (B) 2,555 hours

    (C) 3,650 hours

    (D) 4,015 hours

    (E) 4,745 hours

15. Which of the following represents the ratio of the hours teenagers spend on Work/School to the hours teenagers spend on all activities?

    (A) 17:24

    (B) 7:17

    (C) 7:24

    (D) 24:17

    (E) 24:7

Column A	**Column B**
16. (30% of 60) + 70	(70% of 60) + 30

$$x < 1$$

17. $2x$	x^2

18. Which of the following equals the reciprocal of $a - \frac{1}{b}$, where $a - \frac{1}{b}$ does not equal 0?

    (A) $\frac{1}{a} - b$

    (B) $\frac{-b}{a}$

    (C) $\frac{b}{(a - 1)}$

    (D) $\frac{a}{(ab - 1)}$

    (E) $\frac{b}{(ab - 1)}$

19. The integer n is a multiple of both 5 and 3. Which of the following is (are) true?

    I. n is odd.

    II. $n = 30$.

    III. n is a multiple of 15.

    (A) III only

    (B) I and II only

    (C) I and III only

    (D) II and III only

    (E) I, II, and III

Refer to the following graphs for Questions 20 and 21.

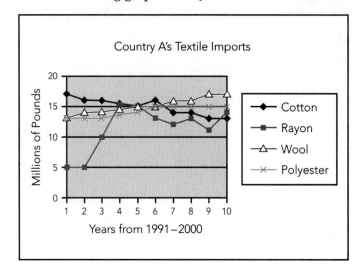

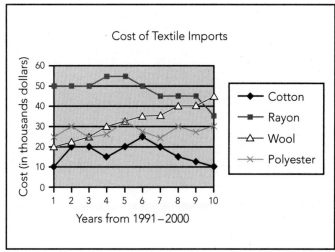

20. What was the approximate average yearly increase in the cost of wool from 1996 to 2000, inclusive?

   (A) $1,250

   (B) $2,000

   (C) $3,300

   (D) $5,000

   (E) $10,000

21. Approximately what percent of textile imports in 1991 came from cotton?

    (A) 18%

    (B) 25%

    (C) 28%

    (D) 35%

    (E) 40%

22. If $x + 3y = 3$ and $(x + y)^2 = 4$, which of the following is a possible value of x?

    (A) -8

    (B) -5

    (C) $\frac{-3}{2}$

    (D) $\frac{3}{2}$

    (E) 5

Column A	**Column B**
$0 < v < w$	
23. $\frac{v}{w}$	$\frac{w}{v}$
24. $100{,}315 \times 90{,}531$	$100{,}531 \times 90{,}315$
$0 < 6x < 2$	
25. x^2	x^4

26. $(2 \times 100) + (5 \times 1) + (6 \times 1{,}000) + (9 \times 10) =$

    (A) 2,569

    (B) 2,956

    (C) 6,259

    (D) 6,295

    (E) 9,526

27. Allie lives 3 km west of Billy's house. Charlie lives 4 km north of Billy's house and 3 km west of Danny's house. What is the distance from Allie's house to Danny's house?

    (A) 4 km

    (B) 5 km

    (C) 8 km

    (D) 10 km

    (E) 12 km

28. $25.86 \times \dfrac{1}{100} =$

    (A) 0.2586

    (B) 2.586

    (C) 25.86

    (D) 258.6

    (E) 2,586

END OF SECTION 4

GRE Practice Test 2 Answer Key

Section 3

1.	A	17.	E
2.	C	18.	C
3.	D	19.	C
4.	E	20.	A
5.	C	21.	C
6.	A	22.	D
7.	A	23.	C
8.	A	24.	E
9.	B	25.	A
10.	E	26.	B
11.	B	27.	domesticated, salubrious
12.	C	28.	B
13.	E	29.	B
14.	D	30.	A
15.	E		
16.	B		

Section 4

1.	B	17.	D
2.	A	18.	E
3.	A	19.	A
4.	C	20.	B
5.	A	21.	D
6.	E	22.	D
7.	A	23.	B
8.	B	24.	A
9.	3	25.	A
10.	D	26.	D
11.	B	27.	B
12.	C	28.	A
13.	C		
14.	E		
15.	C		
16.	A		

Scoring Guidelines

To calculate your approximate Scaled Score, count the number of questions that you answered correctly on the Verbal and Quantitative sections. This is your Raw Score, which can then be converted to a Scaled Score for each section using the table on facing page. Remember that this is just an *approximation* of what you might expect to score on the GRE if you took the test today!

SCORE CONVERSION TABLE FOR GRE GENERAL TEST

Raw Score	Scaled Score	
	Verbal	Quantitative
30	800	
29	780	
28	750	800
27	730	780
26	710	750
25	690	720
24	660	700
23	640	680
22	620	650
21	600	630
20	580	610
19	570	600
18	550	590
17	520	570
16	490	540
15	470	500
14	450	480
13	440	460
12	400	430
11	380	400
10	360	390

Continued on Next Page

9	320	370
8	240	320
7	200	290
6	200	240
5	200	200
4	200	200
0–3	200	200

NOTE: Your actual scaled GRE score may vary by as many as 60 points.

GRE Practice Test 2 Answers and Explanations

Sections 1 and 2—Analytical Writing

Because grading the essays is subjective, we've chosen not to include any "graded" essays here. Your best bet is to have someone you trust, such as your personal tutor, read your essays and give you an honest critique. Make the grading criteria mentioned in Chapter 7, "GRE Analytical Writing Assessment," available to whoever grades your essays. If you plan on grading your own essays, review the grading criteria and be as honest as possible regarding the structure, development, organization, technique, and appropriateness of your writing. Focus on your weak areas and continue to practice in order to improve your writing skills.

Section 3—Verbal

1. **The best answer is A.** The relationship that exists between *zenith* and *peak* can be expressed with the following sentence: "*Zenith* is a synonym for *peak*." Because *urbanity* is a synonym for *refinement*, this choice best expresses the relationship that exists between the words in the question stem.

2. **The best answer is C.** The relationship that exists between *odious* and *hatred* can be expressed with the following sentence: "*Odious* means 'deserving of *hatred*.'" *Culpable* means deserving of *blame*, so this choice best expresses the relationship that exists between the words in the question stem.

3. **The best answer is D.** The context indicates that winning the party's nomination was the senator's ultimate goal. *Pinnacle* refers to the "highest achievement," so it is the best choice.

4. **The best answer is E.** The word *interminable* means "seeming to last forever"; it makes sense that the students would start to whisper and fidget if the speech seemed to go on and on.

5. **The best answer is C.** The word *wily* means "crafty or sly"; therefore, the words in the question stem are synonyms. *Profuse* is a synonym for *abundant*, so this choice best expresses the relationship that exists between the words in the question stem.

6. **The best answer is A.** The word *immeasurable* means "unable to measure; very vast," whereas the word *finite* means "having definable limits." Therefore, *finite* is most nearly opposite in meaning to *immeasurable*.

7. **The best answer is A.** The word *magnanimous* means "very generous," whereas *avaricious* means "very greedy." Therefore, *avaricious* is most nearly opposite in meaning to *magnanimous*.

8. **The best answer is A.** The relationship that exists between *whet* and *sharpen* can be expressed with the following sentence: "*Whet* means 'to *sharpen* or increase.'" *Protract* means "to *prolong*," so this choice best expresses the relationship that exists between the words in the question stem.

9. **The best answer is B.** To be *obdurate* means to be firm, whereas *yielding* means "disposed to comply with." Therefore, *yielding* is most nearly opposite in meaning to *obdurate*.

10. **The best answer is E.** The word *assuage* means "to lessen or ease," whereas the word *exacerbate* means "to intensify bitterness or violence." Therefore, *exacerbate* is most nearly opposite in meaning to *assuage*.

11. **The best answer is B.** The word *garrulous* means "very talkative," whereas the word *taciturn* means "uncommunicative." Therefore, *taciturn* is most nearly opposite in meaning to *garrulous*.

12. **The best answer is C.** The word *laudable* means "deserving praise," whereas the word *contemptible* means "deserving of one's disgust." Therefore, *contemptible* is most nearly opposite in meaning to the word *laudable*.

13. **The best answer is E.** The relationship that exists between *vehement* and *forceful* can be expressed with the following sentence: "*Vehement* means 'very *forceful*.'" *Unstinting* means very *generous*, so this choice best expresses the relationship that exists between the words in the question stem.

14. **The best answer is D.** The context indicates that critics are undecided in their opinion of modern art. *Equivocal* means "ambiguous or uncertain," so it is the best choice.

15. **The best answer is E.** As it is used here, *keen* means to be "sharply aware," whereas *dull* means to be "not sharp." Therefore, *dull* is most nearly opposite in meaning to *keen*.

16. **The best answer is B.** The word *vacillated* means "wavered or showed indecision." The context suggests that the inexperienced teacher wavered between sticking to her lesson plans and taking advantage of spontaneous teaching moments in the classroom.

17. **The best answer is E.** Answer choices B, D, and C are all mentioned in the passage, but only as details supporting the main idea, which is the importance of bicycle use for transportation in urban China. Answer choice A is insufficiently specific because it doesn't mention China. Also, the author describes only a situation; she does not promote, or advocate, any particular program.

18. **The best answer is C.** The author addresses rising car ownership at the beginning of the second paragraph. Increased economic prosperity implies there is more money available and, consequently, more wealthy Chinese to purchase automobiles. Answer choices A and E are not addressed by the passage. Answer choice D is contradicted by the passage. While answer choice B is a plausible assumption, there is not enough evidence in the passage for it to be a credited answer.

19. **The best answer is C.** The word *vilify* means "to defame," and the word *malign* means "to slander." Therefore, the words are synonyms. *Trail* can mean "to *pursue*," so this choice best expresses the relationship that exists between the words in the question stem.

20. **The best answer is A.** The context indicates that the best word for the first blank will be an antonym for "central virtue." That is, something that *honesty* is not. Answer choices A, B, and D are good matches. Now consider the second blank, which should reflect a negative impact on the virtue of honesty. Among answer choices A, B, and D, only *undermined* fits the context.

21. **The best answer is C.** This is a main idea question, so the correct answer choice must reflect the theme of the entire passage. Answer choices B and E are too narrow. The tone of the passage is descriptive and neutral, so words like *promoting* and *arguing* are too strong. Therefore, answer choices A and D are incorrect.

22. **The best answer is D.** This is an implication question, so the correct answer will be strongly supported by the information in the passage. Answer choice D makes explicit the implied link between hormone production and disorders such as diabetes. While obesity and diabetes have been linked, the connection is not made in this passage, so answer choice A is incorrect. Answer choice B is contradicted by the passage.

Answer choice C simply restates the question; it does not address the reasons why. Answer choice E is outside the scope of the passage.

23. **The best answer is C.** Answer choice C is found near the start of the third paragraph. Answer choice A contradicts the passage, and answer choices B and E are outside the scope of the passage.

24. **The best answer is E.** Tone is essential to answering this question; the correct answer choice must have a neutral tone. Answer choices A and B are not neutral; in addition, they are incorrect because specific studies are not mentioned in the passage. While the passage does warn against getting too little sleep, this is not how the argument is developed. Therefore, answer choice C is incorrect. Answer choice D is incorrect because the author does not develop an opinion about non-human sleep. Only answer choice E correctly captures the tone and scope of the passage.

25. **The best answer is A.** The author indicates that the dolphins rely on sonar pulses to "see" and to find food. This implies that the sonar is necessary and used regularly by all river dolphins. Therefore, it can be logically inferred that a device that tracks these pulses could be useful in identifying and tracking the dolphins themselves. Answer choices C and D are contradicted by the passage. Answer choices B and E are not supported by the passage.

26. **The best answer is B.** At the end of the first paragraph, the author states that the underwater acoustic device measures the clicking sounds produced by dolphins and helps with identification and tracking. This best supports answer choice B. The other choices either are not addressed by the passage or are beyond its scope.

27. **The best answer is *domesticated, salubrious*.** First blank: The only word that fits the context of the sentence is *domesticated*; note that the text states that emus live on farms. Second blank: *Salubrious* means "healthful," which is what a domesticated animal might find life on a farm to be. *Palliative* means "tending to soothe," which isn't quite the right relationship; *nugatory* means "minor or insignificant." *Sanguine* means "cheerful," which the emu is not particularly, while *splenetic* means "full of rage"—also a bit too anthropomorphic for this particular avian species.

28. **The best answer is B.** The word *aversion* means "strong dislike," whereas the word *predilection* means "fondness." Therefore, the word *predilection* is most nearly opposite in meaning to the word *aversion*.

29. **The best answer is B.** The word *veritable* means "genuine," whereas the word *bogus* means "not genuine." Therefore, *bogus* is most nearly opposite in meaning to the word *veritable*.

30. **The best answer is A.** The word *veracity* refers to "honesty," which is the opposite of *deception*. *Acceptance* is the opposite of *renunciation*, so this choice best expresses the relationship that exists between the words in the question stem.

Section 4—Quantitative

1. **The correct answer is B.** To solve this problem, draw a diagram and calculate the values in each column, as follows:

Column A:

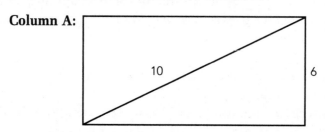

Use the Pythagorean theorem to find the length of the rectangle:

$$10^2 = 6^2 + b^2$$
$$100 = 36 + b^2$$
$$64 = b^2$$
$$8 = b$$

The perimeter of the rectangle is $2(6) + 2(8) = 12 + 16 = 28$.

Column B: An equilateral triangle has 3 equal sides, and the perimeter of a triangle is simply the sum of the lengths of the sides. Therefore, the perimeter of the triangle is $3(10) = 30$, and the quantity in Column B is greater than the quantity in Column A.

2. **The correct answer is A.** To determine a relationship, recognize that $y^4 - 1$ is equal to $(y^2)^2 - 1$. Therefore, you can substitute $y^2 = x^2 + 1$ into $(y^2)^2 - 1$ to get $(x^2 + 1)^2 - 1$, which is equivalent to $(x^2 + 1)(x^2 + 1)$. Use the FOIL method to simplify:

Multiply the First terms: x^4

Multiply the Outside terms: x^2

Multiply the Inside terms: x^2

Multiply the Last terms: 1

Now add the terms together: $x^4 + 2x^2 + 1$.

The quantity in Column A is $x^4 + 2x^2 + 1$, and the quantity in Column B is x^4. Because any number raised to the second or fourth power yields a positive number, the quantity in Column A must be greater than the quantity in Column B.

3. **The correct answer is A.** To solve this problem, recognize that the percentages are the percent of interest the investment will make each year. Assign x as the amount of the inheritance invested at 5% and assign the amount of inheritance invested at 6% as $(15,000 - x)$. Because the total interest earned is the sum of the interest from the two investments, it can be expressed as $0.05x + 0.06(15,000 - x) = 800$. Solve for x:

$$0.05x + 0.06(15,000) - 0.06x = 800$$

$$-0.01x + 900 = 800$$

$$-0.01x = -100$$

$$x = 10,000$$

Thus the quantity in Column A ($10,000) is greater than the quantity in Column B ($15,000 − $10,000).

4. **The correct answer is C.** To solve this problem, first convert the mixed numbers into improper fractions:

$$\textbf{Column A: } 4\frac{1}{8} = \frac{33}{8}$$

$$\textbf{Column B: } 16\frac{1}{2} = \frac{33}{2}$$

Next, recall that dividing by a fraction is equivalent to multiplying by its reciprocal. Therefore, the quantity in Column A $= \frac{33}{8} \times 2 = \frac{66}{8} = \frac{33}{4}$, and the quantity in Column B $= \frac{33}{2} \times \frac{1}{2} = \frac{33}{4}$.

5. **The correct answer is A.** Recall that 1 min = 60 sec. Then set up an equation to convert $\frac{\text{cm}}{\text{min}}$ into $\frac{\text{cm}}{\text{sec}}$ as follows:

$$\frac{x\text{ cm}}{1\text{ min}} \times \frac{1\text{ min}}{60\text{ sec}} = \frac{x\text{ cm}}{60\text{ sec}}$$

Then multiply by y sec to calculate the distance traveled:

$$y\left(\frac{x\text{ cm}}{60\text{ sec}}\right) = \frac{xy\text{ cm}}{60}$$

6. **The correct answer is E.** To solve this problem, first figure out the probability (p) that a person selected at random will have a first and last name that begin with the same letter. Divide the number of people with first and last names that begin with the same letter by the total number of people on the membership list:

$$p = \frac{36}{720} = 0.05$$

Because all probabilities add up to one, $1 - p$ will equal the number of people whose first and last names do NOT begin with the same letter:

$$1.00 - 0.05 = 0.95$$

7. **The correct answer is A.** Because the average is the sum of a group of values divided by the number of values, the average of a, b, and 5 is 4 and can be expressed as $\frac{(a + b + 5)}{3} = 4$. To determine the relationships of Column A and Column B, solve this equation for $a + b$. First multiply both sides by 3. Then subtract 5 from both sides to get $a + b = 7$. Thus the quantity in Column A ($\frac{7}{3} \approx 2.33$) is greater than the quantity in Column B (2).

8. **The correct answer is B.** To quickly solve this problem, calculate the values of the exponential terms in each column:

Column A: $4^5 = 4 \times 4 \times 4 \times 4 \times 4 = 1{,}024$

Column B: $5^4 = 5 \times 5 \times 5 \times 5 = 625$

Because 1,024 is an even number, the greatest prime factor will be 2. Likewise, the greatest prime factor of 625 will be 5. The quantity in Column B is greater than the quantity in Column A.

9. **The correct answer is 3.** Remember to perform the operations in the correct order, as follows:

$$3(x + 4) - 8 = 2x + 7$$
$$3x + 12 - 8 = 2x + 7$$
$$3x + 4 = 2x + 7$$
$$3x = 2x + 3$$
$$x = 3$$

10. **The correct answer is D.** To solve this problem, set x = the number of 1-page memos typed. The number of 2-page memos typed will equal $8 - x$. Add the total number of pages typed from 1-page memos, x, to the total number of pages typed from 2-page memos: $2(8 - x) = 12$. Solve for x:

$$x + 2(8 - x) = 12$$
$$x + 16 - 2x = 12$$
$$x = 4$$

Because the question asks for how many 2-page memos the receptionist typed, substitute $x = 4$ into $8 - x$ to yield an answer of 4.

11. **The correct answer is B.** To determine the relationship, solve the equation $8x^2 = 24$ for x. First, divide both sides by 8 to get $x^2 = 3$. Because the square root of 3 is less than 2, the quantity in Column B is greater than the quantity in Column A.

12. **The correct answer is C.** Because percent decrease is the amount of decrease divided by the original amount, the decrease of the stock's assets can be expressed as $\dfrac{4.03}{(74.02 + 4.03)}$, or 0.05. This is true because the original amount is \$74.02 billion plus \$4.03 billion. Remember that $0.05 = 5\%$.

13. **The correct answer is C.** To solve this problem, you must determine the value of the quantity in each column. Because the probability of an event is expressed as the number of favorable outcomes divided by the total number of possible outcomes, Column A can be written as $\dfrac{9}{18}$. Column B can be expressed as $\dfrac{(3 + 6)}{18}$, or $\dfrac{9}{18}$. Thus, the quantities in Column A and Column B are equal.

14. **The correct answer is E.** The first step in solving this problem is to recall that there are 365 days in a typical year and 24 hours in one day. Therefore, a teenager will spend a total of $365 \times 24 = 8,760$ hours on all activities in one year. Next, notice that in one day, a teenager spends 3 hours watching TV and 10 hours sleeping; therefore, 13 out of 24 hours are spent on those two activities. Set up a proportion to solve:

$$\frac{13}{24} = \frac{x}{8,760}$$
$$113,880 = 24x$$
$$4,745 = x$$

15. **The correct answer is C.** To solve this problem, look at the graph to see that teens spend 7 hours per day on $\frac{\text{Work}}{\text{School}}$. Therefore, the ratio is $\frac{7}{24}$ or 7:24.

16. **The correct answer is A.** To solve this problem, first calculate the value of the quantity in each column. The quantity in Column A is (30% of 60) + 70. Because 30% of 60 can be represented as .30(60), or 18, the quantity (30% of 60) + 70 = 18 + 70, or 88. Similarly, (70% of 60) + 30 = .7(60) + 30, or 42 + 30, which equals 72. Thus the quantity in Column A (88) is greater than the quantity in Column B (72).

17. **The correct answer is D.** To solve this problem, try some test values for x. If $x = -2$, then Column A (-4) is *less* than Column B (4). However, if $x = 0.5$, then Column A (1) is *greater* than Column B (0.25). Therefore, you cannot determine the relationship based on the given information.

18. **The correct answer is E.** Because the reciprocal is the inverse of the quantity, the reciprocal of $a - \frac{1}{b}$ is $\frac{1}{\left(a - \frac{1}{b}\right)}$. Multiply the fraction by $\frac{b}{b}$ to remove the fraction in the denominator as follows:

$$\frac{1}{a - \frac{1}{b}} \times \frac{b}{b} = \frac{b}{b\left(a - \frac{1}{b}\right)} = \frac{b}{(ab - 1)}$$

19. **The correct answer is A.** To answer this question, take each of the Roman numerals independently and eliminate answer choices as follows:

   Roman numeral I: For n to be a multiple of 5 and 3, it must also be a multiple of 15. $15 \times 2 = 30$, which is an even number. Roman numeral I is not always true, so eliminate answer choices B, C, and E.

   Roman numeral II: 15, 45, 60, etc., are also multiples of 5 and 3; therefore, Roman numeral II is not always true. Eliminate answer choice D.

   Roman numeral III: Because $3 \times 5 = 15$, n will also be a multiple of 15. Roman numeral III is always true, and the correct answer choice must be A.

20. **The correct answer is B.** To solve this problem, find the line for wool on the second table. In 1996, the cost of wool was about $35,000, while in 2000 the cost of wool was about $45,000. Therefore, from 1996 to 2000, the cost of wool increased $10,000. There are 5 years in the interval including 1996 and 2000, so the average yearly increase in the cost of wool was $10,000 $\times$ 5 = $2,000.

21. **The correct answer is D.** To solve this problem, first find the total volume of textile imports in 1991, as follows:

    Cotton = about 17 million pounds

    Rayon = about 5 million pounds

    Wool = about 13 million pounds

    Polyester = about 13 million pounds

    Therefore, in 1991, 17 + 5 + 13 + 13 = about 48 million pounds of textiles were imported. Of that, about 17 million pounds were cotton, so $\frac{17}{48} \times 100$ = about 35% of textile imports in 1991 came from cotton.

22. **The correct answer is D.** Use substitution to find the value of x. First, solve $(x + y)^2 = 4$ for y. Take the square root of both sides and then subtract x from both sides to get $y = 2 - x$. Substitute $y = 2 - x$ into $x + 3y = 3$ and solve for x:

    $$x + 3(2 - x) = 3$$
    $$x + 6 - 3x = 3$$
    $$2x = 3$$
    $$x = \frac{3}{2}$$

23. **The correct answer is B.** To solve this problem easily, recall that a larger value divided by a smaller value will be greater than a smaller value divided by the larger value. Because v is less than w, Column B will always be greater than Column A.

24. **The correct answer is A.** You could solve this by multiplying each quantity and comparing. However, you could also solve by thinking about the quantities in the following ways:

   90,531 = 90,315 + 216. Therefore, the following is true:

   100,315(90,531)

   = 100,315(90,315 + 216)

   = 100,315(90,315) + 100,315(216)

   Likewise, 100,531 = 100,315 + 216. Therefore, the following is true:

   100,531(90,315)

   = (100,315 + 216)(90,315)

   = 100,315(90,315) + 216(90,315)

   It is apparent that the quantity in Column A is greater than the quantity in Column B.

25. **The correct answer is A.** To solve this problem, first solve the inequality for x. Divide both sides by 6 to get $0 < x < \frac{1}{3}$. Therefore, x is a fraction between 0 and $\frac{1}{3}$. Recognize that a higher power of a fraction will yield a larger denominator, and therefore a smaller fraction. Thus, the quantity in Column A is larger than the quantity in Column B.

26. **The correct answer is D.** To solve this problem, first perform the operation inside the parentheses:

   $$2(100) = 200$$
   $$5(1) = 5$$
   $$6(1,000) = 6,000$$
   $$9(10) = 90$$

   Add these quantities together to get $200 + 5 + 6,000 + 90 = 6,295$.

27. **The correct answer is B.** To solve this problem, draw a diagram such as this:

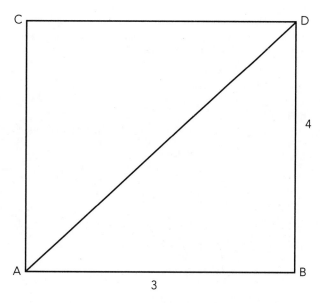

Recognize that Danny's house will also be 3 km west and 4 km north of Billy's house, creating a right triangle. The distance from Allie's house to Danny's house is the hypotenuse, so use the Pythagorean theorem to solve:

$$3^2 + 4^2 = c^2$$
$$9 + 16 = c^2$$
$$25 = c^2$$
$$5 = c$$

28. **The correct answer is A.** Multiplying 25.86 by $\frac{1}{100}$ is the same as dividing 25.86 by 100, which will have the effect of reducing the quantity. You can eliminate answer choices C, D, and E. When dividing by 100, the decimal point is moved two places to the left. Thus $25.86 \times \frac{1}{100} = 0.2586$.

14

GRE Practice Test 3

CHAPTER GOALS

- Take a simulated full-length GRE under actual test conditions.
- Check your results using the Answer Key.
- Review the explanations for each question, focusing particularly on questions you answered incorrectly or did not answer at all.
- Build your test-taking confidence.

The simulated GRE in this chapter contains 58 multiple-choice questions and two essay tasks, divided into four main sections. You should allow approximately 2 hours and 30 minutes to complete the test.

Each of the test sections should be completed in the time indicated at the beginning of the sections, and in the order in which they appear.

There are several different types of questions within each section. Make sure that you read and understand all directions before you begin. To achieve the best results, time yourself strictly on each section.

You should answer each question before you move on to the next question to make this simulated test as much like the actual CAT as possible. Remember to circle your answers on the test so that you can compare your answers to the correct answers listed in the Answer Key on page 390. Carefully review the explanations for any question that you answered incorrectly.

We suggest that you make this practice test as much like the real test as possible. Find a quiet location, free from distractions, and make sure that you have pencils and a timepiece.

Review the Scoring Guidelines on page 391, but remember that your score on the actual GRE will be dependent on many factors, including your level of preparedness and your fatigue level on test day.

361

SECTION 1—ISSUE TASK

45 Minutes

1 Question

You will have 45 minutes to select one topic, organize your thoughts, and compose a response that represents your point of view on the topic that you choose. Do not respond to any topic other than the one you select; a response to any other topic will receive a score of 0.

You will be given a choice between two general issues on a broad range of topics. You will be required to discuss your perspective on one of the issues, using examples and reasons drawn from your own experiences and observations.

Use scratch paper to organize your response before you begin writing. Write your response on the pages provided, or type your response using a word processor with the spell and grammar check functions turned off.

<u>Directions:</u> Present your viewpoint on *one* of the claims made below. Use relevant reasons and examples to support your point of view.

Topic 1

"The highest goal for life or career is not striving to compete, but learning to cooperate."

Topic 2

"While it is easy to give positive feedback to another person or group, it is far more worthwhile to be critical of the work of others."

SECTION 2—ARGUMENT TASK

30 Minutes

1 Question

You will have 30 minutes to organize your thoughts and compose a response that critiques the given argument. Do not respond to any topic other than the one given; a response to any other topic will receive a score of 0.

You are not being asked to discuss your point of view on the statement. You should identify and analyze the central elements of the argument, the underlying assumptions that are being made, and any supporting information that is given. Your critique can also discuss other information that would strengthen or weaken the argument or make it more logical.

Use scratch paper to organize your response before you begin writing. Write your response on the pages provided, or type your response using a word processor with the spell and grammar check functions turned off.

<u>Directions:</u> Critique the reasoning used in the following argument.

The following memorandum was sent to the president of Arbayo Manufacturing from the human resources director.

"In order to reduce the turnover expense to the company associated with recruiting, hiring, and training, Arbayo should adopt a program of screening prospective new employees with multiple-choice tests designed to assess intelligence, emotional aptitude, and overall interests. This technique has clearly benefited Wixmer Bank: Five years ago, 200 recently hired Wixmer employees volunteered to undergo such testing. Five years later, over 80 percent of those employees were still employed at Wixmer, whereas the company as a whole had a retention rate of only 50 percent."

SECTION 3—VERBAL

30 Minutes

30 Questions

This section consists of five different types of questions: Sentence Completion, Analogy, Antonym, and Text Completion with Two or Three Blanks (this is a new question type; you will typically see only one of these questions on your GRE), and Reading Comprehension. To answer the questions, select the best answer from the answer choices given. Circle the letter or word(s) of your choice.

Directions for Sentence Completion Questions: The following sentences each contain one or two blanks, indicating that something has been left out of the sentence. Each answer choice contains one word or a set of words. Select the word or set of words that, when inserted in the blank(s), best fits the context of the sentence.

Example: Because of his --------, Brian's guests felt very welcome and comfortable staying at his house for the weekend.

    (A)   animosity

    (B)   hospitality

    (C)   determination

    (D)   wittiness

    (E)   severity

Directions for Analogy Questions: The following questions contain a set of related words in capital letters and five answer choices. Each answer choice also contains a set of words. Select the set of words that represents a relationship similar to the original set of words.

Example: APPRENTICE : PLUMBER ::

    (A)   player : coach

    (B)   child : parent

    (C)   student : teacher

    (D)   author : publisher

    (E)   intern : doctor

<u>Directions for Antonym Questions:</u> The following questions contain a word in capital letters and five answer choices. Each answer choice contains a word or phrase. Select the word or phrase that best expresses a meaning opposite to the word in capital letters.

Example: CREDULOUS:

> (A) skeptical
>
> (B) naive
>
> (C) spontaneous
>
> (D) sensitive
>
> (E) discrete

<u>Directions for Text Completion with Two or Three Blanks Questions:</u> These questions consist of a short passage with two or three numbered blanks, indicating that something has been left out of the text. Select the word or set of words that, when inserted in the blanks, best completes the text.

Example: Experts believe that humans have ten trillion cells in their bodies that (i) _____ any number of essential genetic elements; scientists often marvel at what incredible (ii) _____ would ensue should the cells become jumbled or misunderstand their purpose.

Blank (i)	Blank (ii)
govern	order
organize	method
dislocate	chaos

<u>Directions for Reading Comprehension Questions:</u> The passages in this section are followed by several questions. The questions correspond to information that is stated or implied in the passage. Read the passage and choose the best answer for each question.

Answer the questions in the order presented.

The Verbal section questions begin on the next page.

1. PILOT : JET ::

   (A) actor : state

   (B) gate : prison

   (C) physician : health

   (D) fence : landscape

   (E) conductor : orchestra

2. FECKLESS : PURPOSE ::

   (A) constant : habit

   (B) eccentric : convention

   (C) inherent : attribute

   (D) innate : possession

   (E) inimical : harm

3. The intern, while --------, proved too unskilled to be permitted to work on his own -------- project.

   (A) reckless . . unsupervised

   (B) enthusiastic . . dedicated

   (C) competent . . autonomous

   (D) excitable . . subsidiary

   (E) responsible . . obscure

4. I put a bandage on the child's finger to -------- the flow of blood from his cut.

   (A) irrigate

   (B) expose

   (C) stanch

   (D) pluck

   (E) obviate

5. HACKNEYED : ORIGINAL ::

    (A) fatuous : intelligent

    (B) incongruous : impossible

    (C) careless : inadvertent

    (D) threatening : forceful

    (E) beginning : inchoate

6. SQUELCH:

    (A) pilfer

    (B) amplify

    (C) gleam

    (D) suppress

    (E) quench

7. INSIPID:

    (A) vivacious

    (B) articulate

    (C) adamant

    (D) dull

    (E) indecisive

8. BANAL : ZEST ::

    (A) fortuitous : grace

    (B) garrulous : speech

    (C) gregarious : money

    (D) grievous : sincerity

    (E) incongruous : harmony

9. NOXIOUS:

    (A) salubrious

    (B) deleterious

    (C) deficient

    (D) complete

    (E) egregious

10. VENERABLE:

    (A) aged

    (B) esteemed

    (C) forgotten

    (D) disreputable

    (E) noble

11. TRACTABLE:

    (A) unruly

    (B) phlegmatic

    (C) acquiescent

    (D) distant

    (E) artful

12. PRAGMATIC:

    (A) ample

    (B) sensible

    (C) impractical

    (D) astute

    (E) exiguous

13. IRASCIBLE : ANGERED ::

    (A) exigent : ignoble

    (B) docile : trained

    (C) exceptional : uncommon

    (D) ethical : mistreated

    (E) estimable : offended

14. France and Spain, while actually very --------, share a common reputation for a more -------- way of life than that experienced by the average harried American.

    (A) similar . . tranquil

    (B) genteel . . guarded

    (C) informal . . substantial

    (D) dissimilar . . serene

    (E) diverse . . traditional

15. DUBIOUS:

    (A) inadvertent

    (B) oblivious

    (C) intentional

    (D) skeptical

    (E) certain

16. Both discipline-based and affection-based parenting methods stand the chance of undermining their own assumptions: Overreliance on external discipline through punishment may (i) _____ the child's independent moral development, while an overly (ii) _____ parenting style may provide the child with the false impression that no one else's needs matter.

Blank (i)	Blank (ii)
occlude	obstreperous
anticipate	indulgent
repudiate	lachrymose

Questions 17 and 18 are based on the following passage.

The polar lights known as auroras are produced when charged subatomic particles, such as protons and electrons flowing from the sun through Earth's magnetosphere, collide with atoms and molecules in Earth's upper atmosphere. For reasons not entirely understood, magnetic storms, called substorms, occasionally occur where the flow of particles greatly increases and the interplanetary magnetic field becomes much stronger. These substorms are frequently visible on Earth because they increase the intensity of the polar lights.

Recently, five identical probes were blasted into orbit in a $200 million U.S. project known as the THEMIS mission. Scientists hope the probes will be able to investigate a number of mysteries about the nature of the substorm instabilities, including when and where substorms begin, how the individual components of the substorm interact, and how substorms power the auroras. The mission's secondary objectives involve understanding and predicting variations in the flux of electrons in Earth's outer radiation belt. These electrons pose a hazard to the safety of both astronauts and spacecraft. Understanding substorm instabilities would thus improve success rates of future space missions.

17. The main purpose of the passage is to

(A) explain why it is important to invest in space research

(B) explain how magnetic substorms interfere with satellite communications

(C) define magnetic substorms and identify a recent scientific experiment to study them

(D) compare two alternative approaches to the study of magnetic substorms

(E) demonstrate that unmanned probes are the best way to conduct research in space

18. According to the passage, all of the following are objectives of the THEMIS mission EXCEPT:

(A) predicting variations in the flux of electrons in Earth's outer radiation belt

(B) understanding how individual components of the substorm interact

(C) guaranteeing the success rates of future space missions

(D) investigating when and where substorms begin

(E) understanding how substorms power the auroras

19. PROPAGATE : MULTIPLY ::

    (A) dilate : decrease

    (B) discern : include

    (C) expect : shift

    (D) precipitate : happen

    (E) deride : excel

20. People traveled hundreds of miles to be in the presence of the -------- and listen to his -------- words.

    (A) scholar . . ludicrous

    (B) dissident . . calming

    (C) extrovert . . fabricated

    (D) miscreant . . joyous

    (E) sage . . astute

Questions 21–24 are based on the following passage.

Despite the ubiquity of computer technology, most people are unaware that
computers exist in two mutually exclusive, distinct categories: analog and digital.
We are most familiar with digital computers, such as laptops. On the one hand,
digital computers process information using a binary number system that allows
(5) them to calculate numbers in an accurate and exact manner. Analog computers,
on the other hand, do not calculate per se; they measure and respond to a
continuously changing input.

Simple analog computers, called astrolabes, were first developed by the
Greeks to solve problems in astronomy. The devices proved very popular and
(10) soon spread throughout the Roman world. By the 10th century, Muslim scholars
had developed the astrolabe into a sophisticated mechanical device capable of
calculating solutions to problems not only in astronomy, but also in astrology,
navigation, surveying, and timekeeping.

Modern scientific opinion was that the ancient Greeks had been
(15) technologically unable to produce a similarly sophisticated computer, until a
discovery was made just over a century ago. In 1900, divers discovered the wreck
of a merchant ship, possibly dating back to 150 BCE, off the coast of the Greek
island Antikythera. In the wreckage, they found the remains of a complex device
apparently a thousand years ahead of its time.

(20) Made of metal, this device, known as the Antikythera mechanism, is
approximately the size of a shoebox. At the time of its discovery, it was in terrible
shape, having been underwater for so long. Its pieces had merged into a broken
mass and experts could discern only that it had something to do with astronomy.

(25) Thanks to a combination of advanced imaging methods and X-ray computer tomography, however, scientists have since discovered much more.

(30) Originally, the mechanism had at least 30 bronze gears with as many as 225 hand-cut triangular teeth. It had three main dials, one on the front and two on the back, respectively marking the astronomical divisions of the Egyptian calendar, the Metonic cycle, and the Saros cycle. Each dial had subdials for greater specificity. For example, the front dial contained a smaller dial that could be adjusted to account for leap years. There were also hands and gearing to account for the movements of the planets.

(35) While the workings of the device are now fairly well understood, researchers are still puzzled by the reason it was made. Some postulate that it, like later astrolabes, was used to create astrological charts, or to set feast days, or even to adjust the lunar and solar calendars. Others have thought it was a curiosity made solely for display. The device's relatively small size and the inclusion of a 3,000 character "user's manual" suggest that the mechanism was created to be portable and functional, but scientists are no closer to knowing for sure and can only (40) wonder at the purpose of its superb design.

21. Which of the following would weaken the author's argument that the Antikythera mechanism was a thousand years ahead of its time?

    (A) Items discovered on the Antikythera shipwreck were found to date back to 500 BCE.

    (B) Similarly complex astrolabes were recently found at a series of archeological sites dating between 100 and 500 CE.

    (C) Complex machines involving pulleys and ropes were found at archeological sites on the Greek island of Antikythera.

    (D) At the time of the Antikythera shipwreck, the island of Rhodes was famous for its collection of scientific devices.

    (E) Ancient Romans were famous for their acquisitions of Greek art and architecture.

22. The author mentions that the front dial of the Antikythera mechanism contained a smaller, adjustable dial (line 30) most probably in order to

    (A) illustrate the complexity of the mechanism

    (B) describe exactly how the mechanism worked

    (C) emphasize the importance of leap years in the study of astronomy

    (D) argue that the mechanism was used only for very specific tasks

    (E) allow readers to imagine what the device looked like

23. The passage's statement that, by the 10th century, Muslim scholars had developed the astrolabe into a sophisticated mechanical device would justify which of the following conclusions?

    (A) Muslim scholars were unaware of other scientific measuring devices.

    (B) Muslim scholars developed a kind of technology that had never been known before.

    (C) There was no need for sophisticated mechanical devices such as the astrolabe before the 10th century.

    (D) The astrolabe's sophistication allowed for more exploration of the physical world.

    (E) Muslim scholars had a need to solve complex problems in astronomy, navigation, surveying, and timekeeping.

24. The passage supplies information for answering which of the following questions?

    (A) Where was the mechanism made?

    (B) What was the primary purpose of the Antikythera mechanism?

    (C) How did ancient scientists know how to use the Antikythera mechanism?

    (D) Precisely how many gears did the mechanism have?

    (E) What is the purpose of computer tomography?

Questions 25 and 26 are based on the following passage.

Modern science fiction movies are often known for their breathtaking special effects. These effects can show us a glimpse of the future, and frequently have tremendous dramatic force. Sometimes, however, special effects can leave the science behind to focus only on the fiction. One of the worst offenders is a film's
(5) depiction of explosions in outer space.

      On Earth, explosions occur in some form of matter, usually air or water. The change in energy level in the matter creates the energy differential known as a *shock wave*. The wave is what creates the characteristic "boom" of an explosion. Since there is very little matter in outer space, the energy transfer never takes
(10) place. Consequently, there is no sound. Further, because air and water are not perfect conduits for energy, they measurably slow the travel of the explosive force. This allows the explosion to unfold in relatively slow motion, which renders it visible to the eye. In space, there is nothing to slow the energy, which would disperse almost immediately. The effect for an observer would be a bright
(15) flash, gone almost as soon as it appeared, and nothing like the great billowing space clouds shown in the movies, suggesting that reality is insufficiently dramatic for cinematic representation.

25. The author's argument is developed primarily by the use of

    (A) an attack on the misuse of scientific discoveries by modern film directors

    (B) a critique of technical developments in science fiction movie special effects

    (C) an example of how science fiction directors distort science to increase dramatic effect

    (D) an analogy between science fiction movie special effect and science education in schools

    (E) a warning against an overreliance on films to teach science to youngsters

26. According to the passage, which of the following is true about explosions in space?

    I. A lack of matter in space allows the energy from an explosion to travel very quickly.

    II. An explosion in space would be visible as a flash of bright light.

    III. Shock waves created by an explosion in space would cause an audible "boom."

    (A) I only

    (B) II only

    (C) I and II only

    (D) II and III only

    (E) I, II, and III

27. Chris's interest in his action-figure collection began to) _____ as he completed elementary school and became a preteen; he was growing up.

    (A) improve

    (B) dilate

    (C) exist

    (D) wane

    (E) thrive

28. OBTUSE:

    (A) substantial

    (B) trivial

    (C) immense

    (D) perceptive

    (E) dense

29. QUOTIDIAN:

    (A) circadian

    (B) sporadic

    (C) stark

    (D) adverse

    (E) exotic

30. INUNDATE : OVERWHELM ::

    (A) lambaste : beat

    (B) extricate : tangle

    (C) extol : criticize

    (D) redo : expunge

    (E) fathom : declare

END OF SECTION 3

SECTION 4—QUANTITATIVE

30 Minutes

28 Questions

This section includes three types of questions: Quantitative Comparison, Discrete Problem Solving, and Numeric Entry. For each question, circle the letter of your choice or write your answer as instructed.

General Information:

Numbers: All of the numbers used in this section are real numbers.

Figures: Assume that the position of all points, angles, etc., are in the order shown and the measures of angles are positive.

Straight lines can be assumed to be straight.

All figures lie in a plane unless otherwise stated.

The figures given for each question provide information to solve the problem. The figures are not drawn to scale unless otherwise stated. To solve the problems, use your knowledge of mathematics; do not estimate lengths and sizes of the figures to answer questions.

Directions for Quantitative Comparison Questions: Some of the following questions give you two quantities, one in Column A and one in Column B. Compare the two quantities and choose one of the following answer choices:

A if the quantity in Column A is greater;

B if the quantity in Column B is greater;

C if the two quantities are equal;

D if you cannot determine the relationship based on the given information.

Do not mark answer choice E, as there are only four choices from which to choose.

Note: Information and/or figures pertaining to one or both of the quantities may appear above the two columns. Any information that appears in both columns has the same meaning in Column A and in Column B.

Example: **Column A** **Column B**

$-(3)^4$ $(-3)^4$

<u>Directions for Discrete Problem Solving Questions:</u> Select the best answer for the remaining multiple-choice questions.

Example: If $y = 5x$ and $z = 3y$, then in terms of x, $x + y + z =$

      (A) $21x$

      (B) $16x$

      (C) $15x$

      (D) $9x$

      (E) $8x$

<u>Directions for Numeric Entry Questions:</u> Enter your answer in the box below the question.

Example: Solve the equation for x: $2(x - 3) + 9 = 4x - 7$

    $x =$ ☐

Answer the questions in the order presented.

The Quantitative section questions begin on the next page.

	Column A	**Column B**

w, x, and y are positive
integers and wx = y.

1.	w	y

Working at a constant rate,
machine Y makes x bolts in
0.25 hour and machine Z makes
x bolts in 0.50 hour. (x > 0)

2.	The bolts made by machine Y in 4 hours.	The bolts made by machine Z in 8 hours.

$$x = 2y + 3$$

3.	3x	5y + 1
4.	$\frac{1}{4} + \frac{2}{5}$	$\frac{(1 + 2)}{(4 + 5)}$

5. If a small soda can contains 300 mL of soda, how many liters of soda are in 25 cans?

(A) 0.75

(B) 7.5

(C) 75

(D) 750

(E) 7,500

6. A given street median is planted with trees. Of the 30 trees in the median, 3 are lindens, one-fifth are oaks, 12 are cedars, and the remainder are maples. What is the ratio of lindens to maples?

(A) 1 to 10

(B) 1 to 4

(C) 1 to 3

(D) 1 to 2

(E) 3 to 1

	Column A	**Column B**

$$4 < y < 6$$

7.

Column A	**Column B**
$\dfrac{(4 + y)}{4}$	$\dfrac{(6 + y)}{y}$

Seven one-dollar coins are distributed
among Abby, Bobbie, and Connie
so that each person receives at least
one 1 dollar coin.

8.

Column A	**Column B**
The total number of ways to distribute the coins so that at least 1 person receives at least \$3.	The total number of ways to distribute the coins.

$$x + 5 = 15$$

9.

Column A	**Column B**
$x - 5$	$\dfrac{x}{5}$

10. If $2x + 3y = 18$ and $y = 3$, then $4x =$

(A) 3

(B) 9

(C) 10

(D) 18

(E) 36

	Column A	**Column B**

11.

Column A	**Column B**
The average of a and b	The average of $\dfrac{a}{2}$ and $2b$

12. A rancher wishes to enclose a field that measures 12 feet by 27 feet. He purchases 76 feet of fencing material that must be affixed to posts at the corners, with no two posts being more than 6 feet apart. What is the least number of fence posts he will require to fence in this field?

(A) 10

(B) 12

(C) 13

(D) 14

(E) 18

13. $|14| \times |-2| = ?$

Refer to the following graphs for Questions 14 and 15.

Types of Diets in 1995 (total dieters: 135 million)   Types of Diets in 2000 (total dieters: 210 million)

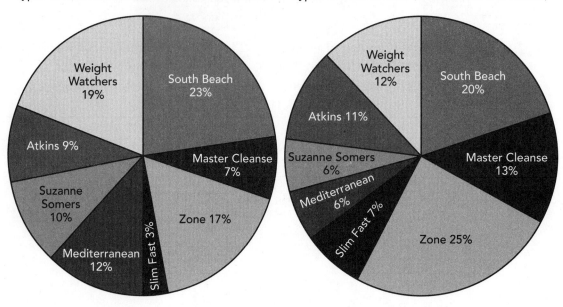

14. In 1995, approximately how many million people were on the Zone Diet?

(A) 12

(B) 16

(C) 23

(D) 27

(E) 35

15. What is the approximate percent increase in the number of Master Cleanse dieters from 1995 to 2000?

(A) 200%

(B) 189%

(C) 187%

(D) 159%

(E) 129%

Column A	**Column B**

The price of a piece of jewelry
is reduced from \$60 to \$40. The
reduced price is then increased
by x% to return it to \$60.

16. x 20

0.02 is less than or equal to $x < .025$.
$0.02 < y$ is less than or equal to $.025$.

17. The absolute value of $x - y$ .005

18. If x is an integer, then the units digit of x squared cannot be

  (A) 0

  (B) 1

  (C) 2

  (D) 5

  (E) 6

19. Which is both the mean and the median of 5 consecutive integers the least of which is x?

  (A) $x + 4$

  (B) $x + 3$

  (C) $x + 2$

  (D) $\dfrac{(x + 28)}{7}$

  (E) $\dfrac{(x + 3)}{2}$

Refer to the following information for Questions 20 and 21.

A poll of 200 students was taken before Centerville College changed the name of its mascot. All 2,000 students indicated which one of the four mascot names they would vote for. The results of the poll are given in the table below.

Mascot Name	Number of Students
Spartans	300
Lions	400
Gophers	800
Knights	500

20. What percent of the students polled chose Spartans in the poll?

    (A) 40%

    (B) 30%

    (C) 25%

    (D) 20%

    (E) 15%

21. If the information in the table were converted to a pie chart, then the central angle of the sector for Lions would measure how many degrees?

    (A) 144°

    (B) 108°

    (C) 72°

    (D) 54°

    (E) It cannot be determined from the given information.

22. What rational number is halfway between $\frac{1}{6}$ and $\frac{1}{2}$?

    (A) $\frac{1}{8}$

    (B) $\frac{1}{4}$

    (C) $\frac{1}{3}$

    (D) $\frac{2}{3}$

    (E) $\frac{3}{2}$

Column A	**Column B**
23. The largest prime number between 65 and 80	The largest multiple of 7 less than 81

Data Set A: 2, 5, 7, 9, 2x
Data Set B: 3, 6, 10, 13, x

24. The mean of Data Set A	The mean of Data Set B

$x + y = 27$
$y - 9 = 23$

25. x	y

26. If $b - c = 5$ and $a + c = 35$, then $a + b =$

    (A) 30

    (B) 35

    (C) 40

    (D) 42

    (E) 50

27. What is the remainder when 7^3 is divided by 9?

    (A) 0

    (B) 1

    (C) 2

    (D) 3

    (E) 5

28. How many positive whole numbers less than 50 are NOT equal to squares of whole numbers?

    (A) 9

    (B) 15

    (C) 43

    (D) 44

    (E) 45

END OF SECTION 4

GRE Practice Test 3 Answer Key

Section 3

1.	E	17.	C
2.	B	18.	C
3.	C	19.	D
4.	C	20.	E
5.	A	21.	B
6.	B	22.	A
7.	A	23.	E
8.	E	24.	C
9.	A	25.	C
10.	D	26.	C
11.	A	27.	D
12.	C	28.	D
13.	B	29.	B
14.	D	30.	E
15.	E		
16.	occlude; indulgent		

Section 4

1.	D	17.	D
2.	C	18.	C
3.	D	19.	C
4.	A	20.	E
5.	B	21.	C
6.	C	22.	C
7.	D	23.	A
8.	C	24.	D
9.	A	25.	A
10.	D	26.	B
11.	D	27.	B
12.	D	28.	C
13.	28		
14.	C		
15.	B		
16.	A		

Scoring Guidelines

To calculate your approximate Scaled Score, count the number of questions that you answered correctly on the Verbal and Quantitative sections. This is your Raw Score, which can then be converted to a Scaled Score for each section using the table on page 392. Remember that this is just an *approximation* of what you might expect to score on the GRE if you took the test today!

SCORE CONVERSION TABLE FOR GRE GENERAL TEST

Raw Score	Scaled Score	
	Verbal	Quantitative
30	800	
29	780	
28	750	800
27	730	780
26	710	750
25	690	720
24	660	700
23	640	680
22	620	650
21	600	630
20	580	610
19	570	600
18	550	590
17	520	570
16	490	540
15	470	500
14	450	480
13	440	460
12	400	430
11	380	400
10	360	390

Continued on Next Page

9	320	370
8	240	320
7	200	290
6	200	240
5	200	200
4	200	200
0–3	200	200

NOTE: Your actual scaled GRE score may vary by as many as 60 points.

GRE Practice Test 3 Answers and Explanations

Sections 1 and 2—Analytical Writing

Because grading the essays is subjective, we've chosen not to include any "graded" essays here. Your best bet is to have someone you trust, such as your personal tutor, read your essays and give you an honest critique. Make the grading criteria mentioned in Chapter 7, "GRE Analytical Writing Assessment," available to whoever grades your essays. If you plan on grading your own essays, review the grading criteria and be as honest as possible regarding the structure, development, organization, technique, and appropriateness of your writing. Focus on your weak areas and continue to practice in order to improve your writing skills.

Section 3—Verbal

1. **The best answer is E.** The relationship that exists between *pilot* and *jet* can be expressed with the following sentence: "A *pilot* is a human who controls a jet, directing it where to go." Eliminate answer choices B and D because the first word does not refer to a human. A *physician* does not necessarily control or direct *health*, so answer choice C can also be eliminated. A *conductor* controls and directs and *orchestra*, so this choice best expresses the relationship that exists between the words in the question stem.

2. **The best answer is B.** The relationship that exists between *feckless* and *purpose* can be expressed with the following sentence: "*Feckless* means 'lacking in purpose.'" *Eccentric* means "lacking in convention," so this choice best expresses the relationship that exists between the words in the question stem.

3. **The best answer is C.** The words that best fit in the blanks should suggest a contradiction between the intern's perceived ability and his actual ability to perform a specific task. While he was *competent*, he was, nonetheless, not skilled enough to work *autonomously*. The other answer choices are not supported by the context.

4. **The best answer is C.** The word *stanch* means to "stop the flow of," which best fits the context of the sentence.

5. **The best answer is A.** The relationship that exists between *hackneyed* and *original* can be expressed with the following sentence: "*Hackneyed* is an antonym for *original*." *Fatuous* is an antonym for *intelligent*, so this choice best expresses the relationship that exists between the words in the question stem.

6. **The best answer is B.** The word *squelch* means "to crush or silence," whereas the word *amplify* means "to increase or make louder." Therefore, *amplify* is most nearly opposite in meaning to *squelch*.

7. **The best answer is A.** To be *insipid* means to be "dull," whereas to be *vivacious* means to be "high-spirited." Therefore, the word *vivacious* is most nearly opposite in meaning to the word *insipid*.

8. **The best answer is E.** The relationship that exists between *banal* and *zest* can be expressed with the following sentence: "*Banal* means 'lacking *zest*.'" *Incongruous* means "lacking *harmony*," so this choice best expresses the relationship that exists between the words in the question stem.

9. **The best answer is A.** To be *noxious* means to be "unwholesome or harmful," whereas to be *salubrious* means to be "favorable to health or well-being." Therefore, *salubrious* is most nearly opposite in meaning to *noxious*.

10. **The best answer is D.** The word *venerable* means "highly esteemed or respected," whereas the word *disreputable* means "not respectable." Therefore, *disreputable* is most nearly opposite in meaning to *venerable*.

11. **The best answer is A.** To be *tractable* means to be "easy to control or work with," whereas to be *unruly* means to be "disobedient." Therefore, *unruly* is most nearly opposite in meaning to *tractable*.

12. **The best answer is C.** The word *pragmatic* means "practical," whereas the word *impractical* means "not capable of being put to use." Therefore, *impractical* is most nearly opposite in meaning to *pragmatic*.

13. **The best answer is B.** The relationship that exists between *irascible* and *angered* can be expressed with the following sentence: "*Irascible* means 'easily *angered*.'" *Docile* means "easily *trained*," so this choice best expresses the relationship that exists between the words in the question stem.

14. **The best answer is D.** The words that best fit in the blanks should suggest a contradiction between France and Spain's perceived differences and the common reputation that they share. In addition, the word for the second blank should be an antonym for *harried*. Only answer choice D includes a word pair that is supported by the context.

15. **The best answer is E.** To be *dubious* means to be "skeptical or uncertain," whereas to be *certain* means to be "sure or absolute." Therefore, *certain* is most nearly opposite in meaning to *dubious*.

16. **The best answer is *occlude; indulgent*.** Too much discipline may stunt a child's moral development; too much leniency may make the child self-centered. *Occlude* means "to block," while *indulgent* means "lenient." To *anticipate* is to "come before," to *repudiate* is to "denounce"; *obstreperous* means "noisy," while *lachrymose* means "tearful."

17. **The best answer is C.** The passage contains a very general description of magnetic substorms and a scientific mission to learn more about them. While the topics in answer choices A and B are discussed, they are details mentioned only in passing. There is no mention of two alternative approaches to the study of substorms (answer choice D) and the author makes no argument about the best way to conduct research in space (answer choice E).

18. **The best answer is C.** This is an EXCEPT question, so your goal is to identify the one answer choice that does NOT appear in the passage. While improving the success rates of future space missions may be an outcome of the THEMIS mission, it is a possible consequence of an objective, not an objective itself. The passage does not indicate that the success rate is guaranteed. All of the other choices are listed as goals of the mission.

19. **The best answer is D.** The relationship that exists between *propagate* and *multiply* can be expressed with the following sentence: "*Propagate* means to 'cause to *multiply*.'" *Precipitate* means "to cause to *happen*," so this choice best expresses the relationship that exists between the words in the question stem.

20. **The best answer is E.** The best word for the first blank should be a person whom others would travel hundreds of miles to see. Both *scholar* and *sage* seem appropriate. However, only *astute* fits in the second blank, as it is unlikely that people would travel hundreds of miles to listen to a scholar's *ludicrous* words.

21. **The best answer is B.** If similar mechanisms were found that were separated from the Antikythera mechanism by only a few centuries, then the device would not be a thousand years ahead of its time. Therefore, answer choice B is best. The other choices are either outside the scope of the question or are irrelevant.

22. **The best answer is A.** The passage states that the dials had subdials for greater specificity. That, along with the increasing level of detail in the passage, indicates that answer choice A is the best answer. The passage does not talk about the importance of leap years in astronomy, nor does it describe exactly how the mechanism worked; therefore, answer choices B and C are incorrect. Answer choices D and E are implicitly contradicted by the passage.

23. **The best answer is E.** This is a strengthen question; therefore, the correct answer will make the statement more likely to be true. Answer choice E explains why (if vaguely) Muslim scholars would bother to make a complex mechanism that performs those certain tasks. We don't have enough information to know if answer choices A and D are true. Answer choices B and C are contradicted by the passage.

24. **The best answer is C.** The last paragraph mentions a 3,000-character "user's manual" that would allow contemporary scientists to use the mechanism. This best supports answer choice C. The passage does not say where the mechanism was made or what tomography does, so choices A and E are incorrect. The passage states that the primary purpose of the device and its exact physical description are still unknown, so eliminate answer choices B and D.

25. **The best answer is C.** The generally descriptive tone of the passage eliminates answer choices A and E, which are too negative. The passage also does not address the role of movies in education, so answer choice D is not correct. Instead, the passage describes how explosions would occur in space and how that differs from explosions on Earth (and, by extension, in the movies). This best fits with answer choice C.

26. **The best answer is C.** This question asks you to choose which of three statements is true, based on the passage. The answers are found in the second paragraph. The author states that there is nothing to slow the energy from an explosion; therefore, it would disperse very quickly. Thus Roman numeral I is true. The author also states that the effect of an explosion for an observer would be a bright flash, so Roman numeral II is true. While the author writes that shock waves from an explosion cause a "boom," she also writes that those waves are not heard in space. Therefore, Roman numeral III is false. Consequently, only Roman numerals I and II are true.

27. **The best answer is D.** The context indicates that Chris was growing up, and therefore likely to lose interest in his action-figure collection. The word *wane* means to "decrease in intensity," so it is the best choice. The other answers are not supported by the context.

28. **The best answer is D.** To be *obtuse* means to be "lacking intellectual clarity," whereas to be *perceptive* means to be "keenly aware." Therefore, *acute* is most nearly opposite in meaning to the word *obtuse*.

29. **The best answer is B.** The word *quotidian* means "occurring daily." The word *sporadic* means "occasionally." Therefore, *sporadic* is most nearly opposite in meaning to *quotidian*.

30. **The best answer is E.** The word *inundate* means "to *overwhelm*." Therefore, the words in the question stem are synonyms. *Lambaste* is synonymous with *beat*, so this choice best expresses the relationship that exists between the words in the question stem.

Section 4—Quantitative

1. **The correct answer is D.** To solve this problem, pick values for x and compare the quantities. The quantity in Column B is larger when $x > 1$; the quantities in Column A and Column B are equal when $x = 1$. Because the value of x is not specified, you cannot determine a relationship between the columns.

2. **The correct answer is C.** To solve this problem, multiply the constant rate of each machine by the time stated. Machine Y will make $\left(\dfrac{x\,\text{bolts}}{0.25\,\text{hr}}\right) \times 4$ hr, or $16x$ bolts. Machine Z will make $\left(\dfrac{x\,\text{bolts}}{0.5\,\text{hr}}\right) \times 8$ hr, or $16x$ bolts. Thus the quantities in Column A and Column B are equal.

3. **The correct answer is D.** To solve this problem, translate $3x$ into an equation in terms of y. To do so, substitute $x = 2y + 3$ into $3x$ to get $6y + 9$. While the quantity in Column A appears to be greater, when $y \leq -11$, then the quantity in Column B would be greater. Because the value of y is not given, a relationship cannot be determined.

4. **The correct answer is A.** To solve this problem, determine the value of the quantity in each column. To determine the quantity in Column A, find a common denominator that is a multiple of 4 and 5; in this case 20 is the LCD. Multiply $\frac{1}{4}$ by $\frac{5}{5}$ and $\frac{2}{5}$ by $\frac{4}{4}$ to get $\frac{5}{20} + \frac{8}{20}$, which equals $\frac{13}{20}$. To determine the quantity in Column B, complete the operation within the parentheses first to get $\frac{3}{9}$, or $\frac{1}{3}$. Thus the quantity in Column A ($\frac{13}{20}$) is greater than the quantity in Column B ($\frac{1}{3}$).

5. **The correct answer is B.** To solve this problem, first figure out how many milliliters (ml) you have in 25 cans of soda by multiplying $\frac{300 \text{ mL}}{\text{can}}$ by 25 cans to get 7,500 ml. Recall that 1 L = 1,000 mL. Multiply 7,500 mL by the conversion of $\frac{1 \text{ L}}{1,000 \text{ mL}}$. The mL's cancel out, giving you $\frac{7,500 \text{ L}}{1,000}$. Because dividing by 1,000 moves the decimal point 3 spaces to the left, you end up with 7.5 L.

6. **The correct answer is C.** To solve this problem effectively, you will need to know the number of maples in the median. The problem gives 3 lindens, $\frac{30}{5} = 6$ oaks, and 12 cedars, for 21 trees altogether; this means the remaining 9 must be maples. If there are 3 lindens for every 9 maples, then the ratio must be 3 to 9, which reduces to 1 to 3.

7. **The correct answer is D.** To solve this problem, pick values for y and substitute them into each equation. For example, when $y = 4.5$, $\frac{(4 + y)}{4} = 2.125$ and $\frac{(6 + y)}{y} = 2.333$. In this case, the quantity in Column B is greater. However, when $y = 5$, $\frac{(4 + y)}{4} = 2.25$ and $\frac{(6 + y)}{y} = 2.2$ and the quantity in Column A is greater. You cannot determine a relationship between the two quantities based on the given information.

8. **The correct answer is C.** To solve this problem, set up a distribution list as follows:

Abby	Bobbie	Connie
$1	$1	$5
$1	$2	$4
$2	$2	$3
$2	$3	$2

Recognize that no matter how the money is distributed, one person receives at least $3; therefore, the quantities in Column A and B are equal.

9. **The correct answer is A.** To determine the relationship, solve the equation $x + 5 = 15$ for x. Subtract 5 from both sides to get $x = 10$. Substitute this value into the equations in Column A and Column B. The quantity in Column A (5) is greater than the quantity in Column B (2).

10. **The correct answer is D.** To solve this problem, substitute $y = 3$ into $2x + 3y = 18$, as follows:

$$2x + 3(3) = 18$$
$$2x + 9 = 18$$
$$2x = 9$$
$$x = \frac{9}{2}$$

Next, substitute $\frac{9}{2}$ for x in $4x$ and solve:

$$4\left(\frac{9}{2}\right) = \frac{36}{2} = 18$$

11. **The correct answer is D.** To solve this problem, first translate the words into their mathematical equivalents, remembering that the average is the sum of the values divided by the total number of values:

The average of a and b translates into $= \frac{a + b}{2}$

The average of $\frac{a}{2}$ and $2b$ translates into $\frac{\left(\frac{a}{2}\right) + 2b}{2}$

Simplify the values by using the distributive property as follows:

Column A: $\frac{a + b}{2} = \frac{a}{2} + \frac{b}{2}$

Column B: $\frac{\left(\frac{a}{2}\right) + 2b}{2} = \frac{\left(\frac{a}{2}\right)}{2} + \frac{2b}{2} = \frac{a}{4} + b$

Now use test values for a and b. Let $a = 4$ and $b = 1$. The quantity in Column A would equal 2.5 and would be greater than the quantity in Column B, which equals 2. Now let $a = 1$ and $b = 2$. The quantity in Column A would equal 1.5 and would be less than the quantity in Column B, which equals 2.25. Therefore, you cannot determine the relationship based on the given information.

12. **The correct answer is D.** When dealing with complicated geometry problems, it is helpful to draw a diagram. In this case, you would draw a rectangle measuring 12×27. Now label the posts. You know that there must be one post at each corner, and on the shorter sides there will need to be one post between the corner posts to ensure that no span is longer than 6 feet without being secured. For the longer stretch, you will need

one post 6 feet from the northwest corner, one 12 feet in, one 18 feet in, and one 24 feet in. This will leave only 3 feet between the last post and the northeast corner, but this is unavoidable. Label posts on the other long side the same way, and count: There will be 14 posts required in all.

13. **The correct answer is 28.** To solve this problem, recall that absolute values are always positive. Therefore, you can ignore the negative sign in front of 2 and solve, as follows:

$$|14| \times |-2|$$
$$= 14 \times 2 = 28$$

14. **The correct answer is C.** To solve this problem, note that the Zone dieters make up 17% of the total percentage. You are given that there were 135 million dieters in 1995. At this point you could calculate 17% of 135 million, but it will be quicker to note that 20% of 135 million is 27 million, so 17% will be slightly less than 27 million. Only answer choice C works.

15. **The correct answer is B.** In 1995, 7% of the total percentage was on the Master Cleanse diet. Therefore, 0.07 × 135, or 9.45 million people were on the Master Cleanse diet. In 2000, 13% of the total percentage was on the Master Cleanse diet. Therefore, .13 × 210, or 27.3 million people were on the Master Cleanse diet. The difference between the two numbers is 17.85 million. So the fraction is the difference over the original number, or $\frac{17.85}{9.45}$, which simplifies to 1.88888, or 1.89. Multiply by 100 to get 189%.

16. **The correct answer is A.** To determine a relationship between the columns, you must determine the value of the quantity in each column. Find the difference between the reduced price, $40, and the increased price, $60: 60 − 40 = 20. Divide the difference by the reduced price and multiply by 100 to find the percent increase. The quantity in Column A (50) is greater than the quantity in Column B (20).

17. **The correct answer is D.** To solve this problem, try some test values for x and y that fit within the parameters stated. If $x = 0.02$ and $y = 0.025$, then $|x - y| = |0.02 - 0.25|$, or 0.005 because absolute values are always expressed as positive numbers. Thus Column A and Column B are equal. However, if $x = 0.021$ and $y = 0.023$, then Column A (.002) would be less than Column B (.005). A relationship cannot be determined from the information provided.

18. **The correct answer is C.** To solve this problem, find examples of squares in which the units digit is equal to the answer choices in order to eliminate answers: $10^2 = 100$, so eliminate answer choice A; $1^2 = 1$ and $9^2 = 81$, so eliminate answer choice B; $5^2 = 25$, so eliminate answer choice D; $6^2 = 36$, so eliminate answer choice E. There is no example that allows you to eliminate answer choice C, so it must be the correct answer.

19. **The correct answer is C.** If x is the least of the integers, the remaining integers are $x + 1$, $x + 2$, $x + 3$, and $x + 4$. Remember that the median is the middle value of a series of numbers. In this series, $x + 2$ is the median. Calculate the mean as follows:

$$\frac{[x + (x + 1) + (x + 2) + (x + 3) + (x + 4)]}{5}.$$

Simplify this equation:

$$(5x + 10) = 5x + 10 = x + 2$$

The median and the mean equal $x + 2$.

20. **The correct answer is E.** According to the information given in the table, 300 students voted for the name Spartans. Therefore, 300 out of 2,000 students voted for Spartans. Because you are looking for a percentage, set up a proportion and solve for x, as follows:

$$\frac{300 \text{ students}}{2,000 \text{ students}} = \frac{x \text{ percent}}{100 \text{ percent}}$$

$$30,000 = 2,000x$$

$$15 = x$$

21. **The correct answer is C.** According to the information given in the table, 40 students voted for the name Lions. Therefore, 400 out of 2,000 students voted for Lions. First, calculate the percentage of the whole pie chart represented by Lions by setting up a proportion and solving for x, as follows:

$$\frac{400 \text{ students}}{2,000 \text{ students}} = \frac{x \text{ percent}}{100 \text{ percent}}$$

Cross-multiply and solve for x:

$$40,000 = 2,000x$$

$$20 = x$$

You now know that 20% of the students voted for Lions. Because there are 360° in a circle, find 20% of 360:

$$360 \times 0.2 = 72$$

22. **The correct answer is C.** A rational number is any number that can be written as a ratio; in other words, it is a fraction. So simply determine the fraction that is exactly halfway between $\frac{1}{6}$ and $\frac{1}{2}$. One way to do this is to find the average, as follows:

$$\frac{\left(\frac{1}{2} + \frac{1}{6}\right)}{2} = \frac{2}{6} = \frac{1}{3}$$

Another way to solve this problem is to find the Lowest Common Denominator (LCD):

$$\frac{1}{2} = \frac{3}{6},\text{ so the LCD is 6.}$$

The value that is halfway between $\frac{1}{6}$ and $\frac{3}{6}$ is $\frac{2}{6}$, which is equivalent to $\frac{1}{3}$.

23. **The correct answer is A.** To solve this problem, calculate the value of each of the quantities. Find the largest prime number between 65 and 80 by counting down from 80: 80 is even, so obviously not prime; 79, however, is prime. The smallest multiple of 7 less than 81 is 77. Therefore, the quantity in Column A is greater than the quantity in Column B.

24. **The correct answer is D.** While at first glance it would seem that Data Set B would be greater, it is actually impossible to tell. If x is 10,000, for example, then Data Set A will clearly have a higher mean than Data Set B. On the other hand, if x is strongly negative— $-10,000$, for example—then Data Set B will definitely be the larger set.

25. **The correct answer is A.** To solve this problem, simplify the second equation:

$$y - 9 = 23$$
$$y = 32$$

Now substitute 32 for y in the first equation:

$$x + 32 = 27$$
$$x = -5$$

Therefore the quantity in Column A is greater than the quantity in Column B.

26. **The correct answer is B.** To solve this problem, use substitution.
If $c = b - 5$, then substituting this equation into $a + c = 35$ would yield $a + b - 5 = 35$. Add 5 to both sides to get $a + b = 40$.

27. **The correct answer is B.** To solve this problem, first find 7^3 as follows:

$$7 \times 7 \times 7 = 343$$

Then use long division to find the remainder when 343 is divided by 9. Take the dividend (343) one digit at a time starting from the left. Because 9 does not divide evenly with 3, use the first two digits (34). Find the biggest multiple of 9 that is less than 34, in this case 9×3, or 27. Subtract 27 from 34 to get a remainder of 7. Next, "bring down" the next digit of the dividend (3) to get 73. Find the biggest multiple of 9 that is less than 73, or $9 \times 8 = 72$. Subtract 72 from 73 to get a remainder of 1. Because there are no more digits in the dividend, 1 is the final remainder.

28. **The correct answer is C.** To solve this problem, first find all the whole number squares less than 50:

$$1^2 = 1$$
$$2^2 = 4$$
$$3^2 = 9$$
$$4^2 = 16$$
$$5^2 = 25$$
$$6^2 = 36$$
$$7^2 = 49$$

This leaves 43 remaining positive whole numbers that are less than 50 and are not squares of whole numbers.

APPENDIXES

GRE Vocabulary List

Although the following is by no means a comprehensive list, it does contain words that have appeared on actual GRE tests, each followed by a sentence or sentences appropriately using the word or a derivation of the word. The words are included here because they have been selected by experienced GRE instructors as representative of the vocabulary level that is expected to appear on the GRE.

A

Abate   to reduce or lessen
> *After blowing fiercely for hours, the hurricane winds at last began to abate.*

Aberration   a deviation or departure from the norm
> *Harry's low grades in chemistry are an aberration; he is typically an A student.*

Abeyance   temporary inactivity or suspension
> *For some time now, the dissenters have been held in abeyance; they have suspended all protests.*

Abjure   to forswear or abstain from; to give up
> *Once King Edward VIII abdicated the throne to marry a commoner, he abjured all of his former titles.*

Abrade   to wear down or rub away the surface of something
> *Years of exposure to the sea spray had abraded the face of the cliffs.*

Abridge   to reduce the length of or diminish in scope (for example, written text)
> *The author recently published an abridged version of his original 600-page novel.*

Abrogate   to end or do away with something
> *It is unlikely that the senator's push to abrogate any rights regarding free speech will be supported.*

Abscond   to withdraw and hide, typically to avoid arrest
> *The fugitive absconded to Canada in an attempt to avoid arrest in the United States.*

Absurd   extremely ridiculous or completely lacking reason
The idea that Samantha would fail her test was completely absurd; she had studied for hours and was completely prepared.

Abysmal   very profound or deep; very bad
Despite all of the advertisements promoting the new product, its first-quarter sales were abysmal.

Accretion   a gradual increase in the amount or size of something
Increased organic matter accumulation has led to an increase in the accretion rate in the Mississippi Delta.

Acquisitive   characterized by a strong desire to gain or retain information or objects
The acquisitive nature of the chimpanzee makes it appear almost human.

Acrid   harsh or bitter taste or smell
Sean immediately turned the engine off when he smelled acrid smoke billowing from beneath the hood of his car.

Acute   quick and precise, intense; sharp, keen
The acute pain in Sarah's wrist kept her from performing even the simplest activity.

Henry was an acute observer; he quickly learned the rules of the game.

Adhere   to stick fast; to remain in support of
In order to maintain order in his classroom, Mr. Blume required strict adherence to the code of conduct.

Adjacent   in the nearest position; next to
Chase took a new job in downtown Chicago, but purchased a house in an adjacent suburb.

Adroit   showing skill and experience
Steve was considered an adroit negotiator; he was often able to settle disputes when others had failed.

Aesthetic   appealing to the senses because it is beautiful
The aesthetic quality of the painting was more appealing than its historical significance.

Affinity   natural attraction; inherent similarity
Michelle's affinity for getting straight to the point made her a popular editor at the publishing house.

Alienate   to isolate oneself from others or another person from oneself
Gregg often felt alienated from his classmates because of his illness.

Ambiguous   unclear or capable of having more than one meaning
The student's <u>ambiguous</u> answer left the professor wondering whether the student had studied the assigned material.

Ambivalent   characterized by uncertainty; unable to decide between opposites
His inability to show emotion left her feeling <u>ambivalent</u> about their relationship.

Amenable   responsive to suggestion; willing
Josh was <u>amenable</u> to eating dinner early; he was ravenous.

Amiable   friendly and pleasant
Joe was very <u>amiable</u>; as a result, he made friends easily at his new school.

Anachronism   something existing or happening out of its time in historical order
Her yearning to be nothing more than a housewife seemed an <u>anachronism</u> in today's society.

Annotate   to provide with extra notes or comments
In order to ensure the credibility of his students' sources, the professor asked the students to <u>annotate</u> their bibliographies.

Anomaly   something that is different from the norm
The botanists were excited when they discovered the unique flower; it was a complete <u>anomaly</u>.

Apathy   a lack of any emotion or concern
Mary appeared quite <u>apathetic</u> at her trial; she seemed unconcerned by the jury's guilty verdict.

Ardor   intense feelings; passion
Scott's <u>ardor</u> for Julianne increased as he spent more and more time with her.

Articulate   *v.* to clearly explain. *adj.* the quality of being able to speak clearly
Young children often find it difficult to <u>articulate</u> exactly what they are thinking.

Ascribe   to attribute to a specific source; to assign a characteristic
It is not unusual to <u>ascribe</u> jealousy and pettiness to one's critics.

Asperity   roughness or severity
The <u>asperity</u> of the desert climate in Death Valley prevents many people from visiting for extended periods of time.

Assay   *n.* an analysis or examination. *v.* to subject to analysis; to examine
The diplomat carefully <u>assayed</u> the situation prior to making a decision.

Assert   to demonstrate power; to defend a statement as true
It is often necessary for a parent to <u>assert</u> his or her authority over an unruly child.

Assimilate   to incorporate into; to make similar
Many immigrants desire to <u>assimilate</u> quickly into their new community.

Assuage   to lessen or ease
Mandy often used food to <u>assuage</u> her loneliness, a habit that led to her problem with obesity.

Assiduous   characteristic of careful and persistent effort
The journey to earning good grades is an <u>assiduous</u> one; consistent effort must be put forth.

Assumption   something believed to be true without proof; unstated evidence
Because Jennifer wore glasses every day, we <u>assumed</u> that she had poor eyesight.

Aver   to declare as true; to maintain
The politician continued to <u>aver</u> that he was more experienced than his opponent, despite evidence to the contrary.

Aversion   strong dislike
Kelly has such an <u>aversion</u> to strenuous exercise that she never goes to the gym.

B

Banish   to force to leave
The deposed dictator was <u>banished</u> from his native country.

Benevolence   an inclination to be kind or charitable
Mr. Horn's <u>benevolence</u> made him a beloved school principal; his generosity and understanding far exceeded that of his predecessor.

Benign   kind, mild, harmless
Katherine was relieved to discover that her tumor was <u>benign</u>; she would not require surgery after all.

Bequest   the act of passing on; something that is passed on
This collection of rare manuscripts was donated to the library as a <u>bequest</u> from Professor Austin.

Bereft   deprived or despondent
Jill was <u>bereft</u> when she discovered that the coveted role had been offered to another actress.

Blithe   carefree or joyous; casual
Ellen's <u>blithe</u> and outgoing attitude made her one of the most popular students on campus.

Bolster   *n.* a narrow cushion. *v.* to support or strengthen
The small business owner secured a low-interest loan to <u>bolster</u> his financial situation during a period of expansion.

Brazen   bold or shameless; insolent
His often <u>brazen</u> behavior at work led to his being reprimanded on a regular basis.

Burgeoning   thriving or growing rapidly
Although it was completely undeveloped a year ago, the vacant land is now home to a <u>burgeoning</u> commercial area, complete with a new shopping mall.

C

Cadge   to beg
The destitute man was relegated to <u>cadging</u> meals from local restaurants.

Capricious   impulsive; prone to sudden change
Jill's sudden move to Hollywood was considered <u>capricious</u> by the rest of her family.

Castigate   to punish or criticize severely
Jason was <u>castigated</u> by his teacher for turning in his assignment late.

Catalyst   something that causes something else to happen, usually without being directly involved in or changed by the process; a trigger for an event
Our classmate's recent job offer served as a <u>catalyst</u> for the rest of us to update and submit our resumes.

Censure   *n.* a formal criticism or intense disproval. *v.* to express a formal criticism
The prosecuting attorney was <u>censured</u> for a conflict of interest arising from his personal relationship with the plaintiff.

Chronicle   *n.* a detailed narrative. *v.* to document or record
Several biographers have <u>chronicled</u> the life of Albert Einstein, one of the world's greatest physicists.

Circumspect   mindful of potential consequences; prudent
A wise investor is <u>circumspect</u> about fluctuations in the market.

Cite   to quote as an example or proof
The company <u>cited</u> a 10 percent increase in sales as evidence that their new advertising campaign was achieving the predicted results.

Coalesce   to unite or come together
The different factions <u>coalesced</u> to form a strong group opposed to the current regime.

Coerce   to force or threaten someone into thinking a certain way; to compel
The jury did not hear the man's taped confession during the trial because police had coerced him into admitting that he had committed the crime.

Cogent   convincing and reasonable
The teenager's cogent argument for a later curfew persuaded his parents to push it back to midnight.

Cognitive   relating to conscious intellectual activity such as thinking, reasoning, and learning
Entering college at the age of 14, the teen had cognitive abilities far beyond most of her peers.

Coherence   the quality of being logical and clear
The essay lacked coherence; it did not flow logically from one concept to the next.

Coincidental   occurring by chance
The coincidental meeting of two old friends was a pleasant surprise for them both.

Commensurate   corresponding in size, degree, or duration
He refused the job offer; the salary did not seem commensurate with his related skills and experience.

Complaisant   showing a willingness to please; obliging
Eager to earn a large tip, our waiter was unusually complaisant.

Comprise   to consist of; to include
Students enrolled in the music program comprised the university marching band.

Concede   to admit or reluctantly yield; to surrender
The presidential candidate decided to concede defeat based on the latest poll results; he was too far behind to win.

Conducive   contributive; favorable
The noisy restaurant was not conducive to holding intimate conversations.

Consternation   alarm or fear
To her consternation, she found that she'd forgotten to bring her assignment to class.

Converge   to meet or come together at a common point
Ambulances, police cars, and fire trucks quickly converged on the scene of the accident.

Convivial   festive and sociable
There was always a convivial atmosphere at the annual holiday party.

Cordial   friendly; gracious
The doorman at the luxury hotel <u>cordially</u> greeted all arriving guests.

Correlate   to have corresponding characteristics
According to researchers, the length of time a student studies is roughly <u>correlated</u> to the grades that the student receives.

Corroborate   to confirm, to substantiate with evidence
Further laboratory tests <u>corroborated</u> the scientist's theory that taking vitamins could help to maintain a person's good health.

Countenance   *n.* facial features or expression.
The teacher had a stern <u>countenance</u> that intimidated many of her students.

Credulous   easily deceived; believing too readily
Even the most <u>credulous</u> person would not believe the story that Mike had concocted.

Cryptic   mystifying; hidden or concealed meaning
The <u>cryptic</u> hieroglyphics on the Rosetta Stone were finally deciphered using the Greek writings also found on the stone.

Culmination   completion or climax
Finishing the marathon in less than four hours was the <u>culmination</u> of months and months of training for Elaine.

Culpable   deserving of blame; guilty
Despite his claims to the contrary, the senator is likely <u>culpable</u> of misappropriating funds.

D

Debilitate   to weaken or impair
Bob's broken leg left him <u>debilitated</u> and unable to attend school.

Decimate   to destroy large numbers of; to inflict great damage upon
The rain forest is being <u>decimated</u> at an alarmingly fast pace; it is estimated that it could be completely gone within 40 years.

Decry   to denounce or criticize
A loyal fan of classical music, Megan <u>decried</u> all popular rap and hip-hop artists.

Defamation   a malicious or abusive attack on one's character
The celebrity sued the tabloid for <u>defamation</u> of character when the magazine published a story replete with lies.

Delve   to deeply search through
Many philosophers and scientists <u>delve</u> into the secrets of the universe.

Demise   the end of existence; death
The <u>demise</u> of the dinosaurs is a topic of much debate among paleontologists.

Denigrate   to speak ill of; to belittle
You should not <u>denigrate</u> a person whose opinion differs from yours.

Depict   to represent or describe
Many people disapprove of how Native Americans are <u>depicted</u> in old Westerns.

Deplore   to condemn; disapprove of or regret
Environmental advocacy groups <u>deplore</u> deforestation and industrial pollution.

Derision   use of ridicule to show contempt
Joe's harsh <u>derision</u> of his pesky younger brother set everyone on edge at the dinner table.

Derivative   *adj.* copied or adapted. *n.* something derived
There are zero-calorie sweeteners available that are <u>derivatives</u> of real sugar.

Desultory   inconsistent and irregular, aimless
The project leader's rather <u>desultory</u> speech left the team members uncertain of how to proceed.

Dexterity   skill and ease of movement, especially of the hands; cleverness
It took great <u>dexterity</u>, but the politician managed to evade answering every difficult question that the reporters threw at him.

Diatribe   an abusive, insulting verbal attack
The environmental activist launched into a lengthy <u>diatribe</u> against the developers who wanted to build a new mall in place of the city park.

Didactic   intended for the purposes of moral teaching or instructing, even when such instruction is not necessary or welcome
Professor McFarland's <u>didactic</u> presentations in the classroom tended to bore some students and outrage others.

Dilate   to make larger; expand
Jesse's pupils began to <u>dilate</u> as the sun set and the room darkened.

Diligent   continuously putting in great effort
Ben <u>diligently</u> trained for the marathon, running at least 40 miles per week.

Disabuse   to free someone of believing something that is untrue
I hope that this most recent scandal will finally disabuse the public of its notion that the senator is infallible.

Discern   to differentiate or distinguish; to perceive
The moon's distance from Earth makes it difficult to discern most of the features on the surface of the moon with the naked eye.

Disconcerting   unsettling
Linda had the disconcerting habit of staring at the ground whenever she spoke.

Dislodge   to remove from a former position
The small earthquake dislodged several tons of rock from the mountain.

Disparity   the state of being different or unequal
There was much disparity between my perception of the judicial process and the actual manner in which the process worked.

Disperse   to scatter or spread out
The crowd began to disperse as the concert came to an end.

Dissemble   to disguise or conceal
The platoon's efforts to dissemble their preparations resulted in a swift ambush of the enemy the following day.

Dissident   *adj.* disagreeable. *n.* one who disagrees
It took hours of careful diplomacy for the staunch political dissidents to reach an accord.

Dissipate   to drive away; scatter
The wind helped to dissipate the smoke from our campfire.

Dissonance   lack of harmony; discord
Band leaders know immediately by the piercing dissonance that a wrong note has been played.

Diverge   to move apart, or extend in different directions; to differ in opinion
Though they agreed on most things, their opinions diverged on the topic of abortion rights.

Divest   to get rid of
Howard was extremely lucky; he divested himself of $10 million worth of electronics stock days before its value plummeted.

Docile   easy to train or teach
The normally docile students became very rowdy as the day's pep rally drew near.

Dubious   unsure, skeptical
Mike was very dubious when his older brother, infamous for playing pranks, told Mike that he had a surprise for him.

E

Eccentric   *adj.* departing from convention. *n.* one who deviates from the norm
Mary's style, considered to be very <u>eccentric</u> when she was young, led her to become one of the most popular fashion designers of all time.

Eclectic   combining elements from many different sources or styles
Jenny's <u>eclectic</u> taste in movies ranged from musicals to comedies, dramas to action films.

Effrontery   rude and presumptuous behavior
The general was unaware that his imperialist <u>effrontery</u> was only breeding contempt among the colonists.

Egregious   noticeably bad or offensive
William committed an <u>egregious</u> error when he failed to mention his wife during his acceptance speech.

Eloquent   very clear and precise; quality of being skilled in clear and precise speech
Julie's valedictorian speech was quite <u>eloquent</u>; she clearly articulated her hopes and dreams for a prosperous future.

Elucidate   to clarify
Recent efforts to <u>elucidate</u> the text on certain ancient scrolls have yielded curious new perspectives on the political history of Babylon.

Emancipation   the act of freeing or liberating
Minor children may petition a court for <u>emancipation</u> from their parents if they provide evidence of alternate housing and income.

Emollient   *adj.* softening or soothing. *n.* a softening agent
Sarah rubbed an <u>emollient</u> over her dry, peeling, sunburned skin.

Empirical   based on or provable by observation and experiment
The hypothesis had to be backed up by <u>empirical</u> evidence in order to be considered credible.

Emulate   to follow an admirable example; imitate
As she entered law school, she hoped to <u>emulate</u> the success of her sister, who was already a prominent partner in a law firm.

Endorse   to support or sign
The sports superstar was paid more than $10 million to <u>endorse</u> the new athletic shoe.

Engender   to give rise to; originate
Professor Evan's good nature <u>engendered</u> a positive attitude among his students.

Enigmatic   unexplainable, puzzling
The Mona Lisa's <u>enigmatic</u> smile is legendary.

Entity   a discrete unit or being
Though the corporations worked in conjunction with each other, they remained separate legal <u>entities</u>.

Enumerate   to state things in a list
At his performance review, the employee listened to his boss <u>enumerate</u> several ways he could improve his performance in the workplace.

Ephemeral   temporary, fleeting
Considered a "one-hit wonder," the pop star enjoyed only <u>ephemeral</u> fame.

Equivocal   uncertain or ambiguous
Many lengthy court battles could be avoided if the legislature took more care to avoid <u>equivocal</u> language in the criminal statutes.

Erudite   learned; having great knowledge
After earning three doctoral degrees, Dr. Kidman was considered one of the most <u>erudite</u> professors on campus.

Esoteric   understood by few people; mysterious
Most of the subject matter in the novel is quite <u>esoteric</u>; the author is forced to overwhelm the reader with too much background information.

Espouse   to choose to follow or support something
Abraham Lincoln was famous for his refusal to <u>espouse</u> slavery in the North.

Estimable   admirable; deserving of esteem
His first attempt at writing a novel was <u>estimable</u>; nearly 1 million copies of the book were sold.

Ethical   in line with the principles of right and wrong
Only the most <u>ethical</u> people would return money from a wallet they find in the street.

Euphemism   an inoffensive expression substituted for one that is deemed offensive
The word borrowing is sometimes used as a <u>euphemism</u> for stealing.

Exacerbate   to intensify bitterness or violence
The terrorist attacks <u>exacerbated</u> the already strained relations between the two countries.

Exceptional   having uncommonly great qualities
Kevin was an <u>exceptional</u> basketball player, and received many offers to play at the collegiate level.

Excoriate   to denounce; to chafe
The film critics excoriated the film that was supposed to be that year's biggest blockbuster, emphasizing how overrated it was.

Exculpate   to remove blame; acquit
The defendant was exculpated of the homicide charges when new evidence was found at the crime scene.

Exhort   to urge or try to persuade
After graduating from college, Diana exhorted her parents to lend her the money to start her own business.

Exigent   demanding immediate attention; urgent
In the exigent circumstances of the coup d'état, thousands of troops were dispatched to the capital city.

Explicate   to explain or make comprehensible
The graduate student was unable to successfully explicate his thesis; therefore, he did not earn his degree.

Expunge   to get rid of or erase
The speeding infraction would be expunged from John's driving record after he paid a $600 fine and kept a clean record for one year.

Extant   currently existing
There are few extant copies of the Gutenberg Bible, four of which are in New York City.

Extenuating   partially justifiable
Extenuating circumstances surrounding the motive for the assault meant Sean would serve less jail time.

Extol   to praise or glorify
Ever the proud mother, Anna extols her child's accomplishments to no end.

Extrovert   a person characterized by concern with things outside of himself or herself; an outgoing or gregarious person
In order to be successful as a salesperson, you must be somewhat of an extrovert.

Extricate   to free or disentangle
It took rescue crews several hours to safely extricate all of the passengers from the plane that had crashed earlier in the day.

Exultant   gleeful because of success
The exultant crowd cheered the soccer team on to victory in the World Cup.

F

Fallacy   an error in reasoning
It is a common <u>fallacy</u> that first-year law students spend every waking moment studying.

Familial   relating to the family
Her <u>familial</u> ties kept her from moving too far away from the town in which she grew up.

Fathom   *v.* to come to understand the meaning of something. *n.* a measure of distance equal to six feet
The complexity of the situation made it difficult to <u>fathom</u> a simple outcome.

Fatuous   foolish or delusive; smug
We ignored Brendan's <u>fatuous</u> remarks about politics; he spoke strictly from opinion with no regard for the facts.

Feckless   lacking in purpose; careless
Because more than half of the legislators are not running for reelection this fall, pundits predict another <u>feckless</u> session of the State House.

Feign   to fabricate or deceive
She <u>feigned</u> astonishment when she walked into her surprise party; her best friend had previously told her about the event.

Feint   *n.* a deceptive, diversionary action. *v.* to make a deceptive show of
The robbers used some smoke bombs in the parking lot as a <u>feint</u> while they discretely took money from the cash drawers.

Fidelity   faithfulness or allegiance; often used to denote faithfulness in a romantic relationship, or faithfulness to a particular religion
I admire dogs for their unshakeable <u>fidelity</u> to their owners.

Florid   flushed with color; ornate
The stark realism of neoclassicism in painting replaced the <u>florid</u> idealism of the Rococo period.

Foil   to keep from being successful
Her plans were often <u>foiled</u> by her failure to plan ahead.

Foment   to incite or agitate
Ryan tried to hold his tongue; he knew that one of his sarcastic remarks would <u>foment</u> a fight that he didn't want to start.

Forage   to search for food or provisions
During the cold winter months, many wild animals are forced to <u>forage</u> for scarce food.

Formidable   capable of arousing fear or awe
The current championship team was a <u>formidable</u> opponent for the yet unranked team.

Fortuitous   happening by accident or chance
The defenseman scored easily with a quick shot after the puck's <u>fortuitous</u> bounce toward him.

Forum   a public meeting place; a medium for open discussion
The mayor held an open <u>forum</u> for discussion to learn what the people thought of his new proposal.

Fracas   a noisy fight; a brawl
James was arrested for disorderly conduct after getting into a <u>fracas</u> outside the restaurant this weekend.

G

Gainsay   to deny or contradict
There can be no resolution if all you do is <u>gainsay</u> each of my suggestions.

Garrison   a military post; the troops stationed at a military post
The <u>garrison</u> was currently home to nearly 400 troops.

Garrulous   very talkative
The normally <u>garrulous</u> teenager was very subdued at the party; she barely spoke to anyone.

Genre   a type, class, or category
His favorite <u>genre</u> of music was classic rock, but he also enjoyed jazz quite a bit.

Gist   main idea
I'm in a hurry, so please tell me the <u>gist</u> of the story.

Glib   seemingly slick and clever, but lacking sincerity
The president's <u>glib</u> speech about the financial state of the company resulted in a general sense of unease among the members of the staff.

Gratuitous   for no reason or at no cost
Her <u>gratuitous</u> acts of kindness earned her fondness and respect within the community.

Gregarious   sociable; enjoying the company of others
It's a wonder Lynn can get a word in edgewise when speaking with her extremely <u>gregarious</u> sister.

Grievous   causing grief or pain; serious
The spokesperson knew he had made a <u>grievous</u> error when he prematurely announced that all of the victims had survived the accident.

Guile   cunning; shrewdness
I employed all of my guile to convince my housemates that I truly deserved the largest bedroom in the house along with the house's single parking spot.

H

Hackneyed   unoriginal, overused
The hackneyed plot of the television show led to its cancellation after only three episodes.

Harrow   to torment or cause suffering and agony
The prospect of a beach landing in broad daylight harrowed the troops for days before the battle.

Hierarchy   a way to rank or place things in order
The business's hierarchy allowed room for all employees to advance within the company if they worked hard enough.

Heterogeneous   made up of dissimilar elements; not homogeneous
Switzerland has a heterogeneous culture, in which German, French, and Italian influences are intermixed.

Hypothesis   a tentative explanation that can be tested by further investigation and experimentation
The graduate students working on the project presented a viable hypothesis regarding the outcome of their experiments.

I

Idiosyncrasy   a peculiar characteristic
One of the most annoying idiosyncrasies of the computer is that it must be completely restarted every two hours.

Immutable   not subject to change
People should know that their freedom is not immutable and must be protected whenever necessary.

Impending   threatening to occur
We changed our tee time to later that afternoon because of the impending rain.

Imperturbable   hard to excite or upset, very calm
Kevin's imperturbable demeanor during the storm helped keep his wife and children calm.

Impetus   a stimulus encouraging a particular activity
The upcoming race provided the impetus she needed to expand her training regimen.

Implosion   a violent, inward collapse
A careful <u>implosion</u> of the old stadium would prevent damage to adjacent structures and onlookers.

Inadvertent   unintentional, often related to carelessness
His <u>inadvertent</u> pull of the lever started a chain reaction of leaks throughout the building's plumbing.

Inchoate   poorly formed or formless
His <u>inchoate</u> political opinions were based largely on ignorance.

Incinerate   to set fire to and burn until reduced to ashes
The leaves were <u>incinerated</u> quickly in the raging campfire.

Incongruous   inconsistent; lacking in harmony
Carrie's colorful joke was <u>incongruous</u> with the deep conversation going on around her.

Incorrigible   impossible to change or reform
The child was <u>incorrigible</u>; he refused to listen when his parents repeatedly told him to stop teasing the dog.

Indigenous   native; innate
The Maori are the <u>indigenous</u> people of New Zealand.

Inevitable   impossible to avoid; predictable
After spending the weekend doing everything but studying, it was <u>inevitable</u> that she would fail her exam.

Infer   to conclude from evidence
Mr. Mauro was able to <u>infer</u> from his employee's attitude that she was not satisfied with her job.

Ingenuity   cleverness or imagination
The world relies on the <u>ingenuity</u> of people such as Bell and Edison to conceive of tomorrow's technology.

Inherent   naturally occurring, permanent element or attribute
The risks <u>inherent</u> in driving a car are surprisingly greater than those associated with riding in an airplane.

Inimical   harmful or unfriendly
Doctors agree smoking is <u>inimical</u> to good health and longevity.

Innate   possessed at birth; a natural characteristic
Linguists still don't know why humans have an <u>innate</u> capacity for language while other animals do not.

Inscrutable   difficult to understand; having an obscure nature
Science still has little explanation for the <u>inscrutable</u> origins of matter and energy in the universe.

Insinuate   to subtly imply or insert
Andrew attempted to <u>insinuate</u> himself into the conversation by replying to a question that was not directed at him.

Insipid   dull; lacking in flavor or zest
Waiting in line for the movie, I was forced to listen to an <u>insipid</u> conversation between two young girls who could not decide which actor they found most attractive.

Insular   isolated; narrow-minded
The villagers displayed the typical <u>insularity</u> of small communities.

Integral   essential or necessary
The quarterback was an <u>integral</u> part of the football team's seven-game winning streak.

Intercede   to mediate, or plead on another's behalf
When Kelly learned that she had become the prime suspect in a police investigation, she called upon her lawyer to <u>intercede</u>.

Interpolate   to insert or introduce between, often to falsify
No one can be sure what fanciful stories were <u>interpolated</u> into the old chronicle by medieval scribes.

Intractable   difficult to manage; stubborn
Paul's <u>intractable</u> temper landed him in jail after a brief altercation with a police officer.

Inundate   to quickly overwhelm or exceed capacity
The government was <u>inundated</u> with requests for help after the hurricane destroyed or damaged over 10,000 homes and businesses.

Inure   to cause to accept something that is undesirable; habituate
Every winter it snows heavily in this area, but by now I am <u>inured</u> to the harsh climate.

Invariable   not subject to question or change; constant
Judge Owens is famous for his <u>invariable</u> demeanor, which is lauded by prosecution and defense counsel alike.

Irascible   easily angered
Grizzly bears are <u>irascible</u> beasts, which one would do well to avoid.

J

Jovial   full of joy and happiness
Noelle was in a <u>jovial</u> mood for weeks after getting engaged to her high school sweetheart.

Judicious   sensible, having good judgment
Kate's decision not to take the job was quite <u>judicious</u> because she had no previous marketing experience.

Juxtapose   to place things next to each other in order to compare or contrast
The artist <u>juxtaposed</u> some of his early sketches with some of his later works to show how much his style had changed over time.

K

Keen   quick-witted, sharp
His <u>keen</u> sense of smell allowed him to figure out what was for dinner long before he reached the kitchen.

Kudos   praise for achievements
The volunteers all received <u>kudos</u> for their work at the homeless shelter.

L

Lambaste   to scold or criticize sharply; to beat
The critics <u>lambasted</u> the author's newest novel, saying he had become lazy in the wake of his last book's success.

Languish   to exist in a dreadful or gloomy situation; to become weak
The convict had been <u>languishing</u> in prison for nearly 20 years.

Latter   the second of two thing mentioned; nearer the end
My parents offered either to buy me a new computer or to pay for a trip to Europe for my graduation, and I chose the <u>latter</u>, having never been abroad.

Laudable   deserving praise; favorable
Jenny's efforts to raise money for breast cancer research were <u>laudable</u>.

Lavish   *adj.* elaborate and luxurious. *v.* to freely and boundlessly bestow
He showered her with <u>lavish</u> gifts of jewelry and clothes in an attempt to win her over.

Lenient   easy-going, tolerant
Sarah's parents were not <u>lenient</u> at all when it came to grades; she was expected to earn straight A's.

Lethargic   deficient in alertness; lacking energy
Linda was <u>lethargic</u> all day; she had not slept at all the night before.

Listless   characterized by a lack of energy
During his long illness, Michael became very <u>listless</u> and spent most of his time in bed.

Loathsome   offensive, disgusting
His <u>loathsome</u> behavior ultimately resulted in his being fired; his employers had received numerous complaints from his coworkers.

Loquacious   very talkative or rambling
My plans for a quiet dinner were disrupted by a <u>loquacious</u> patron seated at the next table.

Lucid   easily understood; clear
The speaker presented a series of <u>lucid</u> arguments in favor of the antismoking law.

Ludicrous   laughable or foolish
Mark's <u>ludicrous</u> budget estimations resulted in large financial losses for his company.

M

Magnanimous   courageous, generous, or noble
Coach Davis was <u>magnanimous</u> in defeat and congratulated the winning team on a game well played.

Malevolent   purposefully wishing harm on others
The villain in the movie was a <u>malevolent</u> old man who would stop at nothing to gain power over the citizens in his community.

Manifest   *adj.* clearly recognizable. *v.* to make clear. *n.* a list of transported goods or passengers used for record keeping
The airline workers' dissatisfaction with their wages <u>manifested</u> itself as a two-week-long strike.

Mar   to inflict damage or blemishes on
The surface of the antique table was <u>marred</u> during the move from the storage facility.

Melancholy   *adj.* glum. *n.* deep contemplative thought
Reid attributed his <u>melancholy</u> mood to the weather; it had been raining for nearly a week.

Melodramatic   overly emotional or sentimental
"I'm never talking to you AGAIN!" she exclaimed <u>melodramatically</u> to her sister.

Mercurial   prone to sudden unpredictable change; volatile
Michael had a very <u>mercurial</u> temperament; he could go from cheerful to irate in a matter of moments.

Metamorphosis   a transformation or change
The new CEO vowed that the struggling business would undergo a complete <u>metamorphosis</u>, and that it would soon be thriving and successful.

Meticulous devoting a high amount of attention to detail
Janine was <u>meticulous</u> about her appearance, refusing to be seen in public without makeup.

Mettle courage
The troops showed their <u>mettle</u> in the face of armed combat.

Minuscule extremely small; unimportant
The acceptable error for this test is <u>minuscule</u>, so the research team takes the utmost care in executing it.

Miscreant villain; evildoer
In typical fairy tale style, the heroine of the story overcomes the local <u>miscreant</u>, teaching him a lesson and earning the esteem of the townspeople.

Mitigate causing something to be less intense, forceful, or harmful
The County Road Commission authorized the use of extra snowplows to help <u>mitigate</u> the hazardous road conditions.

Mollify to calm down or alleviate; to soften
The experienced referees attempted to <u>mollify</u> the angry players before a fight broke out.

Munificence the act of liberally giving
The soup kitchen was able to feed more than one thousand homeless people every day, thanks to the <u>munificence</u> of the community.

N

Nascent just beginning to exist
Brett's <u>nascent</u> career in politics ended before it began when the public learned that he had been arrested for the purchase of narcotics.

Negligent characterized by carelessness and neglectfulness
His often <u>negligent</u> behavior led to his being replaced by a more diligent manager.

Negligible meaningless and insignificant
The difference between the two brands of baby food was <u>negligible</u>; both offered the same nutritional value.

Nostalgia a bittersweet longing for the past
Every time I hear that song, I feel a wave of <u>nostalgia</u> for my college days.

Noxious unwholesome or harmful
Environmentalists protested the construction of a new factory that would emit large quantities of <u>noxious</u> gases into the atmosphere each day.

O

Obdurate   firm, stubborn
The governor was <u>obdurate</u> in her beliefs that schools needed additional funding for their art and music programs.

Obscurity   the condition of being unknown
The 1962 hit single propelled him from relative <u>obscurity</u> in the Canadian north to fame and fortune in Los Angeles.

Obsolete   no longer in use; outmoded or old-fashioned
Telegrams became <u>obsolete</u> with the development of the Internet.

Obtuse   lacking intellectual clarity; blunt, or slow-witted
My law professor insinuates that his students are incredibly <u>obtuse</u> if they don't know the answer to one of his questions.

Obviate   to render unnecessary
The brand-new underpass <u>obviates</u> the railroad crossing gates at the intersection.

Odious   arousing or deserving strong hatred
The <u>odious</u> crimes committed by the gang members put them at the top of the cities most-wanted list.

Onerous   very troublesome or oppressively difficult
The police had the <u>onerous</u> task of somehow convincing the assailant to set his hostages free.

Ostracize   to eliminate from a group
Coworkers have <u>ostracized</u> the young welder since he first spoke out against the union.

P

Paradox   a self-contradiction; something that appears to be self-contradictory, but is nonetheless true
It was a strange <u>paradox</u> that adding more capacity to the network actually reduced its overall performance.

Paragon   an example of excellence
Mother Theresa was a <u>paragon</u> of piety and generosity.

Parse   to break down into components
Mrs. Antoinette assigned our French class 100 sentences to <u>parse</u> into subject, verb, and tense.

Penchant   a tendency or fondness
Her <u>penchant</u> for designer clothes was something that her meager salary could simply not support.

Pedantic   characterized by a narrow concern for detail, particularly in academics
> *My history teacher's hopelessly <u>pedantic</u> lectures left the class in a state of utter boredom.*

Perceive   to become aware of something, usually through the senses
> *<u>Perceiving</u> the sadness in his voice, I asked him if anything was wrong.*

Percolate   to slowly pass through
> *Mountain spring water is generally safe to drink because it has spent decades slowly <u>percolating</u> through porous layers of rock.*

Peripatetic   *adj.* moving or traveling from place to place. *n.* one who travels frequently from place to place
> *My grandmother loves to hear stories from the <u>peripatetic</u> salespeople who occasionally come to her door.*

Periphery   the outermost boundary of an area
> *Paul jogged daily along the <u>periphery</u> of the lake, enjoying the view of the water as he worked out.*

Perjury   knowingly lying under oath
> *Witnesses whose intent is to deceive the court with their testimony may later be found guilty of <u>perjury</u>.*

Perpetuate   to prolong the existence or idea of; to make everlasting
> *That a high grade point average leads to a high standardized test score is a myth <u>perpetuated</u> among some educators.*

Pertinent   relevant or appropriate
> *Our professor warned us to read chapter eight very carefully; the information was <u>pertinent</u> to what would be found on our exam.*

Peruse   to examine or review something
> *Each day Liz <u>perused</u> the want ads in the newspaper, desperately trying to find a job.*

Pervasive   capable of spreading or flowing throughout
> *Because we lived on a farm, it was impossible to avoid the <u>pervasive</u> smell of cow manure at certain times during the year.*

Phenomenon   observable fact or event; an unusual, significant, or outstanding occurrence. Plural is *phenomena*.
> *Many cosmological <u>phenomena</u> have yet to be fully explained.*

Pith   significance, importance
> *Politicians seem to have a knack for obscuring the <u>pith</u> of an issue.*

Placate   to calm
> *The waitress tried to <u>placate</u> her angry patron by offering him a free meal.*

Placid   calm or quiet
The placid lakeside resort in the mountains of Colorado was my favorite place to get away from it all.

Plagiarize   to copy another's work and pretend that it is original
The journalist was sued for plagiarizing an article from another writer and selling it to a national magazine.

Plausible   reasonable, likely
Her reasons seemed highly plausible; nonetheless, her friends found it hard to accept her unusual tardiness.

Plethora   excess or overabundance
The library has a plethora of books on the Civil War.

Poignant   profoundly moving; incisive
The audience sat stunned, moved to silence by the speaker's poignant remarks.

Polarity   the possession of two opposing attributes or ideas
The novel was based on the ironic polarity of the identical twins.

Postulate   to put forth or assert
Karl Marx postulated that Communism was the only successful way to organize the economy; he was wrong.

Pragmatic   practical
She was pragmatic in her approach to applying for the job; she thoroughly researched the company prior to her interview.

Precarious   in a dangerous state, lacking security or stability
Many start-up companies find themselves in a very precarious position when seeking additional funding.

Precedent   an example or event that is used to justify similar occurrences at a later time; custom arising from long-term practice
The student broke her family's long-running precedent and attended the University of Colorado instead of Colorado State.

Precipitate   to cause something to happen very suddenly or prematurely
The bombings precipitated a massive wave of antiterrorism among the people of the target country.

Precept   a guiding rule or principle
The fraternity's founding precepts were love and equality among all of its brothers.

Preclude   to prevent or make impossible
John's embezzlement conviction precluded him from getting another high-powered accounting job.

Precursor   one that precedes or suggests the approach of another
The peasant uprisings of earlier decades are now considered to be <u>precursors</u> of the French Revolution.

Presage   an omen or other warning sign
Some sailors believe that a red sky in the morning is a <u>presage</u> of storms coming that day.

Prescience   foresight; the power to see the future
The captain's <u>prescience</u> for trouble at sea prompted him to replace the old life jackets he had on board.

Presume   to take something for granted as being fact
Many college graduates with high grade point averages <u>presume</u> that finding employment will be easy.

Prevaricate   to lie
It was obvious that Emily was <u>prevaricating</u> when her story changed slightly every time she told it.

Probity   integrity and uprightness
It is important that those working at the clothing store display <u>probity</u>, for it would be far too easy for greedy employees to take whatever they wanted from inventory.

Prodigal   wasteful; extravagant
Gone are the days of <u>prodigal</u> expenditures on social services by the government.

Profuse   plentiful or abundant
After her foolish mistake, Maria offered <u>profuse</u> apologies.

Progeny   offspring or product
My great-grandfather is proud of his extensive <u>progeny</u>.

Prognosis   forecast or prediction
The economic <u>prognosis</u> was bleak; it looked like the recession had only just begun.

Proliferate   to grow or increase rapidly
Computers, like any other technology, <u>proliferate</u> rapidly as production costs decrease and materials availability increases.

Promulgate   to proclaim; usually in reference to rules or laws
At the Board meeting, the town trustees <u>promulgated</u> some new zoning regulations.

Propagate   to cause to multiply or spread
The newly introduced plant species began to <u>propagate</u> quickly in the humid environment.

Prototype   an original form of something
The prototypes of countless sports cars will be debuted at the auto show next week.

Protract   to lengthen or prolong
Our train trip was annoyingly protracted by a series of unexplained delays.

Prowess   great skill or ability in something
Chandler's athletic prowess was overshadowed by that of his legendary older brother, who was named MVP all four years of his high school football career.

Prudish   exaggeratedly proper; righteous
My prudish mother wouldn't allow me to wear miniskirts, no matter how hot it got in the summer.

Q

Quaff   to drink heartily
After a long day at work, Chad quaffed multiple beers while waiting for his dinner.

Querulous   characterized by constant complaining or whining
The losing candidate's querulous remarks regarding his opponent were not included in the newspaper article.

Quixotic   unpredictable and impractical
The quixotic nature of the weather in April requires that you carry an umbrella with you wherever you go.

Quotidian   ordinary, occurring daily
Cell phone use has become a quotidian part of our existence; it's hard to imagine that only 20 years ago cell phones were used primarily in emergencies.

R

Rancor   bitter resentment
The prisoner's rancor was increasingly evident in his malicious glance at the warden.

Recalcitrant   stubbornly resistant; defiant
Joanna seemed to morph overnight from a polite child to a recalcitrant teen.

Recluse   someone who is withdrawn from society
Although the movie star has been in countless blockbusters, she lives as a recluse and refuses to give interviews or appear at publicity events.

Recompense   *n.* payment in return for something. *v.* to award compensation to
You are certainly entitled to some <u>recompense</u> after all of your hours of hard work.

Reconciliation   the reestablishing of cordial relations
It took hours of negotiations to bring about <u>reconciliation</u> between the two parties.

Recondite   difficult to understand
Many students feel it is more helpful to read the textbook than attend the professor's <u>recondite</u> lectures.

Refute   to prove to be false; to deny the truth of
The testimony provided by the prosecution's star witness <u>refuted</u> the statements previously made by the defendant.

Relegate   to refer or assign to a particular place or category
The journalist was <u>relegated</u> from investigative reporting to writing obituaries after submitting too many substandard articles.

Renounce   break; reject
Because of the scandal, the senator <u>renounced</u> all ties to the disgraced lobbyist.

Reparation   compensation given to make amends
Some countries were unable to pay the <u>reparations</u> demanded after the war.

Reproach   to express disapproval
Zach's wife <u>reproached</u> him for spending all of his time watching sports on TV.

Repudiate   to reject or refuse as valid
Ellen <u>repudiated</u> the accusation that she had cheated in order to pass her exam last week.

Resolute   definite, determined
Kelly is <u>resolute</u> in her decision to run a marathon this year, despite her current inability to run more than one mile without a break.

Resplendent   dazzling or brilliant in appearance
The bride looked absolutely <u>resplendent</u> walking down the aisle in her white gown.

Resonant   strong and deep; lasting
The <u>resonant</u> voices of the choir rang out through the concert hall.

Resurrect   to bring back to life
Each summer, Renaissance festivals try to <u>resurrect</u> the spirit of the Middle Ages across the country.

Rhetoric   effective use of language; a style of speaking or writing
The politician used his <u>rhetoric</u> to be voted into office, but whether he will actually use his power constructively remains to be seen.

Rigor   strictness or severity
The nature of the study demanded extreme <u>rigor</u> in setting up the experiments.

S

Sage   one revered for experience and wisdom
It is not wise to disobey the teachings of the tribal <u>sages</u>.

Sanctimonious   feigning piety or righteousness
After a few years, the <u>sanctimonious</u> preacher was finally exposed and run out of town.

Sanction   *n.* authoritative permission. *v.* to give official approval to
Our research proposal received official <u>sanction</u> from the university last week.

Satirize   to insult using witty language
Television shows such as Saturday Night Live <u>satirize</u> many people and current events.

Sedulous   persevering, industrious
In spite of the declining poll numbers, the senator's campaign manager remained <u>sedulous</u> to the end.

Skepticism   an attitude of doubt or disbelief
Miranda's claims to be a psychic were met with <u>skepticism</u> by her friends and family.

Solace   comfort, safety
Paul sought <u>solace</u> from the cold near the roaring fireplace in his living room.

Solicitous   concerned; thoughtful
For a week after my surgery, my <u>solicitous</u> neighbors brought me meals so I wouldn't have to cook.

Specious   appearing to be true or genuine but actually deceptive
Despite sounding credible, all of Jordan's arguments were <u>specious</u>.

Speculate   to theorize on the basis of inconclusive evidence
The tabloids have been <u>speculating</u> for months that the celebrity couple is getting a divorce.

Spontaneous   arising without apparent external cause; unrestrained
Charlotte's <u>spontaneous</u> laughter caused an uncomfortable pause in the conversation; nothing that had been said was meant to be funny.

Squelch   to crush or silence
The dictator <u>squelched</u> any sign of rebellion by making it public that those who spoke out against him would be jailed indefinitely.

Stanch   to stop or check the flow of
Carrie pressed a towel firmly onto the wound to <u>stanch</u> the flow of blood.

Static   fixed or stationary
The typically <u>static</u> price of corn rose dramatically when a major drought hit the Midwest and millions of acres of crops were lost.

Stint   a length of time spent in a particular way
Samantha's two-year <u>stint</u> as a court reporter was one of the most fascinating jobs she ever held.

Stoic   indifferent or unaffected
Kevin's <u>stoic</u> expression gave no clue about what he was thinking.

Subjective   depending or based on someone's personal attitudes or opinions
I think that my best friend is the greatest actress in the world, but my opinion of her is rather <u>subjective</u>.

Substantiate   to validate or support
I had to provide a list of all sources used in my research paper to <u>substantiate</u> the fact that I didn't plagiarize.

Subsume   to contain or include
The new Corporate Policy Manual now <u>subsumes</u> both the Customer Contact Manual and the Internal Procedure Manual.

Subvert   to undermine, ruin, or overthrow
My desire to go to class was <u>subverted</u> by my body's need for more sleep.

Surfeit   an overabundance or excess
The farmer donated his crop <u>surfeit</u> to a charity dedicated to feeding the poor.

Susceptible   easily influenced or likely to be affected
People who don't wash their hands frequently are much more <u>susceptible</u> to illnesses than are those people who regularly wash their hands.

Synchronized   occurring at the same time and at the same rate
The lights in the show were <u>synchronized</u> with the pulsing rhythm of the music.

T

Tacit   using no words
With a smile, Rob's girlfriend implied <u>tacit</u> approval of his gift of a dozen roses.

Tangential   slightly connected; superficially relevant
Chandra's <u>tangential</u> remark added nothing relevant to the conversation.

Temperance   moderation and self-restraint
When the constitutional prohibition of alcohol was lifted, citizens were left to manage their own <u>temperance</u>.

Tenuous   very thin or consisting of little substance
My sister has a <u>tenuous</u> grasp of physics; she does not completely understand how the physical world works.

Torpor   state of physical or mental sluggishness
No amount of incentives or creature comforts could lift the cloud of <u>torpor</u> that had overcome the office.

Tout   to promote or solicit
Salespeople tend to <u>tout</u> the obvious benefits of a product, while distracting from any negative aspects of ownership.

Tractable   easy to control or work with
Teachers are charged with the powerful task of molding <u>tractable</u> young minds.

Transcend   to go above and beyond; to rise above
Through luck and hard work, he was able to <u>transcend</u> his humble origins.

Transgress   to exceed or violate
Joel has repeatedly <u>transgressed</u> the laws against using a cell phone while driving.

Transpose   to reverse the order of; interchange
When I copied down her telephone number, I foolishly <u>transposed</u> two digits.

U

Unalloyed   pure; complete
The detectives needed more than four hours to extract the <u>unalloyed</u> version of events from the witness.

Unilaterally   performed in a one-sided manner
When the high school principal failed to respond to numerous requests for more information, the school board <u>unilaterally</u> terminated his contract.

Unprecedented   having no previous example
The coffee shop franchise launched new locations at an <u>unprecedented</u> rate, opening an average of eight new stores per day across the country.

Unstinting   very generous; bestowed liberally
Sometimes the boss's <u>unstinting</u> praise of our work can be construed as disingenuous.

Urbanity   refinement and elegance
Cindy's <u>urbanity</u> was apparent in the way she dressed herself—classic clothes with a touch of style.

Utilitarian   useful or practical
The workers' coveralls were very <u>utilitarian</u>, but had no regard at all for style or looks.

V

Vacillate   to swing or waver
In an emergency situation there is no time to <u>vacillate</u>, so first responders are taught appropriate courses of actions for a myriad of crises.

Variegated   having a variety of colors or marks
Calico cats have <u>variegated</u> coats of many shades of brown, tan, black, and white.

Vehement   forceful; displaying extreme emotion
In spite of <u>vehement</u> protests from his parents, Joey left Harvard and moved to Los Angeles to become an actor.

Venal   corruptible, open to bribery
The success of mafia crimes relies on a steady supply of <u>venal</u> police officers and judges.

Venerable   highly esteemed or respected; commanding respect
Dr. Sanford, a most <u>venerable</u> professor, received a standing ovation at his retirement party.

Veracity   truthfulness
The <u>veracity</u> of his alibi was questioned when several witnesses saw him fleeing the scene of the crime.

Verbose   wordy; long-winded
Most students were yawning and half-asleep by the end of the dean's <u>verbose</u> commencement speech.

Verisimilitude   the quality of appearing to be true or real
Carol added several specific details to her story to lend it <u>verisimilitude</u>.

Veritable   genuine or authentic
After months of privation in the wilderness, the Andersons enjoyed a <u>veritable</u> feast of turkey, mashed potatoes, stuffing, and carrot cake.

Versatile   having many uses or a variety of abilities
She is a very <u>versatile</u> singer and is equally comfortable singing operatic arias or country-western ballads.

Vilify   to make negative statements about; to malign
She was <u>vilified</u> in the press as "the other woman" in the divorce case of a married actor.

Vindicate   to clear someone or something from blame
The suspect was <u>vindicated</u> when the person who actually committed the robbery turned himself in.

Virtually   in almost all instances; simulated as by a computer
Surviving a plunge over Niagara Falls in a barrel was <u>virtually</u> impossible prior to the invention of reliable foam padding and rigid plastics.

Vituperate   to criticize in an abusive way
The senator condemned and <u>vituperated</u> his political opponents in a series of angry speeches.

Voluminous   large in volume or bulk
He produced a <u>voluminous</u> amount of published works during his 50 years as an author.

Voracious   excessively greedy; ravenous
After his two-week wilderness camping trip, Pat had a <u>voracious</u> appetite.

W

Wane   to gradually decrease
Randy's interest in his baseball card collection began to <u>wane</u> as he got older.

Wary   cautious and untrusting
Emily threw a <u>wary</u> glance at the man who had been following her for nearly five blocks.

Whet   to sharpen or stimulate
Before a large meal, I like to <u>whet</u> my appetite with a little wine and cheese.

Wily   very sly, deceptive
The <u>wily</u> salesperson convinced my friend to purchase a car that was well beyond my friend's financial means.

X

Xenophobic   distrustful of strangers or foreign people
Before traveling abroad, I had a <u>xenophobic</u> mistrust of all people who weren't American.

Z

Zealous   very passionate or enthusiastic
As a dedicated and honest attorney, Kara remained committed to the
zealous pursuit of the truth.

Zenith   the peak point
Winning the Academy Award for Best Actor was the zenith of the actor's
career.

<u>APPENDIX B</u>

Glossary of GRE Math Terms

This glossary includes many of the concepts tested on the GRE Quantitative section. We recommend that you thoroughly review difficult mathematical concepts, and refer to this glossary as necessary during your preparation.

A

Absolute Value   A number's distance on the number line from 0, without considering which direction from 0 the number lies. Therefore, absolute value will always be positive.

Acute Angle   An angle less than 90 degrees.

Adjacent Angle   Either of two angles having a common side and common vertex. For example, in the following figure, angles *a* and *b* are adjacent angles:

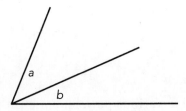

Arc   A portion of the circumference of a circle, as shown in the following figure:

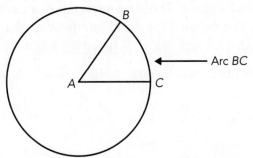

The complete arc of a circle has 360°.

Area   The number of square units that covers the shape or figure. Following are the formulas for the area of some common figures:

- Square: side (s) squared (s^2)
- Rectangle: length (l) times width (w) ($l \times w$)
- Circle: pi (π) times the radius (r) squared (πr^2)
- Triangle: one half the base (b) times the height (h) ($\frac{1}{2} b \times h$)

Arithmetic Mean (*see* Average)   The average of a group of values. Calculate the arithmetic mean by dividing the sum of all of the values in the group by the total count of values in the group. For example, the average of the 3 test scores 82%, 83%, and 87% is equivalent to (82 + 83 + 87) divided by 3; 252 ÷ 3 = 84.

Associative Property   A mathematical property whereby the grouping of numbers being added or multiplied can be changed without changing the sum or the product. The associative property of multiplication can be expressed as ($a \times b$) $\times c = a \times$ ($b \times c$). Likewise, the associative property of addition can be expressed as ($a + b$) $+ c = a +$ ($b + c$).

Average (*see* Arithmetic Mean)   The arithmetic mean of a group of values. Calculate the average by dividing the sum of all of the values in the group by the total count of values in the group. For example, the average of the 3 test scores 82%, 83%, and 87% is equivalent to (82 + 83 + 87) divided by 3; 252 ÷ 3 = 84.

B–C

Base   In geometry, the bottom of a plane figure. For example, in the right triangle that follows, AC is the base:

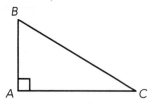

In algebra, the base is the number that is raised to various powers. For example, 2^3 indicates a base of 2 raised to the power of 3.

Circumference   The distance around a circle. The circumference of a circle is equal to pi times the diameter (πd). The formula for the circumference of a circle can also be expressed as $2\pi r$, because the diameter, d, is twice the radius, r.

Collinear   A term referring to points that pass through or lie on the same straight line.

Commutative Property   A mathematical property whereby the order of numbers being added or multiplied can be changed without changing the sum or the product. The commutative property of addition is expressed as $a + b = b + a$. Likewise, the commutative property of multiplication is expressed as $a \times b = b \times a$, or $ab = ba$.

Complementary Angles   Two angles for which the sum is 90 degrees.

Congruent   A term describing any shapes or figures, including line segments and angles, that have the same size or measure. For example, in the triangle below, sides *AB* and *BC* are congruent, and angles *A* and *C* are congruent:

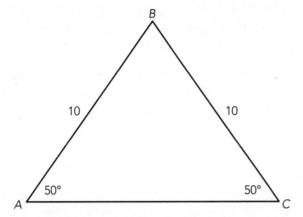

Coordinate Plane   A plane, typically defined with the coordinates *x* and *y*, where the two axes are at right angles to each other. The horizontal axis is the *x*-axis, and the vertical axis is the *y*-axis, as shown in the following figure:

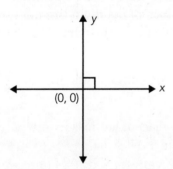

You can locate any point (*x,y*) on the coordinate plane by an ordered pair of numbers. The ordered pair (0,0), where the *x* and *y* axes meet, is the origin.

The coordinate plane is divided into four quadrants, as shown in the following figure:

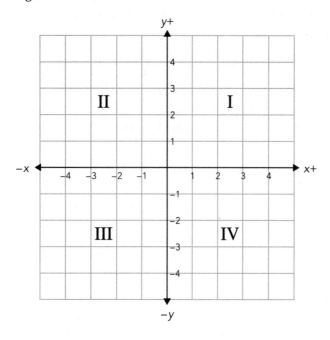

D

Decimal   The point that separates values less than 1 from those greater than 1. In our number system, digits can be placed to the left and right of a decimal point. *Place value* refers to the value of a digit in a number relative to its position. Starting from the left of the decimal point, the values of the digits are ones, tens, hundreds, and so on. Starting to the right of the decimal point, the values of the digits are tenths, hundredths, thousandths, and so on.

Denominator   The bottom part of a fraction. For example, in the fraction $\frac{3}{4}$, 4 is the denominator.

Diagonal   A line segment that connects two nonadjacent vertices in any polygon. In the following rectangle, *AC* and *BD* are diagonals:

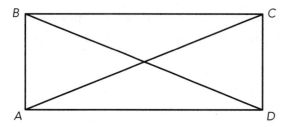

Diameter   A line segment that joins two points on a circle and passes through the center of the circle, as shown in the following figure, where AB is the diameter:

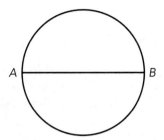

Distributive Property   A mathematical property observed when an expression involves both addition and multiplication. The distributive property is expressed as $a(b + c) = ab + ac$, where the variable a is distributed to the variables b and c.

Divisible   Capable of being divided, usually with no remainder. For example, 6 is divisible by 2, because when 6 is divided by 2, the result is 3 with no remainder.

E–F

Equilateral Triangle   A triangle in which all of the sides are congruent and each of the angles equals 60 degrees.

Exponent   A number that indicates the operation of repeated multiplication. A number with an exponent is said to be "raised to the power" of that exponent. For example, 2^3 indicates 2 raised to the power of 3, which translates into $2 \times 2 \times 2$. In this instance, 3 is the exponent.

Factor   One of two or more expressions that are multiplied together to get a product. For example, in the equation $2 \times 3 = 6$, 2 and 3 are factors of 6. Likewise, in the equation $x^2 + 5x + 6$, $(x + 2)$ and $(x + 3)$ are factors.

FOIL Method   A method of multiplying two binomials, such as $(x + 2)$ and $(x + 3)$, according to the following steps:

Multiply the **FIRST** terms together: $(x)(x) = x^2$

Multiply the **OUTSIDE** terms together: $(x)(3) = 3x$

Multiply the **INSIDE** terms together: $(2)(x) = 2x$

Multiply the **LAST** terms together: $(2)(3) = 6$

Now, combine like terms to get $x^2 + 5x + 6$

Fraction   An expression that indicates the quotient of two quantities. For example, $\frac{2}{3}$ is a fraction, where 2 is the numerator and 3 is the denominator.

Frequency Distribution   The frequency with which a data value occurs in any given set of data.

Function   A set of ordered pairs where no two of the ordered pairs has the same x-value. In a function, each input (x-value) has exactly one output (y-value). For example, $f(x) = 2x + 3$. If $x = 3$, then $f(x) = 9$. For every x, only one $f(x)$, or y, exists.

G–H–I

Greatest Common Factor (GCF)   The largest number that will divide evenly into any two or more numbers. For example, 1, 2, 4, and 8 are all factors of 8; likewise, 1, 2, 3, and 6 are all factors of 6. Therefore, the greatest common factor of 8 and 6 is 2.

Hexagon   A six-sided figure, shown below:

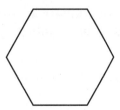

Hypotenuse   The leg of a right triangle that is opposite the right angle. For example, in the right triangle in the following figure, *BC* is the hypotenuse:

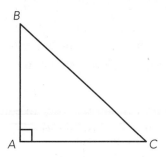

The hypotenuse is always the longest leg of a right triangle.

Improper Fraction   An integer combined with a fraction. For example, $2\frac{1}{2}$ is an improper fraction (*see also* **Mixed Number**).

Inequality   A mathematical expression that shows that two quantities are not equal. For example, $2x < 8$ is an inequality that means that $2x$ is less than 8. Likewise, $3a > 17$ is an inequality that means that $3a$ is greater than 17.

Integer   Integers include both positive and negative whole numbers. Zero is also considered an integer.

Interior Angle   The angle inside two adjacent sides of a polygon. The sum of the interior angles in a triangle is always 180 degrees.

Irrational Number   A number that cannot be exactly expressed as the ratio of two integers. For example, π (3.14) is an irrational number.

Isosceles Triangle   A triangle in which two sides have the same length.

J–L

Least Common Denominator (LCD)   The smallest multiple of the denominators of two or more fractions. For example, the least common denominator of $\frac{3}{4}$ and $\frac{2}{5}$ is 20.

Least Common Multiple (LCM)   The smallest number that any two or more numbers will divide evenly into. For example, the common multiples of 3 and 4 are 12, 24, and 36; 12 is the smallest multiple, and is, therefore, the least common multiple of 3 and 4.

Like Terms   Terms that contain the same variable raised to the same power. For example, $3x^2$ and $10x^2$ are like terms that can be combined to get $13x^2$. Also, $-x$ and $4x$ are like terms that can be combined to get $3x$.

Line   A straight set of points that extends into infinity in both directions, as shown in the following figure:

Line Segment   A figure representing two points on a line and all of the points in between, as shown in the following figure:

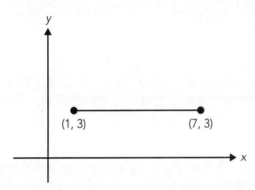

M–N

Median   The middle value of a series of numbers when those numbers are in either ascending or descending order. In the series (2, 4, 6, 8, 10) the median is 6. To find the median in an even set of data, find the average of the middle two numbers. In the series (3, 4, 5, 6) the median is 4.5.

Midpoint   The center point of a line segment. To find the midpoint of a line given two points on the line, use the formula $\left(\dfrac{[x_1 + x_2]}{2}, \dfrac{[y_1 + y_2]}{2} \right)$.

Mixed Number   A number that combines an integer with a fraction. Mixed numbers are also called **Improper Fractions**; $1\frac{1}{2}$ is a mixed number.

Mode   The number that appears most frequently in a series of numbers. In the series (2, 3, 4, 5, 6, 3, 7) the mode is 3, because 3 appears twice in the series and the other numbers each appear only once in the series.

Number Line   The line on which every point represents a real number. On a number line, numbers that correspond to points to the right of zero are positive, and numbers that correspond to points to the left of zero are negative. For any two numbers on the number line, the number to the left is less than the number to the right.

Numerator   The top part of a fraction. For example, in the fraction $\frac{3}{4}$, 3 is the numerator.

O–P

Obtuse Angle   An angle that measures greater than 90 degrees and less than 180 degrees.

Octagon   An eight-sided figure, shown as follows:

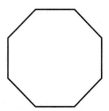

Parallel   A term that describes two distinct lines that lie in the same plane and do not intersect. Two lines are parallel if and only if they have the same slope. For example, the two lines with equations $2y = 6x + 7$ and $y = 3x - 14$ have the same slope (3) **(see Point-slope Form)**.

Parallelogram   A quadrilateral in which the opposite sides are of equal length and the opposite angles are equal, as shown below:

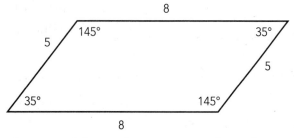

The sum of the angles in a rectangle is always 360 degrees.

PEMDAS   An acronym that describes the correct order in which to perform mathematical operations. The acronym PEMDAS stands for Parentheses, Exponents, Multiplication, Division, Addition, and Subtraction. It should help you to remember to do the operations in the correct order, as follows:

P First, do the operations within the *parentheses*, if any.

E Next, do the *exponents*, if any.

M, D Next, do the *multiplication* or *division*, if any.

A, S Next, do the *addition* or *subtraction*, in order from left to right, if any.

Pentagon   A five-sided figure, shown as follows:

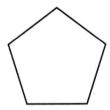

Percent   A fraction whose denominator is 100. The fraction 25/100 is equal to 25% and can also be expressed as 0.25.

Perimeter   The distance around any shape or object. Following are the formulas for the perimeter of some common figures:

- The perimeter (P) of a rectangle is equivalent to $2l + 2w$, where l is the length and w is the width.
- The perimeter of a square is $4s$, where s is the length of a side.
- The perimeter (P) of other polygons is the sum of the lengths of the sides.
- The perimeter (P) of a triangle is the sum of the lengths of the sides.

Perpendicular   A term describing two distinct lines whose intersection creates a right angle. Two lines are perpendicular if and only if the slope of one of the lines is the negative reciprocal of the slope of the other line. In other words, if line a has a slope of 2, and line b has a slope of $-\frac{1}{2}$, then the two lines are perpendicular.

Point   A location in a plane or in space that has no dimensions.

Point-slope Form   The equation of a line in the form $y = mx + b$, where m is the slope and b is the y-intercept.

Polygon   A closed plane figure made up of at least three line segments that are joined. For example, a triangle, a rectangle, and an octagon are polygons.

Polynomial   A mathematic expression consisting of more than two terms. $2x^2 + 4x + 4$ is a simple quadratic equation, and also a polynomial.

Prime Number   Any number that can only be divided by itself and 1. That is, 1 and number itself are the only factors of a prime number. For example, 2, 3, 5, 7, and 11 are prime numbers.

Probability   The likelihood that an event will occur. For example, Jeff has three striped and four solid ties in his closet; therefore, he has a total of seven ties in his closet. He has three chances to grab a striped tie out of the seven total ties, because he has three striped ties. So, the probability of Jeff grabbing a striped tie is 3 out of 7, which can also be expressed as 3:7, or $\frac{3}{7}$.

Proportion   A mathematical statement indicating that one ratio is equal to another ratio. For example, $\frac{1}{5} = \frac{x}{20}$ is a proportion.

Pythagorean Theorem   This theorem applies only to finding the length of the sides in right triangles, and states that $c^2 = a^2 + b^2$, where c is the hypotenuse (the side opposite the right angle) of a right triangle and a and b are the two other sides of the triangle.

Q–R

Quadrilateral   Any four-sided polygon with four angles. A parallelogram, a rectangle, a square, and a trapezoid are all examples of quadrilaterals.

Quotient   The result of division.

Radius   The distance from the center of a circle to any point on the circle, as shown below in the following circle with center C:

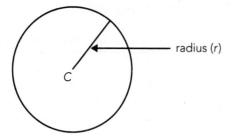

Ratio   A mathematical comparison between two quantities. A ratio of 1 to 5, for example, is written as either $\frac{1}{5}$ or 1:5.

Rational Number   A fraction whose numerator and denominator are both integers and the denominator does not equal 0.

Real Number   Any rational or irrational number, used to express quantities, lengths, amounts, and the like. All real numbers correspond to points on the number line. All real numbers except zero are either positive or negative.

Reciprocal   Given a number, n, the reciprocal is expressed as 1 over n, or $\frac{1}{n}$. The product of a number and its reciprocal is always 1. In other words, $\frac{1}{3} \times \frac{3}{1} = \frac{3}{3}$, which is equivalent to 1.

Rectangle   A polygon with four sides (two sets of congruent, or equal sides) and four right angles. All rectangles are parallelograms.

Right Angle   An angle that measures 90 degrees.

S–T

Sequence   An *arithmetic* sequence is one in which the difference between one term and the next is the same. For example, the following sequence is an arithmetic sequence because the difference between the terms is 2: 1, 3, 5, 7, 9. A *geometric* sequence is one in which the ratio between two terms is constant. For example, the following sequence is a geometric sequence because the ratio between the terms is $\frac{1}{2}$: 16, 8, 4, 2, 1, $\frac{1}{2}$.

Set   A well-defined group of numbers or objects. For example, {2, 4, 6, 8} is the set of positive even whole numbers less than 10.

Similar Triangles   Triangles in which the measures of corresponding angles are equal and the corresponding sides are in proportion, as shown in the following figure:

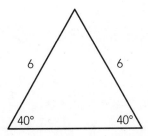

Slope   The change in y-coordinates divided by the change in x-coordinates from two given points on a line. The formula for slope is $m = \frac{(y_2 - y_1)}{(x_2 - x_1)}$, where (x_1, y_1) and (x_2, y_2) are the two given points. For example, the slope of a line that contains the points (3,6) and (2,5) is equivalent to $\frac{(6-5)}{(3-2)}$, or $\frac{1}{1}$, which equals 1.

Slope-intercept Equation $y = mx + b$, where m is the slope of the line and b is the y-intercept (that is, the point at which the graph of the line crosses the y-axis).

Special Triangles   Triangles whose sides have special ratios. The following are angle measures and side lengths for special right triangles:

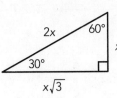
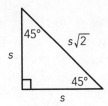

30-60-90 Triangle   45-45-90 Triangle

Square   A number multiplied by itself. Squaring a negative number yields a positive result. For example, $-2^2 = 4$.

Square Root   Given a number, n, the square root is written as $\sqrt{n}$, or the non-negative value a that fulfills the expression $a^2 = n$. For example, the square root of 5 is expressed as $\sqrt{5}$, and $(\sqrt{5})^2 = 5$.

System of Equations   A group of two or more equations with the same set of unknowns. In solving a system of equations, try to find values for each of the unknowns that will satisfy every equation in the system.

Triangle   A closed plane figure having three sides and three angles.

V–Z

Volume   A measure of space or capacity of a three-dimensional object. The formula for the volume of a rectangular solid is $V = lwh$, where l = length, w = width, and h = height.

y-intercept   The point at which a line crosses the y-axis in the (x,y)–coordinate plane.

Additional Resources

The purpose of this book is to help you prepare for the GRE. While this book provides you with helpful information about the test and realistic practice materials to get you ready for the real thing, the following additional resources might be useful in your preparation:

ETS

Educational Testing Service (ETS) is the entity that creates and administers the GRE tests. The official GRE website at www.gre.org offers a wealth of up-to-date information about the GRE. Once you get to the Test Takers section of the website, you can download the POWERPREP® software, find out about test locations and fees, register for the test, learn about your score report, order additional score reports, and more.

Practicing to Take the General Test, 10th edition (ISBN 0886852129), published by ETS, is a great source of practice material for the GRE. This book is usually available at all the major bookstores. Pick one up as a great complement to *McGraw-Hill's GRE*.

Advantage Education

Advantage Education offers many programs for students planning to go to graduate school, including programs that prepare students for the GRE, as well as admissions counseling. To learn about individual tutoring, workshops, courses, and other programs, visit www.AdvantageEd.com, or call Toll Free 1-888-737-6010.

Textbooks and Human Resources

High school and college textbooks are extremely valuable resources. The content areas tested on the GRE Quantitative section are the same content areas that you've been studying in school. Hence, textbooks cover many of the relevant skills and subjects you will need for success on the GRE. If you do not have your textbooks, your school library should have copies that you can use.

Don't forget to talk to professors and students who have some experience with the GRE. They might be able to shed some additional light on getting ready for the test. It is in your best interest to be as well prepared as possible on test day.

SOFTWARE AND INFORMATION LICENSE

The software and information on this CD-ROM (collectively referred to as the "Product") are the property of The McGraw-Hill Companies, Inc. ("McGraw-Hill") and are protected by both United States copyright law and international copyright treaty provision. You must treat this Product just like a book, except that you may copy it into a computer to be used and you may make archival copies of the Products for the sole purpose of backing up our software and protecting your investment from loss.

By saying "just like a book," McGraw-Hill means, for example, that the Product may be used by any number of people and may be freely moved from one computer location to another, so long as there is no possibility of the Product (or any part of the Product) being used at one location or on one computer while it is being used at another. Just as a book cannot be read by two different people in two different places at the same time, neither can the Product be used by two different people in two different places at the same time (unless, of course, McGraw-Hill's rights are being violated).

McGraw-Hill reserves the right to alter or modify the contents of the Product at any time.

This agreement is effective until terminated. The Agreement will terminate automatically without notice if you fail to comply with any provisions of this Agreement. In the event of termination by reason of your breach, you will destroy or erase all copies of the Product installed on any computer system or made for backup purposes and shall expunge the Product from your data storage facilities.

LIMITED WARRANTY

For questions regarding the operation of the CD please visit: http://www.mhprofessional.com/techsupport/

McGraw-Hill warrants the physical disk(s) enclosed herein to be free of defects in materials and workmanship for a period of sixty days from the purchase date. If McGraw-Hill receives written notification within the warranty period of defects in materials or workmanship, and such notification is determined by McGraw-Hill to be correct, McGraw-Hill will replace the defective disk(s). Send request to:

Customer Service
McGraw-Hill
Gahanna Industrial Park
860 Taylor Station Road
Blacklick, OH 43004-9615

The entire and exclusive liability and remedy for breach of this Limited Warranty shall be limited to replacement of defective disk(s) and shall not include or extend to any claim for or right to cover any other damages, including but not limited to, loss of profit, data, or use of the software, or special, incidental, or consequential damages or other similar claims, even if McGraw-Hill has been specifically advised as to the possibility of such damages. In no event will McGraw-Hill's liability for any damages to you or any other person ever exceed the lower of suggested list price or actual price paid for the license to use the Product, regardless of any form of the claim.

THE McGRAW-HILL COMPANIES, INC. SPECIFICALLY DISCLAIMS ALL OTHER WARRANTIES, EXPRESS OR IMPLIED, INCLUDING BUT NOT LIMITED TO, ANY IMPLIED WARRANTY OF MERCHANTABILITY OR FITNESS FOR A PARTICULAR PURPOSE.

Specifically, McGraw-Hill makes no representation or warranty that the Product is fit for any particular purpose and any implied warranty of merchantability is limited to the sixty day duration of the Limited Warranty covering the physical disk(s) only (and not the software or information) and is otherwise expressly and specifically disclaimed.

This Limited Warranty gives you specific legal rights; you may have others which may vary from state to state. Some states do not allow the exclusion of incidental or consequential damages, or the limitation on how long an implied warranty lasts, so some of the above may not apply to you.

This Agreement constitutes the entire agreement between the parties relating to use of the Product. The terms of any purchase order shall have no effect on the terms of this Agreement. Failure of McGraw-Hill to insist at any time on strict compliance with this Agreement shall not constitute a waiver of any rights under this Agreement. This Agreement shall be construed and governed in accordance with the laws of New York. If any provision of this Agreement is held to be contrary to law, that provision will be enforced to the maximum extent permissible and the remaining provisions will remain in force and effect.

SYSTEM REQUIREMENTS - PC: Microsoft Windows 2000, XP, Vista; Intel Pentium III processor (450 MHz recommended) or better; 256 MB RAM; Display capable of 800 x 600 resolution and 16-bit color; Windows compatible sound card. Apple Macintosh: Mac® OS X 10.2.8, 10.3.x, 10.4.x, 10.5.x; Power PC processor (G3 or higher recommended), any Intel Processor; 256 MB RAM.